Atlantic Passages

UNIVERSITY PRESS OF FLORIDA

Florida A&M University, Tallahassee
Florida Atlantic University, Boca Raton
Florida Gulf Coast University, Ft. Myers
Florida International University, Miami
Florida State University, Tallahassee
New College of Florida, Sarasota
University of Central Florida, Orlando
University of Florida, Gainesville
University of North Florida, Jacksonville
University of South Florida, Tampa
University of West Florida, Pensacola

ATLANTIC PASSAGES

Race, Mobility, and Liberian Colonization

ROBERT MURRAY

University Press of Florida
Gainesville · Tallahassee · Tampa · Boca Raton
Pensacola · Orlando · Miami · Jacksonville · Ft. Myers · Sarasota

Publication of this paperback edition made possible by a Sustaining the Humanities through the American Rescue Plan grant from the National Endowment for the Humanities.

Copyright 2021 by Robert Murray
All rights reserved
Published in the United States of America

First cloth printing, 2021
First paperback printing, 2023

28 27 26 25 24 23   6 5 4 3 2 1

Library of Congress Cataloging-in-Publication Data
Names: Murray, Robert, 1983– author.
Title: Atlantic passages : race, mobility, and Liberian colonization / Robert Murray.
Description: Gainesville : University Press of Florida, 2021. | Includes bibliographical references and index.
Identifiers: LCCN 2020023366 (print) | LCCN 2020023367 (ebook) | ISBN 9780813066752 (hardback) | ISBN 9780813057736 (pdf) | ISBN 9780813080284 (pbk.)
Subjects: LCSH: Slaves—Emancipation—United States. | African Americans—Colonization—Liberia. | Blacks—Liberia. | Atlantic Ocean Region—Race relations. | Liberia—Emigration and immigration. | Liberia—History.
Classification: LCC DT633 .M87 2021 (print) | LCC DT633 (ebook) | DDC 966.62/02—dc23
LC record available at https://lccn.loc.gov/2020023366
LC ebook record available at https://lccn.loc.gov/2020023367

The University Press of Florida is the scholarly publishing agency for the State University System of Florida, comprising Florida A&M University, Florida Atlantic University, Florida Gulf Coast University, Florida International University, Florida State University, New College of Florida, University of Central Florida, University of Florida, University of North Florida, University of South Florida, and University of West Florida.

University Press of Florida
2046 NE Waldo Road
Suite 2100
Gainesville, FL 32609
http://upress.ufl.edu

For Amy and Lucy

Contents

List of Figures ix

Acknowledgments xi

Introduction 1

1. "To Be Called a Free Colored Man in the States Is Synonymous with What We Here Term Slavery": Transformative Mobility and Liberian Travels through the United States 23

2. "All Those Things Desirable for a Map to Show": Space, Cartography, and Control in Colonial Liberia 75

3. "Nearly All Have Natives as Helps in Their Families, and This Is as It Should Be": The "Civilizing" Mission of Unfree Labor 113

4. "They Would Dearly Learn What It Was to Fight White Men": Whitening through Violence in Liberia 153

5. "Your Views Cross the Atlantic": Black and White Responses to Settler Activism 195

Afterword 223

Notes 227

Bibliography 267

Index 277

Figures

1. Map of the West Coast of Africa 83
2. William Thornton's Plan for Mesurado, 1821 85
3. Map produced by the ACS in 1845 95
4. "A View of Bassa Cove" 99

Acknowledgments

This is a remarkable time to catalog this book's debts. As I sit at my desk in the home that I have scarcely left for weeks due to the COVID-19 pandemic, I have increasingly come to ponder the devolution of my daily routines. In many ways, it is a technological marvel that class and faculty meetings take place remotely with no commute and only the minimal requirement of changing shirts after hopping out of bed. And yet, I have been particularly struck by the duality of this historical moment, in which we are both showing how much can be done with a webcam and halfway decent wi-fi connection and seeing the inadequacies of these wonders. The Zoom meeting is a poor reproduction of the genuine article, and the warm memories of the stimulating conversations over good food and drink that shaped this book are particularly bittersweet. Writing this now has been a useful reminder of the community that supported me and this book, and I can only say that I look forward to reuniting with all of you in person.

This book began its life as a research project at the University of Kentucky under the direction of Joanne Pope Melish. Her sharp intellect and advice continued to shape this book long after I left Lexington. I also thank Erik Lars Myrup, Ronald P. Formisano, Tracy Campbell, and Richard Schein for their support and constructive criticism in that formative stage. Like many graduate students, my thinking and social skills were mutually reinforced by wonderful conversations with colleagues who always had the good sense to know when was the appropriate time to theorize and when was the appropriate time to enjoy a beer and watch basketball. In the marathon of graduate school, Andrew Adler, Amanda Higgins, Patrick and Jenny Lewis, Anthony and Stephanie Miller, Stephen Pickering, and James Savage were instrumental in helping me survive.

My colleagues at Mercy College have helped me understand what it means to be a "teacher-scholar." I have leaned on them as I navigated the complexities of writing while supporting a heavy teaching and service load.

They, too, possess the good sense of knowing when it is time to discuss pedagogy, scholarship, and assessment and when it is time to remember life outside academia. I am particularly indebted to Austin Dacey, K. Patrick Fazioli, Soonyi Lee, Maureen MacLeod, and Andrés Matías-Ortiz. Our little humanities writing group produced many good suggestions on how to revise this book.

I am privileged to work within the same field as some truly remarkable scholars. Beverly Tomek in particular is worthy of note as a model scholar and generous colleague. In reviewing my many emails to her over the years, I am embarrassed by how many times the subject line is asking for a favor. I thank her for always responding to those messages. The anonymous readers made this a much better book. Any remaining errors are my own. I must also thank my editor at the University Press of Florida, Sian Hunter, and her assistant, Mary Puckett, who have been nothing but patient with a first-time author. In fact, the entire staff at the press has been nothing but understanding as I worked to complete this project during a pandemic.

While I am grateful to all the librarians and archivists who assisted me over the years, the Friends Historical Library at Swarthmore College saved an entire research trip by pulling my materials and allowing me to continue my work even as they dealt with water flowing from a broken pipe. I thank the University of Kentucky and Mercy College for supporting my research.

Parts of this book were previously published and have been revised and expanded here. Part of chapter 1 appeared in "Bodies in Motion: Liberian Settlers, Medicine, and Mobility in the Atlantic World" in the *Journal of the Early Republic* 39 (2019). It is reprinted here with permission of the University of Pennsylvania Press. Part of chapter 2 appeared in "The End of Emancipation Street: 'Civilization,' Race, and Cartography in Colonial Liberia" in *New Directions in the Study of African American Recolonization*. I thank the University Press of Florida for permission to reprint it here.

Finally, my greatest debt is to my wife, Amy, who has lived with these pages far longer than any mere mortal could withstand. She has been a constant reminder that there is more to life than tapping away on a keyboard even as she has been my most studious, supportive, and correct companion/critic. I learned to type with a cat in my lap, and Amy learned to accept that the cat she brought into our home simply likes me more (now we have two cats). It has been quite the journey from Virginia to Kentucky to New England to New York. In 2016, we welcomed our daughter, Lucy, into our lives. Even as she has greatly improved the quality of my life, I cannot say that her presence accelerated the completion of this book. For that, I must again thank Amy, who through Herculean efforts managed to entertain a toddler and bought me precious moments of a quiet house to concentrate on my work. Now, that work is completed and the house is filled with a frenetic child, noise, and the stresses of a global pandemic. Of all the people on the planet, I am glad that I am sheltering in place with you two.

Introduction

In any other place, at any other time, it would assuredly have been an odd dinner party. The guest, Horatio Bridge, an officer of the U.S. Navy, listened intently and recorded every detail from his host: the average temperature of the place, the number of residents, the looks of its cattle, and how the locals rested upon their heels. While he did not record what he ate, he did note that his host bestowed upon him a collection of monkey skins and other "curiosities." In taking these detailed observations of his surroundings, Bridge was only following the instructions of his lifelong friend Nathaniel Hawthorne. Bridge described his host, John Brown Russwurm, as a "man of distinguished ability and of collegiate education," an affirmation of Russwurm's talent if not exactly effusive praise for a fellow graduate of Bowdoin College who had even joined the same literary society as Bridge and Hawthorne.[1]

What brought Bridge and Russwurm together in September 1843—and piqued Hawthorne's interest—was the colony of Liberia. Bridge served aboard the USS *Saratoga*, Matthew C. Perry's flagship for the little Africa Squadron, four ships dispatched by the United States to combat the illegal Atlantic slave trade in 1843.[2] Hawthorne cared little for any supposed benefits from America's military intervention in the Atlantic slave trade, but he did see the financial gain to be had in a book deal. Before sailing, Hawthorne suggested that his friend keep a journal of his African adventures, which they would subsequently publish with Hawthorne serving as editor.

Hawthorne was especially interested in Bridge's journal, as his tour of duty would place him near the settlements of African Americans first established by the American Society for Colonizing the Free People of Color (the American Colonization Society or ACS) in 1822. Hawthorne entreated Bridge to include copious details about his experiences in this colony of Liberia, believing that "if, in any portion of the book, the author may hope to engage the attention of the public, it will probably be in those pages which treat of Liberia."³

With growing national anxiety over slavery and abolitionism, Hawthorne was gambling that an exposé on the ACS and its African colony would find a ready readership. The ACS was formed in December 1816 by a group of prominent white men in Washington, D.C., who styled themselves as philanthropists following the path established by Paul Cuffe, an Afro-Indian sea captain who argued that the establishment of African American colonies along the western coast of Africa could stymie the Atlantic slave trade and spawn "legitimate" commerce.⁴ Cuffe passed away in 1817 before the society was a year old. If the early black-led emigration efforts had found cautious acceptance among the nation's burgeoning free black population, the white-led ACS, filled and governed by many slaveholders, seemed a plan designed solely to prop up American slavery by removing its most ardent opponents to distant shores. From its earliest days, controversy surrounded the society and its African colony.

Those "pages which treat of Liberia" were, indeed, a significant portion of the work, as sixteen of its twenty-two chapters dealt with some aspect of Liberia, including Bridge's dinner with Russwurm. Russwurm was a former editor of the *Freedom's Journal*, the first African American newspaper in the United States, who had earned the scorn of most free people of color when he reversed course and endorsed colonization. Russwurm had emigrated to the colonial capital, Monrovia, in 1830 to serve as editor of its newspaper, the *Liberia Herald*. But at the moment that Bridge found himself sitting at Russwurm's table, the former editor was serving as agent and governor of the independent colony established by the Maryland State Colonization Society (MSCS) at Cape Palmas, nearly three hundred miles southeast of Monrovia.⁵

Apparently, the main topic of dinnertime conversation was the governor's recent expedition seventy miles into the interior. This was not an insignificant distance, as the majority of the Liberian settlements hugged the coast. Russwurm impressed his dinner guests with tales of encountering a powerful "tribe" in the "Bush," and although he could not secure an escort for further exploration from the mighty "king" of this group, the African leader was impressed enough by Russwurm and his entourage to dispatch his son to the coast "to see the *black-white* people and their improvements." The "black-white people," it turned out, were none other than the African American settlers of the Liberian colonies. The West African neighbors and inhabitants of Liberia, who conceived of themselves as "black," recognized the significant cultural differences between themselves and these newly arrived Americans. To African eyes and ears, the Liberian settlers prayed to a Christian God, spoke English, wore Western-style clothing, constructed Western-style dwellings along grid-pattern streets, and, in short, behaved in the manner they associated with the European and Euro-American tradesmen and sailors who had been traveling down the western coast of Africa for centuries. And so as Liberian settler Diana James succinctly wrote to her former enslaver in 1843 about the customs of the Africans, "they call us all white man." Instead of operating as binaries, as they often are presented, the whiteness and blackness of these African American settlers operated simultaneously. In their African enclave, the African American settlers were the "black-white people."[6]

Even more surprising, although he supported the removal of free people of color from the United States owing to the hardened and seemingly immutable racial lines drawn there, Bridge paradoxically recognized that something different was afoot in the Liberian settlements he visited and that the "race" of the African American settlers was perhaps not so immutable after all. For Bridge and most white supporters of colonization, the "colored people of America, or any other part of the world, may be regarded as borrowed from Africa, and inheriting a natural adaptation to her soil and climate."[7] In other words, people of African descent, regardless of their temporal or physical distance from Africa, held a "natural" affinity and place in that land of their ancestors. It was a central tenet of colonizationist rhetoric that this relocation to western Africa actually constituted a "homecoming" for these settlers; for the readers of Bridge's journal, they were informed that Liberia "may indeed be called the black man's paradise." But after these repeated affirmations of unchanging and unalterable racialized—and masculine gendered—blackness, a blackness "borrowed" from Africa, Bridge then paradoxically noted that "blackness" was perhaps *not* a mutually shared identity between the settlers and their African neighbors.[8] Indeed, Bridge was so struck by the prejudices held by many of the Africans against the settlers, and vice-versa, that he actually employed the rhetoric of "race-mixing" to describe the relations between the two groups: "Many of the natives look with contempt on the colonists, and do not hesitate to tell them that they are merely liberated slaves. On the other hand, the colonists will never recognize the natives otherwise than as heathen. Amalgamation is scarcely more difficult between the white and colored races in America, than it is in Africa, between the 'black-white' colonist and unadulterated native."[9]

This book examines the ramifications for these African American settlers, the Americo-Liberians, of becoming white and black through their Atlantic mobility. This is not to suggest that those African Americans who relocated to Liberia somehow desired to be white, conceived of themselves as white, or hoped to "pass" as white after their arrival in Africa. In other words, this is not a story of black people wishing they were white. But it is a story of a society hoping to replicate similar privileges for itself in Africa that exclusion from whiteness had prevented its denizens from enjoying in the United States. Instead of simply crossing over some black/white divide, these settlers employed their morphing racial identity and the fascination with their African whiteness found in the United States (and fueled by accounts like Bridge's) as a useful tool to mold themselves into exotic others while simultaneously escaping associations with primitivism. As the harbingers of Christianity and Western culture in "benighted" Africa, existence in Liberia transformed its African American inhabitants from the perceived bottom rung of American society into the "civilizers" of a continent, a cultured and elevated identity to which many Anglo-Americans found themselves awkwardly acquiescing.

Centering this examination on the African American settlers' race and mobility sheds new light on race, the colonization movement, and Liberia. A critical first step is reestablishing Liberia as a significant and evolving point within the Atlantic world, instead of its usual interpretative role as the *end* of a transatlantic journey. While scholars have not ignored life in the colony of Liberia, most have focused on the lived experiences *within* the colony.[10] The oceanic journey of these settlers is largely perceived as the culmination of their transatlantic peregrinations rather than just the beginning.[11] Certainly Liberia was an impoverished location with a high mortality rate that would make it a permanent resting place for many previously mobile Atlantic subjects, but for those who survived the acclimating fever, the wars, and the poverty, it was not necessarily the end. Whether as disgruntled former settlers, paid spokesmen for the ACS, visitors returning to childhood abodes, emancipators looking to free family from the chains of slavery, or students seeking medical degrees, Liberian settlers returned to the United States with no interest in resuming their formerly downtrodden place in American society.

In his history of African American journeys to Africa, James Campbell asserts that Africa is paradoxically a site for people of African descent to negotiate and conceptualize their relationship to the United States. Travel between Africa and the United States meant that negotiation played out on both sides of the Atlantic. Liberia's idealized role as African America further complicated settlers' identities. Both black and white colonizationists shared a vision in which Liberia would function as a new United States, one with inverted power dynamics in which the settlers would enjoy the privileges of American whiteness in Africa and Africans would function as societal mudsills. These relations of power have led James Sidbury to conclude that Liberia ironically provided a place where black Americans could "become more fully American." Similarly, Bronwen Everill argues that Liberia was "'more American than America,' since only in Africa could the African descendant practise unfettered Christianity, participate in democracy, own his land, and engage in modern life." The African whiteness of the settlers underscores the missing racial element of Sidbury's and Everill's claims: Liberia offered black Americans a place where they could be more fully *white* Americans. Of course, mobility disrupted the settlers' Americanness as they pressed to see whether that identity created *outside* the United States could travel back and exist *within* the United States. Liberians' claims on that American identity were complicated and shaped by their African residence, a point Everill underscores. As occupants of a colony of a private benevolent society rather than an actual territory of the United States, Liberia's settlers were left to develop their own institutions, usually founded upon American models, and emphasize their commercial success and parallel colonial experiences—the troubles of Monrovia were often conflated with the early problems of Jamestown—to engage the United States. In examining the "Americanness" of the settlers, the violence of the colonial space, and the agricultural practices of the colony, Everill's work in particular laid the foundation for this book.[12]

This book builds upon these scholars' insights to argue that Liberia provided settlers with a set of "tools" to negotiate new relationships with the inhabitants of the United States. Settlers could not fully turn their backs on Africa because it was their residence there—and the claims they made regarding their African experiences—that undergirded their negotiations. The transatlantic travels of Liberians ensured that these were not just metaphorical arguments shouted across the Atlantic Ocean, and these "negotiations" had practical applications for the lives of settlers in both the United States and Africa.

Liberian narratives like Bridge's and the numerous publications of the ACS ensured that word of the colony's racial constructions returned to the United States. An umbrella organization, the ACS was an evolving tapestry of state auxiliary societies that cobbled together disparate supporters of slavery, conservative antislavery advocates, evangelicals concerned with missionary efforts in Africa, and supporters of black uplift who believed that it could only be achieved through separation and the establishment of an independent African American republic among the nations of the world.[13] The sinew that connected these discordant constituents was a shared assumption that the unchecked growth of the number of free people of color within the United States would spell unmitigated disaster for the nation due to increased racial violence. Whether in the form of free peoples' involvement in slave insurrections or clampdowns by uncompromising whites who would never grant equality or freedom to African Americans, the violence predicted by ACS prophets foreshadowed an uncompromising race war with distinct and hardened battle lines. In positioning the ACS as an organization whose members both supported and opposed slavery, I turn away from the vexing question of whether the ACS was a proslavery or antislavery society.[14]

Despite momentary bursts of "neo-colonizationist" scholarship aimed at rehabilitating the antislavery credentials of the ACS, the majority of scholars examining antebellum black activism have categorized the colonization movement as an "idea championed by White racists who did not want to interact with free Blacks on an equal basis and plotted to forcibly remove Blacks from the United States before they gained American citizenship and posed a real threat to Southern slavery."[15] For scholars, "emigration" usually denotes the movement of black-led organizations who were frustrated by the racial oppression of the United States and sought freedom beyond its borders. Such a rigid binary fails to address intellectual crossbreeding between the movements, the very real conservative antislavery wing of the ACS, and essentially transforms those emigrants who decided to relocate to Liberia as either unwitting dupes of white racists or activists intentionally trying to undermine black uplift (charges that were actually brought against the settlers). An organization as diffuse, decentralized, and constantly evolving as the ACS looked in far more directions than Janus and defies such simplistic declarations regarding its stance on slavery, especially since its primary concern was not support or opposition to slavery but the great question of freedom.[16]

The driving question for many colonizationists was not slavery but rather whether free black Americans could coexist with white Americans.[17] Such an issue fostered deep divisions within the organization, as members arrived at vastly different answers to that question. Some perceived of blackness as inherently degraded, violent, and valueless, a needless threat to slavery and white society that colonization could remedy; others argued that degraded blackness was an artificial product of white society and that only through separation from whites, who would never allow for peaceful coexistence, could African Americans find uplift; still others perceived Liberia as a case study in black capacity and believed that African American uplift in the United States could begin only with evidence of a sophisticated and "civilized" republic of African Americans. Even supporting the creation of an independent black republic, as Brandon Mills astutely noted, could allow white people to simultaneously support "black self-determination and disenfranchisement at the same time." Regardless of their respective paths to colonization (and there were many more), many white Americans considered the possibilities of free black existence within the United States and concluded that separation offered the greatest benefits. For an institution committed to the literal whitening of America, it must have come as a bit of a surprise to its members that the ACS was also apparently whitening Africa.[18]

Since the first meeting of the ACS, colonizationists had assumed that "degraded" free blacks would also become the vehicle of African uplift and "civilization" by establishing "colonies, composed of blacks already instructed in the arts of civilized life." There is a duality here that has always perplexed and intrigued scholars of Liberia. How could such an uncivilized and violent class in America form the civilizing backbone of a rejuvenated and Christian Africa? Marie Tyler-McGraw found this transformation more indicative of "alchemy." Claude A. Clegg III referred to it as "a tortured logic geared more toward effecting their ends than to proving the intellectual cogency of their position."[19] The arguments, however, can be explained by the low regard with which most colonizationists held Africa, as they repeatedly affirmed that the lowest of the low in America were still far superior to the greatest in Africa. The true logical fallacy of colonization lay in its supporters' understanding of race. Colonization was a complex sociospatial argument that asserted that merely inhabiting the space of Liberia was transformative and "civilizing" for all parties. The racial morphing of the Americo-Liberians played a critical role in how white colonizationists perceived their respective "civilization" across the Atlantic.[20]

Understanding this elevation for those who entered the space of Liberia requires a more complex notion of "whiteness," divorced from phenotype and the presence of people of European descent—a "whiteness" without "whites."[21] The ACS, after all, was an organization nominally founded on the principle of uncompromising conflict among fixed and intractable races. Yet, colonizationists proved remarkably adept at holding the same contradictory understanding of race as a societal construction that Bridge employed in his journal; they could see only unending and unchanging racial conflict within the United States even as they pondered the evolution of race in Liberia and what it meant for the "black-white" settlers across the Atlantic Ocean.[22] This was the central paradox at the heart of many colonizationists' thinking: a surprising understanding of race as a product of a given society and a simultaneous rejection that different constructions were possible within American society. In the context of Liberia, whiteness was produced by the settlers' Western cultural practices. The same set of circumstances did not produce the same racial identity in the United States at the same time, but colonizationists within the United States were not only aware of the racial adaptations in Liberia but also used the African whiteness of their settlers as a propaganda tool. For example, Samuel Wilkeson, general agent of the ACS in 1839, proclaimed in one tract: "The Liberian is certainly a great man, and what is more, by the natives he is considered a white man, though many degrees from that stand—for to be thought acquainted with the white man's fashions, and to be treated as one, are considered as marks of great distinction among the Bassa and other nations."[23]

Clearly, some colonizationist leaders were dismissive of these Africans' conflation of the performative aspects of Western culture with whiteness; the African Americans were "many degrees" from becoming white in Wilkeson's eyes. Although there were a few rare exceptions of white colonizationists embracing these African notions, one being Moses Sheppard, who holds an integral place in the following pages, one should not assume that an *awareness* of the Americo-Liberians' whiteness in Africa equated to an *acceptance* of that identity. Most white colonizationists, steeped in ideas of white supremacy, assumed that the whiteness of the Liberian settlers reflected their neighboring Africans' concession that these newcomers to the continent represented an advanced cultural vanguard clearly superior to their own and worthy of emulation.

In reality, most of the Liberian Africans were not overly impressed with their newly acquired Americo-Liberian governors, as attested by the constant strife between settlers and Africans. The violent conflicts between Americo-Liberians and Liberia's indigenous peoples have led Tunde Adeleke to conclude that the settlers adhered to a European model of "civilization" and imperialism. In doing so, he joins a chorus of Liberia's nineteenth-century critics who argued that the settlers functioned merely as surrogate whites in Africa, an argument undergirded by the settlers' African whiteness. Christine Whyte has challenged Adeleke's construction as overly simplistic given the complexities of Liberia. Yet, she counters that Liberian imperialism must be understood by examining the settlers' "shared history" of slavery, reasons for emigration, and "shared racial identity with native-born Africans." Not all of the settlers experienced slavery in the same way—let alone the colony's small population of freeborn settlers—and a "shared racial identity" was a far more complex notion than Whyte suggests.[24]

Although some African Liberians sought acculturation and adopted Western cultural practices, many Africans desiring educational opportunities and acquaintance with what they termed "white man's fash" were seeking economic opportunity only. The ACS land claims constituted much of the former "pepper coast," named for the melegueta pepper.[25] The West African coastal dwellers there had engaged in the commercial networks of the Atlantic for centuries before the arrival of the first ACS ships. While disrupting the balance of power in the region's commercial enterprises, the creation of Liberia also signaled the establishment of missionary-run schools for African children that offered access to literacy, command of English, and Western cultural practices, all desired commodities for these coastal middlemen. The arrival of the colonists likewise provided work for laborers. There were many reasons why Africans sought the educational and economic opportunities of the Americo-Liberian settlements that did not reflect an assumption of the settlers' supposed superiority.

While the Africans' racialized identity was not meant to convey superiority, the African American settlers, in turn, used their African whiteness as part of a broader effort to establish an ambiguous identity somewhere between white and black based upon their perceived elevated status in Africa. The Americo-Liberians proved remarkably adept at holding the colonization societies accountable for their celebration of the settlers, especially when they returned to the United States. As Elizabeth Pryor has ably demonstrated, the public conveyances of the early nineteenth century's "transportation revolution"—stagecoaches, trains, steamships—were notorious locations for antiblack aggression and violence. Black activists identified mobility as a marker of citizenship, and travel became a significant theater of operation for the era's civil rights leaders who were especially concerned with newly created segregated seating arrangements.[26] Liberian settlers skirted around the citizenship debate, but they were likewise uninterested in riding in the Jim Crow Car. Here, the celebrated whiteness of the settlers came home to roost for colonizationists, who found themselves acquiescing to Liberian demands for different treatment based upon their elevated position in Africa. Once colonizationists had celebrated the whiteness of their African American settlers, they could not easily return to interacting with Americo-Liberians as they did with other African Americans. The prophets of unending racial conflict found themselves opening their homes, their wallets, their social networks, their resources, and their schools to African Americans.

In turning our analytical gaze to the cross-Atlantic peregrinations of Americo-Liberians, however, we must also examine this Atlantic world—what many scholars have dubbed the "black Atlantic"—in detail. In reexamining Liberia as a node of the broader Atlantic world instead of the end of the journey, this book suggests new avenues for integrating studies of whiteness with "black Atlantic" scholarship. Paul Gilroy, in his transformative work *The Black Atlantic: Modernity and Double Consciousness*, sought to untether "black" from its usual conflation with "Africa" and push it into the watery mobile world of the Atlantic Ocean. Gilroy's "black Atlantic" is fluid and adaptable. The horrors of the slave trade produced a mobile population that eschewed national divisions by finding resonance and commonality in the shared experience of New World slavery. The significance of this call to interpret the Atlantic "as one single, complex unit of analysis" cannot be understated.[27]

Fissures have developed in the black Atlantic model, however, many resulting from scholars of Africa or the non-Anglophone black Atlantic privileged by Gilroy.[28] Most critically, for a scholarship dedicated to hybridity, fluidity, and mobility, why must this be an inherent and unchanging "black" Atlantic? That scholars now take seriously the contributions of the enslaved and formerly enslaved in shaping Atlantic societies is a groundbreaking evolution in the field, but can "black" be deterministically defined as the enslaved, the manumitted, and their descendants?

And questions have even arisen within the Anglophone black diaspora about the utility and commonality of that diasporic identity built upon a shared history of terror and enslavement. Indeed, those scholars who have read the letters of Liberian settlers have often been struck by their strong connections to American homelands rather than to a broader diasporic identity. On the other hand, others have noted that certain settlers emphatically affirmed Liberia and Africa more broadly as their "home," rather than the United States. Colonization spurred a fundamental debate in America: where was "home" for African Americans? White colonizationists emphatically answered "Africa"; African Americans overwhelmingly responded "America." The opinions, thoughts, and letters of those who lived in Liberia were marshaled by each side. In reality, some settlers thought of the United States as their home, others embraced Africa, many waffled between the two, and others found neither answer convincing and kept on moving.[29]

It is unsurprising that black Atlantic scholars have turned their analytical gaze toward Liberia, along with its Anglo cousin, Sierra Leone. Founded in 1792, Sierra Leone shared many similarities with Liberia as a settler society consisting of African diasporans. Padraic X. Scanlan notes that British abolitionism as manifested in Sierra Leone was aggressively militarized and expected to wring profits from the labor of "liberated Africans," enslaved peoples freed from illegal slave-trading vessels, who now owed a supposed debt to the British. Readers will find many parallels with this book's description of Liberia. Yet, there were significant differences. As the product of a private benevolent society, although one deeply entwined with the federal government, Liberia's governance and relationship to the United States was far more murky and complicated than the British model once the crown took over Sierra Leone in 1808. Significantly, while one can debate its relative merits, Sierra Leone was at least founded on antislavery principles, whereas Liberia was created to solve the "problem" of free people of color.[30]

Liberia and Sierra Leone embody the constitutive elements of the black Atlantic—a space for mobile members of the African diaspora crossing the Atlantic to establish a new "home"—and Liberia holds a particularly significant, if not always acknowledged, place in Gilroy's *The Black Atlantic*. Whether embracing or rejecting, running to or running away from, most of the intellectual elites spotlighted by Gilroy as indices of the black Atlantic, including Frederick Douglass, Martin Delany, Edward Wilmot Blyden, and Alexander Crummell, dedicated significant time, ink, and energy to thinking about Liberia as a space, a nation-state, an idea, or a lived experience. In the Atlantic networks of mobility, Liberia was an important hub, even if scholars must remember the dangers of conflating one particular juncture of the Anglophone African American Atlantic with *the* black Atlantic or *the* black diaspora.

Yet, in refocusing our scholarly lens on this important Liberian node of the black Atlantic, "black" suddenly becomes a more diffuse and nebulous concept, necessitating a renewed examination. Perhaps most curiously, whiteness studies and black Atlantic scholarship have rarely intersected.

This is especially peculiar given their nearly simultaneous meteoric rises within the academic community and the shared challenges raised to each discourse as their practitioners floundered to delineate the contours of the "black diaspora" and "black Atlantic," on the one hand, and "whiteness," on the other. These have been two different discourses passing in the night; the complete dearth of scholarly attention to any intersections of these two prolific topics of academic study intrinsically suggests the allure of formulaic binaries even in fields whose practitioners are the most vocal in eschewing them. Where the black Atlantic goes, whiteness can only impede, interrupt, or challenge; the two seemingly never walk hand in hand. But if we are to take seriously the whiteness of the African American settlers in Liberia, whiteness can no longer merely stand in for white supremacy exercised by Europeans and their descendants, and the "black" qualifier of the "black Atlantic" must be questioned and probed and can no longer refer simply to an assumed cohesiveness founded on enslaved pasts or presents.

Americo-Liberians were noted for their ability to pragmatically shape their identities.[31] While the Liberian settlers sought an elevated status above their formerly degraded station when traveling to the United States, their ability to do so depended heavily upon class and their social connections within the United States. Gender further shaped these complicated and fluid dynamics. Colonizationist rhetoric, centered on a mission to tame African "savagery," was heavily skewed toward idealized masculine tropes of dominance. Furthermore, as conservative colonization societies sought settlers to travel the United States in order to lecture to mixed-sex groups of potential settlers, they specifically targeted male settlers as the only suitable candidates to perform these tasks. Women were likewise excluded from opportunities for educational pursuits, which provided another principal means by which Liberian settlers returned to the United States with the support and patronage of colonizationists. Whiteness in Africa was a powerful tool to bring to the negotiating table, but it was not a dominating claim that trumped everything else. Gender and class placed obvious constraints on its exercise by women, the poor, and those without the personal connections of an influential patron.[32]

This book proceeds broadly and thematically. Chapter 1 establishes the trajectories of several Liberian settlers' travels in the United States, what they wanted to accomplish, how they fared, and what they actually attained. It traces how the settlers' whiteness became entangled with arguments regarding their relative "civilization" and the power that provided to certain well-positioned settlers to make claims for an elevated status during their stays abroad. Here, I join other scholars who have reminded us that focusing solely on the overwhelming rejection of emigration to Liberia by African Americans obscures the motivations and thinking of those settlers who did choose to go there.[33] They sought a liminal position between antipodal whiteness and blackness that they often described through negation; they hoped to remain undefined and unfixed and in this manner slip through American society's racialized norms. This slippery and ever-changing approach, however, neither ensured settlers' success nor guaranteed a similar experience for all.

Of course, the same ships that returned Liberian settlers to their American roots could, and did, bring native Africans across the Atlantic for their own American adventures. The resulting exchange between the two societies shaped racial consciousness not only in the United States but also within the Liberian colonies themselves. Differing definitions of whiteness were at work in these Atlantic societies, and the constant exchange between the two reshaped each one's perceptions of race. While the focus of this chapter is on the watery networks linking the United States and Liberia, this should not be interpreted as denying the broader network of connections in which this node of the Atlantic world was situated. The harbors of Liberia were filled with vessels from a multitude of nations; in addition to the treaties and negotiations with numerous African groups to expand Liberia's territory, the settlers also were sandwiched between French colonial incursions to their east and Sierra Leone to the northwest; there were British recruiters trying to secure workers for their Caribbean colonies; there were rumors that Brazil planned to establish its own African colony to relocate its enslaved population. Although the subject of this chapter is the critical and constant interchange between colony and metropole, it is important to note that this is but one channel of a vast array of Atlantic intercourse and mobility.

Chapters 2 through 4 examine the practices by which the Americo-Liberians established their African whiteness.[34] These constituted a perceived command and control of the space, the employment of degraded African labor, and the use of multifaceted violence against Africans. Chapter 2 examines the geographic and spatial logic that undergirded colonization. At its heart, colonization is an argument about space, or as Nicholas Guyatt eloquently summed, "a form of 'racial improvement' that sees space as a solution to the problem of race."[35] By occupying the "civilizing" space of Liberia, degraded American blackness was transformed into exotic, and "civilized," whiteness. One of the keys to this transformation was projecting

Liberia as a tiny United States—despite the environment's and Africans' best efforts to defy this transplantation—in which Americo-Liberians served as masters. Critical to the perception of elevated settlers, on the one hand, and degraded Africans, on the other, was that "heathen" Africans be separate and beyond the limits of "civilization," so as to not taint the area with their "barbarity," while simultaneously being subject to the control of the settlers. A critical element of whiteness is the effort to control nonwhites, and a constant propagandist refrain of colonizationists was the "influence" the settlers held over Africans, as evidenced by their African whiteness. Cartography and maps of Liberia proved useful tools in this complex dance of establishing separation and togetherness, distance and control, simultaneously.

Chapter 3 focuses on Liberia's labor regime. If geography was used to rhetorically separate African from Americo-Liberian, then the expansive use of coerced, unfree, or debased African labor in the colonies "returned" them to the "civilized space." The spatial separation of Americo-Liberians and Liberian Africans had to be established discursively because of the obvious and overwhelming presence of Africans in the American settlements. Labor provided a tool for explaining how Africans had been brought "back" into a place they had never actually left. Like the discourse on space, the rhetoric surrounding the Liberian labor system attempted to project Africans as separate from the settlers but under their control. In this case, the literal command of black bodies undergirded the whiteness of the Americo-Liberians.

Two broad charges leveled against Liberian settlers' labor practices dominated the discourse in the United States. First, the settlers were supposedly lazy and preferred engaging in trade to the hard work of farming. Not only did this charge emanate from the image of the "lazy freed slave" circulating in the Atlantic following British abolition in the Caribbean, but accusations of settlers refusing to farm were common complaints voiced by the colony's administrators. However, the situation on the ground was far more complex. Liberia's coastal soils are rather poor, a fact many settlers commented on. Also, Liberian settlers *did* engage in agriculture and even tried their hand at producing indigenous crops. The "failure" of Liberian agriculture was a failure only when measured against the pipe dreams of American backers who concocted a completely unrealistic agrarian vision for the colony.[36]

The second charge, that the settlers utilized slave labor, was even more explosive. Slavery was made unconstitutional and illegal from the first days of the colony, but as in other places of the nineteenth-century Atlantic, there were many degrees of freedom and unfreedom in Liberia. Although chattel slavery was outlawed, there were a large number of labor options available to those settlers in the best position to capitalize on them. The African system of pawnship, whereby individuals, often women and children, were held in bondage as collateral for loans or their labor was used to pay off a debt evolved in the Liberian context into a form of indentured servitude. This resulted in a large number of Liberian households utilizing African youths as domestic servants. Additionally, illegally enslaved Africans liberated by the U.S. Navy, called "recaptives" or "Congoes,"[37] were deposited in Liberia regardless of their actual points of origin; many of these "Congoes" found themselves bound to Liberian settlers under terms of service familiar to American audiences. There was also the simple option of hiring African laborers for particular tasks and paying them substantially reduced wages. Ideologically, Liberia actually needed to uplift two separate populations: indigenous Africans *and* African American settlers. The bridge between these two groups lay in the "civilizing" capacity of labor. Working for the settlers within various states of unfreedom would bestow "civilization" upon native Africans; settlers would find uplift through their command of indigenous black labor.[38]

In addition to thinking about the spatial control over Liberia and the labor of its inhabitants, the Liberian settlers also projected their power and control over Africans through the threat of force and violence. Chapter 4 explores the multifaceted forms of violence that rocked the colony, characterizing day-to-day life in intimate settings as well as within larger conflicts. Liberia was an expansionist space continually looking to enlarge its influence and territory along the coast and into the continent's interior. These conquests involved numerous instances of aggression and violence, and the settlers quickly utilized their often-violent interactions with Africans to establish their cultural separation from Africans and celebrated their victories as evidence of their power and control. In addition, such violent excursions provided martial glory to the settlers and their cause. Americo-Liberians celebrated their military organizations and were very proud of their ranks, such distinctions having been denied them in the United States. The projected and assumed threat of being swallowed by "barbaric" neighbors papered over the many societal divisions that threatened to break Liberian society apart: freeborn settlers often quarreled with their formerly enslaved neighbors, Northerners and Southerners were dismissive of each other's respective homes, and some settlers arrived in Africa with economic advantages that others did not share. The violence likewise reinforced colonization's masculine projection, as settlers heroically defended their outpost of "civilization" against what they argued was aggressive heathenism. The violence between Americo-Liberians and Africans became a source of criticism for those opposed to colonization, who argued that the settlers were not so much exercising "influence" over Africans as violently repressing them. Although this book separates these arguments regarding space, labor, and violence into three distinct chapters, there are obviously significant areas of overlap between them, and readers will find elements of each in every chapter.

Turning its lens away from the space of Liberia, chapter 5 reexamines the overwhelming rejection of colonization by free people of color in the United States, the evolution of the colonization societies, and the agency of the settlers in enacting these changes. For scholars, the trajectory of free black people's rejection of colonization follows a fairly standard narrative, from early hopeful flirtations with Paul Cuffe and his idea for black-led migrations to the resounding rejection of the white-led ACS. Indeed, scholars have noted that the colonization movement's conflation of "Africans" with people of African descent led free blacks to drop "African" from the names of their institutions in favor of a "colored" identity and dramatically shaped their determination to define and secure citizenship within the United States.[39] This chapter certainly does not challenge the unpopularity of colonization with free African Americans. It does, however, add nuance to this narrative. The figure of the successful Liberian settler, traveling through the United States with lighter restrictions than other African Americans and lecturing on the possibilities of life in Africa, posed a substantial obstacle to those who desired to fight for African American rights in the United States. The blanket denunciation of African American settlers in Liberia and their accomplishments undermined the agenda for black uplift in the United States. The result was a meandering course in which colonization's critics often celebrated the colony while denouncing colonization, portraying the settlers as unfortunate, but resilient, victims deceived by the white racists in charge of the ACS. The independence of Liberia made this a problematic line of attack, and many critics switched to denouncing the Americo-Liberians as simply white surrogates attempting to carve up Africa for Western imperialism.

Therein lay the difference between the few who elected to depart for Liberia and the vast majority who remained. For the majority of African Americans, the spatial argument of the colonizationists, the idea that they were debased, immoral, and depraved in the United States but could be civilization's vanguard in Africa, was laughable and offensive. Those few who saw possibility in Liberia emphasized the performative possibilities of the colony: the ability to draw up their own maps, command their soldiers in battle, and travel through the United States with an African servant to symbolize their rank. Significantly, the small number of African Americans who willingly chose to emigrate to Liberia were often racially ambiguous.[40] They saw opportunity in the undefined and evolving racial identities of the Atlantic.

Chapter 5 also examines the settlers' roles in changing the colonization societies. One of the aspects that makes the ACS difficult to define was the evolving nature of the organization itself. While other scholars have commented upon changes within the ACS, such as the great antislavery/proslavery schism within the Society that came to the forefront during the 1833 national convention, most have placed the onus of these changes on the white leadership.[41] This work adopts a different approach and argues that the African American settlers forced the hands of colonizationists and led them to adopt changes. Far from being fools tricked by whites, the Liberian settlers were intimately aware that colonization was a multifaceted movement, and they sought to create changes that recognized and supported black uplift. For many settlers, there was no difference between abolition and colonization, and they vocalized their frustrations with abolitionists' focus on the ACS leadership. Settlers worked with colonizationists committed to black uplift and attempted to drive out those who did not favor such reforms. This is why so many Americo-Liberians were critical of the charges brought against the colonizationist movement by African Americans and white abolitionists. For the Americo-Liberians, it was more important to recognize that certain white colonization leaders would work toward the goal of black uplift and to secure *their* support than to denounce the movement as a whole because it included supporters of slavery or black subjugation.

This book focuses on the experiences and beliefs of the African American settlers and Africans in the colony of Liberia and on its earliest years as a republic after independence in 1847. Readers will notice that while I examine Liberia and Liberians broadly, I often focus my analytical gaze upon the independent colony of Maryland in Liberia, established by the MSCS in 1834. The MSCS desired to shift colonization in a more antislavery direction and did not believe it could accomplish this goal within the confines of the ACS—a telling argument regarding the respective antislavery chops of that latter organization—and thus established the model for independent state action, which they termed the "Maryland Plan." Nominally, the ACS collected funds, support, and settlers through its state auxiliaries before dispatching official expeditions; the Marylanders retained control over their state donations to establish and support Maryland in Liberia. The effort would spark additional rebellions from other state and regional colonization societies. This diffuse collection of Liberian "colonies"—which is a more accurate description, given that Liberia was not a single "colony"—were brought together under the 1839 constitution of the "Commonwealth of Liberia," with the exception of Maryland in Liberia, which remained independent until 1857.[42]

The result of these changes was a dramatic decentralization of the ACS and its African colonies. The African geography found itself, in addition to its own Maryland, with a Kentucky, Virginia, Louisiana, and Mississippi.[43] Because of its decentralized, state-oriented approach, many scholars have examined the colonization movement through state studies, and we have excellent monographs examining the movement in Pennsylvania, Maryland, North Carolina, Mississippi, and Virginia.[44] This book focuses less on the peculiarities of particular organizations within the colonization movement than on the broad process of race-making within Liberia and how this affected Americo-Liberians and their colonizationist sponsors in the United States. I often discuss Maryland in Liberia not because it is a more interesting settlement but rather because many of the central figures of this work—those individuals who best capitalized on the advantages derived from their African whiteness—settled there.

Because my project centers on the creation of race in Liberia and its effects both there and in the United States, it does not proceed as a chronological history of the colonization societies or of the Americo-Liberian settlements in the traditional sense. This is also not strictly a history of the African Liberians who lived, worked, traded, and otherwise engaged with the Americo-Liberians. Although I do take seriously the racial categorizations of these West Africans and place them at the center of this argument where they rightfully belong, a history of the Africans in Liberia is a different book. Indeed, even the use of the word "African" is a bit misleading as it is more a creation of the African diaspora in the western hemisphere than of Africa itself. The arrival of the African American settlers to the region reinforced an understanding that those groups who had inhabited the area before the settlers shared certain cultural traits that they identified as "black"; the other common identity to signify these native Africans was "countrymen." The whiteness of the Americo-Liberians was established in opposition to this "countryman" identity, but a conceptualization of a shared "otherness" differentiated from the Western settlers did not necessarily create a uniformed African identity.[45] Today, Liberians recognize at least sixteen ethnic groups: Gola, Kissi, Bassa, Belleh, Dei, Grebo, Krahn, Kru, Gbandi, Gio, Kpelle, Loma, Mandingo, Mano, Mende, and Vai. Speaking in nearly twenty languages from at least three different family groups and possessing their own characteristics, cultures, and motivations, these different groups at various times found the Americo-Liberians useful allies, bitter enemies, aggressive trading partners, overbearing educators, annoying interlopers, and beneficial mediators in their conflicts with each other and with the settlers.[46]

Unfortunately, the majority of the settlers and visitors to Liberia were not especially interested in ethnographic differences, and their accounts reflect their generalizations. Liberia was a project in colonialism, and its backers, white and black, joined with other colonizers in obsessing over ideas of "civilization," "heathenism," "barbarity," and "savagery." Such hierarchical ordering of societies was obviously contested, and I have emphasized the constructed nature of these ideas in the text. However, most accounts written by settlers and visitors, with very few exceptions, refer to Africans simply as "natives" or "heathens." As identifying individuals or groups is often impossible, I am unfortunately left with the equally generic "African" to denote these men and women.

Even when non-Africans *did* attempt to identify indigenous peoples, their classifications are often problematic. The nautical Krumen, a Liberian group famed for their seamanship, are illustrative. Their skills ensured that the Krumen were some of the few African Liberians explicitly identified by white observers. However, Westerners were actually part of the process of creating "Krumen," rather than merely identifying a preexisting group. The Krumen speak a dialect of the Kru language family along with the Grebo peoples of Cape Palmas, who likewise hold a prominent place in this book, and many other coastal dwellers who sought nautical work. While they did not conceive of themselves as a single people, these African sailors shared some linguistic and cultural similarities. Western sailors, however, were uninterested in these nuances and lumped together the many African identities that went to sea as "Krumen," or "Kroomen" as they often spelled it. The Krumen identity actually evolved out of these classifications. Since many peoples were identified as "Krumen," I have elected to use the shortened "Kru" to emphasize the broader and evolving identities of those who may not have conceived of themselves as "Krumen."[47]

Also problematic is Western travelers' widespread use of sobriquets and nicknames for Africans. Occasionally, the purported name of the individual is recorded along with their nickname; in this manner, we know that "King Freeman," the ruler of the African village attached to Russwurm's colony, was actually named Pah Nemah. I have elected in this book to enclose the Western sobriquets within quotation marks to denote that these are artificial creations. While a famous leader such as Pah Nemah remains in Liberian memory, this book is likewise built upon obscure persons who appear briefly in colonial accounts, as hewers of wood and drawers of water, and are always listed by their Western nicknames. Similarly, I often employ the term "Americo-Liberian" to denote the African American settlers and their children regardless of time frame, whereas this term is usually reserved to denote the generations proceeding from the first African American settlers. I employ it simply as a shorthand to differentiate between Liberians of American descent and African Liberians.

Finally, any scholar writing about the creation of race is left to ponder the implications of enclosing "white," "black," or "race" in quotation marks, to emphasize their constructed nature, or of not enclosing them, to emphasize the lived experience of individuals. To understand that blackness was a creation of a particular society at a particular time does not mean that to be defined as "black" lacked real-world effects. Examining whiteness in two different, though intimately connected, societal contexts crisscrossing the Atlantic Ocean makes answering this question doubly difficult. I occasionally employ "Euro-American" and "African American" to add variety to the narrative and underscore that these are creations of particular societies, but I find it an inelegant solution that possibly could be construed as asserting some sort of nonexistent racial purity. All of this being said, the emphasis of this project is to examine the bending of racialized identities in the lives of these people, and I have elected to eschew quotation marks, aside from instances in which I want to underscore the artificial construction of these identities or replicate the language of my subjects.

Race proved a fluid and adaptable form of identity in the Atlantic world. The experiences of Martin Delany, one of the bellwethers of the black Atlantic, underscore the point. Delany did visit the independent Republic of Liberia in 1859 after many years of denouncing colonization, Liberia, and the Americo-Liberians themselves.[48] Having embraced black-led emigration during the 1850s, Delany initially rejected Africa as a potential home for African Americans. However, he eventually changed course and supported the establishment of an African American colony in the Niger Valley region of Africa, and he sought funding for an exploratory expedition from the National Emigration Convention that he had helped found in 1854 and from prominent abolitionists. All declined to provide financial assistance for an African colony. Delany and his expedition partner, Robert Campbell, found themselves forced to accept aid from colonizationists, who provided the company with free passage on one of their vessels bound for Liberia on the condition that the exploring party stop briefly in Liberia and report on life there.[49]

In his official report of the expedition, Delany did his best to defuse his admittedly awkward arrival in Liberia, given his previously published remarks that its citizens were the puppets of white racists. The irony that Martin Delany of all people found himself in need of Liberian assistance was not lost on the good citizens of that republic. A committee of Monrovia's most prominent citizens dispatched a message of welcome as he traveled toward their city from his landing point at the northwestern town of Robertsport: "The undersigned citizens of the city of Monrovia, having long heard of you and your efforts in the United States to elevate our down-trodden race, though those efforts were not unfrequently directed against Liberia, are glad to welcome you, in behalf of the community, to these shores."[50]

This African voyage obviously influenced Delany's novel *Blake: Or, the Huts of America*, published in serialized form between 1859 and 1862. Although Delany had apparently started writing the work earlier, the book's descriptions of slave trading on the African coast and its mobile Atlantic protagonist, a thinly veiled surrogate for the author, who organizes African Diasporic communities for a grand multinational slave revolt, demonstrate knowledge gleaned from his own African voyage. In *Blake*, light-skinned Cuban quadroons serve as black double agents by posing as whites. These rebels "of the fairest complexion among the quadroons were classed as white," but behind the white mask they remained united with their black brethren. Ifeoma Nwankwo notes that Delany's notion of "blackness" in this novel rests upon a shared political commitment and identification with the black community rather than upon phenotype or culture.[51] In framing blackness as a choice for those of the "African race" who were "classed as white," Delany directly referenced the sorts of racial metamorphoses available in this amorphous Atlantic society.

In fact, his obsession with these racialized "choices" was present even before he sailed for Africa. In his keynote address at the 1854 Emigration Convention, Delany asserted that the entire world's destiny would be dependent upon a great racial struggle, "a question of black and white; and every individual will be called upon for his identity with one or the other."[52] Delany was clearly uncomfortable with the shades of gray in which the Atlantic system and its inhabitants existed, and he sought to draw clearer lines in the future struggle between black and white. Much like the quadroons of Cuba in *Blake*, all would cast their lot with either black or white and be done with the confusing space in between. For Delany, a decisive and final choice had to be made. For the Americo-Liberian subjects of this study whose existence vacillated between these two extremes, there were always more choices to be made and paths to be taken that, much like the Atlantic world, did not have such irremediable ends.

1

"To Be Called a Free Colored Man in the States Is Synonymous with What We Here Term Slavery"

Transformative Mobility and Liberian Travels through the United States

Although the racial hierarchy within the Liberian colonies was contested, unstable, and changing, most Liberian settlers did conceive of their trek across the Atlantic Ocean as a transformative move. This determination to steer their own destiny had characterized the African American settlers since the ACS dispatched its maiden voyage in 1820. While colonizationists celebrated the sailing of the *Elizabeth*, confusion reigned supreme aboard. The Society had not adequately outlined its vision for the relationship between the American-based organization, its representatives in Africa, and the settlers. Most settlers assumed that they would constitute any governmental body established in Africa. The society's agent, Samuel Crozer, disagreed. Additionally, the ACS's initial foray into Africa was largely supported through federal funds appropriated by the U.S. government following the enactment of the Slave Trade Act of 1819. Section 2 of the act authorized the president of the United States "to make such regulations and arrangements as he may deem expedient for the safe-keeping, support, and removal beyond the limits of the United States" of the "recaptured" Africans, and President James Monroe determined that the ACS's proposed colony provided a removal point well "beyond the limits of the United States." Thus, in addition to ACS agent Crozer, the *Elizabeth* sailed with government agents Samuel Bacon and John Bankson. Unfortunately, not only had the three white agents failed to establish the outlines of colonial governance with the settlers, but they did not even agree among themselves on how the colony would function.[1] The government agents assumed that the settlers were essentially laborers contracted by the United States to build a station for recaptured Africans; the ACS agent thought he commanded an expedition of settlers who were also coincidentally prepared to fulfill certain obligations for the federal government to establish the new colonial beachhead; the African American settlers believed they were members of an expedition to establish a colony that they would govern themselves.[2]

This confusion was a recipe for disaster for those aboard the *Elizabeth* following their arrival in Sierra Leone in March 1820. On the voyage across the Atlantic, the white agents had attempted to assert their control by reading their abbreviated instructions from the ACS, which primarily addressed the amount of land to be issued to colonists according to familial size. Based upon this responsibility, the agents asserted that they were the only ones authorized to negotiate with African leaders for the purchase of territory. A heated debate among the settlers was moderated only by the activism of Reverend Daniel Coker, an instrumental figure in the establishment of the African Methodist Episcopal Church, who was also the son of a white English indentured servant and an enslaved African. Coker, an early adherent of Paul Cuffe's ideas, found himself serving as the middleman between the agents and the settlers. Before sailing, Coker had impressed the government and ACS agents who put him in charge of loading the *Elizabeth* and invited him to bunk in their cabin.[3] Unfortunately, their planned destination, John Kizell's settlement on Sherbro Island, a thirty-mile-long and fifteen-mile-wide island just off the mainland, proved sickly and undeveloped. Kizell had to import fresh water from the mainland and morale deteriorated further.

Although a native of the area, Kizell had been sold into South Carolina slavery early in his life, served the British during the American Revolution, relocated to Canada, and returned to Sierra Leone in 1792 with other black Nova Scotians. One did not have to travel far to locate Americans near Freetown, the capital of Sierra Leone. One substantial cluster of American merchants and slave traders was located north of Freetown along the Rio Pongo. British officials in Sierra Leone were apparently so fearful of American colonial encirclement that they began raiding the factories during the War of 1812 and spent the following decade expanding Freetown's influence in the region.[4]

In Paul Cuffe's early sailings along the African coast to establish contacts in the region, he had organized the Friendly Society of Sierra Leone with the hope that the mercantile group would be able to break British trade monopolies and provide material assistance to future African American emigrants. Kizell was president of the Friendly Society when he met with John Mills and Ebenezer Burgess, two agents the ACS had dispatched to Africa in 1818 to survey potential sites for the planned colony. The agents became enamored of Kizell. In reported extracts of Mills's diary published posthumously in the ACS's annual report, the agent gushed, "We may safely trust our friend K. No man's heart can be more ardent for the success of our object, and no man in Africa could probably be so useful to us under present circumstances." Little wonder that the *Elizabeth* turned for Sherbro Island once the governor of Sierra Leone, still concerned about American influence, offered little assistance to the American enterprise.[5]

Disease swept among the settlers and the death toll rose. Christian Wiltberger, who sailed with the second ACS expedition aboard the *Nautilus*, listed five men, eight women, and eight children among the dead at Sherbro. Concomitant with the rising mortality rate, tensions, already high, rose even further. Although he arrived after the abandonment of Sherbro Island, assistant agent Wiltberger was forced to deal with the fallout from the first expedition. He evidently found those trials intriguing enough to transcribe the diary of Elijah Johnson, an *Elizabeth* settler, into his own journal from onboard the *Nautilus*. In so doing, Wiltberger created a combined rendering of the affairs of the first two expeditions. While the means by which Johnson's account survived leads to serious questions regarding the accuracy of transcription and possible editing on the part of the transcriptionist, the text offers some intriguing details. Amid the voyage, Johnson vis-à-vis Wiltberger notes that Coker had organized a Methodist congregation that would not be subject to white Methodists nor Richard Allen's authority. Given Coker's history and rivalry with Allen, this is not entirely out of character. In addition to mentioning Coker's defense of the white agents, including an argument presented by Coker that it was God's will that he bunked with the agents so that he could report on their activities to the settlers, Johnson's diary unveils a contentious voyage. John Fisher whipped his wife on deck; Richard Butler cut Francis Creecy with a knife; William Milton and Butler had a fight about cooking that terminated when Butler threw the pot overboard.

But beyond the scrapes and arguments commonplace to cramped living situations, there were darker conflicts at work. "Today Charles Francis's daughter had a fight and Mr. Bacon went down between decks and took the youngest and tied her and whipped her." What six-year-old Abigail Francis had to do with this altercation is unclear. It is equally unclear why Bacon administered corporal punishment on a settler's child. Was this part of the agent's campaign to reassert white dominance over the expedition? Was Bacon acting in his capacity as an Episcopal priest and former schoolteacher to correct a wayward child? Of course, performing this function would challenge the legitimacy of Coker's newly established ministry among the settlers.[6]

Once at Sherbro and its accompanying lean times, the ACS agent charged Creecy with stealing provisions. The agent intended for Coker to oversee the trial, but Creecy profusely objected to being tried by a "mulatto." Racial politics were afoot, and while Creecy perhaps did not believe he should be judged by the light-skinned Coker, it was probably Coker's close relationship with the agents that enraged Creecy. Even more problematic, the settlers again challenged the authority of the white agents to negotiate the purchase of land from Sherbro's African leaders. At a meeting held at Kizzel's church, Jonathan Adams proclaimed to Bacon, "Mr. K, the King, & head men, are waiting for our Agents, and they will not let a *white* man have the land, but the head man whom they give the land to must be a *black* man." Kizzel rose and exclaimed, "You misunderstood me," but Bacon was already convinced that Kizzel sought to water the seeds of discord sprouting vines among the settlers. Considering the Africans' previous and subsequent willingness to negotiate with Europeans and Anglo-Americans, Kizzel was probably being truthful when he announced that Adams had misunderstood.[7]

The abandonment of Sherbro did not solve the embryonic colony's racial problems. Remarkably, the ACS still had not determined the colonial hierarchy and the relationships between settlers, ACS agents, and government agents by the time the *Nautilus* sailed into Sierra Leone one year after the *Elizabeth*. Writing to the ACS from the Fourah Bay settlement in that colony on April 17, 1821, ACS assistant agent Christian Wiltberger found himself in a bind. He wrote, seemingly startled by his own ignorance, "I find I have come out here in much ignorance as to what is my duty as respects the Society's affairs or the connexion there exists between the Government and Society, and Agents and how we stand related to the people as Society's Agents and they to us." The impetus for his concern was the claims of two leaders of the settlers, soon to be destined for prominent positions in colonial governance, Colin Teague and Lott Cary, who explained to the agents that they considered the colonists independent of the ACS. After explaining the muddled affair in Sierra Leone, a befuddled Wiltberger could only ask for directions from home, as the only thing he could discern was that "the people do not consider themselves under the Society at all or it having any thing to do with them."[8]

By the fall of 1821, it seemed that the settlers would secure their independence through attrition alone. All three agents from the *Elizabeth* passed away in Africa. The *Nautilus*, which had sailed with two government representatives, Jonathan Winn and Ephraim Bacon, along with the ACS agent Joseph Andrus and his assistant, Wiltberger, fared slightly better. In April 1821, Andrus and Bacon negotiated with "King Jack Ben" of Grand Bassa for the purchase of territory southeast of the future site of Monrovia. Bacon's published diary notes the same questions of land ownership broached by the misunderstanding between Adams and Kizzel on Sherbro. Believing that the Bassa leader would find commonality with "American blacks," Andrus and Bacon informed the leader that they wanted "to get land for the black people in America, to come and sit down upon. . . . We told him that the people were very many, and required much territory; that a few white men only would come along, to assist and take care of them." After delivering this early encapsulation of the white man's burden, Andrus and Bacon set about the hard business of negotiation. After four days, a deal was struck and the agents distributed trade goods among the African participants. Bacon dutifully recorded "Jack Ben's" response to one particular trade good given to his son: "The king was much pleased at seeing his son with trowsers on; the people said, 'He gentleman all one white man.'" Unfortunately, the agent did not linger on that choice of words. That the Americans, agents and settlers, and Africans were thinking of "white" and "black" in very different terms during these early days of settlement is clear. Although successfully negotiated, Andrus and Bacon's agreement called for annual tributes to the African leader, and the ACS managers refused to support such an arrangement. The negotiations fell apart, and the luck of the *Nautilus*'s agents soured. Andrus and Winn passed away within weeks of concluding their negotiations with "Jack Ben," while Bacon returned to the United States in ill health.[9]

The administration fell to Wiltberger, himself ill and ineffective, in Sierra Leone until the arrival of Eli Ayres, representing both government and society, in the autumn of 1821. In December, while Ayres was down the coast negotiating the purchase of territory, Wiltberger prepared the settlers for relocation by issuing supplies and clothing; it did not go well. Settlers Francis and Lucy Posey found themselves doubly angry with Wiltberger when he refused Lucy's request for supplies after she arrived late to the distribution. Wiltberger recorded in his journal for December 12, 1821, "She made great to do about it." The next day, Francis knocked at Wiltberger's door. Answering, the agent supposed Posey's arrival stemmed from the previous disputes over supplies and immediately shut the door between himself and the settler. But Posey had actually arrived to receive a payment owed to him by Wiltberger. The agent refused to open the door for the settler, apparently upset at Posey for "abusing me in the most shameful manner." Wiltberger threatened to remove the Poseys from the list of those who would receive society support; Posey retorted, "Do it as quick as you please" and stormed off without payment. Wiltberger's journal soon was filled with accounts of altercations with settlers accompanied by signed statements from witnesses.[10]

By December 17, the settlers began holding formal meetings and established a society under the telling name "American African Union Society" with a leadership committee that included Cary, Teague, Johnson, and Coker in order to formally present settler grievances to the agents. Wiltberger was rescued from negotiating with the settlers by Ayres's return from negotiating with the Dei leaders of Cape Mesurado. Nakedly showcasing American naval power in the form of the USS *Alligator*—the warship was in the region to suppress the slave trade and Lieutenant Robert Stockton volunteered his services to the ACS—the negotiators were able to secure the embryo of Liberia for roughly $300 worth of trade goods. Wiltberger recorded in his diary, "They [Stockton and Ayres] had to make use of much planning and scheming to get the place and they state we are indebted to Captain Stockton." After the return of Ayres, the American African Union Society attempted to insert themselves into colonial governance by issuing formal declarations of their intent to negotiate with the agents on behalf of several settlers, including the Poseys. Ayres flatly rejected the authority of the group "to regulate the conduct of the people," instead claiming the judicial authority over the people for himself. Between January and May 1822, the society shuttled those emigrants who were willing to leave the British colony for Perseverance Island, a small island in the Mesurado River lying between the cape and the mainland. The settlers were unhappy with their agents; the Africans were unhappy with the settlers.[11]

Finding themselves sick, isolated, and undersupplied, Ayres and Wiltberger abandoned the island to seek reinforcements from America, leaving Elijah Johnson in charge of the settlement. Finally under the leadership of someone they considered their own, the settlers crossed the river and established their beachhead on the cape. It was this site, which Johnson and Cary were rapidly preparing for war against neighboring Africans, to which Jehudi Ashmun arrived in 1822. Ashmun led a combined expedition of African American settlers and recaptured Africans. Unaware that Ayres and Wiltberger had departed for the States, Ashmun carried an appointment from the ACS to serve as agent in the absence or death of Ayres. Although Ashmun's reputation would remain decidedly mixed among Liberian settlers for years after the end of his tenure as agent, there were at least several settlers who remembered Ashmun fondly for his assistance in defending Mesurado from early African assaults and expanding the settlement beyond its nascent boundaries. Yet, he too clashed with the settlers. After a brief return of Ayres as the society's agent in 1823, which was only notable for his further angering the settlers by assigning town lots without regard to plots already in possession, Ashmun returned to the seat of power and attempted to restrict rations for those settlers who did not consistently contribute two workdays each week to public projects.[12] The settlers found this a hard bargain, and upon finding the agent unmovable in his conviction simply raided the storehouse to forcibly secure their rations. Letters poured in from the colony charging the agent "with oppression, the neglect of obvious duties, the desertion of his post, and the seizure and abduction of the public property." The colonial administration held only a tenuous position of power in Africa, and the managers of the ACS determined that only an armed warship with a special inspector, Ralph R. Gurley, commissioned to report on the state of affairs could rectify their strife-riddled colony.[13]

Gurley, a minister from Connecticut and a graduate of Yale who, over the course of fifty years of involvement with the ACS, beginning in 1822, would serve as traveling agent, secretary, corresponding secretary, vice president, and honorary life director, set about establishing regulations for aiding widows, orphans, the sick, and the despondent. He established a channel of communication by which settlers could directly communicate with the managers of the ACS. Most importantly, he reorganized the civil constitution of the colony to create a colonial advisory council consisting of settlers; previously, the constitution had called only for a board of the society's (white) agents to "determine all questions relative to the government of the Settlement." This 1824 reorganization laid the groundwork for a colonial administration consisting of settlers with an ACS-appointed agent atop the pyramid. Gurley deserves credit for seeing leadership potential in the rebellious settlers when many other Anglo-American colonizationists refused to cede power to the settlers. Ashmun doubted the "qualifications of the settlers for any share in the concerns of government" and demanded the creation of a small military guard commanded directly by him.[14]

Back in the United States, the managers of ACS reported at their annual meeting that "in reference to the government of the Colony, the Managers cannot entirely concur in opinion with their Agent [Gurley]." Still, the board admitted, Gurley's actions reinvigorated the struggling colony and hopefully reaffirmed the settlers' faith in the good intentions of the ACS. Those "good attentions" were often put to the test. Until the appointment of Joseph Jenkins Roberts as agent in 1841, the board of the ACS preferred to name white agents, often physicians or missionaries, to oversee colonial affairs. The vice-agents were drawn from settler ranks. Frequent turnover at the top and the long voyage between Africa and the United States meant that while the colonial government at Monrovia would not *officially* have a governor of African descent until Roberts, the *reality* on the ground was that settlers frequently governed their own affairs.[15]

Of course, some white agents still tried to usurp settler power. The Liberian climate had proven insalubrious to Governor John Pinney's health since his arrival there as a Presbyterian missionary in 1833. In September 1834, Pinney resigned his post and, in an effort to retain white leadership over the colony, turned over the title to Ezekiel Skinner, the colonial physician, without Board approval. Vice-agent Nathaniel Brander protested to Pinney that he could not "unconstitutionally impose it [the governorship] on one, not appointed by the Board of Managers nor elected by the suffrage of the people." Brander admitted that his opposition created "a degree of unpleasantry," but Pinney returned to duty as agent. When he formally resigned in May 1835, Pinney did not attempt to usurp settler power again, and Brander took the reins of government until the managers formally named Skinner as their agent. By 1839, all that was left to argue about was the exact amount of time Brander had spent as acting agent in order to determine his compensation. In setting up the colony in 1824, Gurley only recognized the reality on the ground: regardless of the intentions of the ACS leaders in terms of slavery or black uplift, the settlers were going to use the rhetoric and ideology of the society to elevate themselves and secure positions of power. The settlers were not going to be passive participants in the colonization movement.[16]

* * *

What is striking about these early colonial growing pains is the racialized nature of the grievances. Wiltberger's diary laments that certain settlers were prejudicing others' minds against white agents, Creecy would not be judged by the "mulatto" Coker, and some settlers believed that African leaders would not negotiate with any agent of European descent. New arrivals to the West African coast, the settlers and their agents operated with an understanding of racial difference forged in their early-nineteenth-century American experiences.

Almost immediately after their arrival, however, the settlers noticed the indigenous peoples of Liberia called them "whites" and even understood the root cause. Peering beyond the pale of Liberia's "civilized" areas of Americo-Liberian habitation, the editor of the colony's newspaper, the *Liberia Herald*, denounced those Africans "around us and almost within our doors, those who with perfect impunity foster their prejudices.... They look with suspicion upon the colony, and a word from a 'white man' (a generic term for all classes, colors and conditions enveloped in clothing)." Settler George R. McGill, progenitor of one of Liberia's most prominent families, informed the white leaders of the MSCS that the Greboes living at the future site of Maryland in Liberia "express a strong wish to become white men, (i.e. Read & Write)." Although pointing to different behaviors, the settlers understood whiteness was a shifting cultural category reflecting one's association with the behavior, education, literacy, dress, language, and Christianity of the United States or Europe. Transitioning from American racialized lines to murky and fluid African notions of race inflected by cultural practice and performance would be an uneven task for these Americans in Africa. This process would be all the more complicated by settlers' refusal to simply remain in Africa.[17]

Many settlers desired to return to the United States, if only to visit friends and family left behind. Martin Delany eloquently voiced the emotions Africa evoked in travelers and settlers when he visited Liberia. After comparing his initial emotional response at seeing the African coast to a form of intoxication, Delany noted that this embryonic sentiment soon progressed into "a feeling of regret that you left your native country for a strange one; an almost frantic desire to see friends and nativity; a despondency and loss of the hope of ever seeing those you love at home again." And Delany experienced such highs and lows while only a temporary visitor to Africa.[18] Some Americo-Liberians had been forced to leave behind spouses, children, and other family members in bondage, due either to slaveholders being unwilling to emancipate loved ones or to intransigence on the part of free African Americans, and they sought reunion with those they left behind. Others simply desired to visit former acquaintances and see the sights of their earlier years. For some, returning to the United States as Liberian settlers provided opportunities for educational and occupational uplift unavailable to them if they had remained in America. Separated by thousands of miles and with mail services relying upon the erratic and unreliable merchant, naval, and immigrant ships calling at Liberian settlements, such desires were only natural if often beyond the financial means of many settlers.

The vast majority of settlers emigrated from slave states, and other obstacles beyond pecuniary setbacks plagued their minds as they thought of returning home. In letters sent back to former enslavers, colonization society officials, patrons, and sponsors, settlers in the colony sought information on how white Americans would react to their returns. Diana Skipwith and her father, Peyton Skipwith, were two immigrants immediately disillusioned with Liberia who hoped to return on the first ship back to the United States. Foiled in this endeavor, they at least sought to visit their old Virginia plantation to reunite with family and friends. Writing to her former enslaver, Sally Cocke, five years after her arrival in Africa in 1834, Diana sought updates on local conditions. "There was some things that we wish to know, that conserning of the Laws of the Cuntry. We hear from People that they are verry strick and I wrote you conserning of it but never get any letter. I do not know what he will do about it. I expect that he will write to [you] conserning of the mater his self." Twenty years later, John Cocke, Sally's father, still received letters from the formerly enslaved seeking his advice. "I would wish to come over to America," wrote Robert Sterdivant, "where you are if you think it adviseable, to see all the people but not until I hear your advice on the subject." Meanwhile, Nancy McDonogh told her former enslaver simply, "I would be happy to come and see you but I am afraid I would be interrupted by the white people. But if they would not you will be kind enough to let me no so I can come."[19]

Clearly, these concerns reflected a practical recognition of the impediments they might face upon their return to their former homesteads. Laws constricted African American mobility and impeded travel. Liberian settlers occupied a mobile black Atlantic world that, in the wake of the successful Haitian Revolution, had been interpreted as an inherently radical black Atlantic by both fearful white people and hopeful black people. Abolitionists, proslavery advocates, black Americans, white Americans—most Americans, in fact—assumed that migratory black subjects traversing Atlantic pathways adopted and spread abolitionist ideology. Such logic undergirded Martin Delany's novel *Blake*, in which a fugitive from slavery lays the foundation for a multinational slave rebellion through his Atlantic travels. On the other end of the spectrum, South Carolina's 1822 Negro Seamen Act, legislation passed in the wake of Denmark Vesey's Conspiracy, empowered sheriffs to incarcerate any "free negroes or persons of color" employed on ships from Northern states or foreign ports for the duration of the vessel's time in port; eventually, Southern legislatures in North Carolina, Georgia, Florida, Alabama, Louisiana, and Texas followed South Carolina's lead in adopting similar laws. Although inimical in their aims, both Delany's *Blake* and the Southern black seamen laws derive from identical assumptions that radical antislavery activism traversed the Atlantic in the form of mobile black bodies and that these bodies posed inherent danger to the slave regime.[20]

Both Delany and white legislators believed that Atlantic mobility led to racialized transformations. For Delany, blackness was defined as a political and social commitment to the black community; hence, *Blake*'s light-skinned Cubans of mixed ancestry not only participate in the black uprising that is the novel's culmination but also serve as *agent provocateurs* by passing into white society.[21] Initially, South Carolina's 1822 Seamen Act had exempted "free American Indians, free Moors, and Lascars or other colored subjects of countries beyond the Cape of Good Hope," apparently in a nod to maintaining commercial ties to the Indian Ocean. By 1825, however, the South Carolinians were forced to respond to black legal ingenuity, as the legislature complained that people of African descent from Northern states and other Atlantic nations had evaded the Seamen Act by carrying papers identifying themselves as "free American Indians, free Moors, or Lascars"; in particular, the law singled out "mulattoes or mestizos" as the principal perpetuators of this identity fraud.[22] Just as Delany's fictitious racially ambiguous Cubans infiltrated white ranks as part of a black revolution, equally ambiguous sailors adjusted their racialized identities to escape imprisonment upon arrival in Charleston. Both accounts assume a racial metamorphosis capable of visually fooling white people while also concealing an inherent revolutionary blackness. The free movement of Liberians complicates both these assumptions of black Atlantic radicality and what makes this an inherently "black" Atlantic.

Clearly, their African whiteness and malleable identity within the Atlantic context reinforced white concerns regarding mobile Atlantic subjects. And yet, in conceding the United States to whites by relocating to Africa, Liberian settlers also embodied the aspiration many white people had of an idealized all-white American society. Most Southern states required free people of color to register a white guardian's affirmation of their character. As the ACS provided its settlers with documentation to affirm their identity during their travels in the States, the society functioned in the role of surrogate guardian for all settlers.

Conversely, that document that nominally affirmed the need of whites to vouch for free people of color could also disrupt racialized modes of travel. At the same historical moment that the State Department refused to grant African Americans official U.S. passports, Liberians traveling in the United States often carried these strange credentials affirming their Liberian residence. Of course, no one knew whether the white ticket agent would accept such an odd piece of paper bearing signatures of distant colonizationists, possibly stamped with the seal of some local city judge, as evidence that the Liberian settler before them would not have to ride in the Jim Crow Car, but it was an arrow in that settler's rhetorical quiver to claim they were no longer the "degraded black" as imagined by whites.[23]

Also, as inhabitants of a colony of a private society, the Americo-Liberians raised questions about the definition of "foreign negroes." Although the law applied to any individual of African descent not from the slaveholding South, including Northern African Americans, the liminal space of colonial Liberia—not quite Africa, not quite America, not quite its own nation—posed serious problems for interpreting their place in Southern laws. This liminality, combined with the respectability engineered by their residence in Liberia, their usually well-placed patrons in the colonization society, and their own refusal to return to their previously degraded positions within American society, led to a confusing legal dynamic. Little wonder that their letters are filled with repeated requests for legal updates from the United States.

Beyond legal obstructions, African American travelers were also largely at the mercy of white-owned transportation. Whites owned and operated the steamboats, railroads, coaches, and even the vessels that carried the settlers away from Liberia. The Americo-Liberians despised the oft-degraded conditions of their accommodations. Unlike their white counterparts, the Americo-Liberian travelers did not have easy access to legal redress in case of trouble. Of course, Liberian settlers were not the only ones suffering from these degraded conditions, and such concerns were staple complaints of the entire black community. The second issue of the *Freedom's Journal* spotlighted the case of Betsey Madison, a formerly enslaved person from New Orleans who managed to purchase her freedom and that of a friend. Her liberty, however, was tragically cut short after enduring a lingering illness in New York City widely attributed to the "inhuman treatment" afforded her on the ship. Russwurm and his fellow editor Samuel Cornish admitted that while free people of color were widely targeted, they had few options for redress; the editorial simply called upon unspecified "Polished Republicans" to recognize the blight to national honor that such repeated injustices inflicted. It was not a clarion call that inspired confidence that wrongs would be righted. But Americo-Liberians were not simply free blacks in America. Their removal to Liberia under the auspices of a private society meant that while they were not foreign nationals, they had removed themselves from the racialized landscape of America. Conversely, their return, especially for those who had found success and elevated social status in Africa, signaled the capacity of African Americans for improvement, much to the detriment of the race-based arguments undergirding American slavery. The threat of physical violence or of kidnapping and a return to bondage was also very real.[24]

Some whites were sensitive to these problems. Moses Sheppard, a leading Quaker businessman in Baltimore and leader of the MSCS, confided to settler William Polk, then residing in the capital of Maryland's African colony, the difficulties that Ephraim Titler encountered in his attempted return to Monrovia. Titler originally relocated to Liberia in 1834, but the devout cooper soon sought a religious education back in the United States. Trained and ordained under the auspices of the Presbyterian Church, Titler crossed through Baltimore on his way to Norfolk, Virginia, and the awaiting ACS ship. Apparently, the former New Yorker no longer possessed papers identifying his legal status. This caused immediate difficulties in the slave state of Maryland when the boat captain refused to transport Titler without proof of his freedom. Titler called upon Sheppard to affirm his identity, but the captain still refused to bring the Liberian to Norfolk in fear of the hefty fines potentially awaiting him in Virginia. Finally, Sheppard persuaded the captain to take Titler to Norfolk and directly place him on the ACS ship, thus bypassing landfall and not actually "touching" Virginia. Sheppard provided the details of this escapade to Polk "for your information and that of your friends, if any of you should come to this Country you must acquaint yourselves with the laws of the slave states.... Coloured persons have many obsticles to encounter in traveling here." Obviously, Sheppard wanted Polk and his companions to take heed of the restrictions placed upon their mobility in the United States, but it is also intriguing that Titler would forego the step of carrying proof of his identity. Did he assume that relocation to Liberia had removed him from the legal constraints placed on people of color? Or did his Northern birth and Liberian experience lead him to underestimate the trepidation of the South regarding black mobility?[25]

The case surrounding Zion (occasionally spelled "Sion") Harris's 1841 trip to the United States is also illustrative of the problems facing Americo-Liberians traveling in the United States. Harris was a leading figure in Liberia. Born in East Tennessee in 1811, Harris's legal status at the time of his birth is murky. Although free by 1830 when he joined his wife, Martha, in departing for Liberia aboard the aptly named *Liberia*, the ACS records do not indicate Harris's legal status at birth. Ezekiel Birdseye, however, a leading abolitionist from eastern Tennessee, suggested in a letter to Gerrit Smith that Harris had been born enslaved. Harris achieved fame in 1840 while employed as a carpenter at the Heddington mission station in the African interior. At daybreak on March 7, several hundred native warriors attacked the mission. The Heddington defenders amounted to Harris, his wife, who served as a teacher at the mission, Bennet Demery, George S. Brown, the white missionary in charge of the station, and Zoda and Nicky, two African boys who attended the mission school. This little band defended the mission until reinforcements arrived, and they found fame after missionary Brown returned to the United States and published an account of Heddington's defense (this affair is further detailed in chapter 4). Although Brown had portrayed himself heroically as one of the defenders, Harris grumbled in a private letter that Brown had shut himself into his second-story bedroom and did not participate in the fight except to discharge four muskets on Harris's command. Regardless of whether Brown inflated his own role in the affair, Harris became a celebrity of sorts for the missionary and colonization establishment, and he hoped to capitalize on his fame.[26]

In the same letter in which he detailed his account of the Heddington attack, Harris also expressed a desire to visit the United States. "I desire to go to America," he wrote to an ACS official, "to see my frinds who are in East Tenasee, Knox County, and I would like your advice about it whether it would be safe or right.... If you think it difficult to go to tenesee I would like to visit America anyhow, somewhere or other." Harris's father-in-law, George Erskine, although born enslaved, had been taken under the wing of Dr. Isaac Anderson, president of Maryville College in Tennessee, and trained as a Presbyterian missionary. Erskine was personally acquainted with many of the Presbyterian leaders involved in colonization, including Ralph Gurley, whom Harris hoped to meet. While Harris did not leave behind any immediate family in America,[27] the Erskines had, in fact, left behind several family members in Tennessee. Erskine passed away soon after his arrival in Liberia and while on his deathbed had coaxed a promise from his son-in-law to return to the States and retrieve these relations. Clearly, Harris had a ready network of black and white acquaintances.

The opportunity to return to the United States came in the summer of 1841, and after initially traveling to Washington, D.C., the headquarters of the ACS, Harris moved on to east Tennessee in the company of an ACS agent; the society hoped to capitalize on Harris's fame in order to secure more emigrants.[28] By all accounts, the trip was personally successful for Harris and beneficial to the ACS. Harris traveled through Virginia and Tennessee, stopping along the way to encourage his African American audiences to immigrate to Liberia. He persuaded thirteen members of his extended family to return with him. While in Maryville, Tennessee, Harris reunited with Anderson, his father-in-law's old tutor, and addressed a camp meeting at the local Presbyterian church to a crowd reported to be more than one thousand strong. He dined with white benefactors and slept as an honored guest in their homes, traveled with white companions, and spoke to mixed crowds about his African experiences and defense of the mission station. Before his return to Liberia in July 1842, Harris had traveled expansively across the upper South and as far north as Massachusetts. But there were also ample reminders of why Harris had left the United States in the first place and why he swore that nothing could induce him to stay. While Harris visited one relative, a freeman, near Knoxville, several white men entered the home searching for a fugitive from slavery. Harris reported to Birdseye that the slave catchers treated him and his relative "with much harshness," even tearing up the floorboards and ransacking the house in hopes of catching the escapee.

In another brush with American slavery, Harris was obliged to arrange the purchase of one enslaved brother-in-law. Harris's unencumbered travels, public lectures, and repeated tales of African American accomplishments in Africa also riled the area's supporters of slavery. On the Sunday night following Harris's public lecture at the church, Birdseye observed a group of patrollers parading an African American by the church's door, disrupting a meeting held to discuss the importance of Christian missionaries in Africa. The poor man's crime was to appear in the neighborhood without a pass, a charge that surprised Birdseye, as that particular law was irregularly enforced in the Tennessee mountains. The timing of the patrol's sudden determination to curtail African American mobility and the choice of their route past the same church that provided Harris its pulpit at the exact moment that its congregation debated the necessity of "civilizing" Africa seem more than coincidental. Birdseye deduced as much and relayed to his fellow reformer Gerrit Smith, "I thought it not improbable that the attentions shown Harris might have offended them."[29]

While reminders of African American subjugation surrounded Harris even as he enjoyed the hospitality and companionship of white hosts, others worried for the Americo-Liberian's safety. George S. Brown, the missionary whose station had been defended by Harris, had returned to New York City earlier to drum up support for the missionary field in Africa. Whether due to miscommunication, lost letters, or the energetic itinerary, Harris lost contact with Brown, and by November the minister had grown worried over the Liberian settler's fate. He soon placed an advertisement in several newspapers seeking information on Harris's whereabouts, and the *Maryland Colonization Journal* soon echoed the call. The editors of the journal feared that he had been kidnapped and returned to slavery, although they admitted upon reflection that Harris had once fought off hundreds of attackers, and they concluded, "We should fear little for him in a fair field with some dozen kidnappers." Still, some "scoundrel" may have robbed Harris of his identity papers, and he was far too important a colonist to lose to the anonymity of slavery.[30] For settlers, many of whom had found their path to freedom only by leaving the country, a return visit could lead to reminders of their subjugated past or to a disastrous return to chains.

For other returning settlers, the confrontation with their enslaved past was far more direct. Alexander Hance, a free man of color from southern Maryland, had been persuaded by the MSCS's traveling agent to emigrate. He left Baltimore in December 1834 aboard the ship *Bourne* with fifty-eight other settlers, including his wife and two sons, aged one and two. Unfortunately, the family was not complete, as the Hances could only afford to purchase the two young boys, and thus were forced to abandon their three daughters, who remained the property of James Sommerville of Prince George's County, Maryland.[31] The separation weighed heavily on Hance. Three months after his arrival in Maryland in Liberia, Hance was writing to the organization's agent begging him to purchase and send his daughters on to Africa. Hance promised to repay the Board of Managers for the expense and swore that "if it is ten or twelve years to com I Will go Back again to them." A subsequent letter in August from Hance asked the agent to send his love to his friends "both white and colerd" and closed with another plea to free his children. Luckily, his daughters did not have to wait ten years.³²

Hance achieved both success and respect in the Maryland colony's capital of Harper and was elected selectman soon after his arrival. By the following year, he was a member of the governor's council. In the summer of 1837, he felt himself capable of returning to the United States and completing his family. He arrived in Baltimore that fall and presented himself to the Board of Managers of the MSCS at the September 4 meeting, where he was provided with letters of introduction and appropriate paperwork to prevent disruption to his travels. Within days, Hance had arranged a purchase price of one thousand dollars for his three daughters, ages fourteen, twelve, and nine or ten. The MSCS leadership, which had watched the number of emigrants steadily decline with each departing ship from Baltimore, realized that they had an opportunity in Hance's sudden arrival. The board authorized Hance to begin lecturing on Liberia to his old African American neighbors as an official spokesman for the colonization society. The Board of Managers agreed to compensate Hance a salary of no more than $500, surely a motivating factor in Hance's efforts, considering it amounted to half of the purchase price for his daughters. And he ably repaid the board's investment by securing commitments from nearly seventy people who were willing to emigrate that year. When the reunited Hance family left for Liberia aboard the *Niobe* on November 27, they enjoyed the company of seventy-nine other passengers, making it the largest expedition the MSCS had ever dispatched to Harper.³³ The large number of emigrants from southern Maryland and Hance's home county attest to his influence.

Their poorly timed arrival in January 1838 likewise demonstrated the effect that Hance's speaking tour had on the large number of emigrants who came out with him. Maryland in Liberia needed the agricultural produce of both its own settlers and its African neighbors, the Grebo, to achieve sufficiency. At the time of Hance's departure, the harvest of 1836 was disappointing but not disastrous. Unfortunately, while Hance was in the United States, the following year's harvest was much worse and famine struck the Cape Palmas coast. Conditions were so poor that the Greboes, who were normally subject to differing village loyalties, united to set prices for the principal foodstuffs of the area. Thus, the largest expedition the MSCS ever dispatched landed in the midst of famine and strained tensions with the rarely united Greboes. The new emigrants attributed their misfortune to Hance, whom they believed had intentionally misled them. Hance's descriptions of the colony had been integral to their decision to leave the United States for Africa, and the new arrivals directed their displeasure at the man. In a defensive letter to the leaders of the MSCS, Hance noted that although he had rescued his daughters from slavery, he regretted his trip to the United States. Not only were the settlers attempting to excommunicate him from the Methodist Church for deception but, Hance speculated, they "would deprive me of my existence were it in their power."[34]

Nine years after Hance's American sojourn, Charles Scotland made the same return to the United States for exactly the same purpose: to liberate a child from bondage. But whereas Hance had found the assistance of the colonizationists useful in securing his family's freedom and only later incurred the wrath of his fellow settlers, Scotland stumbled much earlier in his efforts to free his child. Scotland had come to the United States at the request of the MSCS, who had learned that settler testimonials like Harris's and Hance's were more persuasive than the proselytizing of their white agents. Although Scotland had not achieved quite the same political success as Hance, he was a well-respected figure throughout the Liberian colonies who had initially settled in Caldwell, a settlement of the ACS, in 1832. Wearing second-hand clothing donated to the settlers by American benefactors, the venerable sixty-three-year-old settler boarded the Baltimore-bound *Kent*, which had just deposited thirteen settlers in Africa. After visiting his old home in Martinsburg, Virginia (now West Virginia), Scotland crossed the border to Frederick, Maryland, and the comfortable home of David Hughes, from which he was to conduct interviews with local African American leaders. During his travels, he collected promises of emigration from his old neighbors, almost all of whom were related to Scotland in some fashion. Regrettably, the aged Scotland had exposed himself to damp weather while riding to Frederick, and he developed chills and a fever his first night there; Hughes, however, was not prepared to have the Americo-Liberian die before speaking to the area's people of color and sent for his own physician to attend Scotland. The settler recovered and conducted his speaking tour on the benefits of emigration across the state of Maryland throughout the summer, ranging as far west as Hagerstown and also addressing the Eastern Shore's African American population. In the meantime, white colonizationists donated funds for the benefit of purchasing his enslaved son, and in September Scotland traveled to Virginia to buy his son's freedom and return to Liberia.[35]

Unfortunately, Scotland had grossly miscalculated his son's desire to leave the United States. To Scotland's "utter astonishment," Medley, his son, planned to remain in Virginia with his free wife and children. Such intentions caught the father off guard, especially in light of Virginia's laws requiring the removal of free people of color. Scotland's conviction that his son and family would return with him to Africa led him to request that the colonization society forward on the payment for Medley. If Medley would not emigrate willingly, then, Scotland assured the board, while apologizing profusely for his son's intransigence, he would purchase his son and as his legal owner forcibly remove the young man to Liberia utilizing the full force of Virginia's slave code to his advantage. And so a Liberian planned to liberate his son from slavery by becoming his enslaver and continuing the cycle of bondage. In a further unexpected reversal of roles, Scotland requested the assistance and presence of the colonization society's white agent in Virginia to fully press his legal claims and convince Medley to remove to Africa without trouble. Completing the sale, Scotland deposited Medley at the home of another white colonizationist, J. W. Reynolds, to gather his family and belongings before departing for Africa; Scotland, meanwhile, continued on to Baltimore to make arrangements for their brief stay and to ensure their passage on the *Liberia Packet*. Perhaps unaware of the circumstances by which the Scotland family found itself in his home, Reynolds reported that Medley and his wife were in "fine spirits and anxious to go with their Father to africa." Perhaps the Scotlands had had a miraculous reconciliation after the father threatened to turn master or perhaps they concealed their true sentiments from their white host. More likely, Reynolds replicated the logic of colonization by conflating African Americans with Africans and assumed that such "returns" to Africa could only bring happiness to the emigrants. Few colonizationists thought that a forced governmental removal to Liberia was likely or practical and thus relied heavily on the assumption that once the colony was established and economically viable, African American settlers would pour into western Africa of their own accord; within this ideological framework, there were no alternatives to "anxious" settlers in "fine spirits." Regardless, the elder Scotland did not provide any time for his prodigal son to change his mind or escape. On November 18, Reynolds placed the young Scotland family—Medley, his wife, Elizabeth, and their young son, John—on the train for Baltimore. By December 1, they had sailed out of Baltimore harbor into the Chesapeake Bay heading east.[36]

* * *

Americo-Liberians returning to the United States confronted their enslaved past, the skeptical gaze of African Americans, and white supporters of slavery, who were provoked by their mere presence, and they were justifiably concerned about the social, cultural, and legal repercussions of their mobility. But many of them also interpreted their journeys to Africa as transformative. Crossing the Atlantic Ocean had allowed them to at least claim—if not permanently take hold of—some of the elements of whiteness, they had built a republic upon a foundation largely constructed of the formerly enslaved, and they believed they represented the vanguard of civilization in "benighted" Africa. While the Americo-Liberians sought an elevated status above their previously degraded station, their ability to do so depended heavily upon their gender, class, and social connections within the United States. The peregrinations of Samuel Ford McGill are illustrative of the racial, social, educational, and cultural possibilities available to those few wealthy and well-placed emigrants able to capitalize on their relocation to Africa.

Scion of one of the first and most prominent African American families in Liberia, McGill had been born in Baltimore in 1815 and emigrated to Africa when his father, George R. McGill, a freeman of color and preacher, relocated his entire family to Monrovia in 1827. Following the establishment of the separate Maryland colony, George McGill was also one of the first immigrants to Maryland in Liberia.[37] At the age of twenty-one, the younger McGill sought a profession befitting his African social status; Maryland in Liberia's first governor, James Hall, was a medical doctor originally from New England, and McGill found his desires drifting toward that profession. However, writing in October 1835 from Monrovia following the destruction of the American settlement at Bassa Cove by the neighboring Bassas under "King Joe Harris," McGill was not particularly in a donnish mood. Addressing Moses Sheppard, McGill regaled his correspondent with the response of the Monrovian settlers to the destruction of the American settlement, namely, the destruction of the African town deemed responsible. McGill joined in the fight and proudly informed his Quaker correspondent that although he could not provide an exact reckoning of the number of African casualties, "there is a certainty of six of them being killed, and I doubt not but many more." The Liberian settler was especially proud that after the assault and destruction of the Bassa town, his fellow soldiers, following in the tradition of American volunteer and militia companies, had voted him from the ranks and into the officer corps as a third lieutenant. It was only after detailing his martial exploits that McGill added to the conclusion of the letter his desire for a medical education and requested the support of Sheppard and Maryland colonizationists.[38]

McGill's letter arrived at a fortuitous time in Baltimore, as the colonization society's agent, colonial physician, and governor in Africa, Hall, had no intention of becoming a permanent resident of that continent and was dispatching a stream of letters to the MSCS both begging that he be replaced and requesting that the society train several colonists to administer to the medical needs of the colony. McGill's plans to become a doctor were well-timed but not without complications.[39] It was left to Sheppard to explain to McGill the requirements of his American education.

> You were I suppose too young when you left the United States to have recollection of the distinction between the whites and blacks it is therefore necessary to apprise you that it will preclude you from associating with the whites, and place you in the degraded class of the blacks. You must not expect to hear the term Mr. McGill from a white man. In the College you must appear as a servant; there is not a medical school in the U. States into which you could be admitted in any other character.[40]

McGill accepted this rather gloomy prediction and made his way to Baltimore to enter that city's Washington Medical College in the fall of 1836 under the patronage of the Young Men's Colonization Society of Maryland. In a telling bit of advice reinforcing the constraints on black Atlantic mobility, Sheppard concluded his letter with the notation, "You must not arrive at any port south of Norfolk, the Laws would subject you to imprisonment."[41] McGill began attending lectures at the medical college in November. The experiment ended predictably. By December, his fellow students had organized, met, and presented a series of resolutions to both their faculty and the colonizationists. Claiming to respond to rampaging rumors that the college had "permitted the introduction of a Negro Boy," the students denounced these reports as slanderous against their faculty members who never would have intended that the "Students of fair complexion should mingle with those of dark skin." The students explained that the "Boy" had been allowed into the college for the purpose of instruction only if he acted in the dual capacity as servant, but they "conceive[d] that this Boy has gone far beyond the limited space granted him, and has encroached as far upon the privilege enjoyed by the students, as to wound their feelings, disgust them by his actions."[42] Thus concluded what surely was a tumultuous semester at Washington Medical College. Perhaps the outcome was inevitable, but one wonders if significant problems emerged from the fact that Sheppard had technically informed McGill that he would only have to "appear as a servant," whereas his fellow students seemed to expect the arrival of a personal valet.

Maryland's colonizationists scrambled for a solution. They attempted to meekly regain the favor of the faculty and students of the Washington Medical College, noting that it "was never the wish of the Board of Managers that Sam. F. McGill should be esteemed an equal; or as claiming privileges at all comparable with the Students but that in the capacity of a Servant, he might, thru the mere magnanimity of both the Professors and Students be gratuitously instructed in the Science of Medicine." Clearly, the colonization society was not interested in securing a thorough education for McGill, hoping instead that he might catch snippets of lectures based solely on the generosity of the white professionals. Equally clear was the fact that McGill, a freeborn man sensitive about his social station and fresh from the martial glory of his African conquests, was not interested in performing the role of a servant.

It is suggestive that McGill requested assistance from Sheppard in securing a medical education only *after* detailing his performance in war against native Africans. Indeed, the request for aid practically appears as an addendum to the letter. The body of the letter is dedicated to establishing McGill as a heroic defender of "civilization" in Africa, a figure portrayed in stark contrast to "heathen" Africans. The letter's text ranges across the political, economic, and military conditions of the colony and their potentials. The net effect was to portray the writer as a colonizer firmly in control over his colonial space. Such a letter signaled McGill's elevation in Africa over "barbaric" blackness, and it should have been obvious to Sheppard and his colonizationist allies that the proud newly elected third lieutenant of Americo-Liberian soldiers would have been very uninterested in behaving as a servant.

Even as the episode demonstrates the activity of whites to constrict African American education even for a student uninterested in permanently settling in the United States, it also underscores the constrained possibilities for Liberian settlers in the United States. If Washington Medical College's student petitioners initially proved the validity of Sheppard's warning that there would be no "Mr. McGill" from white lips, they also found their petition's wording displeasing to their faculty, who had granted McGill permission to attend lectures. Facing backlash from their instructors, the students dispatched a second letter couched in softer terms. Although they still demanded McGill's removal from the college, it was now framed as a "painful duty" and he was referred to as "Mr. McGill." The new petition refocused attention away from McGill's presence as a direct threat to his fellow students' sentiments and instead zeroed in on their ability to secure future employment in the South. They pointed to circulating "prejudicial reports" to argue that once word got out that they had graduated on equal terms with a man of African descent, the students could never practice medicine in a slave state.[43]

Fortunately, alongside the activities of the MSCS Board, Governor Hall had corresponded with a medical acquaintance of his from New England, Dr. Edward E. Phelps, who served on the faculty of the medical college at the University of Vermont. Equally lucky, just as the Washington Medical College students erected a racial wall around their institution, a letter arrived from Phelps inviting McGill to become a private medical student at his home in Windsor, Vermont, a small village located along the border with New Hampshire. Although McGill would be a personal student lodging in his home, Phelps assured the MSCS that he would learn the curriculum of the University of Vermont.[44]

And so McGill trekked to New England with a letter from the MSCS's home agent reminding him that he "must not forget that you are an *African in America*; and in that station, whatever may be your sense of equality with your fellow man, remember, it will be dangerous to show it." The necessity of such a reminder strongly suggests that McGill had demanded an equal footing among Baltimore's medical students and also explains the response of the medical students who had their feelings "wounded" by such demands. The Maryland colonizationists hoped New England would "be a more congenial clime, at least . . . one more friendly to the coloured people in some respects." And it seems that the spectacle of a Liberian seeking a medical degree roused at least the curiosity of Windsor's citizenry. Reports of the hubbub led to grousing on the part of Sheppard. Referencing Alexander Pope's "Essay on Man," in which a group of superior beings "show'd a Newton as we show an ape," Sheppard sardonically grumbled that "a white ape would have attracted as much attention in the good town of Windsor as a coloured Liberian aspiring to science."[45]

Soon after McGill's arrival in Vermont, Phelps resigned his position at the university and recommended that his protégé attend medical lectures at Dartmouth in nearby Hanover, New Hampshire. By the time McGill reached Dartmouth, his transformation into a fully exotic, yet somehow "civilized," "other" was complete. A professor there, hoping to avoid a situation similar to that which engulfed the Washington Medical College, introduced McGill to the student body as a native African because "foreigners of any color are respected." McGill concocted an explanation for his fluency in English and, as he phrased it in his report to the MSCS, "the deception carried the point." In a reversal of the normative "passing" as a means of crossing the color line from black to white, McGill was actually attempting to pass as an African. Such a formulation transformed McGill from a "mulatto" freeman of color seeking to climb the social ladder to an exotic English-speaking African. As such, even if he did not find equality among his fellow students, McGill found a form of acceptance as a curiosity and spectacle. Surveying his newly duped white classmates, McGill breathed a sigh of relief when he determined that he was "not the most ignorant one of the whole, and in a year from this I hope to be attached to the Senior class." In fact, after pondering his predicament for a week, McGill slyly, but without explanation, confided to his MSCS benefactors that his African ruse might prove beneficial in the future.[46]

While McGill took this transformation one step further than most—being told he was an African and then being requested to pass as one—this exoticization of the mobile subject was a weapon of choice for Americo-Liberian settlers traveling abroad. Residence in Africa had transformed them into exotic others, "white apes" according to Sheppard, while their mobility and ambiguity loosened the binds of identity. Colonizationist rhetoric locating Liberians at the forefront of the African civilizing mission also allowed them to shed the tincture of primitivism. In this manner, Hance, Harris, McGill, and others could travel, reside in the homes of whites who would shun other African Americans, and open doors to opportunities previously unavailable to them. Sheppard could grumble about Windsor's citizenry making a spectacle out of a Liberian medical student, but it was that engine of wonderment that paved if not McGill's equality, then at least his acceptance among Windsor's white population and through the doors of Dartmouth's medical college. For his part, McGill disliked the implications but recognized that Liberia and Liberians inhabited a space between white assumptions about Anglo-American civilization and black African barbarity. He wrote to Sheppard, "I have received many invitations, all of which I always made it a point to decline.... I cannot say that my failure to accept them arose from my aversion to society; yet the idea that it was merely a momentary act of condescension, on their part, as well as a desire to see and converse a half savage character, made it rather a pain than a pleasure to be exposed to their solicitations." Obviously, "savage" was a word imbued with significant meaning for Americo-Liberians who conceived of their "civilized" African home as being surrounded by "savage" Africans. Clearly, McGill bristled at being conceived of as even half a savage, but he too found the utility of becoming an exotic "civilized" (or not entirely savage) African in New England.[47]

Relocation to Liberia had provided McGill with opportunities that were overwhelmingly unimaginable for African Americans. Only a few years earlier, James McCune Smith, the first African American to receive a medical degree, had attempted and failed to find similar acceptance among Northern medical schools. He lacked the exoticism and connections of an Americo-Liberian, however, and failed to gain admittance to an American institution. After being denied entrance to several American schools, he was forced to attain his credentials abroad at the University of Glasgow, earning his Bachelor of Arts degree in 1835 and his medical degree in 1837. McGill, utilizing the transatlantic connections afforded by the colonization societies, was able to secure admittance to an American institution—although admittedly with several false starts—at the same historical moment that Smith found those doors closed. On October 22, 1838, McGill along with the rest of his cohort completed his oral examinations to the satisfaction of the faculty and defended his thesis, thus becoming the first African American doctor to receive a medical degree from an American university.[48] To sail out in the fall expedition,[49] he was forced to depart Dartmouth and the United States without his diploma, but James Hall sailed for Maryland in Liberia a few weeks after McGill carrying the document that the Liberian coveted. Clearly, one element of New England life had greatly affected McGill: the weather. Unsurprising for a young man who had spent much his of childhood and adolescence living near the equator, McGill's letters are filled with complaints about New England winters and wonderment that snow remained on the ground in April. And when it came time to write a medical thesis to complete his degree, McGill selected a subject close to his heart though of little use in Liberia: "Direct Physical Effects of Cold."[50]

Beyond finding his muse in Vermont and New Hampshire's snows, McGill busily established his transatlantic network. He corresponded, visited, and associated with prominent whites and counted some of Maryland's leading figures, including John H. B. Latrobe, architect Benjamin Latrobe's son, and Moses Sheppard, as his patrons and friends. But McGill found liberty without equality empty, and confrontations like the one he endured at Washington Medical College angered him. After his return to Africa,

McGill communicated with a white colonizationist seeking his advice on how to best persuade African Americans to emigrate. Describing the obstacles facing people of color in the United States, McGill recalled his travels across the country: "I have visited the States as a free Liberian under circumstances the most favorable, and even then felt that to be called a free colored man in the States is synonymous with what we here term slavery.—it is a kind of freedom which the unwearying kindness and courtesies of our *best and most undoubted colonization friends* can hardly render agreeable—we never breath freely again until the goodly bark conveys us once more to the shores of our but happy home."[51]

McGill chaffed under the category "free colored man," and his studies in the United States subtly altered his style of writing. In letters to his white friends and benefactors, he increasingly categorized those African Americans living in the United States as "your colored population," renouncing any connection between himself and those he believed unwilling to or incapable of grasping true freedom. By 1842 and after several more visits to the United States, McGill wrote to Sheppard that "your Coloured population" were "porr creatures . . . devoid of elevated feelings, their spirits are hardened to oppression, nothing but force can ever expel them from their present servile station in the U. States."[52]

As his graduation neared, McGill wrote to the MSCS to seek their advice regarding the timing of his return to Liberia. "My anxiety to see friends & home and above all my anxiety to leave the U.S. strongly urge my departure; on the other hand justice to myself and fellow Colonists render a longer stay necessary." The problem was that McGill believed himself deficient in "clinical knowledge," and a stay in Baltimore working among that city's African American population would provide valuable experience.[53]

Baltimore had, in fact, already contributed greatly to McGill's clinical knowledge. Controlling black bodies held great significance for McGill's and the broader medical profession's claims to scientific knowledge. Doctors used their familiarity with the human body and the power to wield the scalpel to emphasize their scientific stature and authoritative claims to medical knowledge in juxtaposition to folk medicine, midwives, and traditional healing practices. At this time, the only legal means in most states to acquire bodies for dissection was via executed prisoners, and the growing demands of medical students far outstripped this meager supply. The deficiency was filled by grave robbers and "resurrection men." Seeking the easiest targets, resurrectionists largely disturbed the graves of the poor, indigent, and unknown, meaning a disproportionate number of the cadavers on nineteenth-century dissecting tables were black. Baltimore, with its large black population, became notorious for its grave robbing.[54]

When McGill undertook his transformative journey to New England, he did not travel alone but relocated in the accompaniment of two deceased males who were more than likely African Americans from Baltimore. The neophyte doctor did not realize that he should have brought along bodies of both sexes, leading to a letter to Baltimore colonizationists with instructions to procure the bodies of two young black women, preferably teenagers. The graves were robbed in the spring of 1838, and two deceased black Baltimoreans were on Dartmouth's dissecting tables by July. No correspondence from McGill voiced any hesitations, regrets, or sentiments for the four black cadavers instrumental in his education.[55]

A few white leaders of the colonization society feared that McGill would desire to stay in the United States after his medical training and become a "King among beggars."[56] Such concern was greatly misplaced. McGill was uninterested in becoming a Baltimore king, especially if his rule only extended over that city's people of color. To quote the new doctor, "A short stay in Balt. would enable me to obtain this, and even though some lives might be sacrificed, it would not make much difference providing I use every exertion to save—To hurry the departure of some of your Colored population out of this world would not be so great a crime."[57] McGill seemingly lacked any recognition that he was once a member of Baltimore's African American population; relocation to Liberia allowed him to shed that particular identity. But if the death of "some" of the African American population "would not be so great crime," some people were then presumably salvageable, but who? A member of one of Liberia's most prosperous families and John Brown Russwurm's brother-in-law, McGill, who in addition to these advantages had also been born free, received an education, and was an accepted member of Maryland's colonization elite, predictably found salvation possible for those African Americans most like himself, but only if they elected to seek liberty in Africa. Not surprising, given that at the time of his studies there were only two African American students at Dartmouth, McGill became acquainted with fellow black student Thomas Paul. The educated New Englander quickly caught the Americo-Liberian's eye as someone "who possesses qualifications sufficient to render him a conspicuous character if placed in a situation where an opening existed for promotion." Unfortunately, McGill noted that Paul was an abolitionist in the mold of Garrison and seemed uninterested in emigration. But McGill still held hope as Paul was "sensible of oppression and I hope it may drive him to seek refuge in Africa. He would in my opinion prove an ornament to our Colony, and no persuasions of mine shall be spared in inducing his removal from this 'cradle of liberty.'" And so McGill condemned part of the African American population to ignoble death by his inexperienced hands while simultaneously pressuring those he deemed worthy to undertake the transformative migration to Liberia.[58]

In fact, McGill generally loathed abolitionists because he, like his white colonizationist companions, attributed to their influence the widespread rejection of Liberia by educated and affluent African Americans like Paul. Tellingly, the freeborn Americo-Liberian believed that most abolitionists focused on slavery rather than equality and lacked what he termed "true Thompsonian spirit,—which I believe holds amalgamation as one of its principal doctrines." Although British abolitionist George Thompson was a fervent opponent of the ACS, McGill preferred Thompson's reformist vision that extended beyond abolition to include social equality.[59] As a freeborn man of color, McGill's disdain for abolitionists "with perhaps a few exceptions" stemmed from his demand for social and political equality beyond the demise of slavery. For McGill, abolition was only a necessary progression on the correct path for people of color to attain equality "unless from mental or pecuniary deficiencies he be constrained to forgoe them."

Of course, conceding that equality could be forfeited by a lack of mental faculties or class reveals that McGill was not so much an advocate of equality as he was an outspoken advocate for the treatment of those people of color like him—learned, financially comfortable, male, and "gentlemanly"—as white men. In an argument foreshadowing W.E.B. Du Bois's "Talented Tenth," McGill sought to open the doors of privilege and education to leading intellectuals. The end of slavery was only the first step in this program, and for those white New Englanders unfortunate enough to engage McGill in a debate on abolition, the Liberian settler always took great delight in observing his foe's nausea at the "blessing" it would be to follow abolitionism's logic to its natural Thompsonian conclusion; one of these late-night debates among students ended abruptly when McGill made "a rather serious" proposal to his opponent for his sister's hand in marriage.[60]

Unsurprisingly, when McGill finally did ask for a woman's hand in marriage who was not the sister of some unsuspecting white abolitionist, he proposed to twenty-year-old Lydia Nickolson, a freeborn resident of Baltimore and of mixed ancestry—someone exactly like McGill.[61] The engagement was broken off twice before Nickolson finally agreed to marry the love-struck McGill, and the nuptials required the intercession of both his father and Baltimore friends. It seems that the major point of contention was McGill's determination to return to Africa; Nickolson apparently was not as enamored of the idea of leaving the United States as she was of McGill. If McGill embodied the litany of possibilities that Liberia presented to those able to grasp them, then his young bride tragically epitomized what emigration to Africa meant for many other African American settlers. Soon after her arrival in Liberia, Nickolson contracted an illness that defied the best efforts of her doctor husband and died on July 12, 1843, seven months after first setting foot in Africa.[62] McGill was crushed and confided to Latrobe that because of his wife's death his "best and most determined principles . . . have been tested I must confess." However, McGill decided that moving his young bride to Liberia ultimately was the only alternative. "I yet could not have acted otherwise. I could not or rather would not have resided in the United States nor could I have left one of my race there for whom affection was entertained. I would have sacrificed much very much to have averted danger, but my liberty would have been a sacrifice entirely too great."[63]

These travels of an Americo-Liberian medical student expose the results of Liberia's developing racial hierarchy and the importance of class there. McGill did not conceive of himself as white as he sought to rescue those "of my race" from American subjugation. Yet, if he did not claim a "white" identity, he obviously also did not lay claim to an American blackness. Not only did he find the idea of being referred to as a freeman of color more akin to slavery, McGill even struggled to interact with black Americans, both the living and the dead who ended up on his dissecting table. He distanced himself from those Americans of African descent who voluntarily, as he saw it, remained under the heel of white oppression. The black janitor of the Washington Medical College in Baltimore, a Mr. Golden, was seemingly repulsed by McGill's haughty attitude. After conversing with Golden, Sheppard reported to McGill the janitor's summation of the Americo-Liberian as a "proud nigger." Although claiming to have shown Golden respect, McGill also belittled the janitor's own claims to medical knowledge based upon his experiences in the position, a servant of the college, that McGill had originally intended to occupy in his own quest for a medical education. McGill wrote, "His being Dr. Golden did not elicit from me the degree of Reverence which was generally paid him, by those who had partaken of his *nostrums*, consequently he might have supposed me emulous to acquire superior medical information to what he possessed." Intriguingly,

Golden seems to have been providing medical attention, undoubtedly to Baltimore's black community, based upon the knowledge gleaned from his custodial position. Rather than acknowledging Golden's significance to this community to which McGill once belonged, McGill instead framed their interactions as an unraced professional challenging a quack.[64]

In attempting to describe this racialized vacillation, one scholar has credited McGill with advancing a "radical and new African American identity" that presented a pan-African ideology twenty-five years before Alexander Crummell, Edward W. Blyden, and Martin Delany proposed their versions of it, even going so far as to suggest that McGill was an instrumental figure in the development of these figures' own ideas.[65] But McGill's writing and thinking does not exhibit the same commitment to pan-African ideas as those of the later authors. Rather, McGill really did not care for Africans or his fellow settlers. Emigration had opened doors to McGill that would have been completely unavailable to him had his father elected to remain in Baltimore. Possessing numerous advantages, the McGill family exemplified the possibilities of Liberia. But McGill scoffed at the formerly enslaved and uneducated settlers who constituted the majority of Liberia's population. A common practice among missionary teachers to combine classrooms of native and settler children especially earned his scorn, as he believed that the children of settlers were just as likely to become "savage" as the Africans were likely to become Christian.

After the death of his brother-in-law, Governor Russwurm, McGill took over the reins of colonial government, soon alienating himself even further from his fellow settlers. In a letter to the MSCS, McGill notes that, while the colony had increased its size in the numbers of settlers, "I really cannot discover any material increase in intelligence respectability or self dependence." Minimally, McGill recognized that the deficiencies he perceived in his fellow colonists were not a result of their inherent debasement; rather, he pointed an accusatory finger at the racialized organization of the United States, the institution of slavery, *and* the colonization society's inability to educate its settlers. "These same people are now snatched suddenly from the plantations and uninstructed and unimproved are expected by the simple passage across five thousand miles of ocean to be fit to fulfill the functions and duties of free and enlightened citizens."[66] McGill simply failed to recognize that the "simple passage of five thousand miles" *had* been transformative; not only had that passage transformed American blackness into African whiteness, but that initial act of relocation had also enabled the "mulatto" son of a Baltimore lay Methodist minister to secure a medical degree from Dartmouth College and count many prominent whites within his circle of friends. It was his status in Africa that had provided McGill with the tools and connections necessary to secure the requisite education to "fulfill the functions and duties of free and enlightened citizens." The class-conscious McGill foresaw an African Republic of educated men like himself with little room for uneducated settlers.

As far as his thoughts on Africans, McGill's emotions ranged from bemusement at their lack of "civilization" to outright disdain and loathing.[67] In 1840, while employed as the colony's physician in Harper, McGill wrote to MSCS officials expressing the settlers' concerns regarding what they considered preferential treatment of Africans on the part of missionary teachers. Many settlers were upset at the number of native African children who were receiving educations at the hands of the limited number of teachers, and McGill notified his superiors, "I am inclined to the opinions of the residents of the Southern States in relation to their blacks they had better remain in a happy state of ignorance."[68] Not only is this a remarkable sentiment for a man of color who disliked abolitionists for their lack of dedication to racial equality, but it likewise does not sound like the progenitor of pan-Africanism.

Instead of some early form of pan-Africanism or radical African American identity, McGill is better understood within the context of his and his fellow Liberians' African existence. With the arrival of the African American settlers and their attempts to re-create the United States in Africa with themselves in charge, the settlers and Africans shaped and challenged one another's understanding of race. Like many other settlers who found uplift and transformation through Liberian emigration, McGill expressed amazement that most enslaved persons refused to accept freedom based upon the promise of emigration. "Twere I the slave," McGill informed a white American friend who coincidentally was also a slaveholder, "there is nothing that I would not give . . . in return for freedom." Of course, McGill conceded that he had never been held in bondage and had given up understanding the mentality of enslaved persons as something unattainable and an "unnecessary" digression. Conversely, McGill easily imagined himself in the role of slaveholder and did not see such a position as beyond his imaginative powers. "Even were I myself a slave-holder, all my earthly means vested in slaves it is indeed questionable whether I could not once bid them go free, and there suddenly reduce myself to beggary." The obstinacy of enslaved persons unwilling to relocate to the hardships of an impoverished colony surrounded by antagonistic displaced Africans and a guaranteed encounter with the "African fever" eluded McGill, but he could easily picture himself as a slaveholder to better understand their opposition to abolition. Even if most Americo-Liberians were more aware of the transformative properties of their journey across the Atlantic Ocean than McGill was, all understood that returning to the United States with their privileged African positions would require a negotiation with their American hosts. But having tasted the privileges of racialized power, Americo-Liberians ranging from those like McGill, who were most able to bring their privileged position to the United States, to Alexander Hance and Charles Scotland, who directly confronted black deprivation in their efforts to free their children from bondage, were very uninterested in returning to their previous positions in the racial hierarchy of their former home. They mobilized their exotic and civilized identity to accomplish these goals.

* * *

Settler William Polk understood the racialized implications of his new position in Africa when he passed word along to his former friends and neighbors, writing, "I would not exchange homes with them on no condition unless they could make me as the white man." It is significant to note that Polk was not requesting to "become" a white man but rather to be treated *as* white. These were individuals not concealing their identity but rather seeking to use their privileged African position to springboard their demands for a similar treatment in the United States. For Polk and settlers like him, there would be no going home except with the privileges of whiteness, and the African whiteness of these settlers provided a tool by which they could make their demands.[69]

Polk's letter eventually fell into the hands of Moses Sheppard. Noting Polk's condition that he would never return to the United States unless he enjoyed the privileges that whiteness afforded, Sheppard confided, "I have expected you to be one of the respectable settlers and I have no doubt of my expectation being fully accomplished, you will then be a white man, for freedom and independence make a white man, not colour." What Polk made of this conflation between freedom and whiteness went unrecorded, but letters continually poured into Maryland from Polk requesting that his old friends and relatives join him in Africa. Polk was no longer interested in being a "beast of burden" for white people.[70]

Unfortunately for Polk, few of his old Eastern Shore acquaintances followed his advice and immigrated to Liberia. By August 1836, Polk confided that while he was sorry for the condition of America's people of color, he had almost decided to cease writing them altogether, as he could think of no other remedy than emigration. "If they come they come or if they stay they stay," he shrugged. Conversely, the postscript of his letter betrayed any semblance of nonchalance acceptance. Writing to African Americans in Maryland via a white MSCS official, Polk declared, "If they will come out . . . and stay as long as I have been and then want to go back they ought to be sent out to the Southern states as Slaves." Perhaps this condemnation to the slave South reflected a rhetorical flourish, but Polk obviously dismissed those African Americans who were unwilling to brave the same obstacles he encountered to "be out of the white peoples hands altogether." Of course, Polk was not alone in these emotions; shock, betrayal, frustration, and confusion characterized many Liberians' letters as they pondered why most African Americans were unwilling to vacate their homes and subjugation for liberty in foreign Africa.[71]

George McGill, Samuel's father, voiced this understanding completely when he wrote to the Board of Managers of the MSCS while his son attended Dartmouth. Expressing the same bewilderment as his son that most African Americans declined the colonizationists' invitations to emigrate, McGill informed the board, "You can tell them [African Americans] that here I can toe point with their masters the unighted states & English Comodors Captains agents are only my Eaquals when they come here and as such they treat me, as proof when the purtomac friget was here I slep on board one night in the cabin with Capt Nicolson of Baltimore I supd Brakfasted & dined with him in his cabbin, such is the case of a collrd gentleman in Liberia, when he came on shore I treated him accordingly." The elder McGill clearly understood that within the geographical confines of Liberia, he could not only make claims of equality with white naval officers but actually had the power to create that equality. In Africa, he was a colonial administrator, the founder of a trading firm, a schoolteacher, a vice-agent, a respected settler with many prominent white friends in the United States, and a white—with contested meanings—in Africa. Horatio Bridge agreed with McGill. In relaying his Liberian experiences, Bridge noted, "The white man, who visits Liberia, be he of what rank he may, and however imbued with the prejudice of hue, associates with the colonists on terms of equality. This would be impossible (speaking not of individuals, but of general intercourse between the two races) in the United States." As individuals, Americo-Liberians were not content to leave those "terms of equality" in West Africa when they visited the United States, but bringing their privileged African status across the Atlantic would require laying claim to the mantle of "civilization." In this negotiation, their African whiteness helped.[72]

Although their whiteness was confined to the western coast of Africa, Americo-Liberians, especially those with the stature of the McGill family, could travel in the United States with an idiosyncratic whiteness through their associates and friends who would ensure their treatment as a sort of "honorary" white in small social settings. Sheppard, the same individual who had reminded Samuel McGill that he should never expect the words "Mr. McGill" from a white man, had written to McGill's father the same day that he penned that rather pessimistic forecast to his son. Acknowledging that he had prepared the younger McGill for the worst, Sheppard, aware of Liberia's racial constructions, confided to the elder McGill that his son would "be regarded as a white man by a very numerous and respectable circle, but the habits and usages of Society, alas prejudices, will prevent him being treated as such in our public and common intercourse." Throughout McGill's travels in the United States, Sheppard and the white colonizationist leaders continually worked to ensure McGill received preferential treatment as a white man in every instance they could influence; most of these clandestine mechanics occurred without the knowledge of the socially conscious McGill. Edward E. Phelps, McGill's mentor, could see no possibility for the Liberian settler to reside in his house "for the reason, that I could not at all times ask him to my table, without making a great deal of talk, or in other words, I dare not, in this case, brave public opinion, altho I cannot, in principle defend the position." Although he lacked the backbone to stand up to public scrutiny for boarding an African American within his household, Phelps did promise to train the Americo-Liberian for medicine, even at the cost of losing all of his other students. Indeed, Phelps thought this outcome likely and determined that he would have to pass along his other private students to other doctors as they would not take an African American "as a chum," a concern that coupled with the experiences in Baltimore underscores why McGill was introduced as an exotic English-speaking African to the medical students at Dartmouth. But even as McGill encountered obstacles, his path to New England was plowed with deep furrows of whiteness by his Maryland patrons, Sheppard in particular. As a Liberian settler, McGill lacked the official state documentation proving his freedom, and the captain of the vessel originally employed to take the Americo-Liberian to New England refused to take him as a passenger out of fear of violating Maryland's laws regarding the transportation of undocumented people of color. The colonization leaders created documents confirming McGill's identity as an Americo-Liberian and slyly wrote to the owners of the ship that McGill was a cabin passenger and should be treated without distinction to his race. As McGill sailed for Boston, he unknowingly raced letters speeding toward New England colonizationists and acquaintances of the MSCS leadership requesting that they meet McGill. And when Lydia Nickolson initially rejected McGill's proposal for marriage, his white benefactor suggested that the mixed-race Nickolsons were notorious for the delight they held in "fooling" whites and that McGill was just another white fool to Lydia.[73]

Clearly, McGill represented the apogee of Liberian society and was not representative of Americo-Liberians as a whole. The experiences of Dempsey R. Fletcher, a man who shared all the privileges of African whiteness and masculinity with McGill but not his social class, highlights the constraints that could be placed on this transatlantic mobility. For a class-conscious man incapable of seeing the world through the eyes of the enslaved, McGill selected a fascinating student. Fletcher had been born enslaved in Perquimans County, North Carolina, along the eastern coast, and had emigrated at the age of five with twelve other kinsmen per the requirements of the will of their enslaver who had disappeared at sea. Fletcher and McGill shared one trait: they had both immigrated to Liberia as children. But the similarities largely ended there. Not only was Fletcher not of mixed ancestry—at least not to the degree that he was classified as a "mulatto"—but his family developed notoriety in the Caldwell settlement of Liberia. His relative Driver Fletcher was sentenced to nine months in prison in 1838 for grand larceny, and three years later he received a year-long sentence for stabbing someone.[74] While McGill enjoyed the fruits of a well-placed family, Fletcher was orphaned soon after arriving in Liberia. He could write phonetically, however, an impressive talent given his background and a commodity within a colony of the formerly enslaved, and he was employed by a trader. James Hall, the MSCS agent in Africa, saw potential in the youth and hired him to work for the society in Maryland in Liberia.[75] When McGill returned to Africa, he took on Fletcher as a student.[76]

The MSCS had hoped that McGill would provide the foundation upon which to erect an African medical school, and taking on Fletcher as a student certainly supported that mission. But McGill only vocalized a more restrictive vision of Fletcher's employment as an assistant druggist. "I have taken a student of medicine under me, but cannot yet form any idea of his capacity—yet I entertain hope that he soon be sufficiently qualified to assist me as an apothecary." Fletcher evidently undertook his studies with the understanding from McGill and Governor Russwurm that he would study two and half years in Africa and one and half years in the United States, and then he too would acquire a medical degree like McGill. Unfortunately, Fletcher, the formerly enslaved man from North Carolina, did not have the same contacts within the colonization society as the better situated McGill, and he languished at his post in Africa for five years. After repeated letters, Fletcher finally found a patron of sorts in James Hall, who, while he did not actively intercede on behalf of Fletcher as others had done for McGill, at least nominally brought up the prospect before the Board of Governors of the MSCS, who voted in March 1845 to fund Fletcher's medical education in the States. After so many years of effort, Fletcher was understandably ecstatic and gushed to MSCS President Latrobe, in a letter that contained a revealing mistake regarding the number of his supporters, "I never supposed that I had any friends so far distant that would interest them himself thus far for my prosperity and success."[77] Fletcher was to follow McGill's exact footsteps and begin studies in Vermont under Phelps before moving on to the lectures at Dartmouth. Unfortunately, the letters and records for Fletcher do not indicate whether he was also forced to "pass" as an African as McGill had. The Faculty Records for the College of Medicine parenthetically note Fletcher as an "African," but there is no indication whether this reflected deception, his residence in Africa, or a racialist conflation of an "African" with a person of African descent.[78]

While book collections, surgical instruments, and financial assistance had flowed to New England while McGill was in residence through Sheppard's patronage, Fletcher was largely on his own. Whereas McGill was noted by colonizationists and white faculty members alike for his intellect and gentility, Fletcher was construed as an intellectually inferior man.[79] These white advisers' discussions of Fletcher usually pointed to his deficiency as a student as the reason for his problematic academic career, but the correspondence regarding Fletcher is also more racially tinged than the letters about McGill. While the Washington Medical College students only saw a "negro boy," the colonizationists rarely racially identified McGill, and usually only as a means of introduction before racial categorizations evaporated from the text. Conversely, Fletcher, who Sheppard described as "perfectly black with a negro face but possessing mind," was often racialized in correspondence. Indeed, the most extended correspondence between Sheppard and Fletcher while he was in New England stemmed from Sheppard's curiosity regarding the racial hierarchy in that location. This inquiry was probably spawned by Fletcher's report of his arrival at Dartmouth, in which he noted that "the general treatment I received from the class was better than I expected; yet reason forbid my using that degree of intimacy with the same freedom which I could have had I not been a negro." Upon receiving this news of Fletcher's reception, Sheppard wanted to know more. "You are now in a location where it is avowed that colour is disregarded and among a people who are advocates of equality, you are therefore in a situation to impart the information I wish to obtain. Your colour being unmixed gives you an advantage in this respect that Dr. McGill did not possess." Determined to quantify equality, Sheppard asked Fletcher to assign a number between one hundred and zero, one hundred meaning that every New Englander treated him with dignity and zero signifying that no one treated him in this manner. Fletcher placed the number at twenty-five, noting that more cordiality was extended to him while engaged in individual interactions than in group settings, and thus he tended to avoid group engagements in which "I supposed my absence would be preferable."[80]

Suggestive of Fletcher's state of mind, he wrote colonization officials that his plan of withdrawing from groups was so that if forced into an altercation, he could justify his actions on the grounds of self-defense. Years later, after his return to Africa, Fletcher wrote to Sheppard, tellingly calling him one of his "transatlantic friends," to note the value of his American education. While such trips to the United States or England were necessary to acquire this knowledge, Fletcher admitted, "There was not a day while I was in the United States that my mind was free from suspicion or from embarrassment. If I was eulogized for my acquirements, I thought [it] to be flattery & unsound, if spoke contempedly of—I thought I deserved it and had no right to be in America."[81] Needless to say, he found Northern prejudice to differ only in degree rather than in kind. Like McGill before him, Fletcher found himself engaged in debates with white abolitionists regarding the merits of colonization. Yet, class and birth separated the two Liberians. McGill rarely mentioned poor people, except to deny their existence in New England as evidence of his need to operate upon Baltimore's impoverished African American population. In breaking down the 25 percent of the Northerners who engaged with him on some platform of equality, Fletcher noted that two-thirds of them were the most prominent men in the area. These individuals were probably of the same group as Dr. Phelps and Dartmouth physician Dr. Reuben Mussey in whom McGill found comfort and whose power and privilege were secure enough to allow for the intrusion of a Liberian settler in their lives without loss of respect, so long as he did not sit at the dinner table. The remaining one-third of Fletcher's comrades, however, were "the least cultivated in literature," a class absent from McGill's circle of friends.[82] Even as he struggled to find the same acceptance among the upper classes as McGill had, Fletcher exhibited far more dexterity at coexisting with the lower classes.

Several Maryland colonizationists had opposed sending their colonists to New England for fear of abolitionists influencing them to remain in the United States. While McGill eventually escaped most of their suspicions, although not to the point of providing the resources for his clinical work in Baltimore, Fletcher was not so lucky. By October 1846, less than a year after Fletcher's arrival in Vermont, Phelps was convinced that the Liberian had fallen in with "bad company." The ill-defined term had previously suggested abolitionists, but Phelps's primary complaint about Fletcher's social circle centered on expenditures rather than any indication from Fletcher that he no longer desired to return to Liberia. Fletcher's friends apparently encouraged him to spend freely on "ice creams and beers and oysters" (hopefully not in the same sitting). The menu does not suggest refined company and reinforces the notion that Fletcher found a place among the lower classes that McGill neither desired nor found comfortable. Perhaps these were the middle-class abolitionists the Marylanders so feared would tempt Fletcher with the perks of an American residence. More likely, Fletcher's friends were lower-class whites who were unperturbed in sharing a beer with an African American. Class-conscious Phelps, who had expressed such concern about how society would view an African American dining at his table, could only assume that those who would share their table were "bad company."[83]

Just as McGill left Dartmouth early, so too did Fletcher request an earlier examination so he could make the fall expedition to Liberia.[84] To make his ship, Fletcher requested and received a private examination before the end of the semester on October 29, 1846, and he arrived in Liberia a newly minted doctor aboard the *Liberia Packet* on January 23, 1847.[85] Clearly, Fletcher did not find quite the same acceptance among white elites as McGill had enjoyed through his connections. Phelps chaffed at Fletcher's culinary excursions, seemingly forgetting that McGill, upon whom Phelps lavished praise, had requested similar "spending money" while he was in residence in Windsor. Perhaps Fletcher was not McGill's equal in intellect and manners, but there is something suggestive in the way the same whites who had favored and patronized McGill's endeavors so dismissed the "perfectly black" formerly enslaved man. Nor did Fletcher's writing exhibit the same elasticity in his racial identity as McGill's; African Americans never appear as "your coloured population." Lacking such a circle of upper-class intimates as McGill possessed, it is unsurprising that the lowly born Fletcher would be comfortable among the least-cultured denizens of his neighborhood and could enjoy beer and ice cream with this class in a manner utterly foreign to McGill.[86]

And yet, for all of the constraints placed upon Fletcher, he still acquired the same medical degree as McGill. Clearly, the "mulatto" McGill received favorable treatment based upon racialist assumptions that the "more white" the subject, the greater the capacity for culture and civilization. Robert Breckinridge, a leading colonizationist, made this point in his article "Hints on Colonization and Abolition; with reference to the black race," published in 1833. "This whole class of mulattoes is to be considered and treated as distinct from the blacks. They consider themselves so; the blacks consider them so, and all who have opportunity of comparing the two cannot doubt that the former are the more active, intelligent, and enterprising of the two. They look upwards, not downwards. They are constantly seeking, and acquiring too, the privileges of the whites."[87] Regardless of the dubious veracity of Breckinridge's claims that all mixed-race individuals conceived of themselves as "distinct from the blacks," such racial constructions were common among antebellum whites. Within this framework, then, perhaps it is not as startling that Fletcher found impediments where McGill did not but rather that he was supported to the degree that he was.

The African whiteness of Liberians only roughly made the journey across the Atlantic to the United States. The resounding course of Liberians traveling through the United States was to demand some rudimentary forms of equality, especially in terms of their mobility. If they could not bring their whiteness along for the trip, they attempted at least to occupy a liminal space in which they bore greater respect from the white Americans they encountered on their journey. The result was not a unified or uniform response, as race, class, gender, and personal and kinship networks all shaped Americans' responses to the products of Liberia's engine of respectability.

A few years after Fletcher's return to Liberia, Sheppard sat down to explain his foray in African American medical patronage to a fellow Quaker residing in a slave state. After detailing the extent of his involvement in McGill's case, Sheppard admitted that Fletcher had not received the same diligence and attention. But Sheppard claimed that it was not racialist assumptions or class that deterred him from taking the same interest in Fletcher, but rather that it was simply unnecessary. Having established the path to respectability and a liminal space between whiteness and blackness, Sheppard simply noted that "the way was opened" for Fletcher. Indeed, although on a smaller scale, Fletcher too received the benefits of Sheppard's patronage. Before returning to Liberia, he met with Sheppard in Baltimore. Sheppard apparently hoped to establish the new doctor's transatlantic network and invited Dr. W. W. Handy, a member of the faculty of the Washington Medical College who had attempted to find a place for McGill there, to join him and Fletcher for tea. As he did for McGill, although again with less frequency, Sheppard maintained his correspondence with Fletcher after the Liberian's return to Africa. Writing to Fletcher in the wake of the political debates on the Compromise of 1850 and the growing sectional animosity within the United States, Sheppard attempted to describe the raging battle in the States. In a perfect summation of the alchemic possibilities of Liberia, Sheppard grew frustrated with his efforts to describe the contemporaneous state of affairs and concisely concluded his letter with one final note: "I congratulate you on your not being a nigger here."[88]

Both McGill and Fletcher attained a singular accomplishment: a medical degree from an American university. In being the first black medical students to receive official degrees, both were intimately aware that they represented the apogee of African American uplift and that many eyes were fixed in their direction to ascertain their capabilities. Even following in McGill's wake, a solicitous Fletcher had written the MSCS, "You are aware of my anxiety to obtain what is supposed by many to be denied coloured people not from physical but mental disorganization, together with the ebony hue."[89] Most pro-colonization ideologies projected spatial-racialist assumptions that "civilization" and ability were predicated upon geography and location. Liberia was the ultimate civilizing mission, capable of civilizing both African Americans and Africans by their mere presence within its borders. The issue for colonizationists turned on whether those societal dregs of the United States—the free blacks—were inherently inferior or only environmentally so. For those advocates who attributed the problem to the social hierarchy of the United States, free blacks' interaction with white culture would prove to be a blessing for Africa. White colonizationists who performed this intellectual acrobatic maneuver conceived of slavery as providing an "apprenticeship" of sorts in white American society. Even if African-Americans lagged behind whites in civilization, so this logic proceeded, they far excelled native Africans in cultural achievement. Hence, Robert Breckinridge's 1851 address before the Kentucky Colonization Society in which he classified slavery as a "type of training" for African

Americans in the cultural practices of Euro-Americans.[90] The problem the ACS soon discovered was that the operations of a full-fledged colony in Africa necessitated more skill than apprenticeships in slavery could provide. Colonial administration required literate and skilled administrators, schoolteachers, mechanics, and, as highlighted in this chapter, physicians.[91]

Utilizing the colonizationist argument that life in Liberia bestowed respectability, the settlers sought financial support in returning to the United States to acquire trades and skills previously beyond their reach. Although the colonizationists publicly proclaimed settler Anthony Wood's 1844 visit to the United States as a trip solely "to induce some of his old friends and associates to join him in Africa," the formerly enslaved blacksmith actually sought "mechanical instruction" in addition to completing his lecture circuit—apparently in the form of gunsmithing, a skill Samuel McGill considered imperative to the survival of a colony surrounded by "savages." Lott Cary envisioned a lecture trip to Virginia combined with a business venture to sell Liberian coffee in Richmond and to purchase a vessel to make the annual runs between Liberia and the United States. Major Bolon (occasionally spelled "Bolin"), a Baltimore shipwright, sought promotion in a dramatic fashion. Employed by the MSCS to build two schooners in Liberia for the purposes of coastal trade, Bolon requested that upon completing the vessels he be allowed to command one ship on a transatlantic voyage back to Baltimore. Despite his grandiose plan, Bolon recognized that perhaps certain white citizens of Baltimore would not look favorably upon a black captain entering their port. Incredibly, his solution to this logistical problem was to suggest that he take on a white mate. Perhaps he planned for this white sailor to adopt the visage of captain upon their arrival in port, but Bolon never disclosed why he thought that Baltimore's whites who would not allow an all-black crew to enter their port would embrace with open arms a vessel that contained a white subordinate to a black captain. Tellingly, Bolon did not offer any other possibility aside from his captaining the ship, and equally suggestive is the fact that the MSCS leadership left that particular letter unanswered (although interestingly both the *Maryland Colonization Journal* and the *African Repository and Colonial Journal* did reprint the letter).[92]

And so too did Americo-Liberians chafe at segregated railroads. A settler traveling through Richmond displayed both confusion and indignation when a railroad clerk demanded to know his height to fill out the pass that would allow him onto the train. This anecdote led Moses Sheppard to sarcastically comment to his Liberian correspondent, "Next time you come they'll weigh you."[93] All of which was succinctly summed in settler Andrew Hall's statement to a colonization official: "I find it is true what you told me in your office that I would not be willing to come back to America to be called a negro."[94] Intriguingly, Hall places the origins of his statement with a colonization official, specifically referencing a conversation held in the man's office (all of the MSCS leadership were men). Was this promise of the ability to shed a "negro" identity standard fare for the MSCS sales pitch to prospective emigrants? And this promise was predicated not on never returning to the United States but on never returning "to be called a negro." The tantalizing unanswered question in Hall's letter is under what identity he would be willing to come back to the United States if "negro" was unacceptable. The resounding answer of Liberians traveling through the United States was to secure a form of racial equality based upon recognition of their experiences in Africa.

* * *

Journeys to the United States were not limited to Americo-Liberians, however, as the American settler colonies in Africa likewise provided a port for Africans to sail to the United States. Not only did many Africans find employment on the European and American sailing vessels plying the African coast, but a few Africans also found themselves exploring American cities. If the insertion of African Americans into western Africa disrupted the existing racialized organization of that space, the mobility of Africans exploring the United States could equally expose these travelers to the racialized organization of America—an exposure that greatly challenged the supposed racialized dominance of the Americo-Liberians.

Not all visiting Africans went necessarily by choice. On February 14, 1834, the MSCS and the three leaders of the nearby Grebo towns formally ratified the deed of sale establishing the future Maryland in Liberia. These three "kings," Pah Nemah ("King Freeman"), Weah Bolio ("King Will"), and Baphro ("King Joe Holland") were the principal rulers on Cape Palmas. The agent of the MSCS, James Hall, lacked both the manpower and the military strength to repulse a potential assault, and so he negotiated the next best thing: a son from each ruler. Hall confided to the MSCS, "This measure cost me much trouble & coaxing—I wrung them one by one." Hall informed the fathers that he would dispatch the boys to the United States, where they would be taught to read and write, a desirable skill for Africans. In private, Hall confided that while he hoped that the children *would* receive an education and "civilization" in the States, his primary concern was to ensure the possession of hostages that would make their fathers think twice before launching an assault against the nascent colony. Although "Freeman's" son took ill in Monrovia before making the Atlantic crossing, "John Cavally" and "Charles Grahway"[95] found themselves in the original Maryland by April.

The MSCS immediately concocted a strategy to circulate the young Africans among various churches, in hopes of drumming up support for colonization, and then envisioned a broader trip in which the two youths would barnstorm across the northeastern United States in the company of two minister brothers, John and Robert Breckinridge, and raise funds for the society in New York, Philadelphia, Boston, and New Haven.[96] The trip was not a financial success; few Northerners contributed and the traveling companions ran into difficulty while in Boston from William Lloyd Garrison, who lambasted the trip from the pages of the *Liberator*. Ironically, despite their ideological differences, both Garrison and the Breckinridges could agree that the "African princes" offered little incentive for evangelicals to open their purses. Garrison only briefly mentioned their presence in his account of the colonizationist mission to Boston. While Garrison privately called the two Grebo youths "those young humbugs,"[97] Robert Breckinridge confided in a letter to Sheppard that the boys, "while of no use to us, are ruining, as fast as may be." Of course, perhaps the colonizationists expected a bit too much from two youths who had never been to the United States and could not speak English. And putting them under the watchful eyes of the Breckinridge brothers, two conservative Presbyterian clergymen, certainly did not make for a cordial traveling expedition.

Robert Breckinridge was a slaveholder originally from Kentucky who was attracted to colonization through its dual promise of "civilizing" Africa through Christianity, thus appealing to his Protestantism, and of finally creating an all-white American republic, thus appealing to his affinity for whiteness. For myriad reasons, from his racialist perspective, Breckinridge found the Africans unsettling and their continued residence in the United States a possible disaster without white patronage. He recommended in his report to Sheppard: "These two african boys ought to be separated, or they will never learn our language; they ought to be put under the sole care of *white* men; they ought to be taught how to work, as well as how to read, & write; and they ought to be placed if possible, in the country. Excuse this freedom; but if we are not wise, we shall raise up the very worst & most powerful enemies in these boys."[98]

In an assuredly unpleasant manner, the two Africans traveled through the United States' largest urban areas. While these journeys were under the supervision of two stern ministers, the two youths had at least one unsupervised evening in an American city that summer. At the completion of the fundraising travels for the MSCS, the two boys were boarded together in Baltimore at the home of James Ward, an African American minister, despite Breckinridge's unsolicited advice. After some sort of undisclosed dispute with the reverend, "Charles" and "John" absconded one evening and spent at least one night on the streets of Baltimore before locating the home of an MSCS board member. Their American tour ended abruptly when "Charles" died suddenly of an "effusion upon the lungs." The funeral for "Charles" was held at the house of the MSCS's home agent on November 19; a newspaper advertisement in the *Baltimore Patriot & Mercantile Advertiser* invited the entirety of the city's African American population to attend. The surviving child was quickly dispatched on the next ship for Africa on December 14, 1834, to notify the deceased boy's parents that the society had treated them fairly and spared no expense to ensure their wellbeing. But they were not the only Africans to make this journey.[99]

As other Africans repeated this journey, an expanding knowledge of the Atlantic world and the societal structure of the United States also led to African challenges of the colony's racial structures. While the Americo-Liberians would remain generically "white" to most Africans, whiteness remained a malleable cultural construct to those Africans. As the settlers hoped to utilize their colonial powers and tools of whiteness to keep Africans in a subordinate position within the colony, expanding access to that colonial space provided Africans with their own tools to challenge settler dominance. Education proved a critical battleground here, as the establishment of schools for African children became a ubiquitous demand of African leaders engaging in treaty negotiations with the Liberian leadership. Clearly, Africans believed these opportunities to understand Western cultural practices and gain fluency and literacy in English offered these coastal traders advantages in their mercantile negotiations. But the knowledge gained in these schools also proved useful in challenging settler dominance. By 1838, colonist Nathan Lee was writing back to the United States to complain about African children attending the missionaries' schools: "it is Sur much as ever we can do to pass without being terribly abused it is the cry of the Natives Moss Specials these young lads calling us Slaves." Lee's solution was to remove African children from the schools in favor of the settlers' children to ensure that every Americo-Liberian child received the education denied him or her in the United States. Not only did limited classroom space and qualified teachers leave many settler children without teachers, but Western education elevated these African youths within their own societies. Given the flexibility of their definitions of whiteness, it is unsurprising that Lee encountered difficulties from schoolchildren, who, once armed with a working knowledge of English literacy and American customs, would have considered themselves the equals—if not the betters—of their settler neighbors, many of whom were formally enslaved. For those "young lads," there was no contradiction in describing the settler culture as "white man's fash" while simultaneously taunting them for their previous enslavement.[100]

The capital of Maryland in Liberia, Harper, was established on the outskirts of Gbenelu, the village of "King Freeman." Obviously, the early years of colonial establishment in Liberia sparked friction between the settlers and Africans. This strained cross-cultural exchange eventually led "King Freeman" to dispatch his main interpreter, Simleh Ballah,[101] on a trip to the United States to see for himself the country and determine the veracity of the claims that James Hall had been making. In addition to fact finding in Baltimore, Ballah was also instructed to deliver an address to the Board of Managers of the MSCS to notify them that "Freeman" appreciated the influx of trade goods and capital into Cape Palmas. Ballah left for Baltimore in early 1836 and addressed the board in June; in return, he received a list of the laws that the board desired to be enforced in their colony. Armed with these instructions, Ballah returned to Cape Palmas in July aboard the *Financier*, but not before a tour of Baltimore that included an obligatory journey to the top of that city's Washington Monument. Perhaps most impressively, Ballah found lavish quarters during his time in Baltimore at the residence of Latrobe, who acted as his tour guide.[102]

"Freeman" was reportedly pleased with the results of his own little exploratory expedition. Utilizing a white missionary as his "hand," he dispatched a letter to the board upon Ballah's return thanking them for their kind treatment of his "eyes" while in the United States. He was pleased with the MSCS's rules for governance and promised to implement them among his people. "Freeman" also reported that Ballah talked about the United States, and "Freeman" determined that it must be a "fine" country. What seemingly struck "Freeman" most forcibly was the economic power of the United States. Although the letter was written less than a week after Ballah's return from Baltimore, "Freeman" reported that "Soon Bello go for Merica first time long way bush & tell all man say he must make fine road & bring plenty trade for Cape Palmas." Here, "Freeman" blended the MSCS colony and the United States, as he was actually referring to a settler expedition that Ballah was escorting into the interior of Africa to secure trade routes. For "Freeman," America was both in the western hemisphere and in the tiny colonial outpost just beyond the pale of his village.[103]

Intriguingly, not only did Ballah return with a greater understanding of the commercial power of the United States after observing the energy of Baltimore's harbor, but he also carried with him a greater understanding of the degraded position that the African American settlers in Liberia held in the United States. "Freeman" reported that "Me hear say you hab plenty slave in you country," and he promptly extended an invitation for all enslaved people in the United States to enjoy freedom on Cape Palmas. It is possible that the white missionary whose hand guided this letter ascribed a pro-colonization spin to "Freeman's" message without the Grebo leader's knowledge, but the sentiment is not out of character. Ballah observed only Baltimore and may have had a poor understanding of the vastness of the slave South, and "Freeman" may have not understood the sheer numbers of enslaved persons to whom he was extending a blanket invitation to settle. The settlement of Maryland in Liberia proceeded more smoothly than did its sister colony in Monrovia because of "King Freeman's" desire to transform Cape Palmas into a bustling entrepôt. He hoped that the establishment of Harper would provide the necessary stimulus to make Cape Palmas a regular stop for American and European traders. Even if he did not know the true number of immigrants he invited to settle at the cape or ever expressed a desire for them to come to his home to enjoy freedom, "Freeman's" notation that Ballah had observed American society and noted the presence of slavery is a remarkable side effect of the diplomatic mission. These sorts of African mobilities fostered African challenges to the settlers' demands that whiteness bestow similar privileges as it did in the United States and helped Africans challenge Americo-Liberian power.[104]

Even before Ballah returned from Baltimore, an expanded understanding of European and American customs based upon travel and experience within those countries undergirded African resistance to Liberian colonial authority. Immediately following Ballah's dispatch to the United States, Hall grew increasingly frustrated with the large numbers of thefts occurring in his colony. Determined to put a stop to the abuses, Hall held a meeting with local African leaders, pronouncing a new policy in which the settlers would indiscriminately confiscate any African property of equal value to that of the stolen goods. Hall's plan was to force the African community to police its own or be subject to confiscation. The response of "Freeman" and the leaders caught Hall by surprise. "But that what I had proposed was new to them, that they could not learn by their people who had visited the white mans country that any laws of that nature were ever made. That as we were one people & under one flag, I had no right to make one class more than another suffer for all the thefts." Noting the justice system established by the colonists, the Greboes demanded that a similar system be enacted for themselves.

The Greboes considered Maryland in Liberia to be analogous to any "white man's country"—an argument that also indicates the expansive travels of these seafarers—and that the laws in one must apply to the other. In lieu of Hall's abusive system of justice, the Greboes conceded that they would police their own but demanded a place within the colonial judiciary. Thus, Hall gave ground to African legal theory and found himself awkwardly explaining to a Board of Governors in the United States why he had just appointed six Grebo constables and six Grebo justices of the peace to oversee the legal proceedings of Gbenelu. Clearly, an understanding of Western laws enabled these African negotiators to parry a law that would have led to their victimization and to secure a greater role in the colony's judiciary proceedings.[105]

These racialized dynamics of power came to the forefront in 1836, when Ballah returned to Liberia and Hall stepped down as governor and was replaced by John Brown Russwurm. The son of a white, Virginia-born, Jamaican merchant and ambiguously described "Creole" woman, Russwurm was the product of a most remarkable upbringing. Although born in Jamaica in 1799, Russwurm attended boarding school in Canada before relocating to Maine after his father's marriage to the widow Susan Blanchard. For her part, the new Mrs. Russwurm, who already had three children of her own, demanded that John Brown be raised as part of the family. Russwurm graduated from Bowdoin College as one of the first African American college graduates in the United States and moved to New York, where he co-edited *Freedom's Journal*. By the time he replaced Hall as the first African American appointed governor of a Liberian colony—African Americans had *acted* as governors in their position as vice agents, but no colonization society had trusted the top colonial position to a settler—Russwurm had lived in Monrovia for nearly seven years and had served as colonial secretary and editor of the *Liberia Herald*.

Unfortunately, he inherited his predecessor's problem with theft, and Russwurm found himself on the verge of war with the Greboes less than three months after stepping onto the wharf at Harper. In an effort to avoid conflict, Russwurm and the leadership of nearby Gbenelu met, but "King Freeman" refused to address Russwurm directly, preferring to talk only to an accompanying white missionary unassociated with the colonial administration; needless to say, for a man of Russwurm's stature and background, such dismissal was not taken lightly.[106]

The primary problem for the new colonial administrator was the MSCS's store, an agency outpost established to provide settlers with needed goods, which had been raided repeatedly by neighboring Greboes. Colonists had arrested a prominent Grebo leader, a relative of "King Freeman," for these offenses. The spark was applied to this powder keg when another Grebo was subsequently brought before Justice of the Peace Anthony Wood for an unrelated "petty theft." In light of the perceived problem with African thieves, Wood was in no mood for leniency and immediately sentenced the African to be flogged, fined, and incarcerated. Reacting to the imprisonment of a prominent leader and the arbitrary justice doled out to their kinsmen, the Greboes formed an armed mob, sprung the captive from the colony's jail, and closed Maryland Avenue, the main thoroughfare of the colony, which ran through the middle of Gbenelu, effectively cutting the colony and colonists in half by isolating Harper from the outlying agricultural village of Latrobe. The Americo-Liberians found themselves divided in two on either side of "King Freeman's" principal town surrounded by a large force of very angry Greboes.

In this bleak moment, Russwurm arranged for a meeting between himself and "King Freeman" in hopes of avoiding war. Unfortunately, "Freeman" refused to acquiesce to Russwurm's demands to meet and again only addressed the white missionary who had come to observe the proceedings. Fuming, Russwurm suspected that he knew the source of his dismissal: the arrival of Ballah from Baltimore. Just a few months after Ballah returned with information about the state of race relations in the United States, a man of African descent assumed control of Harper's government at a time of heightened tension between colonists and Africans. Believing that "Freeman" and his fellow Greboes dismissed the settlers and himself "from the knowledge which some of his people had acquired from having visited the U. States of the bondage of the people of color," Russwurm "commenced by calling on Simlah Balla & others who had known me in Mesurado, to testify that I came not to reside among them because I was a poor fellow or wanted chop," a Liberian expression for food. As he believed Ballah's report was the reason for the Greboes' sudden lack of respect for the American settlers,

Russwurm wanted to impress upon his audience, using Ballah's testimony, that he was not an impoverished settler fleeing slavery and looking for a meal but rather the representative of the "great men" in America.[107]

In his history of Maryland in Liberia, Richard Hall believes Russwurm was mistaken in his belief that his mixed-race ancestry disrupted the negotiations between himself and "Freeman," as Russwurm was white in Africa.[108] While Hall is nominally correct in that Africans continued to consider the Americo-Liberian settlers as whites even after they received intelligence of the reasons for these newcomers' arrival in Africa, such a construction constrains and reifies whiteness into its prepackaged American form. For Hall, if Russwurm was "white," then "Freeman" could not conceive of him as a refugee person of color fleeing racial oppression in the United States. But this static whiteness lacks the cultural flexibility of the African definition. Nathan Lee was no less a "white man" in Africa because the African schoolchildren taunted him by calling him a "slave." What is also significant about this episode is that it highlights how the Americo-Liberians hoped that their society would function. The Grebo revolt was initiated when an African was brought before a settler Justice of the Peace and summarily sentenced to a corporal and fiscal punishment without a means to challenge the ruling, truly a little America in Africa.

Occasionally, these African visits to the States were more reflective of the diverse Atlantic economic system than of intentional diplomatic endeavors. Thus, six Africans—Kru sailors led by village headman "Prince Will"—found themselves in Baltimore in the summer of 1829 after their efforts to find employment aboard a Mexican ship had been thwarted by a storm that sank their canoe. Picked up by an American ship, the Africans found themselves on an unexpected journey to the United States. Fortunately for them, in the eyes of their American hosts the Kru held a vaunted and practically unparalleled status among African peoples. Coastal dwellers, the Kru had a long association with the sea, and ships plying the Atlantic had counted Kru among their crews for generations before the arrival of the first ACS ship. The entire Liberian coast lacks a natural harbor, and thus nearly every trade good, immigrant, and visitor was rowed ashore by a Kru stevedore. Considering the mortality rate in Liberia, perhaps it is more apt to call the Kru the "Charons" of Liberia.[109]

Many visitors found their Kru boatmen, usually wearing only a cloth about their waist and ritually tattooed and scarred, unsettling, but it is a testament to the hybridity of these middlemen that they carried credentialed letters of introduction for themselves signed by other European and American captains attesting to their talent in unloading and loading a vessel. The colonizationists favored the useful Kru, not only for their nautical skill but also because the Kru were often the most fervent allies of the American settlements, as the establishment of the Liberian colonies ensured steady work for these talented sailors. Thus, when the shipwrecked Kru arrived in Baltimore, the ACS immediately arranged a meeting with "Prince Will" and his brother "Walker" in Washington, D.C., before their return to Africa. While the ACS crowed that such a visit was designed to provide them with greater knowledge of the African coast and its navigation, and there were few people more qualified to perform this task than the Kru boatmen, certainly "Prince Will" and "Walker" also gleaned useful information on America from these travels.[110]

* * *

What then to make of these migrating Liberians in the Atlantic context? The Americo-Liberian experience highlights how whiteness rarely functioned as an analytical panacea for all race relations, as it became entangled in national ("American") and cultural ("civilization") identities. Of course, only at the fringe of American society, this tiny colonial outpost in western Africa, was it even possible for these settlers to *claim* these identities that were routinely denied them in the United States. And such a transformative migration should remind scholars that while the social relations that create race are contextually confined to certain times and places, mobility inherently disrupts this process by catapulting individuals and peoples into new locations. The concerns of Americo-Liberians about how they would be received in the United States and the conditions upon which they would return underscore their unwillingness to return to America "to be called a negro." Being able to "toe point" with whites in Africa, they sought an ameliorated liminal position between white and black in America. Having founded their argument for the removal of America's free black population upon spatial assumptions that their "civilization" would increase abroad, the prominent white leadership of the colonization societies found themselves supporting these Liberian visits to American soil to accomplish tasks often beyond the reach of other African Americans. Liberians traveled with white society officials, resided in their homes, and counted them among friends who would "treat them as white" within intimate circles. Yet, these alchemic journeys were, in turn, shaped by time, place, colorism, gender, class, and social standing.

There were opportunities for male settlers of even relatively modest means to secure colonization society patronage to fund their returns to the United States. Beyond the educational requirements necessary to run a colonial administration, the colonization societies' use of settler testimonials to combat colonization's overwhelming negative image among African Americans provided opportunities for "respectable" settlers to travel around the United States and lecture. "Respectable" obviously functioned as a loaded term reflecting a settler's relative economic success in the colony and continued support for colonization. Hance and Scotland were certainly not as well-off as the McGills, but they had not succumbed to crippling poverty like many of their compatriots, and they maintained a positive outlook on colonization. Of course, educational institutions, specialized mechanical training, and traveling lecture tours to address mixed-race and mixed-sex audiences combined with the already established masculine leanings of the colonization societies and led them to seek out male settlers to perform these tasks. While the Americo-Liberians' African whiteness was born from movement, it could only roughly survive the return to America with money and status in its pockets—preferably the pockets of men like the travelers spotlighted in this chapter.

Ultimately, life for settlers hinged on the multifaceted and evolving interpretations of what defined "white" and where in the Atlantic it could travel. Sion Harris understood this. Writing to the colonization society in early 1848, several years after his initial return to his native Tennessee, Harris was in the midst of arranging a second tour of the United States with colonization officials. He was hopeful for the possibilities of securing more emigrants for the newly minted Republic of Liberia, which had declared independence the year before. "I am able to do much more than I did when I was there before," he informed his ACS correspondent. "I am more experienced about Africa more convinced that this is the collard man's home." Harris was certain that he could turn aside all of the criticisms thrown against colonization and Liberia. But it was not the promises of an independent nation-state that steeled his conviction that he could triumph in any debate with colonization's opponents; instead, it was the performance of the actions that had led to the creation of his African whiteness and those actions with the greatest resonance in America that would serve as his rhetorical trump card. "Sinate & the Representatives met yesterday we have 2 houses now & the oath was ministered to the President & a salute of 24 guns[.] if But slow we are climing[.] how is it possible that a collard man can say he is free in America when these things that I see & enjoy and pertake he cannot talk about[.] that is the reason they are so easy whipped in conversation." A show of political élan with a splash of martial adornment: the things in which Harris could observe and participate defined him as "free."[111] Americo-Liberians and their allies mobilized Liberia's space, violence, and labor to create what Harris experienced. The following chapters explain how they accomplished these goals.

2

"All Those Things Desirable for a Map to Show"

Space, Cartography, and Control in Colonial Liberia

For all of his faults, no one ever accused Henry Clay of thinking small. The architect of the "American System" had been intimately connected with the ACS from its inception, attending its inaugural meeting in Washington, D.C. He would serve as its president, a position that primarily functioned as the face of the organization, from 1836 until 1849. The great nationalist legislator was attracted to the heuristic possibilities of the organization and its efforts to highlight the great ill of the developing antebellum society that, if left unchecked, would grow into an American chimera capable of ripping the fledgling nation apart: free people of color. Freedom, specifically black freedom, and not slavery was always the core issue of the organization. A slaveholder himself, Clay was not uninterested in slavery, but he saw in Liberia a panacea for the more troubling problem of degraded free blackness. Liberia offered a place of transformation and the start of a surrogate American empire in Africa.

Liberia would provide the means and space to transform that blackness, "burdened with all of the degrading, brutalized, guilt-ridden meanings," into respectability. Speaking to colonization societies in the late 1820s, only a few years after the establishment of Monrovia, Clay painted an image of a new Africa for his audience. From the Liberian launching pad, a "confederation of Republican States ... like our own" would sprout from the seed of colonists "reared in the bosom of this Republic." The impetus for this African United States would be the example of the colonists themselves, who would "open forests, build towns, erect temples of public worship, and practically exhibit to the native sons of Africa the beautiful moral spectacle and the superior advantages of our religious and social systems." So alike would Africa be to the United States that the Niger River would be easily mistaken for the Mississippi, at least in terms of its steamship traffic. Tiny Liberia, serving as the model to which all Africans would naturally gravitate, would single-handedly create a "civilized and regenerated Africa, its cultivated fields, its coasts studded with numerous cities, adorned with towering temples, dedicated to the pure religion of his redeeming Son, its far-famed Niger, and other great rivers, lined with flourishing villages." With such opportunities in Africa, Clay wondered aloud for his listeners how African Americans could *not* want to emigrate. And Clay pinpointed one of Liberia's mechanisms for attaining respectability: the subjugation and control of indigenous Africans (for it seems that nothing so quickly delineates whiteness than the effort to control blackness). "Here they [African Americans] are in the lowest state of social gradation—aliens—political—moral—social aliens, strangers, though natives. There, they would be in the midst of their friends and their kindred, at home, though born in a foreign land, and elevated above the natives of the country, as much as they are degraded here below the other classes of the community." Although the neighboring Africans had initially revolted against the Liberian incursion into their territory, colonizationists believed that once they had become better acquainted with the settlers and acquired a desire for their arts and culture, the colony would develop a "salutary influence" over its African dependents. Within the United States, free people of color constituted the most "vicious" class, but "transplanted in a foreign land, they [would] carry back to their native soil the rich fruits of religion, civilization, law and liberty."[1]

The colonizationists' argument rested upon a socio-spatial argument regarding the relative "civilization" of Africans. Robert Breckinridge and others considered slavery a great training course in the "civilization" of whites. Once African Americans "returned" to Africa, they would be recognized for their elevated "civilization." Within this new framework, the degraded black American would influence, control, and elevate the degraded black African and, in turn, acquire his or her own respectability. This circular argument was spotlighted in the sixth issue of the ACS's official organ, *The African Repository and Colonial Journal*, penned by the wonderfully named Peachy Grattan. Commenting upon a speech by Leonard Bacon, an early advocate of colonization, Grattan notes that "by civilizing Africa, the degradation of Africans in other countries may be forever and completely removed; and by elevating the character of these exiles, the civilization of their native continent may be easily effected."[2] The uplift of Africa's descendants was predicated upon their "return" to Africa; the uplift of Africa required the "return" of her descendants to control Africans. Thus, Liberia is transformed into a civilizing space in which the mere habitation therein is transformative.

The logic of this argument reflects a transitive moment in American racial thinking. It is impossible to draw a neat interpretive line between the eighteenth-century environmentalist and nineteenth-century biological understandings of race. Biology was informed by earlier environmental theories. It is not coincidental that colonization and Indian Removal emerged as racial remedies for the United States at the same historical moment. Both argued that racial separation was critical for the uplift of nonwhites. Certain proponents of both suggested that it was possible for nonwhites to fully become the equals of whites if they were separated.[3] This was the "civilizing"—or "whitening"—mission of Liberia: it provided a space to transform its immigrant inhabitants from degraded black Americans into something different, something more, even as they, in turn, transformed the colony's African inhabitants. Of course, mobility disrupted this simplistic formula as Liberians, both settlers and Africans, entered the "civilizing" space and then returned to the United States, forcing colonizationists to ponder the implications of Liberians traveling through the United States.

Even more problematic for the ideologies of whites and the lived experiences of African American settlers was the perplexing problem of what constituted "home" and "foreign" within this framework. Clay's wording on African Americans' "home" is confusing and required an impressive set of mental gymnastics on the part of his listeners: "Here they are . . . strangers, though natives. There . . . at home, though born in a foreign land." African Americans are both of and not of America; they are among African "friends" and "home" on that continent despite their foreign birth.

This question of "home" plagued the African diaspora as it struggled to locate the spatial place of blackness within the Atlantic world. It somehow belonged everywhere but Africa and also solely to Africa. Echoing contemporaneous black critiques of the ACS conflation of Africans with African Americans, several historians have traced the "Americanness" of black society. For Americo-Liberians who journeyed either to a "home" or "adopted home" depending upon the author, the relationship between their African lives and the land of their birth was never truly severed. The result was a vision of "home" that straddled both sides of the Atlantic in complicated and complex networks. Some scholars have attempted to solve this problem by arguing that Liberian settlers who were formerly enslaved rarely referred to Africa as home, compared to white colonizationists like

Clay who nearly universally described the relocation to Liberia as a Homecoming for the settlers.[4]

It is, however, not difficult to find declarations of an African homeland in the writings of the newly manumitted. Such ruminations range from Abraham Blackford's estimation that "Africa is the very country for the colored man" to Caesar Chew's command to "tell the colored people that they Better com to Africa for this is the plase ous colord people." And what should we make of Paul Sansay's message that "if any of my friends enquire about me tell them I am under my own vine and fig tree none dare molest nor make me afraid?" By quoting the Old Testament book of Micah, in which God promises the Israelites deliverance from Babylonian captivity and God's temple is rebuilt as the focal point for the gathering of nations, Sansay ties a Liberian homeland that he possesses and owns—a place under his "own vine and fig tree"—to the missionary ideal of the colony that attracted so many evangelicals to the colonization fold. A rare Catholic parishioner in Liberia, Sansay's reference to a text that combined a promise of deliverance from Babylonian slavery with a vision of a future period of peace established by a gathering of distant nations at a place of Christian religiosity seems less than coincidental. If Liberia was not a homeland exactly, Sansay seems to suggest that it was a place of spiritual deliverance, a place in which to establish a sedentary existence, "to sit" under the vine and fig trees.[5]

There is complexity here, as both white and black colonizationists struggled to define "home." And while white colonizationists were more prone to view the relocation to Africa as a racialized "return" to a homeland, the convoluted structure of Henry Clay's address—born here, though foreign through degradation; foreign there, though elevated—reminds us that this question of a "return" also plagued white colonizationists. Liberia offered a means of elevation and respectability, often interpreted through classed and gendered assumptions of a masculine freedom built upon control of movement and people within that colonized space. Within colonizationist rhetoric, the "settlers" are rarely women, despite their obvious presence and overwhelming importance for a sickly colony with a low birth rate. The Connecticut Colonization Society was typical in its statement, "Every man of colour who removes from the United States to our African Colonies, removes from a land of degradation, from a land where his soul is crushed and withered by the constant sense of inferiority, to a land where he may enjoy all the attributes of manhood and all the happiness of freedom."[6]

For white colonizationists and black settlers, the journey across the

Atlantic and existence within that space would be transformative. This journey necessitated a bit of geographic imagination on the part of those who remained in the United States, and, like Clay, they pontificated on a vision of a continent they had never visited. In depicting Africa and Liberia's ripples in a visual manner—a steamboat lumbering down a Niger River bristling with villages and towns—these armchair geographers relied entirely on the reports, images, and maps produced by those who had visited the colony. For their part, the Americo-Liberian settlers mobilized geography in their efforts to establish sovereignty over the territory previously possessed by their African neighbors. The history of cartography is interwoven with the desire to categorize and demarcate an "us" and "them" and subsequently to assign or deny to each group a territory grafted onto a physical landscape.

Numerous scholars have argued that the turn of the nineteenth century marked an epistemological transition in Europe and the West whereby the non-Western "other" transitioned from being a "savage" (noble or otherwise) to becoming "primitive."[7] The turn of phrase is significant. Savagery denotes a horizontal spatial relationship; a side by side evaluation of two things determined by a value judgment. Most importantly, savagery lacks a temporal element. In its spatial construction, savagery assumes an external factor acting upon the "savage," whether that be the economy, environment, government, religion, or ideology. The "savage" can become tamed by changing his or her thinking and adopting "civilized" patterns of life; lines can be crossed within this framework. "Primitive," however, replaces the spatial hierarchy with a temporal one. Within this model of thinking, Europe has simply progressed beyond its neighbors. In the same amount of time as other societies, Europeans attained a higher level of civilization, suggesting something exceptional in their character and something degraded in the character of non-Europeans. Rather than retaining the capacity to pass from savage to civilized, primitiveness suggests an inability to progress from a sort of defect. "Primitives" not only lack Europe's "civilization" but also are from another time.[8]

Intriguingly, the term "primitive" is almost completely absent from the colonization rhetoric presented in the *African Repository and Colonial Journal* and the letters pouring in from Liberia. Whether it was to announce their determination to support their isolated colony "in a distant and almost unknown country and amongst a savage people" or to infer that the abundance of Africa was responsible for its inhabitants' lack of advancement, "savage" and its religious cousin "heathen" were the preferred and most often used descriptors. They were also the adjectives the Americo-Liberian settlers used most often to describe native Africans.[9]

The settlers' letters were filled with less-than-glowing opinions of the indigenous peoples: "The people among whom we live are very ignorant and superstitious"; "the natives about us are a lazy & idol people"; "they are the most Savage, & blud thirsty people I ever saw." Even John Brown Russwurm, a towering figure in African American scholarship who one biographer has characterized as a "Pan-Africanist Pioneer," peppered his official reports with reminders to his employers that "we are in a land of savages."[10] When Samuel F. McGill traveled through New England, he drew upon his experience in Africa when describing his nights without a bed as reducing himself "to sleep every night as a savage." The colonizationists in the States usually argued that the Africans were not inherently brutes but simply "want but long and uninterrupted intercourse with enlightened nations, and the introduction of the Christian religion, to place them on a level with their more wealthy northern fellow-creatures."[11] Within this understanding of the colonizing mission, the continued use of the term "savage" makes sense. Colonizationists held African society up to a European prism and found it wanting, but they assumed that their African American mediators would prove the ideal go-betweens for coercing Africans across the line of civilization. In this way, their thinking reflected a spatial, horizontal interpretation of society and culture; they believed extended contact with and life under the command of the Anglo-American/European surrogates, namely, the African American settlers, would elevate the African savage. The only temporal element would be the cohabitation time required for Africans to adopt settler culture, that is, for them to start sleeping in beds and wearing trousers. For the settlers, "savagery" also offered a useful excuse to embrace violent suppression of indigenous Africans. If neighboring Africans refused to adopt "civilized" manners even after observing such exemplars of Western culture, then what choice did the settlers have but to occasionally resort to warfare and violence to secure their society? The problem lay in explaining how the colonizers could violently suppress their neighbors while simultaneously exerting peaceful influence over those Africans who lived within the confines of the colony. Realities on the ground would prove problematic for lofty rhetoric.

* * *

William Polk found Liberia's capital of Monrovia a most disappointing settlement run by an "ill conducted government & a parcel of distasteful people." The colony had existed for less than a decade when Polk and his fellow emigrants aboard the *Lafayette* arrived in February 1833. Expecting a small colonial outpost, these settlers were less disappointed in the still rough-hewn appearance of the small village than in the quality of the reception they received. The *Lafayette* expedition was the inaugural effort of the MSCS. With the financial backing of the state government, the *Lafayette* left Baltimore carrying nearly 150 African Americans, primarily from Maryland's Eastern Shore, for Africa. The ACS government in Monrovia simply could not handle such a large number of new settlers and dumped the Marylanders in the young settlement of Caldwell, where they suffered from inadequate housing, poor rations, and a high mortality rate. Adding insult to injury, many of the new arrivals complained that rather than aiding their fellow immigrants, the established settlers swindled the naive newcomers out of their rations. It was not an auspicious start for the MSCS and reveals the great disconnect between Henry Clay's vision of an African United States and the reality on the ground. Liberia existed as much in dreams and rhetoric as it did in the physical realm, and reams of paper and gallons of ink were expended trying to account for the difference between the two.[12]

For many settlers listening to colonizationist rhetoric, the entire point of living in Liberia was to acquire the respectability that residence there bestowed upon the inhabitants. These individuals rested their hopes on the alchemic formula of Liberia. In Africa, the settlers could make claims to both whiteness *and* an American national identity utterly unavailable to them in the United States.

Of course, initially for those African Americans, many of whom were formerly enslaved, "white" and "American" were neither flexible categorizations nor ones in which Anglo-Americans had previously included them. However, as vessels repeatedly arrived off the coast of Liberia carrying new settlers to a deathtrap of a colony, most newcomers, in a trend that would continue until the establishment of the independent Republic of Liberia in 1847, identified themselves not as Liberians but rather as "Americans." Like most settler societies, colonial Liberia strove to re-create its mother country in a new land. Settlements were erected utilizing American-patterned street grids, along with the names, farming techniques, churches, civic institutions, clothing, and culture of the United States. Often, these early teleportation efforts bordered on the absurd. William Thornton, architect of the U.S. Capitol, presented a plan in 1821 for the proposed town of Mesurado, the future Monrovia, that curiously combined the realities of a besieged military post with the sweeping avenues and public squares of L'Enfant's vision for Washington, D.C. Thornton foresaw a future Liberian capital with a similar grid pattern of streets, including a grand avenue similar to the Mall but renamed "Emancipation Street," and intersecting diagonal avenues all convening in an enormous circle, much as L'Enfant drafted for the American capital. But whereas L'Enfant's squares and circles were designed as public spaces, the focal point of Liberia's capital was a twelve-foot-tall tower that would function as an arsenal, complete with circular defensive wall and battery; the great space between the fort and streets centered less on the idea of public gatherings and more on providing a clear field of fire for the fort's defenders. Thornton envisioned the capital of Monrovia as another District of Columbia, but with the ever-present potential of being overrun by enemies. Apparently, there was some concession that enlightened city planning, on the one hand, and bloodshed, on the other, were strange bedfellows, and a note scribbled at the bottom of the plan underscored that "only one half the town on this Plan, reserving the other part of the site for a more mature plan." Thornton's effort to drop the District of Columbia into western Africa, however, is indicative of this broader dream to reconstruct the United States in Africa.[13]

But situated near the equator with a large polyglot population of Africans, Liberia never fully functioned as the new United States the settlers and their white benefactors hoped for.[14] The transportation was incomplete, inadequate, and challenged by the locals, who did not care for the expansionist trajectory of the Liberian colonies. Despite all of the Liberian dreams, the colony was a hybrid space on the ground.

* * *

Of course, one could draw the map in such a way as to reinforce the imagined Liberia rather than the real one. Another primary goal of mapping colonial Liberia's territory was simply to bring it into existence. Within the borders of a place named "Liberia" were more than a dozen ethnic groups whose tongues drew from at least three different language groups; none conceived of themselves as "Liberians." Even the name "Liberia" was an effort to overturn existing European naming practices, bring the colonial entity into being, and assert control over this new creation. As European exploration moved down the western coast of Africa, European naming practices followed a pattern of exploitive commodification; the cartographic list of locations—the slave coast, the gold coast, the ivory coast—inextricably linked the map to economy.[15]

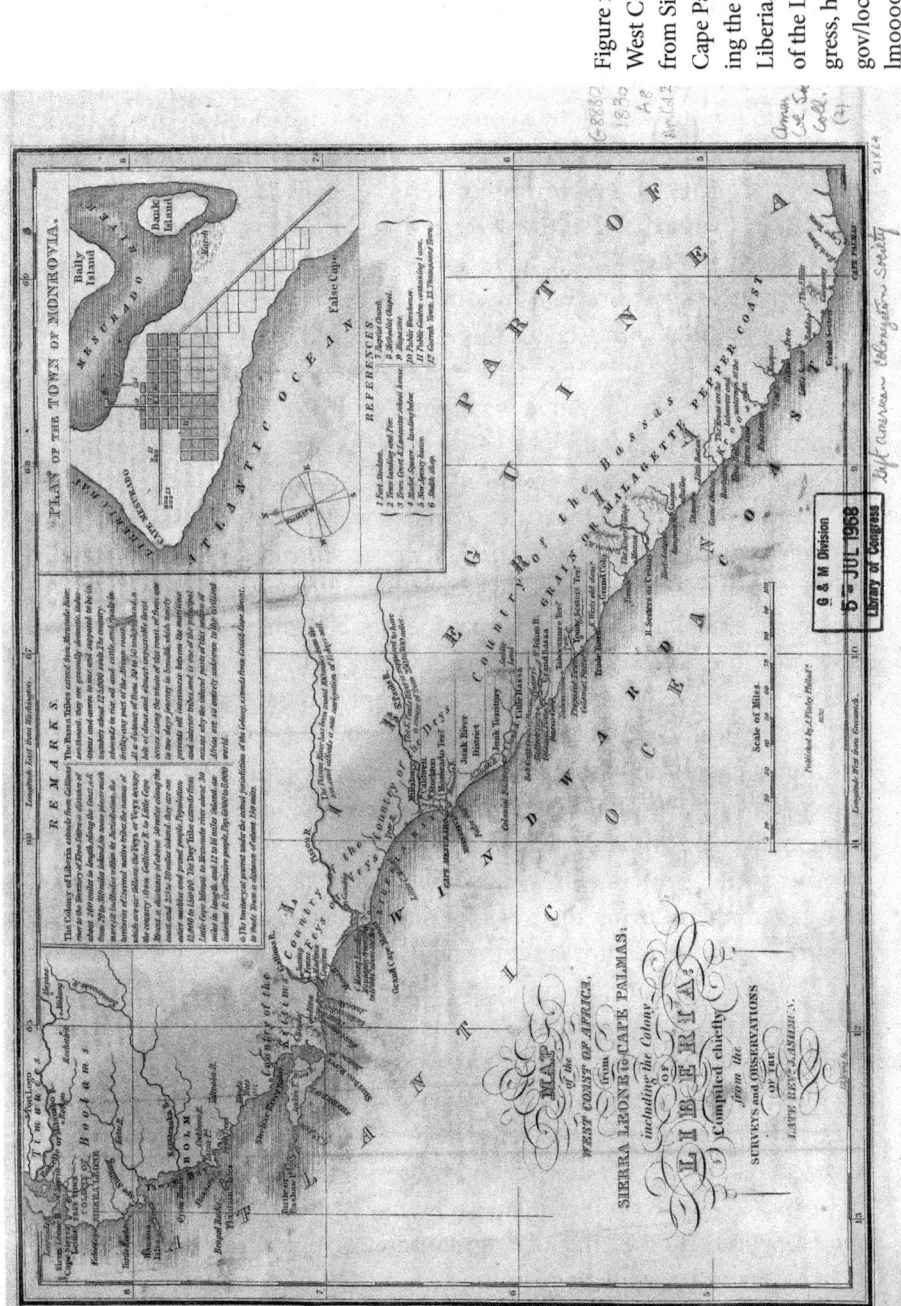

Figure 1. Map of the West Coast of Africa from Sierra Leone to Cape Palmas, including the Colony of Liberia, 1830. Courtesy of the Library of Congress, http://hdl.loc.gov/loc.gmd/g8882c.lm000002.

While European names had focused on exploitive commodification, the colonizationists had to appeal to a higher moral authority to secure volunteers and money for their colony (despite their own plans for extracting money from the territory). Hence, "Liberia" and its newly named geographic features—Monrovia, Clay-Ashland, Millsburg, Caldwell—shifted away from the economic exploitation of resources and toward boosterism and highlighting the colony's connections to emancipation, freedom, for both white and black people, and the United States. That is not to suggest that economic exploitation was not part of the plans for colonial Liberia, but rather than exporting the raw materials of Africa, Liberia would develop much as a tiny United States and export finished goods and agricultural produce on those steamships that Henry Clay envisioned.

Settlers joined with Clay in this economic vision. James C. Minor reported home in 1833, "Our infant commerce is stretching out her hands and inviting the weary wanderers of the Ocean to call. If your readers will peruse the Liberia Herald they will see for themselves the number of vessels that arrive and depart in the course of a month." An 1830 map of the colony, drawn from the measurements of governor Jehudi Ashmun, in addition to asserting Liberian sovereignty over African territories, included remarks that likewise asserted the capacities of the colony for modernized economic exploitation, crowing that the "country abounds in rice, [palm] oil, and cattle, and rivals in fertility any part of the African coast."[16] This was an economic vision of farmsteads supplying goods to well-managed and thoughtfully laid-out communities through the network of rivers before being passed on to ships from the Americo-Liberian settlements along the coast. Unsurprisingly, these were the geographic features—rivers and settlements—prioritized on the ACS map.

And so the settlers and white colonizationists mustered an imaginative geography to bring their colony into existence and grant themselves control over their territory and the land, attempting to wrangle what they could not control on the ground into something they could manage on paper. Even as the Americo-Liberians and colonizationists depicted the American settlements as linear, orderly, neatly delineated by the lines on the map, and carved out of the wilderness in the images they prepared, they likewise reinforced images of their African neighbors as disorderly savages. As sovereignty extended to possession of the land by "us," so too did private possession of the land rely upon a Lockean notion of investing labor into the soil through agriculture.[17] Despite the poor quality of the coastal soils, an overwhelming lack of the draft animals with which

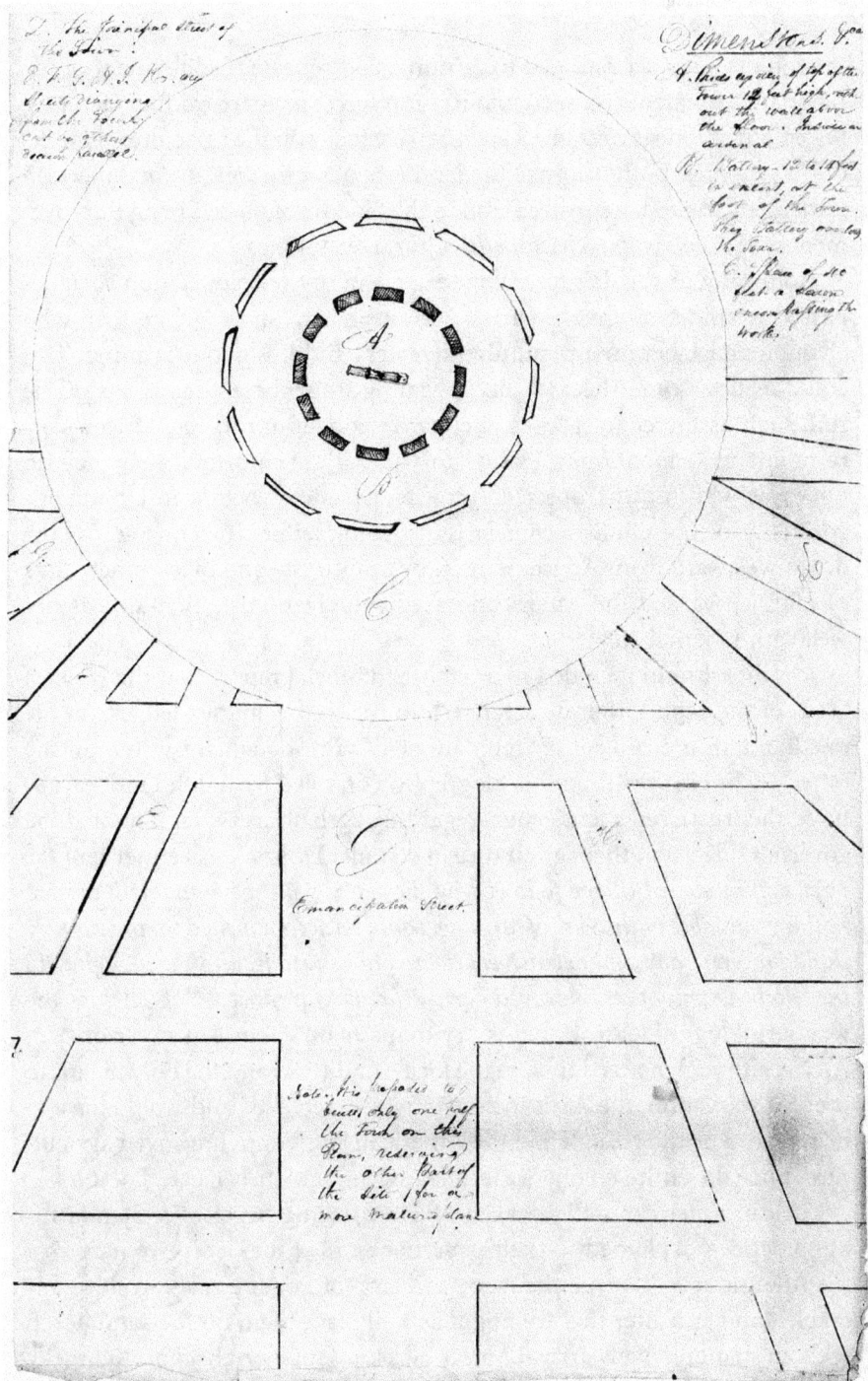

Figure 2. William Thornton's Plan for Mesurado, 1821. Courtesy of the Library of Congress, https://www.loc.gov/item/93505782/.

the settlers were accustomed to farming, and repeated belittlement of the Liberian settlements by anti-colonization forces as mere trading factories, the colonizationists presented an obsessive focus on the agricultural merits of the colonies, both to prove the land's capacity for long-term American settlement and to lay further claim to the land through civilizing improvements over the savage African agricultural techniques.

Comically, as the day-to-day management of the colonization societies passed to ministers, missionaries, and businessmen, the white men who championed Liberian agriculture knew less and less about farming. This could lead to some sheepish backpedaling from these champions of the soil, such as merchant Moses Sheppard's addendum to his African correspondent: "I mentioned Prunes to you[.] I am informed that they do not grow within the Tropics."[18] But even as letters written to Liberia advocated growing plum trees near the equator, letters traveling across the ocean westward from Africa, written by both white and black inhabitants of Liberia, warned the American-based colonizationists that all was not well with Liberian soil.[19]

Jehudi Ashmun included in a published official report that the "richest lands of the cape, either degenerate into rocky, precipitous ledges, on the one hand, or are subject to inundations of salt or stagnant water, on the other." Ashmun's posthumous biography, compiled by Ralph Gurley, captured the frustrated agent's angst regarding agriculture when it quoted the governor's decision that agriculture in colonial Liberia "was either *that the wretched modes of tillage followed by the natives must be adopted; or that nothing valuable in the way of farming, could be accomplished till the country should be generally and extensively cleared of its woods, and the plough with the whole system of an improved agriculture be introduced.*"[20] Such was the wonderful logical legwork necessary to maintain American superiority in Africa; although better suited to the local conditions and the only means to prevent starvation, the African system was "wretched" and would have to be replaced by the plough and the American "system of improved agriculture" once the entire colony was somehow miraculously cleared of jungle.

African American settlers at Cape Palmas, facing criticism of their farming practices, explained to their governor in 1844 the deceptive nature of the Atlantic soil: "Its true the 1st or 2nd crop of Potatoes will produce tolerable good and after that we might as well plant them on the sand beach without manure." New arrival Moses Jackson sent word back to Kentucky in 1846 that Liberians considered a fifteen-acre farm a large establishment. Based upon those gloomy agricultural prospects, Jackson could not recommend that his friend join him in Liberia until he could observe more of the colony.[21] The ACS received these reports and prophesized to the American public in 1838 "that agriculture will open a certain and unfailing source of comfort and competency" based upon "astonishingly and almost incredibly rapid improvements" in farms along the St. Paul's River;[22] in 1839, "the colonists are now prepared, with the aid of suitable beasts of burden, to commence the business of cultivating the soil"; and, of course, 1840 was the year that "the progress of agriculture in the Colonies, has been greater the last, than in any former year."[23] Such is the trend for the entire run of the *African Repository and Colonial Journal.* Each new year heralded by an old refrain that agriculture was improving and it would be better than the last. At the same moment in which settler agricultural improvements—modest, fictitious, or otherwise—were trumpeted, African agricultural practices were dismissed as "in a rude and infant state." Not only did the child-like Africans fail to fully utilize the soil, thus justifying its occupation by American settlers, but their gendered division of labor was completely backward: "the labours of their wretched agriculture devolve, almost entirely, on women."[24] A muscular and masculine colonizing effort necessitated an equally masculine agricultural foundation.

Questions of control over space, land, and agriculture were at the heart of the ACS's enterprise from the very beginning. At a March 1, 1820, meeting of the first expedition onboard the *Elizabeth*, the male emigrants congregated at the bow of the ship to hear the terms of land distribution read to them by the ACS agent. This coincided with the settlers' broader disagreements regarding the role of the white ACS agents in the future governance of the colony. Several settlers viewed the white agents of the ACS solely as aides in establishing the colony and surveying land for farming. While Bacon disapproved of this mutiny, he was even more critical of the expedition's female contingent, whom he labeled as "full of evil speaking[;] nothing satisfies them." The expedition's failures at Sherbro Island were framed as spatial and agriculture failures by a group of the expedition's men who lodged a formal complaint with Bacon upon the grounds that their "friends in the United States are looking up to us for the permanent ground work of this establishment" and that Bacon threatened that "ground work" by not securing the land necessary for agricultural production.[25]

The promise of land in the form of two allotments—one in the town and one in the country for farming—was a primary recruiting tool and presumed economic foundation for the colony. This land acquisition was structured on the two-tier "lease and release" conveyance, in which the land was initially "leased" to the settler upon arriving in the colony by drawing previously surveyed and numbered lots and then "released" to them after surpassing a base requirement of "improvement," usually the building of dwellings and cultivation of the soil within a certain time frame.

The laws put in place in 1824, for example, stipulated that settlers should draw a town lot and a tellingly named "plantation." Just as gendered assumptions of masculine agriculture propelled the colonizing mission, the capacity of a colonist to secure a sizable homestead was a function of his family life. "Plantation" lots were nominally five acres, but a married man could draw an additional two acres in the name of his wife and an additional acre for each child who would live within the nuclear family's homestead; the ACS capped the allotment at a ten-acre maximum per family. Although manhood undergirded the civilizing mission by clearing away savagery from the land, the proscriptive "unit" of settlement was the family. The wording of the law makes this clear: "Every married man, besides a town lot, shall have for himself five acres of plantation land, two for his wife, and one for each child, if they are with him: *Provided*, That no single family shall have, in all, more than ten acres."[26] The man draws the lot, the children are "with him," but the addition of two acres for the wife added considerable economic weight to the household.

Many settlers chaffed at these restrictions on land and also this meager definition of a "plantation." When settler Anthony D. Williams took over colonial governance in 1836 upon the departure of ACS agent for the United States, he expanded the allotments of farmland to twenty acres. His reasoning for expanding the grants of farmland was to facilitate grazing and the creation of a Liberian population of livestock for farming. Of course, if the ACS ran out of available land in the colony with these larger allotments, Williams reasoned that "the expense and difficulty of obtaining more will not be found very great." In other words, there was always more African land to seize and control.[27]

To exchange the certificates of their land for actual title deeds, the settlers had to cultivate two acres, the town lot had to be cleared and enclosed "with a good fence," and a "legal house" had to be built for the family's habitation within two years. For those wondering what constituted a "legal house," the ACS notified its settlers that African architecture just would not do. A "substantial" or legal house must be of sufficient extent to accommodate the family, be made of stone, brick, or "of frame or logs, [be] weatherboarded, and [be] covered with tile or brick." Of course, someone would have to build all of those steam engines for the river traffic envisioned by

Clay and load those ships with goods, and the ACS granted an exemption from maintaining a "plantation" for all approved "mechanics" and tradesmen who lived in the town.[28]

There was a significant disconnect between the rules put forward by the colonization societies in the United States, the actions of their colonial administrators, and the expectations of the settlers. In 1836, Tolbert Major reported his disappointment when he failed to receive the forty acres he expected upon arrival due to confusion over the requirements for "improved" land. Lewis Crook, a member of the inaugural *Elizabeth* expedition, became ensnared in the colony's complicated land system when he failed in farming near Monrovia. By 1835, he was tending a farm in Millsburg, several miles up the St. Paul's River from Monrovia. Unfortunately, the distance between Monrovia and Millsburg apparently precluded word from reaching him that the governor planned to sell his town lot to pay off a debt of thirty-three dollars. The struggling Crook was dismayed at this loss of property, especially as he thought the Board of Managers of the ACS had ordered that no settler land be sold in the colony for the purposes of repaying debts. Only after the sale did someone inform him that the ban on seizing land for debt restitution applied only to land drawn after 1833. He wrote to the board hoping to reclaim his lost town lot and to also chastise them. In addition to the system of land distribution that intentionally separated each settler's allotment into two distinct and distant parcels and the society's failure to adequately convey the laws of the colony to its settlers, Crook was also displeased at the board's treatment of the old settlers. He had fought in the 1822 war and been severely wounded. "What do they think of the old Settlers of the Colony? Would there have been any colony established if we had not shed our blood? Can ever any people suffer as we have suffered? Am I not a cripple having been shot in the year 1822 . . . and do I now deserve a pension? Either in lands as so many others did. Look at the United States soldiers!" Unfortunately, his claims for respect based upon civilizing violence and American analogs was all for naught. Crook died of "decline" in 1835, the same year that he dispatched his plea to the board.[29]

The complicated, multitiered system generated significant paperwork, both in the need for the many forms to sufficiently document the process and also the letters of complaint from the settlers who found the process confusing and unfair; both were sources of consternation for the colonial governor. Paper and earth were often at odds with one another in Liberia.[30]

* * *

If our aforementioned settler William Polk had decided to take a stroll from Maryland in Liberia's capital of Harper to his five-acre farm lot in 1839, he would have at least found the names he encountered comforting reminders of home. Setting out upon the main thoroughfare, Baltimore Street, Polk would have navigated the familiar grid pattern of many American cities. If he had looked to his right southward down Brice Street, one of four streets that bisected the peninsula, he might have caught a glimpse of the Atlantic Ocean and the small island the settlers named Auburn Island, which functioned as an African burying ground. Crossing over Brice, Etting, and Murray Streets, each dotted with frame houses similar to those found in the United States, Polk would have passed Hoffman Square on his right. The public square housed the handsome two-story Agency House, home to the colonial government; on his left, directly across the road from the Agency House, was a small gun emplacement pointing up the cape into the interior. Farther on his left, Polk could see the settlement's economic lifeline, its wharf and agency store, hugging the shore. Across the water, Greboes planted cassava on the peninsula formed between the Atlantic Ocean and Hoffman River. Here, as the road left Harper, it changed its name to "Maryland Avenue" and provided the principal highway of the colony. With the barrel of the fort's cannons pointed squarely at his back, Polk would have walked east and quickly discovered the reason for the cannon's orientation. Maryland Avenue cut like a knife through the mass of native buildings forming the Grebo town of Gbenelu, whose leader was "King Freeman." Emerging on the other side of Gbenelu, Polk would have to pass through a smaller satellite Grebo village that the settlers called "Dury's Town" before entering the more familiar-sounding agricultural village of Latrobe, with its frame schoolhouses supported by the Ladies' Society for Education in Africa sitting atop a coastal hill, the Presbyterian and Methodist mission stations, the receptacles for newly arrived immigrants, and the agency farm, home to both the house of the official in charge of the society's experimental farm and the colony's jail. Farther to the north, along the Hoffman River, he may have been able to just make out the rectangular Episcopal school contrasting sharply against the cluster of cylindrical structures of the Grebo hamlet "Joe Wah's town," named for its leader. If he had looked south, toward the ocean, wedged between the Ladies' school and Fair Hope Presbyterian mission, Polk would have noted a fourth small Grebo settlement nestled along the beach.

Here, it would have made sense for Polk to turn left and walk northward along Thomson Street. Continuing east along Maryland Avenue would bring him near the colony's school for settler children and on to the hilltop mission station of the Episcopal Church, Mount Vaughn, and the more-imposing heights of Mount Tubman, which served as a fortified agency station and main defensive outpost for the settlers who farmed the easternmost lots of the settlement. But in turning left onto Thomson Street and keeping the agency farm on his left, Polk may have exchanged words with his neighbor on the right-hand side of the street, Anthony Wood, whose dialect betrayed his enslaved birth in the West Indies and subsequent illegal importation into Maryland. Proceeding along Thomson Street until it dead-ended at Duncan Street, at which point he would have taken a right and resumed his eastward journey, Polk would have encountered more familiar-sounding voices from Annapolis and the Eastern Shore.[31] Ultimately, Polk's eyes and ears would have found the entire walk of less than a mile filled with recognizable names, dialects, frame and stone houses, and a settlement established like any other on the American frontier. The only disruptions to this idyllic American landscape would have been the clustered African huts of Gbenelu and its satellites filled with Grebo-speakers attired in the local dress that most American settlers considered nudity.

At least, that is what would have happened according to the map. In 1838, colonial secretary James Revey, a member of the *Elizabeth* expedition, sketched a territorial map of Maryland in Liberia and a more localized view of Harper and Latrobe. The map conveys an American settlement built upon precision and scientific measurements. The importance of ships, both as economic engines and bearers of new settlers, is demonstrated by the recorded depths of the various points near Cape Palmas along with markings for dangerous submerged rocks. A pair of anchors symbolically sketched northwest of the cape, where the bottom was reportedly "sandy," mark the prime anchorages for visiting ships and the most direct route to the settlement's wharf along the protected northern side of the peninsula. Each section of Maryland Avenue as it turns from its east-west axis to a precise northeast-southwest direction is measured in rods. The settler farm lots, nearly all perfect rectangles, are numbered and labeled with their appropriate owners and acreage. In combining two maps, one of the settlement and another of the entire territory claimed by Maryland in Liberia, Revey visually demarcates certain spaces as "civilized" Western-style private possessions while claiming the land outside of the neat rectangles as potential areas for settler expansion. The only impediment to settler expansion as projected by the map is Mother Nature.

The blank spaces of the page besieging the settler's rectangular plots are labeled with explanations for the end of the settlement's agricultural progress; "low land" and "sandy" soil to the south of the farms nearer the ocean, "salt mangrove marshes" to the north and west along the Hoffman River, "swamps" near Mount Vaughn. In contrast to American expansionism, the four African settlements are seemingly fed by a single field planted with cassava, which Revey dismisses as a potential source of agricultural expansion due to sandy soil. There is no other notation of native possessions aside from the "native cemetery" on tiny Auburn Island and the navigational hazard of the "Devil Rocks or the Natives sacred rocks."[32]

The entire mapmaking project was intimately connected to economic exploitation and the exertion of control. The governor of Maryland in Liberia submitted the map along with a report noting that the impetus for creating the map with its anchors and accurate soundings of the harbor, along with dangerous submerged rocks, was the near loss of a German trade vessel off the coast. In a subsequent letter, Revey underscored that the map was designed to convey the most important elements of the colony to its American board: the spread of Christianity—"civilization"—via missionary stations and the economic potential of the colony, namely, farms, waterways, and anchorages for ships. Without those ships purchasing the commodities funneled through Harper's wharf, the colony could not long survive. The governor also hoped that the leaders of the MSCS would "be able to form a pretty good idea of your territory in Africa": economy and territorial control portrayed visually on the same map.[33]

The most striking images, however, are the architectural drawings that symbolize the most significant buildings of the colonies: the agency structures, missionary stations, schools, and military fortifications. Presumably, Revey attempted to accurately depict the aesthetics of each structure within the confines of his artistic ability. The frame two-story Agency House sits directly across from the squat, rectangular, single-story agency office. While many of the schools are depicted in a similar manner as the agency office, the mission stations vary from the Presbyterian Fair Hope station, complete with triangular roof and what appears to be a porch, to the neighboring boxy two-story Methodist outpost named Mount Emory. The various outbuildings of Mount Tubman, sitting dutifully on their hilltop, are encircled by a wooden palisade to provide protection to settlers defending the outpost. There is symmetry and order to the settlers' cartographic world.

Revey's map projects savagery in the form of chaotic African settlements. In contrast to the careful street axes and farm lots of the American town, African settlements are written off as a jumbled and disorganized conglomeration of triangles. Although the triangular shape vaguely echoes that of African domestic construction—round buildings with conical thatched roofs—there is little effort to reconstruct the architectural flourishes depicted in the American frame buildings. A larger Grebo town simply has more triangles than a smaller one. In keeping with the settler tradition of employing only Anglicized names, each settlement was rechristened as the possession of that particular village's leader. Thus, the main African settlement of Gbenelu (which translates as "big town") was identified as "King Freeman's Town." This caused Grebo political organizations—a hierarchical system based upon age and gender in which the nominal village leader, the *wodoba*, was really the first among equals of the oldest and most revered men in the village—to mutate into a European monarchial system, complete with "kings," that was more familiar and recognizable to the settlers.[34] This system was more recognizable, but for the American settlers steeped in a republican tradition denied them in the United States, it was not necessarily up to their standards of civilized governance. In comparing the sister projects of Sierra Leone and Liberia, one settler thought the republican traditions of the United States were paramount for colonial success, as the formerly enslaved persons of the British Empire were "but imperfectly civilized."[35] Foisting an Anglicized name and monarchy upon neighboring Africans certainly did not equate to respect.

In employing these symbolic images on his map, Revey was part of an evolutionary cartography that began in the earliest years of the colony. Published nearly a decade before Revey's map, the 1830 map of Sierra Leone and Liberia compiled from the notes of Ashmun utilized squares to represent the location of Monrovia's neighboring African villages. Yet, this early published map likewise ensured the differentiation and isolation of "Gurrah Town" and "Thompsons Town" by employing a cluster of squares set apart and differently organized than the neat grid pattern of Monrovia.[36] An official map published by the ACS in 1845 not only continued the tradition of ignoring African place-names but also followed Revey's logic and represented those African towns nearest Monrovia with small triangles, although in this case even large African settlements were marked by no more than three triangles. By decreasing the number of pseudo-huts, this map diminishes the scope of the African habitation as compared to Revey's, which at least depicted many such symbols for large towns. Hence, even the largest African settlement seems microscopic compared to the grand grid pattern of Monrovia.[37] In their representations of the coast, both ACS maps utilized circles or squares to mark the locations of various African towns, mission stations, slave factories, and trading camps. Despite their agrarian mission, neither map dedicates any ink to demarcating African agricultural fields as Revey had done. The resulting effect is to portray the Liberian coast as empty space open for settler expansion aside from the occasional small dots and triangle of African habitation. Even Revey's half-hearted attempt to name the peninsula across from Cape Palmas as a Grebo agricultural site concealed more than it retained.

Revey was correct in at least one regard: the soil on that peninsula probably was very sandy. The poor coastal soils of the Liberian colonies forced their rice-dependent populations into an expansive system of crop rotation, meaning overgrown fields interpreted by American settlers as wasted territory were viewed by Greboes as active rice fields that were simply fallow.[38] The Greboes at Cape Palmas grew more than cassava, and they certainly thought they possessed more arable land than Revey drew for them on his map.

There are echoes here of the English legal argument of *vacuum domicilium*, in which land that was not properly "subdued" by human improvement was declared vacant. Such ideas of "proper" land use had provided legal justification for the acquisition of American Indian land by the earliest European settlers in North America. In many ways, this "America in Africa" was designed to be a repeat performance.[39]

And much like in the United States, assumptions of native land misuse led to calls for the creation of reservations. On January 10, 1846, Hilary Teague introduced a resolution to the council of Liberia, the pre-independence commonwealth's legislature, which neatly replicated the logic of Indian Removal in the United States without acknowledging those American roots. Much as Andrew Jackson presented Indian Removal during his first annual address to Congress in 1829, Teague argued that neighboring Africans' "irregular and unsettled mode of life" was greatly "inconvenienced" by settler society and agriculture. Thus, just as Jackson argued that removing American Indians to their own established territory would gradually allow them to "cast off their savage habits" if they were free from the power of the United States and contact with white people, Teague's resolution argued

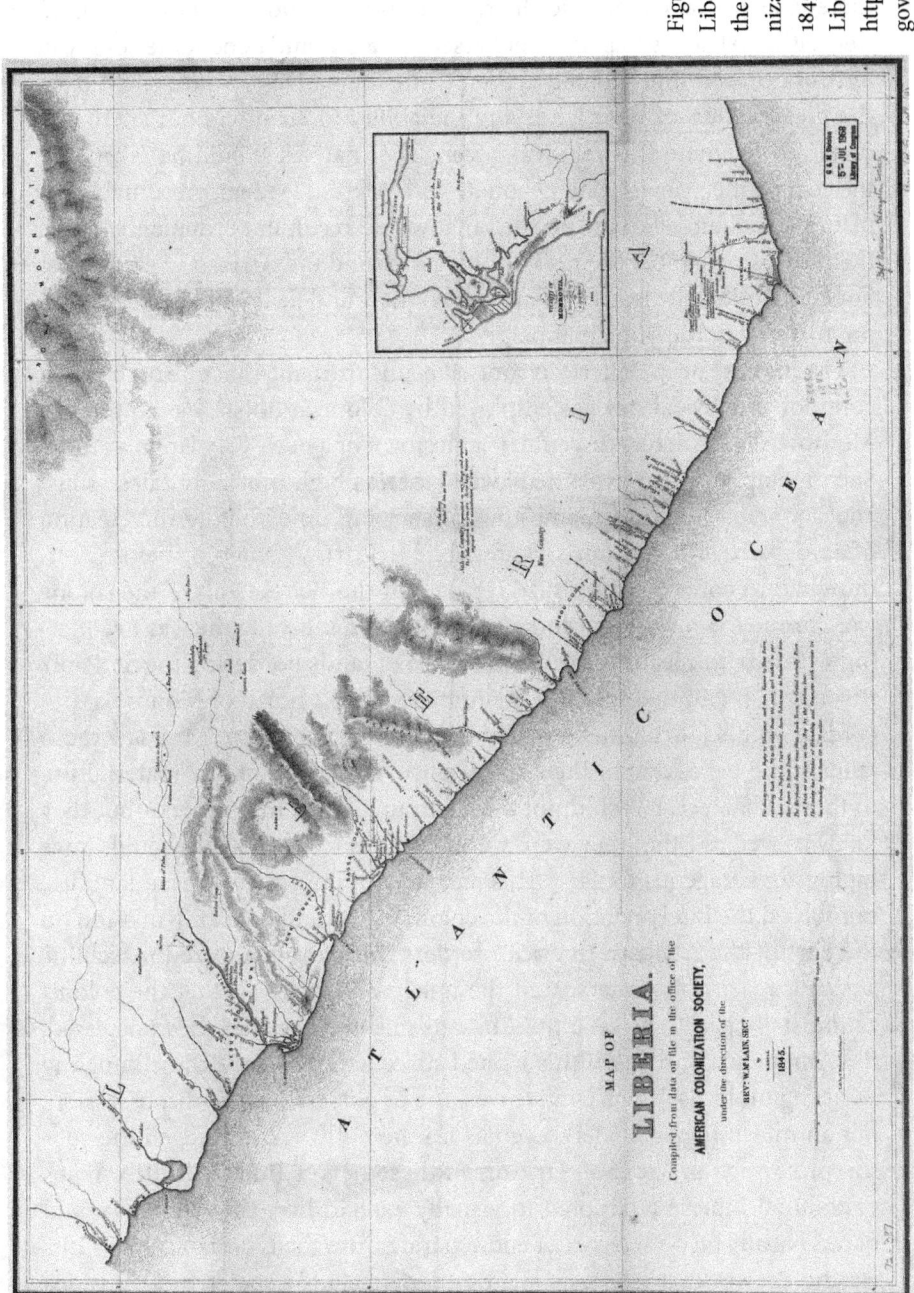

Figure 3. Map of Liberia produced by the American Colonization Society in 1845. Courtesy of the Library of Congress, https://lccn.loc.gov/96684984.

that "nothing will have a more direct and powerful tendency to civilize and improve them than permanent settlements on lands assigned them by public authority, and secured to them as well the improvements they may make thereon as the lands, beyond the reach of private and illegal interference." Relocating Africans to permanent reservations would benefit the colony in terms of preserving valuable timber, while the natives would benefit from the preservation of their lands and the ability to farm without encroachment. To facilitate this removal, a census of natives should be taken and the governor empowered to negotiate with African leaders, presumably explaining to them all of the benefits that would result in permanently fixing them to a single plot. The resolution passed, and the African United States hoped to follow the lead of its mother country and deal with its indigenous populations in the same manner.[40]

Given these deep American roots, it is unsurprising that one of the most common rhetorical devices employed by colonizationists was to refer to Monrovia as a nineteenth-century Jamestown or a new "City Upon a Hill."[41] Such metaphors also explained away Liberia's high mortality rates as just another setback, akin to Jamestown's "starving time," before the creation of an expansive American-style republic in Africa. One year before Ashmun had to concede in his 1826 report that the richest soils of the colony were prone to erosion and contamination from saltwater, he was negotiating with African leaders for the purchase of lands bordering the St. Paul's River, which emptied into the Atlantic Ocean just north of Monrovia. Recording in his journal the ongoing negotiations, he wrote, "If I saw those lands to be necessary to their subsistence, or indeed of any material use to them whatever, I should not ask them to give them up to us—but they knew as well as I that they were wholly useless to them—but would prove highly advantageous to us."[42] This narrative of improper African land use reinforced the interpretation of the colony as a grand civilizing mission on the part of the African American settlers through maximized masculine agriculture. It also underscored the image of separation that the colonizationists hoped to project: the Africans misused the land they possessed; the Americans purchased this wasted space and displaced these bungling African landlords. The narrative was one of possession and dispossession, not an intermingled society, even as it inherently acknowledged the central proximity and role of Africans in these negotiations. All three maps of colonial Liberia attempted to visually explain how the Africans could paradoxically be both a part of and separate from the Liberian colony. This was no easy task, as the maps had to demarcate the society's possessions and present a comforting space for potential African American settlers to Liberia who were distributed maps of the colony as part of the propaganda campaign to entice more settlers.[43]

The early 1830 map especially highlights the remarkable transition of the territory from African to an Americo-Liberian possession. In this early map, "the territory at present under the actual jurisdiction of the Colony" of Liberia is shaded in red. The lexical element of this early map, however, in a display that the later maps eschewed, acknowledges African claims even as the chromatic message of possession simultaneously negates those claims. Within the red shades of Liberian hegemony, there are telling designations of certain areas as the "Country of the Veys," the "Country of the Deys," and the "Country of the Bassas." Additionally, in a nod to the old European names for the region, the font and display of "Liberia" stands alongside the older commodity-based names for the region: "Part of Guinea" and "Grain or Malagette Pepper Coast." The publishers hoped that the map would convey that "the Colony of Liberia extends from Gallinas River to the Territory of Kroo Settra: a distance of about 280 miles in length." Awkwardly, an asterisked notation admitted that the territory under "actual jurisdiction" of the colony extended only 150 miles, itself a very generous summation of the extent under the supervision of the tiny American settlements. The remarks assert that the "territories of several native tribes" are included within the "jurisdiction" of Liberia. The whole cartographic execution of the 1830 map is remarkable evidence for the significance of mapmaking in the practice of colonization. The shading of the map, running roughshod over African territorial claims and European names, makes a powerful argument for the appropriation of the territory by the ACS, even more powerful than if they had ignored those counterclaims. This is all the more remarkable given the map's textual concession that the "actual jurisdiction" of the colonial government was not as great as that portrayed. Perhaps the greatest testament to the power of this map's negation of African and European challenges to ACS hegemony over the territory is the complete absence of any reference to the "pepper coast" or "Country of the Bassas" on later maps.

These later maps leave little question as to the name of the territory presented; for Revey, the larger territorial map is emblazoned with an unquestionable "Maryland in Liberia," while the ACS map projects "Liberia" in an equally impressive font. These later renditions leave no space for combative African claims to sovereignty and territorial possession. The ACS map has wiped away the African ethnicities, leaving behind only the names of settlements and substituting the old African "countries" with the new American imports for spatial organization and governance: Mesurado County, Junk County, and Bassa County. Behind the facade of scientific calculation of geographic metes and bounds lay the intentions of the mapmakers; in this case, the ACS desired to include all of "such boundaries & the various settlements . . . as would be an advantage. We ought to have a good map . . . one showing all the land owned, & the settlements, & all those things desirable for a map to show."[44] Presumably, anything undesirable would be excised to reinforce the importance of settlements and land possessed. The map of Maryland in Liberia follows this trend in focusing on land ownership and downplaying ambiguity.

* * *

The effect of these cartographic representations is to constrict Africans to isolated settlements within the territorial confines of the American colonies, under the control of the Americo-Liberian settlers but not really a part of the colonial hierarchy. They lack agricultural fields and habitations beyond their charted towns; they belong in their villages, and the rest of the territory belongs to the settlers. Even the images produced of the Liberian colonies reinforce this "part of, but separate" spatial construction. An image titled "View of Colonial Settlement at Cape Montserado," published in early issues of the *African Repository and Colonial Journal*, depicted Monrovia for its American audience.[45] Carved from the surrounding forests along the cape, the frame houses of the village stand out against the open sky. Not content with one flag, the colony flies two colonial flags of the ACS, both heavily inspired by the flag of the United States. In the foreground, an American vessel is anchored and the water is plied by African vessels, presumably the Kru stevedores who handled and ferried every good and passenger to and from Liberian wharves.[46]

Yet, one looks in vain for other inhabitants of the colony. The actual settlement is devoid of any human habitation; the Africans perform the menial labor for seemingly omnipresent overlords, but they are outside the immediate confines of the Western-style settlement carved from the African wilderness. They labor but reside somewhere outside the American town, somewhere beyond the tidy frame structures arranged neatly in rows in their own separate settlements of messy triangles. The African villages next to Monrovia so prominently noted on the ACS maps have disappeared in this image. But, of course, Africans never actually disappeared from the American settlements, and the expansive intermingling of the inhabitants

Figure 4. "A View of Bassa Cove." Courtesy of the Library of Congress, https://lccn.loc.gov/2003670327.

reinforces the artificialness of specifying certain spaces as "African" within an "American" world.

Foregrounding Africans against a colonial backdrop was a common motif that visually set the stage and immediately established for the viewer that these were civilized places surrounded by savagery. A lithograph of the Bassa Cove settlement, a venture of the Young Men's Colonization Society of Pennsylvania that replaced the destroyed Port Cresson in 1835 (see chapter 4), followed the pattern of the Monrovia image. Supposedly based upon the sketches of colonial physician Robert McDowall, the image eventually graced the membership certificates of the Pennsylvania Colonization Society. Once again, Africans are placed in front of the colonial backdrop to set the scene, although this time they appear in states of leisure rather than performing the work of the colony. The frame houses of the American settlement starkly contrast to the thick jungle, which obscures in its foliage a few possible African structures and highlights the progress of American civilization to carve itself from the African jungle. There are figures closer to the American buildings than the foregrounded Africans, but they are distant and indeterminate.

Livestock, a rarity in colonial Liberia, walk along the shore, indicating the introduction of superior American agricultural practices. In this image of Bassa Cove, the Africans are exiled from the enlightened embrace of the American settlement by a fence, one of the required improvements in colonial Liberia. Much like the unoccupied Monrovia, the interior of the palisaded settlement is devoid of inhabitants; the exterior is the place for the African.[47]

Two sketches of Monrovia and Bassa Cove defy this easy separation. Although they are undated and unsigned, the buildings represented in them suggest that they date to the 1850s and were produced by someone who had actually traveled the Liberian coast. These images include the conical roofs of African dwellings along the shore of both Cape Mesurado and Bassa Cove. In the image of Monrovia, these are presumably the dwellings of the Kru sailors who lived close to the town landing. At Bassa Cove, the Africans are neighbors to the American settlement, but their close proximity in the 1850s is absent from the lithograph from the 1830s.[48] For many settlers, this constant contact with Africans was considered a liability for the colony. Writing soon after his arrival in the Maryland colony in July 1838, at the same historical moment that Revey was confining chaotic Africanness to the triangles on his map, settler Stephen Smith reported problems with the colony: "But as for my part I am not pleased with the arangment of the cooney [sic] one the reason is this that wee are al among the natives and thear is a nof [enough] of them heare to tend every foot of land that is heare and tha heave as much rite to the land as wee heave and as tha become inlightened theare woold require more room and wheare is it to come from."[49] Sampson Caesar was also startled by the omnipresence of Africans in Monrovia, although he found them a useful, though disconcerting presence. "The natives are numerous in this place and they do the most of the work for the people in this place they will Steal every Chance."[50]

Complaints regarding native thefts were common in settler discourse, and such was the root of the case *Commonwealth of Liberia v. Quaggi*, argued in the colonial courts in February 1840. Settler William Cook lived in the small hamlet of Marshall, southeast of Monrovia at the mouth of the Junk River. In the trial, Cook deposed that "Quaggi" had come to his house "in the night" and called inside that "he had some fish." Cook answered the door and was immediately seized by several unseen assailants. He was robbed of his possessions. While the trial focused on the burglary, the episode reveals the interconnectedness of societies within Liberia. Not only did Cook know "Quaggi," but it was apparently not unusual for "Quaggi" to arrive in the middle of the night with fish, presumably to sell. Cook saw nothing amiss in this late-night visitor and threw open his door without suspicion. *Commonwealth v. Barpha* likewise involved theft, this time of

D. B. Warner's canoe from Monrovia. Warner apparently spied an unknown figure sailing away on his canoe but could not identify or catch the culprit. He immediately went to "King Peter's" town to inquire about his vessel but found no information there. Upon returning, however, Warner spied his canoe pulled onto the bank. Warner returned with the bribe of two brass kettles and this time "Barpha" was presented to him as the thief. The court decided that "Barpha" should be imprisoned for two months and hired out. Again, this was an intimately connected society. Warner knew precisely where to go and how to get the information he desired, although one ponders whether "Barpha" was the actual thief or merely a convenient scapegoat for someone interested in acquiring a couple of kettles.[51]

Revey's own map of Maryland in Liberia inadvertently disputes the rendered separation between Africans and Americans. At the margins of the map, beyond the range of settler explorations, Revey still managed to include rough points of interest. Well to the north of the American settlements, "King Cavas Dominions" were reported to have populations between three and four thousand. Such information could only come from interviews with Africans who had traveled to the interior. Even more explicitly, Revey was forced to estimate the course of the river near the seaside village the Americans called "Fishtown." He dutifully transcribed above the meandering stream "Course of the Fishtown River as described by the natives."[52]

* * *

Liberia was a creolized space, bringing Westerners and Africans into close contact within a new environmental and spatial context for both parties. In many ways, settler insistence on proper Western attire or a daily life structured around Western institutions—Christian churches in particular—reflected an understanding that for all of their best efforts, Liberia simply would not function like an American state plopped down in West Africa. While Revey dutifully noted the frame structures of the settlers on his map, the construction requirements of the new colony were such that African building designs, which were faster and easier to build as they better utilized local resources, were employed. Thus, Tolbert Major and his fellow settlers found themselves being placed in a "thatch house" after arriving in the American settlement at Bassa Cove. Even the first settlers of Revey's Maryland in Liberia lived in native African dwellings as they established the colony.[53]

And while the settlers could sweat in their Western clothing poorly adapted to life near the equator and demand that their public buildings be differentiated from local buildings through the use of frame designs, they also had to eat. For all of their dismissal of African agricultural practices and repeated requests for livestock to plow fields, the local foodstuffs of rice and cassava and the poor soil required the settlers to adapt their farming techniques to local customs. The lack of draft animals and proper plows was a ubiquitous complaint in settler letters and reports back home. Despite the colonizationists' best efforts, North American oxen, mules, and horses proved to have short life spans in equatorial Africa. A few examples drive home the point. Writing in 1836, George Crawford thought he knew the source of Liberia's woes: "As it respects the colony it is not as flourishing as I could wish. I am not prepared to say from what cause tho I think chiefly owing to want of horses to plough." From Kentucky, Liberia, Moses Jackson wrote back to his native Kentucky in 1846: "they use neither horses mules nor oxen and they say that these animals cannot stand it perform labour in this Climate." Jackson was skeptical about the colony's future without livestock. "Now sir," Jackson informed his correspondent, "you may judge how a man feels who has been raised to the use of these animals in Cultivating the ground and you also judge how things are progressing here."[54]

Since American agricultural practices proved to be poor transplants in African soils, Americo-Liberian farmers adapted and adopted local methods and products. Governor Russwurm inadvertently reported in 1839 the breadth of Liberia's creole culture observable in the Agency Farm's garden: "It is almost repetition to say, that not much ought to be expected in farming till the colonists have some kind of working teams, and no sensible man can doubt but their introduction would have a beneficial effect.... At present, on the Agency, we have plenty of water melons, cantelopes, ocra, tomatoes, eggplants, peas, beans, peanuts, corn, and other garden vegetables growing besides potatoes cassadas and plantains."[55] Many of the more successful settler farmers utilized African workforces, and much of the labor in the colony was performed by Africans.[56] Even as colonists adjusted their worldview to simultaneously recognize and deny their new reality in Africa, so too did numerous Africans adapt and adopt the culture of their newly arrived neighbors, friends, enemies, sexual partners, and employers.

Just as many Africans equated whiteness with education and culture, the ability to become a "Merica man" and alter nationality exhibited a similar commitment to elasticity; practicing "white man's fash" also had the power to alter nationality. Liberia was an important hub in the Atlantic world, and its inhabitants found themselves connected to this Atlantic geography and its representations. And, occasionally, engaging in these expansive networks was not entirely optional. The example of "Yellow Will,"[57] another of Polk's neighbors in Harper, is illustrative. "Will" lived at the southern end of Brice Street, on top of the bluffs looking across the narrow channel to the island where the Grebo buried their dead. We know the location of "Will's" dwellings because Revey decided to include them on his map.

While one colonial governor labeled "Will" an "ordinary head man," the sobriquet suggests racial ambiguity and European or Anglo-American ancestry. A visiting missionary in 1854 described him as "a large yellow man." "Will" followed in the footsteps of his people and went to the sea aboard the litany of European and American vessels trading along the coast. "Will" apparently found both employment and trouble in the British colonial outpost of Fernando Po located near Sierra Leone.[58] Although the expansive use of sobriquets of Africans by Europeans and Westerners makes positive identifications difficult, it seems likely that the same "Yellow Will" who would earn the Americo-Liberians' trust in the 1830s as they established Maryland in Liberia near his home of Half Cavally found himself in a British colonial courtroom in September 1827 for receiving stolen goods, along with his fellow "kroomen" "Peter," "Ben Kroo," "Jack Freeman," and "John Freeman."[59]

Events occurring in the following year suggest why "Yellow Will" was back home at Cape Palmas when the American settlers arrived there in 1834. "Will" had found employment aboard the HMS *Eden*, a British sloop of war patrolling the western coast of Africa looking for vessels engaged in the Atlantic slave trade. In November 1828, the HMS *Cornelia* and *Eden* captured the slave ship *Neirseé* (also called the *Estafette*), which had 280 enslaved persons onboard. The French captain and sailors were put below and a skeleton crew—consisting of "Yellow Will" and eight other Kru sailors and native Sierra Leoneans, six British sailors, and the liberated wife of one of "Will's" companions—was put in place to sail the vessel to Sierra Leone. Unfortunately, the French sailors escaped on Christmas Eve and wrested control of the vessel back from their British captors; "Yellow Will" was stabbed twice, in the thigh and in the hand, in the melee. The slave ship sailors reversed course and sailed their vessel and recaptured cargo of enslaved, which now included shackled free Africans and British sailors, to the island of Guadeloupe in the Caribbean. Secretively, they landed in the middle of the night on January 23, 1829, and marched the entire party three miles inland to a sugar plantation, excepting the British sailors. The French slave traders, apparently squeamish about continuing to hold their

European captives, put the sailors in an open boat and kicked them off into the sea. Fortunately, they reached the neighboring island of Dominica, the small British possession between Guadeloupe and Martinique, and sounded the alarm regarding the fate of the *Neirseé* and her human cargo. Soon letters of inquiry were dispatched from the British governor to his French counterpart on Guadeloupe.[60]

The free Africans on Guadeloupe fared worse in their accommodations. The French slave ship captain and his island confederate separated the ten free Africans from the rest of the enslaved peoples and secured them in a loft above the boiling house of the sugar plantation. Unfortunately, "Sarah," the recaptured wife of the Sierra Leonean "Thomas George," was kept with the other enslaved Africans, suggesting the enslavers more greatly feared the men as potential fomenters of revolt. From this plantation, the enslaved people were sold off in small groups to the island's sugar magnates. The free Africans were likewise exposed to sale in their isolated loft, but they were cultural middlemen, well-traveled products of the Atlantic, and far better equipped to challenge the terms of their sale than the others. Minimally, all could speak English to some degree, and several were apparently entirely fluent. At least two could likewise read English; another, "James Paterson," could write.[61] Four claimed to be Christians. Thus armed with these cultural weapons, they proceeded to play the only card at their disposal in this most disproportionately balanced game: they screamed at every potential buyer that they were actually free, Englishmen, and "Subjects of the King of England." To a certain degree, the tactic worked. Although the captain punched, bludgeoned, and threatened to "kill them like sheep if they spoke English"—and apparently severely kicked "George" after he attempted to intercede and prevent the sale of his wife—the free Africans remained the only unsold prisoners after a week. Potential purchasers were not necessarily thrilled about this challenge to their authority. One man examining the lot disliked "Will's" repeated protests that he was an Englishman and delivered the kick instead of the captain, asserting his power to buy them anyway if he so desired. Yet, the prospective buyer decided that the English-speaking prisoners were more trouble than they were worth and passed on purchasing.[62]

Eventually, the free Africans could no longer delay and were apparently purchased by an English planter, or someone claiming to be English, who based his right to purchase these subjects of the English King on his own claims to that nationality. The Sierra Leoneans were skilled artisans—carpenters and one mason—and they were put to work on the plantation plying their trades. Unfortunately for "Yellow Will" and his Kru compatriots, nautical skills were not in high demand on the sugar plantation and they found themselves working in the boiling house, carrying water and fuel for the fires and filling hogsheads with sugar. With such skills and backgrounds, however, they remained dangerous property and their enslaver ensured that the formerly free Africans were separated from the remainder of his enslaved property each night and slept in their own isolated quarters. Three weeks passed in this manner for the newly enslaved "Yellow Will" and his companions.

But the British were not only sending letters to the French governor. To his credit, the British governor of Dominica named the *Eden* Africans as "free British subjects," thus reinforcing and giving credence to their claims for an English nationality. Although internally the British government seemed to separate the Sierra Leone Africans from the Kru sailors—the royal judge responsible for taking the depositions of the Africans made sure to provide quotation marks around the title "Englishmen" for the Kru deponents, a formality he ignored for the Sierra Leoneans—so long as the Kru and Sierra Leoneans remained confined to the same room, the Kru would continue to reap the benefits of being lumped in with the "free British subjects." The fact that the British governor not only dispatched letters to Guadeloupe but also soon had a British warship trolling the waters near Guadeloupe looking for the slave ship also probably aided the Africans. On February 13, two men arrived at the plantation to speak with the owner, apparently revealing that the British were making inquiries. The planter decided that his English-speaking property were liabilities. The nine Africans were brought to the beach to be placed in a sloop, but on their way an unnamed woman from the island who spoke English informed the Kru that they were just being relocated to another French island to be further buried under the anonymity of slavery. Who this female slave was or how she came to deliver the message to the Kru but not to the Sierra Leoneans went unrecorded, but when the sloop arrived, "Yellow Will" and his fellow countrymen decided that they preferred the devil they knew to the one they did not and fled back to the quarters on the plantation.

The Sierra Leoneans risked the sloop and were brought out into the channel between Guadeloupe and Dominica before being put into an open boat and cast off into the Caribbean like their British counterparts. With three oars, three loaves of bread, a bit of salted fish, and a single flask of water they were directed south toward Dominica. Obviously unfamiliar with this part of the world, the Africans requested the location of a harbor; the

French responded that "they must find one as they could." In the meantime, the plantation owner was apparently displeased to find that three of his problematic Africans had returned to him. He called upon one of the two unnamed visitors from the "big Town," apparently an English speaker, and informed the Africans that "they could not be sold, but might be quite sure they were only going back to the English." The following night, the same process that had led to the release of the Sierra Leoneans was repeated for "Yellow Will" and the others; fortuitously, both boats of Africans successfully navigated the channel to Dominica.[63]

Here was the mobile nineteenth-century black Atlantic at work: free Sierra Leonean and Kru Africans preventing their illegal sale into slavery on a French island through their cultural weapons and claims of Englishness acquired from work and education in the British colony, erroneously warned of impending duplicity by a supposedly "French" enslaved woman who spoke English, and cast about on a circuitous journey that brought them from the coast of Africa to Guadeloupe, Dominica, and then back to Africa. It would be a stretch to assume that the tactics adopted by the free Africans to combat their sale into slavery inherently constituted a well-reasoned construction of identity—desperate times call for desperate measures—but there is something suggestive both in the tactic and its relative success. The West African understanding that race and nationality were permeable membranes based upon cultural practices reinforces the theory that "James Paterson," who adopted a completely Anglicized name, spoke and wrote English fluently, professed to be a Christian, and was permitted to visit a nearby church while enslaved on Guadeloupe, believed himself an Englishman when he denounced his imminent sale to potential buyers. Even as Westerners like the Guadeloupe planters were beginning to conceive of race as biologically innate in the mid-nineteenth century, these West African middlemen scared them.

Clearly, their ability to forestall sale and secure freedom had to do with more than simply speaking English. The sobriquet "Yellow Will" suggests racial ambiguity and perhaps indicates that "Will's" liminality started with his birth. Minimally, if the "Yellow Will" of Cape Palmas was the same one who escaped from Guadeloupe, the episode explains his familiarity with the language and customs (and judicial system) of the British, his willingness to adopt a European identity when it best suited his interests, and also perhaps why he no longer found working for the British African squadron an appealing occupation and returned home to Cape Palmas in time for the inaugural expedition of the Maryland State Colonization Society to splash ashore there on February 13, 1834.[64]

With such a background, "Yellow Will" was recruited by MSCS agent James Hall to serve as an interpreter between the Americans and the Greboes situated at Cape Palmas. He fulfilled this duty faithfully and earned the respect of the colonists as an impartial and dedicated interpreter. He certainly cut an imposing figure; when Horatio Bridge observed a formal meeting between the settlers and Africans during his time at Cape Palmas, he recorded that the official interpreter was "dressed in a crimson mantle of silk damask, poncho-shaped, and trimmed with broad gold lace."[65] "Will's" integrity must have been impressive as Maryland's governor repeatedly probed "Will" to no avail to disclose the secret discussions and plans of his people during the early negotiations between the settlers and the Africans living at Cape Palmas. After another round of interrogations examining "Will" for the clandestine intentions of the Greboes, "Will" informed the governor tellingly, "I am this countryman, not an American, I work for you to get money not to betray my own people. When I join the Americans I shall leave my own people. I can't have a heart for both sides." In describing himself, "Will" employed the common African descriptor "countryman," an identity reflecting their older residence in the region and the Americans' newcomer status. Within a year, "Yellow Will" had fulfilled his pledge and relocated to Harper, living at the western tip of the Cape.[66]

Given the value of an earlier English identity that had prevented his permanent sale into slavery, it is not shocking that "Yellow Will" found an American identity equally useful. In highlighting his ability to become an American through adopting the culture and customs of the settlers, "Will" underscored the significance of space in cultural identity. It was not enough to wear a coat and speak English to become an American. "Will" had to relocate and place himself within an American space: the settlement of Harper. This was the inverse formulation of the map's basic assumption of Liberian territorial sovereignty; whereas the colonizationists and settlers viewed the entire space as Liberian aside from isolated African settlements, "Will" conceived of the space as inherently African, and an American identity could be attained only through relocating to one of the isolated American settlements.

Crossing what he perceived to be a permeable line, "Yellow Will" literally crossed into the settlement of Harper and settled in a frame house. Apparently, "Will's" property included a number of other dwellings or buildings, as Revey actually drew a cluster of houses on his map along the edge of Brice Street and inked the words "Yellow Wills houses" next to them. Soon, those houses were graced with a set of American chairs from Oliver Holmes, Jr., an Anglo-American vice-agent for the MSCS who had returned to the States, replacing the "country chairs" (African products) in the home and symbolically representing the change from African to American. "Will's" two sons attended Thomas Savage's school attached to the Episcopal mission station at Mount Vaughan; in addition to being a missionary, Savage was also a trained doctor and "Will" had hopes that at least one of his sons may also become a doctor. "I feel myself an American," he supposedly wrote in 1837, "and am determined at all times to be on their side and adopt their fashion." To emphasize his conversion, he signed his letter "With Much esteem I am yr. obt. Srvt William Hall or Yellow Will of Cape Town." "Will/Hall" likewise expressed a desire to see the United States, probably on different terms than those under which he saw Guadeloupe. Of course, the words of "Yellow Will" may be, in fact, those of any number of possible amanuenses. Upon receiving the chairs from Holmes, "Will" supposedly ended his thank-you note with "hoping that God may bless you for your goodness to me in this thing." It is the only reference to the Christian God among his writings, and other colonial correspondence does not mention "Yellow Will" as a Christian convert. The phrase may have been inserted by the writer to convey "Will's" thankfulness in terms that would resonate with American ears or perhaps it suggests the missionary's influence on one of "Will's" educated sons, who would have made natural choices as scribes for "Will."

There are, however, other indications of a West African author, or at least someone familiar with the creolized Liberian English—the use of "book" to denote a letter, for example—to argue that these pro-American sentiments and hopes for assimilation originated from "Yellow Will." A visitor in 1854 recorded "Yellow Will" as expressing these sentiments: "Merica man been here twenty years, and yet . . . we are two people. We want one school for both. I want bring our people . . . half round, by and by bring em whole round. Not do this all at once."[67] Of course, in forging this American identity, "Will" received positive reinforcement from the United States. Unsurprisingly, given his large coterie of African correspondents, Moses Sheppard wrote to "Will" in 1842 reemphasizing his adoption of a new nationality after interviewing McGill, who was visiting the United States. "I hear good palaver for you, Dr McGill speak me you like Merica man, White man peak [Sheppard envelopes all English speakers, including the settlers, as "white man"]. Yellow Will big Merica man."⁶⁸ The point here is not to claim that nationality or whiteness were flexible categories that individuals could select at will; the complete abandonment of home to live with strangers certainly highlights the severe measures required to accomplish the transformation, and "Will's" exceptional addition to the Revey map suggests that he was singular in his willingness to adopt "white man's fash" and "white man peak." Yet, "Will's" addition to the map underscores the ongoing tension between space, nation, and race occurring in colonial Liberia. Although "Will's" frame houses appear on the map, his Anglicized name "William Hall" does not.

Africans like "Yellow Will" conceived of themselves as crossing identifying boundaries based upon performing whiteness; indeed, the argument that inhabiting the colonial space of Liberia would eventually produce an entire continent of "Yellow Wills/William Halls" was a foundational argument for colonizationists even before Liberia was birthed on the maps. The first official report of the ACS, published four years before the establishment of Monrovia, proclaimed that in that imaginary space "the slaves themselves and their posterity shall be converted into a free civilized and great nation." Yet, the ACS seemingly contradicted itself in the same report when it crowed that "colonies, composed of blacks already instructed in the arts of civilized life, and the truths of the gospel" would expand into the interior and incorporate Africans into their civilizing commerce. African Americans needed to leave the United States to acquire civilization—whiteness—but had seemingly been instructed in civilization by their birth and residence in that white space. This harkens back to the mental gymnastics of Henry Clay that began this chapter.⁶⁹ White colonizationists emphasized free black degradation within the United States owing to the obstinate refusal of whites to accept unburdened black freedom, and they underscored the settlers' power to seize the civilizing mantle of whiteness in Africa. This key word, "degraded," mustered to describe the condition of free people of color in the United States, is ubiquitous within white colonizationist discourse.⁷⁰

* * *

In emphasizing degradation, colonizationists historicized their arguments by highlighting ancient African attainments in Christianity, expansively referencing Ethiopia and, to a lesser extent, the mythical kingdom of Prester John. Adding to this religious argument, they celebrated the arts and societies of ancient Africa; here, Egypt was the favorite archetype. For colonizationists, black potential could only be realized beyond the boundaries of the United States.[71] Having received "training" in whiteness coded as "civilization," African American settlers could flourish in Africa and rejuvenate the continent and return it to its past glory. Liberia was able to lift up this Western vanguard because it offered a remarkable educational experience for the African American settlers: a lesson in the control and management of black subjects, the ultimate attainment of respectability for nineteenth-century white Americans.

The tiered system of governance initially established by the ACS, that is, a black colonial structure capped by a white governor, reinforced this idea of managing blackness as Liberia's central goal: management first in the form of managing the settlers and instructing them and then in the form of turning the settlers loose to control Africans. The first report of the ACS utilized this language of management in the form of the white governor's beneficial influence. "The race [free blacks] possesses a fund of good dispositions, and is capable in a proper situation and under proper management, of becoming a virtuous and happy people. To place them in such a situation, to give them the benefit of such management, is the object of your noble enterprize."[72] Much as Robert Breckinridge argued that slavery provided the "training" in arts and civilization for African Americans, so too did residence in Liberia provide the training to control its African subjects.

Here, it is important to remember that the settlers were issued, in the language of the ACS, a "plantation," complete with its nineteenth-century connotations of coerced labor. The white colonizationists delighted in publishing reports "that the chief and people of one of the native tribes in the neighborhood of the Colony, have sought the protection and placed themselves under the authority of the Colonial government. The intelligence that their offers of submission were accepted, was received by them, says the Colonial Agent, with shouts of joy."[73] Just as the single word "degraded" undergirded the foundational spatial argument of colonization, the settlers' "influence"[74] over neighboring Africans signified the Africans' desire to adopt American cultural practices, learned from the guiding hand of the American settlers and their missionary allies.[75] After this initial tutorial in management, the settlers would be in a position to control their black subjects in a similar manner. Thus, the managers of the ACS crowed at their annual convention in 1829: "By this gentleman [Agent Jehudi Ashmun] the Colonists are represented not only as contented and enterprising, but as making rapid progress in the most important public and private improvements, and exerting a salutary and extensive influence over the native tribes. 'These tribes,' he remarks, 'have begun to perceive that it is civilization and religion, which give superiority to man over his fellow man.'"[76]

The settlers, seeking their own opportunities in the colony and products of the same Western religious and cultural assumptions regarding their superiority, did not need any white assistance in projecting a veneer of control over their African neighbors. When the Bassas succeeded in eradicating the American colony at Bassa Cove in an 1835 attack, settler Samson Caesar remained unconcerned. "I can only say," he wrote to a Virginia correspondent soon thereafter, "that we are in no danger of the natives if we manage Right as for own part I feal no fear at all of the natives." Four years later, Russwurm reported to the MSCS that Maryland in Liberia had started to affect the neighboring Greboes. The "Cape Palmas People" appeared to be more "industrious" as thefts had decreased, although Russwurm cautioned that such alterations may actually have been the result of unusually plentiful harvests. Still, "we cannot but indulge the hope, that they are falling in imperceptibly with civilized habits; as there are many symptoms which would indicate such a state. . . . I am of the opinion that king Freeman, Yellow Will, and a few others of the leading men, have found honesty is the best policy in their dealings with us, and if matters depended solely on them, we should be troubled but little with palavers of any kind."[77]

Three years later, with the arrival of the USS *Vandalia* as part of the Africa Squadron, Russwurm grumbled that the American naval officers had "been meddling with *our* [emphasis mine] natives."[78] These lessons in management would largely come to fruition in the form of guiding the labor of Africans. The white colonizationists bellowed about agriculture as the foundation of the colony, but they often omitted detailing precisely whose hands would wield the hoe. Ashmun, who as governor from 1824 until 1828 was largely responsible for securing and expanding the American foothold at Cape Mesurado, followed in this path when he wrote a small tract titled *The Liberia Farmer* in 1825 to aid new settlers in establishing their "plantations," a title he dutifully maintained throughout the pamphlet. Denouncing those who would depend solely on trade for subsistence, Ashmun asked, "Are you so lost to all sense of shame, as to be willing to depend on a half naked Savage to feed you?" Yet, for all of his suggestions regarding clearing the land, tilling, planting, and fencing, Ashmun never fully addressed who would be conducting this labor, a curious oversight given the nature of possessing a "plantation." Peyton Skipwith answered this question in a letter to his former enslaver in Virginia: "There is Some that hav come to this place that have got rich and anumber that are Sufering. Those that are well off do hav the natives as Slavs and poor people that come from America hav no chance to make aliving for the nativs do all the work. As it respects farming there is no Chance for it unless we would get the nativs to work for us and then you must be wit them."[79] There are echoes from the United States here. The colonial elite—the African American settlers—disdained working side by side with their African workforce. Thus, even as settlers and Africans found themselves in close confines and interspersed, the cartographies of the colony emphasized separation and isolation.

As the Americo-Liberians laid down their neat streets reminiscent of their American homeland and battled both the environment and the inhabitants of the land to reconstitute a version of the United States in Africa, their vision did not include a return to the subjugated position they had previously held in North America. In the Liberian adaptation of American society, the African American settlers would occupy the societal positions previously occupied by white people. Of course, this vacated the lowest levels of society that had provided the cheap or unfree manual labor upon which the United States was built. Conveniently for the Americans, however, there was a large pool of "uncivilized" workers nearby. On the other side of the Atlantic, they found whiteness and became Americans in charge of their tiny United States. Obviously, this bode ill for the African inhabitants of these colonies, some of whom challenged this interpretive rendering of the colony by their presence while others attempted to blend into this civilized space. But as "Yellow Will" discovered, even for those who could enter into the American space and adopt Western culture, the map could arrest their motion and fix their identity. He could live in a frame house, but he could never fully become "William Hall."

3

"Nearly All Have Natives as Helps in Their Families, and This Is as It Should Be"

The "Civilizing" Mission of Unfree Labor

Samuel McGill was steamed. Writing to the editors of the *New England Puritan* to defend the Liberian settlers' religiosity, he penned, "I can now select many colonists in Liberia who have trained up more native children in their families as Christians,—now members of the Christian church, than are to be numbered as native communicants in the Presbyterian mission at Cape Palmas." McGill specifically referred to the prevailing system in the colonies whereby Liberian families kept African "apprentices" to perform domestic and manual labor. While chattel slavery was banned by the constitutions and legal systems of the Liberian colonies, a hybrid system developed there combining American concepts of indentured servitude with African practices of pawnship in which the labor of surrogates, usually children, was used to repay debts or held as collateral for securing a loan.[1] Within the Liberian context, this system was further altered by the supposed payment of "civilization" it provided. African parents sought an education in "white man's fash" for their children to secure economic and social advantages in the coastal trades; while certain settlers took the "civilizing mission" of the arrangement seriously, the system primarily funneled labor into the underpopulated colony. Although these "African servants" were usually contracted for a set number of years and enjoyed certain rights and privileges under the various Liberian legal codes,[2] it was, like its American counterpart, a system rife with opportunities for abuse. It was this system of unfree labor, lying somewhere between slavery and freedom, that McGill asserted served as a more effective civilizing force than the Presbyterian missionary outpost named Fair Hope, which was under the direction of J. Leighton Wilson.[3]

Wilson had earned McGill's ire in late 1842, when McGill publicly declared his mission station as specifically lacking the evangelical chops of the Americo-Liberians, because of a long simmering disagreement between McGill's brother-in-law, Governor Russwurm, and the managers of the MSCS, on the one side, and Wilson and his evangelist directors, the American Board of Commissioners for Foreign Missions (ABCFM), on the other. In a nod to the ever-present violence or threat of violence to the colony, the ordinances that governed Maryland's corner of Liberia dictated that all boys and men between the ages of sixteen and sixty residing within the colony be enrolled in the general militia and drill accordingly when called upon by the governor.[4] Although the missionaries were exempted from this requirement, those employed by the mission stations in more secular work, such as laborers and teachers, were not—an unacceptable provision for ABCFM missionary Wilson. The simmering issue came to a boil in 1838 when the colonial administration fined one of Wilson's teachers for dereliction of military duty owing to his absence from the drill field. The resulting squabble between colonization leaders in both Marylands straddling the Atlantic, who refused to concede the manpower from their militia, and the ABCFM missionaries, who classified all in their employ as engaged in the Lord's work, eventually led to a special ABCFM committee chaired by Reuben Walworth, last chancellor of the State of New York, to declare in 1842, "that it is expedient, if not absolutely necessary to the successful operations of the mission, that it [the mission station] should be removed from the territory of the Maryland Colony at Cape Palmas."[5]

McGill clearly had a lot on his mind during a visit to the United States during the summer and fall months of 1842. Not only was he finally successful in courting Lydia, but he also stumped extensively on behalf of colonization. On November 7, in a publicized meeting called specifically for him to lecture on his African experiences, he addressed a large audience at the Light Street Methodist Church in Baltimore. At the completion of McGill's address, MSCS president John H. B. Latrobe proclaimed that there was "no better demonstration of the effects of African colonization than was furnished in the person of Dr. McGill and his father's family." Despite his American successes and rebuttal to Walworth's report printed in the *New England Puritan*, McGill was clearly still agitated about the episode when he returned to Liberia in February 1843. His actions upon arriving at Monrovia, however, suggest that his own recent familial addition weighed most heavily on his mind. While at Monrovia, McGill "procured a native youth to live with [him] at Cape Palmas; he had resided with [his] brother at Monrovia for nearly a year, and understood the English language." Given his new life as a married man, it seems likely that he intended the African youth to serve as a domestic servant. As the vessel sailed onward to Harper, McGill struck up a conversation with Reverend Samuel Hazlehurt of Philadelphia, a white missionary on his way to take over the Episcopal mission at Cape Palmas, regarding the recent squabbles between the missionaries and the civil authorities of the colony. The two men were interrupted in their conversation by the arrival of McGill's newly acquired African youth on the deck, whose presence perhaps reminded McGill of his published claim that settlers like himself made better evangelists than the missionary standing before him. However the conversation progressed, McGill and Hazlehurt engaged in a sort of private wager that speaks volumes about life in Liberia.[6] "At this moment my boy presented himself on deck, and his name was asked by the gentleman—I had not previously selected one, but at the moment conferred on him that of 'Chancellor Walworth,' (he was previous to this known by his native name, which is generally dropped when they live in our colonies)." McGill declared his intention to "place this boy under influences" that would lead the young African to convert to Christianity and thus prove that settler appropriation of African labor offered the surest means of converting the continent.[7]

Like other westerners living in West Africa, McGill believed African "nakedness" was a principal impediment to the attainment of a civilized life. Hence, "since arriving at home, this boy has been clad" and encouraged to attend church. Apparently, as "Chancellor Walworth" "became acquainted with the native boys of Gov. Russwurm's family, who have been for two years creditable members of the Methodist Episcopal Church," the boy joined them during Sunday sermons. In an unsurprising narrative turn, "Chancellor Walworth" "became more serious and depressed in mind" until he underwent a full conversion experience. McGill appended a letter from the local Methodist minister affirming "Chancellor Walworth's" conversion and regular attendance at services and then concluded that the account proved his point that the settlers were "serviceable on this coast in evangelizing the heathen." The editors of the *Maryland Colonization Journal* who published McGill's letter hoped their readers would recognize the account as "a plain and simple narrative . . . of everyday life in the colony."[8] To modern eyes, there are startling parallels to American slavery in McGill's account. For starters, McGill's word choice raises intriguing questions. He did not "negotiate," "contract," or "indenture" the African youth but rather "procured" the lad. Even more jarring, given the history of enslaved Africans and the power to name them within the context of New World slavery, is McGill's complete nonchalance at sardonically renaming his charge after his former antagonist.[9]

Little wonder that the Africans found the Liberian settlers to be closer to the foreign whiteness of Europeans and Euro-Americans than to their own self-conceptualizations of blackness. In the same manner as depictions of the space of Liberia, this system of controlling the labor of black bodies nourished the conceptualizations of Liberian settlers as "civilized." Indeed, McGill and many of his fellow settlers found the whole system of coerced labor a great benefit to their African laborers, much as apologists for slavery within the United States often extolled the institution's benefits for converting its victims to Christianity. Or as historian James Campbell succinctly put it when summarizing the turn toward sugar and coffee production after Liberian independence: "The Liberian countryside bore a more than passing resemblance to the Old South."[10]

Of course, one should also look at the circumstances of McGill's nonchalant acquisition of a servant: the establishment of his familial household in Africa. The attachment of African children to Liberian households was common throughout the colony. It had actually been one of the youths bound to the Russwurms who McGill credited for putting "Chancellor Walworth" on the path toward Christian conversion. It was probably one of these youths who accompanied Sarah Russwurm on at least two different visits and prolonged residences in the United States. It is also possible that Sarah traveled with an orphan of a settler family, but the few references to youths bound to the Russwurm household identify them as African. How her American associates reacted to the unidentified, although assuredly black, "servant" (or servants if she employed two different individuals) raises startling questions regarding the role of African American women in this system of unfree labor. Indeed, one of the troubling elements of Russwurm's visits to the United States was how *little* commentary her travels with a presumably African servant generated among her colonizationist colleagues. Given their propaganda that such relationships bestowed "civilization" and Christianity upon the "heathen," perhaps her contemporaries simply applauded the use of an African servant and thought it unworthy of notation.[11]

Liberia's labor regime, then, provided settlers with additional claims to black bodies and the civilizing mission. In the case of McGill's dispute with the missionaries, he even asserted that Liberians' claims to African labor *trumped* the civilizing credentials of the missionary establishment. Such claims took on racialized importance given the preference of American churches to dispatch white missionaries like Hazlehurst rather than appoint settlers as official missionaries.[12] If spatial categorizations separated African American from African while likewise exerting control over African space, then the labor system of Liberia rhetorically *returned* the Africans to the "civilizing" space of Liberia, which they had never actually left. Nominally, the labor provided the "soft" guiding hand as opposed to the "hard" hand of violence. Of course, the two often worked in concert toward the same end. Within this framework of "civilizing" work, colonizationists of the evangelical slant—even bitter opponents of slavery such as Gurley or Latrobe—supported Liberian labor systems as a means of spreading Christianity. Such logic not only retroactively supported the introduction of New World enslavement of "heathens," American Indians, Africans, or otherwise, thus allowing for the necessity of terminating slavery now that it had fulfilled its divine proselytizing mission, but also endorsed African American superiority over barbaric unchristian Africans. Of course, such thinking was not limited to Euro-American colonization leaders but likewise undergirded the ideology of many African Americans.

This "Ethiopianism" was an affirmation of a divine mission for African diasporans to "restore" Africa to its previous exalted position as a continent of grand, modern, and artistic civilizations (Egypt) or great Christian empires (Ethiopia). Obviously, such ideology appealed greatly to Liberian settlers along with evangelical colonizationists. This sentiment was reinforced when settlers and colonizationists alike opened their King James Bibles and read in the Psalms, "Princes shall come out of Egypt; Ethiopia shall soon stretch out her hands unto God."[13] The African American princes had left Egypt, wandered in the desert of American slavery, found their enlightenment in that wasteland, and were prepared to restore Africa to the dominion of the Christian God.[14] This was a powerful message (and certainly not one limited to colonizationists). These sentiments were perfectly encapsulated by John Revey's letter to Latrobe that accompanied his maps of Maryland in Liberia. If "Avarice & cruelty dragged the African from his home," then "God bringeth good out of evil." African American colonization of Africa clearly represented the "will of heaven" as it brought settlers to "the land of their forefathers, to impart in however small degree the knowledge & religion they received in a Gospel land."[15]

* * *

If the employment of African labor provided Liberians with opportunities to lay claim to their "civilizing" influence over their colony's African inhabitants, then McGill inadvertently acknowledged the unspoken caveat of the argument that African labor "civilized" the laborer: he spoke only of young domestic servants rather than the labor of adults in which conversion was a low priority. McGill's purported conversion of "Chancellor Walworth" is illustrative of the large-scale employment of African youths within Liberian households as domestic servants. Working within the household, these youths would most likely fall under the direction of African American women.[16]

For Africans, these settler women were likewise categorized as "white," although all western-style cultural performances were labeled as masculine. Hence settler Diana James's report that, "they call us all white man." In terms of securing recognition as such in the United States, however, women simply did not have the same opportunities as men to return to the States in order to lay claim to a "civilized" exotic persona based upon their African whiteness. James's correspondence is filled with desires to visit the United States. In 1839 she wrote, "You request of me and my Father to come over to Emerrica but i do not excpect ever to come thire a gain not because i will not but becawse i cannot." Four years later, James had seemingly made peace with her African home after great initial frustration, but she still held hopes for a return: "My mind are [perhaps a subliminal recognition of her twoness?] perfectly at ease & I wish to make Africa my home the longest day that I live. Yet I do not pretend to say that I do not want to come back and see you all." For all of her desires, James never returned to the United States, and although the colonization societies did not prevent that journey from occurring, the mechanisms of that organization did not offer her the same aid that they extended to male settlers. The colonizationists advanced their agendas through politics and public forums dominated by men. In so doing, they limited the role of women and corralled their female supporters into auxiliary societies. The rhetoric surrounding Liberia, from both its Euro-American supporters and African American settlers, focused on a masculine civilizing mission, taming both the landscape of Africa and its inhabitants. If there were many possibilities for some Liberian settlers returning to the States to find patronage, James's failure to ever make that journey highlights a great roadblock to securing passage on that returning vessel for some: gender.[17]

To quote Moses Sheppard, if "freedom and independence make a white man," then gender, poverty, and personal connections placed obvious restraints on such a nominally fluid identity. For women, the capacity to continue their Atlantic peregrinations was largely economic and class-based. Sarah Russwurm was the wife of a governor; Diana James was not. As both a member of the prominent McGill family and John B. Russwurm's wife, Sarah Russwurm had ample opportunities to travel to and from the United States, unlike a majority of the cash-strapped female settlers. These trips were encouraged by her physician-brother who believed they were salubrious for her health. This was the reason for a trip to the United States that culminated in a return to Liberia aboard the autumnal expedition in 1847, the first mention of her accompaniment by an unnamed though seemingly ever-present servant. One year later, both Mr. and Mrs. Russwurm admitted they were in poor health, wracked by political pressures and the birth of four children, and they decided that a shared journey to the United States would prove beneficial to them and their son who would accompany them.[18] Although Sarah had visited the United States before on shorter trips, Dr. McGill prescribed a more protracted residence in the United States in order to provide her with a fuller recovery. John Russwurm desired to see old acquaintances in Maine; his wife desired to perform the same rounds in Baltimore. They agreed to sail to the United States that August, but Sarah would return at a later date than her husband, to be determined by her health. McGill wrote to Sheppard in June of that year with hopes that his old patron could plow the same furrows of respectability for his sister that had supported McGill during his time in the United States. "I have advised her to go northward where she will be more pleasantly as well as comfortably situated than in Balt. In event either or any of them go North will you have the kindness to use your influence to smooth matters for them as much as possible." Wherever Samuel traveled in the United States, he raced letters of introduction from his Maryland patrons to their extended network of friends and colleagues encouraging all to meet McGill and interact with him accordingly. Clearly, McGill desired that a similar network be established for his sister during her time in the United States.[19]

Significantly, Sarah Russwurm would be traveling accompanied by living evidence of Americo-Liberians' respectability and status: her personal servant. It seems that McGill was not asking Sheppard to intercede on behalf of a stranger, either. Sheppard and Sarah Russwurm, if possibly unacquainted in person, had at least corresponded for more than a decade together in a seemingly constant game of one-upmanship in which African "curiosities" crossed the Atlantic in exchange for trinkets and toys for Russwurm's children.[20]

Both Sheppard and McGill clearly hoped that wife would soon follow husband northward, away from Baltimore. Writing in August soon after Sarah Russwurm's arrival in Baltimore, Sheppard confided to McGill his hopes that "your sister may receive the wanted benefit from her residence in the U. States." Still, Sheppard desired that she head northward as soon as possible. "Here no friendship however ardent, no kindness however sincere, could place her perfectly at ease. The attempt at social intercourse here is Embarrassing to both parties; one part of our people are restrained by pride, and the other by ignorance."[21] For his own part, John Russwurm, after staying but a few days in Baltimore, planned to travel northward through Philadelphia and New York before heading on to Maine. Following his visit with family and old friends in North Yarmouth, Maine, he would stay for a week in Boston before traveling to Baltimore and returning to Africa aboard the *Liberia Packet*. He successfully accomplished this circuitous journey, even indulging in the traditional tourist's pastime of complaining about the prices of hotels; he was particularly offended by the $19.25 bill received from Boston's grand United States Hotel ("oh the Yankees!" he exclaimed to James Hall).[22] In the same letter in which he found the United States Hotel to be overpriced, he also noted, "S.E.R. [Sarah Elizabeth Russwurm] and myself both long to see Africa again." Although he did not explicitly note her presence in Maine, the tone strongly suggests that she had accompanied him on this northern sojourn. It seems likely that she also accompanied him on his return to Baltimore, her hometown, where she remained after the departure of her husband aboard the *Packet*; Russwurm was back at his African post by November 1848.[23] Where Sarah and her servant traveled between that time and her own return to Africa in the fall of 1849 is unclear. It seems that she remained for some time in Baltimore despite the wishes of her brother and Sheppard. In February 1849, three months after John Russwurm's return to Liberia, Sheppard reported to McGill his opinion of Sarah Russwurm's American visit: "I fear your Sisters residence here has not been as agreeable as it ought to have been, shut out from the grade of society in which she should have associated she has been confined to that portion of the community to which she did not belong."[24]

Intriguingly, for all his success in establishing a network of colleagues for McGill who would "regard" him as a white man, Sheppard believed that he had failed to perform the same task for Sarah Russwurm. It seems that one of Russwurm's established contacts in Baltimore was James Hall, then serving as the home agent for the MSCS, and his wife. Before the return of Sarah to Africa, the absence of whom her husband freely admitted had "aided greatly to ruffle my temper," the ruffled husband thanked Hall for "your & Miss Hall's kindness & attention to Mrs. R during her long residence in your country." It also seems that Russwurm trusted Hall to serve as the keeper of Sarah's "little money" and directed drafts through Hall for his wife's exclusive use.[25] Otherwise, there is little indication of whom Russwurm interacted with on her American holiday or even whether she remained in Baltimore.

Sheppard's thinly veiled references to Sarah's association with Baltimore's African American population, a society to which he believed "she did not belong," reinforces the understanding that Americo-Liberians' African sojourn had led to an evolution of their racial identity above and different from American constructions of blackness. We unfortunately do not know Sarah's opinion of her American companions; perhaps she was content with her associations or even sought them out. She clearly defied the wishes of her brother and his patron by residing in Baltimore for some amount of time. We also do not know the travel arrangements or official function of her traveling companion, who simply was listed as her "servant." Not only would the employment of a bound African servant during her two residences in America have assuredly projected Sarah Russwurm's class status, but the command of a black body would have strongly resonated with American proscriptions of whiteness. Regardless of her entourage, Sheppard's belief that he and his fellow Quakers had failed Sarah when he had had such previous success with male Liberian settlers underscores that there were gendered constraints placed on these Atlantic citizens' fluid identities. This is all the more reinforced when examining the American journeys of her husband. During his visit in Baltimore, the Board of Managers of the MSCS hosted a grand banquet in Russwurm's honor at the Exchange Hotel. Reminiscing about the dinner years later, the former society president, Latrobe, recalled, "It was ludicrous to see the astonishment of the Irish waiters . . . when they were called upon to render the same service to a colored man that they were in the habit of rendering to the many socially prominent citizens who were his hosts."[26] Latrobe's memory of European servers, denoted specifically as "Irish" with all its concomitant racial, social, and cultural baggage, balking at performing for "a colored man" the same tasks they would for elite whites even as that "colored man" participated in the same social performances as those elite whites highlights the complex relationship among "whiteness," the "black Atlantic," and the ongoing exchange between Liberia and the United States.

Sarah Russwurm may have had the economic and social clout to travel about the United States accompanied by a servant like other elite women, but her husband possessed the additional gendered boost of securing a banquet in his honor and a white waitstaff. What does it mean for conceptualizations of "black" and "white," when the same individual, Latrobe, who described Russwurm as "colored" could likewise scoff at the hotel staff for not interacting with Russwurm in the same manner as his white hosts? The intellectual acrobatics are all the more pronounced when one remembers that Latrobe was president of an organization dedicated to the removal of African Americans from the United States. And at the same time, Sarah Russwurm found herself in the company of Baltimore's African American population to which her white patron no longer believed she belonged.

Perhaps most intriguing about Sarah Russwurm's American travels is the absolute *lack* of ink spilled about her possession of a servant during those travels. Without the *Maryland Colonization Journal* following the journalistic protocols of the day and listing the prominent passengers aboard each departing journey of the *Liberia Packet*, there would be no documentary record that Russwurm arrived in the United States with a servant in tow. For all of Sheppard's hand-wringing regarding his ability to conduct Russwurm in the society he presumed most suitable for her, the presence of this servant never appeared odd or worth mentioning. It was not one of the problems verbalized by Sheppard, and there are no suggestive undertones to his letter. He simply did not believe that Russwurm's performance of an elite white woman, complete with personal servant, could overcome the known reality of her mixed-race Baltimore roots. While the expressed desire to move northward may simply have reflected a desire to remove Russwurm from a slave state, there is also the fact that she and her family were known in Baltimore. Samuel McGill's initial medical foray in Baltimore had failed spectacularly, but he had found success in New England, not because of any supposedly racially enlightened principles held by the locals there but rather because he was an unknown entity, able to pass himself off as first a wonderfully exotic English-speaking African and then an entirely different sort of exotic, a Liberian.

Of course, much of the impetus for African parents to place their children in settler homes like the Russwurms' was to secure a new identity for themselves. These coastal-dwelling Africans sought for their children literacy and an understanding of western cultural practices so that they could cement their position as economic middlemen between coastal traders and African nations living in the interior. The same logic undergirded the complements of "native scholars" filing into the "native schools" of the colonies, which were usually attached to missionary stations. Hence, the final line of the deed of purchase for Maryland in Liberia, signed by "King Freeman," "King Will," and "King Joe Holland," dictated "that free schools shall be established for the benefit of the Children of each village." Harper's "Yellow Will" may have exceeded many of his compatriots' desires to cross over into the American camp, but his decision to send his sons to a missionary school and his hopes that one would become a doctor—along with other Africans' desires for their children to be immersed in western cultural practices—emanated from a shared understanding of the value of being cultural and literal middlemen along the Atlantic seaboard.[27] Settlers like McGill frequently interpreted African desires for western educations as evidence of colonists' cultural supremacy and influence over Africans. Hence, Hilary Teague of the *Liberia Herald* crowed in an 1844 editorial, "The natives are beginning to 'like' civilized manners and habits. *I sen you my piccaninie,* say they. *I want you for keep him, larn him white man fash, pose he no larn, flog him, O no want him go country make fool fash all same me.*"[28]

There seems to have been some efforts at recording native indentures within colonial records, although the destruction of Liberia's archives in the twentieth and twenty-first centuries makes it difficult to ascertain the extent of the colonial government's commitment to such recordkeeping. The surviving minutes of the monthly Court of Sessions, the principal court of the ACS colonies before the creation of new courts under the commonwealth constitution adopted in 1839, provide a bare minimum of information for a single indenture. In March 1838, there is listed "[manuscript torn] ck Lewis a Native Bound to John N. Lewis, aged 7 years." Following the creation of the commonwealth, a more sophisticated court system was built on a foundation of county courts. The more elaborate judicial hierarchy did not lead, however, to more detailed information regarding native apprentices. The November 1839 session for the Court of Montserrado County, the site of Monrovia, recorded the binding of "Peter Ciples aged six years a native boy" to Lewis Ciples. There is, however, evidence that more detailed reports of apprenticeships were compiled within the government office.[29]

Svend E. Holsoe, an anthropologist and expert on the Vai people, transcribed one such report during one of his many research trips to Liberia before the civil wars. The list includes seventeen people bound to seven Liberian settlers, all prominent citizens. In addition to the names and ages of the sixteen natives (one eight-year-old girl, Margaret Graves, includes a notation that she was a colonist), the document includes the settler to whom they were apprenticed, the date of that apprenticeship, and the number of years each apprentice was to serve. The list seems to be compiled from two sources. The first five names—excepting settler Margaret Graves—are the Anglophone names given to the natives, much as they appear in the court records: "Mary Yates," "Jack Lewis," "Sally Barbour," "John Power," and "James Logan." In her work on recaptured Africans, Sharla Fett notes that this sort of naming practice underscores the impossible situation these native youths found themselves in. The use of an Anglophone name underscores the expectation that these bound Africans would adopt Western customs; their identification as "natives" and their bound status, however, denote separateness and subordination.[30] "Yates," "Lewis," and "Barbour" were apprenticed to those families and assuredly picked up their surnames in this manner; "Power" was apprenticed to John Woodland and "Logan" to Anthony D. Williams, the acting governor of the colony. All the natives were listed as being between the ages of twelve and fourteen and all were apprenticed between February and June 1838. "Barbour" and "Logan" were the only ones whose length of service was listed; both were bound for seven years.

Although Holsoe's transcription provides no break in the list and does not mention new source material, the second half of the list holds different information. The remaining eleven Africans are apprenticed to one man, settler James S. Payne, a future president of Liberia. There seems to have been an effort to phonetically record their given names along with their new Anglophone identities, as the list contains derivatives of several common African names: "Douy (alias) Peter," "Zeamu—Jenny," "Binda—Judy," "Gŏawar—Simon," "Zŏŏ—Fanny," "Kenyeä—Mary," "Sando—William," "Margo—Lucky," "Jarvee—Lewis," "Janda—Lucy," and "Marpella—Mary." Their ages range far more dramatically than the earlier entries, with "Douy" being the oldest at thirty and "Marpella" the youngest at one year. Rather than terms of service, the list provides the servants' heights and relative complexions, the latter listed as either "dark" or "light." Most are listed as between five and six feet in height, but assuredly the dark-complected twenty-three-year-old "Sando" caught the eye of the settlers, standing at six feet, nine inches. There is no indication for the change in categories or approach, but a clue lies in the date Holsoe listed for all eleven Africans bound to Payne. While he transcribed "25 Jany45," it is much more likely that these Africans were apprenticed on January 25, 1846, and contrary to the list's title, "Natives apprenticed to Colonists," it is very unlikely that "Sando," "Zeamu," "Jarvee," or any of the others were actually native to the Liberian coast.[31]

The bound children of nearby Africans did not constitute the entirety of the Liberian labor market. Another possible source of labor was the "recaptives" or "Congoes." These were Africans ensnared in the illegal Atlantic slave trade whose vessels had been captured by the U.S. Navy, and they were universally deposited in Liberia regardless of their actual points of origin (in a nod to the western conflation of a vast coterie of peoples into generic and placeless "Africans"). Their official designation as "recaptured" survivors of the slave trade perfectly encapsulates the many gradations between "free" and "slave" in the Atlantic world. The opinions of the Liberian settlers regarding these African castaways were decidedly mixed and always dependent upon their adoption of American cultural practices. Those recaptives who established New Georgia, for example, were looked upon favorably by most colonists. Having been held in Georgia for several years owing to a lengthy court battle before being dispatched to Liberia, many of the New Georgians had adapted to American customs.[32]

Hence, the *Liberia Herald* of September 30, 1843, carried a two-column obituary of "Brother James Young." A part of a cargo of souls involved in the lawsuit, "Young" had languished in Georgia, "but after years of vexatious litigation the voice of liberty prevailed." Of course, "while the suit was pending the marshal distributed them [the Africans] among planters taking recognizance that they should be forthcoming when called for"—the voice of liberty apparently has many dulcet tones—and while being saved from slavery by being enslaved in a different manner, "Young" underwent a conversion experience. Eventually freed and dispatched to Liberia to join others in establishing the recaptive settlement of New Georgia, named in honor of the state that served as the captives' sometimes-enslaver, sometimes-savior, "Young" went on to serve as the minister of the settlement's Providence Baptist Church. The *Liberia Herald*'s obituary concluded that "Young's" "preaching was plain and practical," eminently suited for his audience, and that he exhibited a "deep seriousness and earnestness" reflecting the weight with which he carried his message. "James Young" and his fellow New Georgians were the favorites of the Americo-Liberian settlers due to their broad embrace of American culture, yet "Young's" obituary was prefaced with two articles, "Heathen Customs" and "Tender Mercies of Heathenism," that underscored the general attitude of the settlers toward

Africans. The editor's arrangements of articles bookended a measured celebration of an African Christian's life, with multiple accounts of African barbarity, depravity, and backwardness.[33]

Juxtaposed against the New Georgians were the recaptured Africans from the *Pons* who were deposited in Liberia in December 1845. The *Pons*, an American barque from Philadelphia, was captured by the USS *Yorktown* carrying nearly nine hundred enslaved persons and almost immediately dispatched to Liberia. It seems likely that the list of eleven Africans apprenticed to Payne were actually shipmates aboard the *Pons* rather than natives of Liberia. Having only recently been taken aboard the vessel and lacking the years of forced acculturation in the United States, the *Pons* Africans evoked a decidedly mixed response from the settlers. Matilda Skipwith sympathized with those who died from their limited time aboard the dreadful vessel and noted that several survivors had "embraced the religion of our Savior and [were] making rapid improvements in Education." Despite these positive signs, she affirmed, "Tho I must say of a truth that they are the most Savage, & blud thirsty people I ever saw or ever wishes to see." The *Liberia Herald* agreed with Skipwith's summation. Six months after their arrival, the *Herald* reported an anecdote in which six of the *Pons* Africans were "engaged in clearing away bush on a farm on Bushrod Island," when they happened across a large snake. "As if apprised of the Congo predilection for snake meat his snakeship went off at full speed for the covert of his house," but the Congoes gave chase and successfully captured the snake along with her nest of eggs. "We need not say it was a high day for the congoes," concluded the *Herald*. "It was indeed to him a feast of fat things." A week and half later, the *Herald* claimed that a number of the *Pons* Africans were living in the woods and raiding the settlers' farms at night. Needless to say, the editors attributed the barbarity of these "thieving scoundrels" to their unwillingness to live in the American settlement. "We have considerable sympathy for these people," chided the *Herald*, "and the community in general would willingly assist in taking care of them;—but such is the disposition of some of them that they prefer, notwithstanding you may lavish upon them much care and expense,—to live a wild life in the woods . . . rather than live with the colonists."

Of course, befitting the narrative of the colony's "civilizing" influence, by December 1846, after one year's residence in the colony, those who had elected to remain within the colony proved themselves "of value to their guardians—those remaining in the colony, show no disposition, now to wander off. . . . we find no great difficulty in accustoming them to our habits." In fact, the *Pons* Africans had become a blessing to the settlers at Grand Bassa as additional reinforcements to counter incursions from the neighboring Bassa settlement of Fishtown. The newspaper quoted a supposedly reliable source from Grand Bassa who claimed "our Congoes have really turned our manly; they have thrown more dread upon the Fishmen, (our former antagonists) and the surrounding tribes, than I have ever known exerted upon them before."[34]

Within the layers of these various evaluations of the *Pons* Africans lay many of the assumptions regarding Liberia's capacity to "civilize" Africans. There are jocular accounts of eating a snake and its eggs, a meal certainly unbecoming to the American settlers who were more interested in the length of the snake—reported at fourteen feet—than its culinary qualities. Further, there is the juxtaposition between the "thieving scoundrels" living in the forests surrounding the settlements, and thus beyond the "civilizing" influence of the colonists, and the utility of the *Pons* Africans who remained within the confines of the settlement. There are intriguing parallels between, on the one hand, the *Herald*'s conclusion that the forests shielded those whose "disposition" led them to reject "warm and comfortable quarters" in the American settlements and, on the other, Charles F. Mercer's speech before the first meeting of the ACS in 1818, in which he denounced "newly grown and almost impenetrable thickets which ... shelter and conceal a banditti, consisting of this degraded, idle, and vicious population." Mercer, of course, was speaking about free people of color rather than Africans, but both he and the editors of the *Herald* assumed that the surrounding thickets stood against the civilized open fields of agrarian society.[35]

More relevant to the labor practices of the colony is the reference to the growing utility of the *Pons* Africans who remained in the American settlements under the guidance of "their guardians." Like other receptives, the *Pons* Africans were apprenticed to Liberian settlers, here redefined in the newspaper account as "guardians." Given the undisclosed number who ran away and inhabited the nearby woods, it is difficult to estimate the exact number of apprentices created by the capture of the *Pons*. The *Liberia Herald* reported, "Doctor Lugenbeel, the United States agent, has put them all out with different persons, who have taken them as apprentices. Those under age will be apprenticed under the apprentice act of the colony, and adults will be bound for seven years."[36] There is an element of ownership of these Africans exhibited by the *Herald*'s unnamed correspondent, presumably one of the settlers who received apprentices from the *Pons*. He refers to the group as "*Our*" Congoes and further notes their recent arrival to manhood. The language employed assumes both a collective ownership by the community ("Our") and an individual ownership ("guardians"). Conversely, the recaptives are not embraced for their respective "civilization" in the same way as the New Georgians but are useful merely in countering the violence of an antagonistic neighboring African settlement. More than simply preventing the aggressions of Fishtown, the recaptives projected the violent authority of their American "guardians" onto Fishtown's inhabitants. The correspondent gleefully reported one altercation in which the "Congoes went down to Fishtown and forcibly arrested the thief, a Fishman, and, after giving him a good beating, took his cloth and a cutlass—and it was pretty difficult for us to prevent them from going down to set fire to the Fishtown."[37]

So, the *Pons* Africans discovered their manhood in becoming an extension of American violence even as the American settlers passed themselves off as the moderating influence in control of African barbarity. An intriguing question arises over whether the female captives from the *Pons* could likewise discover their "womanhood" under American supervision. To accomplish that, however, female recaptives would have had to ascribe to American constructions of feminine domesticity and command their own household staffs, a difficult cultural and economic proposition that necessitated marriage to a settler, a matrimonial act that settlers were infamously reluctant to do. In his testimony on the state of affairs in Liberia in the early 1830s, Thomas C. Brown could think of only two settlers married to African women.[38] There were simply far more opportunities for recaptive men to exhibit violence against neighboring Africans than for recaptive women to establish an American-style household.

The *Pons* Africans perfectly demonstrate the interrelatedness between space, violence, and labor at work in Liberia. Mere inhabitance of the space led to increased "civilization"; one means to ensure that the "savages" remained in the "civilizing" space was to bind them in a system of coerced labor, and as an added bonus they subsequently became useful tools in the day-to-day campaigns of violence against Africans. Through these mutually reinforcing "civilizing influences," the formerly "savage" African would find "civilization" and uplift. The arrival of the *Pons* further underscored the racial classifications of Liberia. Just below the column detailing the demise of the snake at the hands of the recaptives, a small announcement declared: "We have been informed that the supplies sent out for the negroes by the 'Pons' will be shortly distributed. We would suggest as the most equitable mode of distribution that reference be made to the court books where the number which each colonist took is registered." In light of Holsoe's transcription, it is telling language that the settlers referred to this registry as a catalog of the "numbers," not names, "each colonist took." While Holsoe's list included both African and Anglophone names, the registry of heights and complexions falls in line with Americo-Liberian thinking. The use of "negroes" to distinguish the *Pons* Africans underscores the associations between racial designations and labor. The settlers generally expressed aversion to the label "negro"; Andrew Hall's declaration that he "would not be willing to come back to america to be called a negro" reflected a broader sentiment among the settlers.[39] When writing to the United States, Americo-Liberians almost universally used "colored" in their correspondence, again underlining that these were not individuals who desired to be "whites" or conceived of themselves as such but rather utilized the tools of their African whiteness to demand an altered position in relation to the United States as respected foreigners. Although there was certainly a great deal of variation—McGill considered the term "free man of color" to be "synonymous" in the United States with slavery—"negro," imbued with associations of enslaved or degraded labor, was rarely employed as a self-identity by settlers.

The classification of the *Pons* recaptives as "the negroes" certainly suggests the labor-oriented lens through which the settlers viewed these Africans. Referencing the "uncivilized" *Pons* Africans as "negroes" separated these individuals from the settlers, while the Americo-Liberians could lay claim to the title of "civilizers" and "masters of negroes." Much like the New Georgians' residence in old Georgia, the *Pons* Africans found themselves saved from slavery by being bound within a different sort of unfree labor. The parallels to the United States in how this "negro" labor was employed become all the more startling when one remembers that in the official language of the ACS, these settlers' farm lots were technically "plantations."

* * *

Further complicating this labor regime were the large numbers of Africans willing to work for settlers or the colonial administration for minuscule wages. These temporary wage laborers were a constant source of disgruntlement for both Americo-Liberian laborers, who found their wages undercut by this competition, and observers of the colony, who pondered the relative merits of the colony's labor system. Samuel Williams, an Americo-Liberian actually writing in defense of the colony, admitted that many of these complaints were legitimate. "Many of the colonists are in want of work to make something to enable them to get the comforts of life, but the natives are employed in preference, because they can live on twenty-five cents per day, while the colonists must have seventy-five cents. Now, this is wrong." Alexander Cowan, a white colonizationist attached to the Kentucky state auxiliary of the ACS, visited Liberia in 1858, one year after the publication of Williams's book, during a period of increased interest in emigration. He delighted in the tidy appearance of Monrovia's streets, ascribing their general appearance to two laws, one that dictated that settlers and Africans be required to give up four workdays a year to perform public service on street cleaning and another that punished criminals charged with theft or larceny with forced labor on the town's streets. The length of time assigned to clean Monrovia's thoroughfares depended upon the monetary value of the stolen goods. The value of the work of a Liberian settler was established at six dollars a month, meaning that if the stolen goods' value equaled six dollars, then the culprit would work for one month. Native labor, however, was valued at three dollars a month, meaning the same crime would result in double the sentence.[40]

Yet, even as Cowan celebrated a system explicitly built upon the assumption of degraded African labor, he concurrently noted that something was not quite right with work in the young republic. The inexpensive African labor created interesting sights for Cowan, especially given the paucity of livestock within the colony, which raised their relative value considerably and led colonists to only begrudgingly risk their beasts of burden. While exploring Monrovia, he noticed that wagons, buggies, and other means of conveyance usually delegated to the work of domesticated animals were in Liberia actually pulled by African laborers: "What a strange sight in a civilized land to see cattle going about the streets, and a line of human carriers doing the work of beasts of burden. Twenty-five to thirty native men in single file carry on their heads the materials for the erection of *a college building!*"

Although he expressed great admiration for the Constitution of Liberia, specifically its provision establishing that "one great object" of the new Republic was to "regenerate and enlighten" Africans, Cowan admitted that in watching the workers trudge up to the new college building, he "did not admire such a levelling practice as an elevating principle to raise the heathen brothers." Despite the assurances of settlers like McGill that the employment of African labor was a sure means to convert their charges, Cowan concluded, "I am afraid the natives are employed because they can be paid in articles of barter, as cloth, tobacco, & c., that the per centage charged on them left a margin for profits, even *for poor labor.*"[41]

Reflecting their American roots and the need for labor in the colony, the Americo-Liberians also codified labor as acceptable punishment for a range of crimes. Initially, these criminals' labor was sold to the highest bidder for that work. Such is what happened to "Barpha," who was found guilty of stealing D. B. Warner's canoe; he was sentenced to "be imprisoned for 2 months and to be hired out." Thus, the colony benefitted economically from criminal activity while its convicted suffered greatly at lax regulations and work conditions that resembled slavery. By November 1838, however, the governing council in the colony had recognized that it needed to "remedy some glaring and mischievous aspects in the present Law of hiring Felons indiscriminately to the highest bidder—by whom they are too often suffered to go." The council created a new government position, answerable to the colony's sheriff, to oversee the convict labor. The problem was not the use of labor as a punishment for a crime but rather the faults of a diffuse system that could easily be abused. The council's minutes made no mention of any voiced concerns for the system as a whole.[42]

Finally, settler children were often bound to unrelated adults in Liberia. As a sickly settlement with high mortality rates, the Liberian colonies and the young republic faced staggering familial crises with large populations of widows, aged parents without children, and orphans. While sick lists and poor funds only modestly mitigated some of these issues, orphans were almost universally placed in the households of adult relatives. If no adult relative was available, however, the children were subsequently placed in the households of settlers. For children without families, the courts usually appointed a separate guardian to serve as their advocate. However, based upon the few surviving court records, it seems that few guardians challenged the terms of the apprenticeships. Within the relatively complete records for 1838–1842, only D. B. Brown asked the court to remove an apprentice from a master who he did not think "was a fit person to keep said Boy as he was a felon."[43]

Unsurprising given the conflation of labor with proselytization, Liberia's missionary establishment likewise engaged in the labor market. In 1837, the Methodist mission began constructing the White Plains Manual Labor School, so named owing to the largess of benefactors from White Plains, New York. The plan, as explained by the head of the Methodist mission, John Seys, was "to obtain a certain number of boys, say from thirty to fifty, between the ages of ten and fifteen inclusive, both colonists and natives, and have them bound as apprentices to the Superintendent of the Liberia Mission of the M. E. Church and his successors in office until they are twenty-one." The pupils/apprentices would gain both an education and a skilled trade. While Reverend Seys was certain that the mixture of settler and native African children in the school would lead to both civilization and mutual respect, it is telling that Seys anticipated that only the orphans of settler children would be bound to his school superintendent; he presumed settler parents with alternatives would not send their children to a school alongside African pupils.

Beyond their liberal and manual educations, the students would also engage in agricultural labor every day in order to feed the mission. Presumably, the labor requirement led to the mission's decision to combine education and indentured servitude, but signed indentures, while reflecting the school's religious foundation, likewise suggest a greater unease with the student body than is revealed by the glowing propaganda of the *African Repository*.[44] In a nod to religion, boys bound to the school were not to "haunt" saloons and other establishments of "ill fame," but they were also required to keep Seys's secrets—whatever those may be—and neither waste nor loan Seys's goods. Additionally, the boys were to obey their master's commands, to "do no damage" to him, and, critically, to report to Seys if they heard of anyone trying to harm him. Clearly, the headmaster was greatly concerned that bodily harm would come to him at the hands of his pupils.[45]

* * *

The result of all of this was a dizzying buffet of labor options fully in line with those of other contemporaneous Atlantic societies. There were remarkable opportunities here for those with the means to capitalize upon them.[46] Within the Liberian colonies, settlers and colonial administrators could utilize bound African labor, both adults and children, hire African laborers at minimal cost, work criminals on public projects, and employ American orphans placed within households.

The colonial accounts of Maryland in Liberia reveal the Liberian labor market in full force. Russwurm's meticulous line-by-line accounts alternate between wages paid to settlers and to largely unnamed African laborers. On February 3, 1838, the colonial agency paid Nathan Lee eight dollars for "country boards" (boards cut in the West African fashion) and

James Martin $5.50 for "plank" (boards for American-style dwellings) and nails. Ten days later, an undisclosed number of "natives" received three dollars for "bringing plank from bush." Full settler names and unidentified "natives" was the prevalent system employed in colonial bookkeeping, with a few exceptions reserved for those Africans most affiliated with the colony. For example, the records for the colonial school supported by the Baltimore-based Ladies Society for the Promotion of Education in Africa reveals a relationship with "Long Tom," who functioned as the building's guard, even as they recorded the labor of unnamed "natives." Trusted African inhabitants of Cape Palmas were also employed as military extensions of the colonial establishment, much like the recaptives in the ACS settlements. Such was the situation in 1838 after "King Freeman" and Russwurm journeyed together up the Cavalla River, where they were fired upon by a group of native Africans determined to maintain control over the river traffic; they also lost their worldly possessions as their vessels were overturned in the ensuing melee (this incident is further detailed in chapter 4).

While both Cape Palmas leaders had seethed at the subsequent theft of their drenched goods and the soaking of their bodies, they had been militarily unable to deal with the culprits, the Barboes of Ploroh. The accidental burning of "Freeman's" town following this incident and the antagonism between the Cape Palmas Africans and Liberian settlers prevented either side from wielding the necessary force to mount an expedition against the Barboes as their respective leaders desired. But "Yellow Will," underlining his commitment to become an American, provided Russwurm with an opportunity to bring the Barboes to the negotiating table to answer for their actions at the river. "Will" proposed kidnapping several Barbo men in hopes of forcing a ransom and securing restitution for the aforementioned indignities. Russwurm tellingly described "Yellow Will" as "my headman," simultaneously affirming "Will's" significant place within the American colony, the patriarchal possession of him, and the intransience of certain settlers to embrace the "Americanness" of "Will"; no official documents utilized "William Hall" in lieu of "Yellow Will." A contract was established with "Will" and seven "resolute men"; although they succeeded in capturing only a single Barbo man, the solitary prisoner was enough to bring the Barboes to negotiations with the colony. For their services, twenty-nine dollars of "sundries" was paid to these "Cape Palmas Soldiers" for capturing the man; "Yellow Will" received eight dollars individually.[47] That the "resolute men" received "sundries" underscores the prevalence of the practice noticed by Cowan one decade later of paying Africans in trade goods rather than cash.

The labor of the public farm, an agriculture experiment station owned by the colonial administration dedicated to testing new crops and growing food for the public good, proved an even more muddled situation. In addition to the aforementioned conglomeration of African and settler labor, the public farm employed a large number of unspecified "boys." On February 3, 1838, Thomas Davenport was paid $1.50 "for work of boys." Davenport and his wife, Frances, were progenitors of a huge emigrant family consisting of their eleven children and two grandchildren. Davenport would certainly have had available children and grandchildren to work the public farm and probably would have found doing so necessary to support such a large family. Yet, in May, just three months later, the manager of the public farm recorded a payment to "Ths. Davenports Sons for work on farm." In fact, Adam and Rudolph Davenport, two of the older sons of Thomas, were listed individually by name, following the usual bookkeeping protocol for settlers by using their full names. It would seem unlikely then that the "boys" were also Davenport's sons. In this light, it is especially intriguing that the entry recorded Thomas Davenport as receiving the payment for the work of others. And Davenport was not the only settler receiving financial compensation for the work of unidentified "boys." Just one month after Davenport's payment, Nathan Harmon was likewise listed as the recipient of wages for "4 day's work of boys." And like the Cape Palmas soldiers who kidnapped the Barbo, the colonial administration paid "sundries" to "Bottle-Beer & boys for work." "Wills boys," presumably the sons of "Yellow Will" who attended the missionary school, were paid "tobacco and mugs" for work.[48]

The term "boys," then, seems reserved for the bound African youths of Liberian households. The fact that Davenport and Harmon were the listed recipients of the wages for the work of their "boys" would suggest a hiring-out system akin to that employed within the context of American chattel slavery. This argument is further reinforced by the fact that many of the settlers were originally from the Upper South, a labor market in which the hiring out of enslaved labor was a common feature. This idea of bound African children working on the public farm is problematized, however, by Lugenbeel, the American agent for recaptured Africans, who visited Maryland in Liberia in November 1845. As part of his visit to Cape Palmas, Lugenbeel observed the public farm and reported, "I was very much pleased to observe several boys at work on the farm, who, I was informed, were orphans and children of poor persons, and were employed and paid for their labor by the Governor." It is possible that "boys" simply referred to any bound youths regardless of whether they were settler or African. Yet, others besides settler orphans worked the public farm in 1845. Indeed, in his December 1845 report, Russwurm complained of the inadequacies of the colonial jail located on the public farm (and rendered on Revey's map of the colony). For those found guilty of petty crimes within the colony, residency at the jail during the night and labor on the farm during the day were standard punishments, hence the location of the jail on the farm. By the end of 1845, however, Russwurm was souring on this system of justice. Writing to the board, he justified the construction of a new stone jail away from the farm because "our present jail system is too lenient . . . confinement at night in a log house on the Farm, and labor there during the day, when they can see & converse with their relatives & friends, is looked upon as a slight punishment."[49] It is certainly possible that Lugenbeel coincidentally observed the farm on a day in which the labor was performed solely by orphans of American settlers; nevertheless, the overarching image of Liberian workers presents a complex workforce of African and American laborers, bound, apprenticed, imprisoned, and nominally free.

In surveying the dizzying array of workers in Liberia, it would be overly simplistic to level their experiences by labeling all as simply "unfree." Clearly, missionaries, settler women, and government officials could all perceive and understand the same apprenticed African child differently. Such distinctions made about the laborers could dictate whether they received wages for that work, or whether those wages were paid to a guardian, or whether in lieu of wages they received a mug and bit of tobacco, all for the same work. And while settler children and criminals could find themselves ensnared within this complex system of unfree labor, they were never perceived as acquiring "civilization" through work like Africans were.

Ultimately, it was the employment of debased and dismissed African laborers that made the whole labor regime susceptible to abuse. This was a central charge of William Nesbit's damning 1855 exposé on Liberia, *Four Months in Liberia: or African Colonization Exposed*. Nesbit, originally a freeman from Pennsylvania, arrived in Monrovia in December 1853 aboard the *Isla de Cuba*. He required only a matter of months to determine that the Liberian republic was not the Promised Land he had been led to believe, thus giving him the title for his book, and he returned to the United States disenchanted with the African nation's prospects. While Nesbit found much to dislike about Liberia, the relations between Americo-Liberians and Africans held a particularly distinguished place in his narrative. "Every colonist keeps native slaves, (or as they term them servants,) about him, varying number from one to fifteen, according to the circumstances of the master. These poor souls they beat unmercifully, and more than half starve them, and all the labor that is done at all, is done by these poor wretches." By noting the preferred use of the term "servants" over "slaves," Nesbit underscored the mixture of labor systems at work in Liberia even as he rejected those distinctions from chattel slavery based upon the lived experiences of the unfree. Unsurprisingly, he also commented upon and denounced the practice of indenturing out the insolvent to fulfill their financial obligations—an extension of the practice of having thieves work on public works that Cowan so celebrated—and the expansive use of the whip.[50]

Significantly, although he resided in Liberia for less than half a year, Nesbit quickly grasped the racial dynamics at work. In one of the most evocative lines in his book, Nesbit denounced the Liberian citizens' displays of religious piety, declaring that they "make a great deal of outward show of religion, but if half that is said of them be true, the best among them are but whited sepulchers." While the biblical reference denoted the Americo-Liberians as evangelical hypocrites, the racial context of Liberia gave added nuance to the settlers as "whited sepulchers." Nesbit joined with other free people of color in the United States in assuming that the Americo-Liberian settlers were little more than black-masked whites hoping to emulate the white enslavers in the United States. Not only were the settlers whitened shells professing religiosity while emptiness filled their souls, but they also did everything to "imitate" the planter class of the United States. Like the enslaved of the United States, the "slaves" of Liberia "occupy small buildings next to their masters' residence, known as the 'negro quarters,' so their imitators in Liberia . . . so exact have they been in carrying out the customs and feelings of their exemplars in this country, that the slave is never allowed to eat or sleep in the master's house, or hut, as the case may be."[51]

Nesbit assumed that the use of "negro" to denote African labor was a simple mimicry of American slaveholders. Yet, just as in the case of the *Pons* Africans, this assignment of identity was far more complex than settlers' simplistic desires to become Southern planters in Africa. If Nesbit understood the oddity of distinguishing "negroes" in a West African settlement of Africans and those of African descent, he missed the embedded social standing implied by the term's relationship to labor. The roots of this conflation of "negro" with "unfree and degraded labor" lay in the experience of New World slavery, and Nesbit assumed that the use of "negro" equated to a desire to be "white" within an American understanding rather than the whiteness of the Liberian context. Nesbit likewise forgot that the origins of the settlers' whiteness stemmed from classification by Africans and that this racial categorization originated from a host of cultural practices, although labor and the interactions with African laborers certainly was a prominent wedge dividing Africans' self-identity as black and these relative newcomers to the coast.

In focusing on the "negro quarters" behind the houses and detailing the procedures by which African children found themselves bound in settler households, Nesbit primarily focused his attention on domestic servants. He was critical of the legal safeguards against enslavement, arguing that Liberia offered far more parallels to American slavery than differences. "These slaves are generally obtained by purchase from the native parents, after arriving at such size and age as to be able to labor, at prices varying from eight to fifteen dollars. After the private transaction between the master and parents, the courts, at the instance of the master, go through some mummery which fastens the fetters upon the purchased child during his natural life." As in the United States, however, there were runaways, and Nesbit celebrated those who would "defy the powers that would enslave them." Unfortunately, Nesbit lamented, the abundance of available labor meant Liberian masters simply arranged a new contract with another African parent. That being said, there was apparently some effort to stop fugitives, and the McGills seemed to hold a special role for Monrovia's citizenry. "A slave owned by James M'Gill," whom Nesbit identifies only by the sobriquet "second president," would apparently "harangue" other natives into staying within their households for a "dash"—although spelled by Nesbit as a "dosh"—the ubiquitous gift through which all Liberian transactions funneled.[52]

Nesbit claimed that little effort was expended to locate and reclaim fugitive Africans, aside from purchasing the services of McGill's "second president," and the occasional references to runaways in the *Liberia Herald* reinforce his claim. There are a few runaway servant advertisements listed in the *Herald*, but these were reserved for runaway settlers. Such advertisements were reminiscent of similar fare in American newspapers, adjusted for the economic realities of Liberia, and underscore that this was a settlement of displaced Americans familiar with the way such things were handled in the United States.

TWO CENTS REWARD!

Keep a good look out.—Ranaway from the subscriber on the night of the 14th, inst. Isaiah Holister, an indented apprentice, of a brown complexion aged about 15 years. Any person apprehending him and delivering him to me in Monrovia, shall receive a Reward of Two Cents, if found out of this County, and if in the County One Cent; but no further expenses whatever in either case. All persons are forwarned from harboring him. D. B. Brown[53]

SIX CENTS REWARD

Ranaway from the subscriber an apprentice named Matthew Matthias. He ran off without any sufficient cause. All persons are warned against harbouring said apprentice. The above reward will be given to any one that delivers him to me at Monrovia; but no expenses will be paid. James Cotton Monrovia, Sept. 15th, 1842[54]

Both Hollister and Matthias were young orphans originally from North Carolina. The large Hollister clan arrived in Monrovia in 1833, resulting in the deaths of parents, Thomas and Loretta, from the acclimating fever. Isaiah must have found shelter with other family or was bound to someone else, as the Court of Sessions did not bind him to Brown until June 1838. Either through an omission of the recorder or perhaps ignorance of the court, the space to record Hollister's age was left blank.[55] Matthias arrived with his father, also named Matthew, aboard the *Criterion* in 1831. While both the senior Matthew and his wife, Elizabeth, survived the acclimating fever, the family patriarch died in 1838 from a fall. Elizabeth remarried, but apparently there were too many mouths to feed in the new family and Matthew was apprenticed to James Cotton at the age of fourteen in March 1839.[56] Despite their 1842 departures from their masters, both lads were recorded in the 1843 colonial census as present in the colony and employed as "apprentices."[57] "D. B. Brown" was almost certainly Dixon B. Brown, originally a blacksmith from Petersburg, Virginia, who had emigrated to Liberia in 1829 and who eventually served as High Sheriff of the colony, filling a position formerly held by Joseph J. Roberts. James Cotton was another freeborn Virginian employed as a carpenter in the colony. Thus, in a manner similar to how orphans and indigent were bound in the United States, two young settler children were apprenticed to two prominent skilled craftsmen upon the death of one or both parents.

It is intriguing that Hollister was noted as possessing a "brown complexion." The inclusion of such information may simply reflect an adherence to the formula of runaway advertisements in American newspapers. It may also be that phenotypical associations were so cemented in the psyches of the African Americans that Brown assumed that Liberia's citizenry would all understand the precise ratio of melanin necessary to produce a "brown" teenager among the multitudes of individuals of mixed-ancestry in the colony. Equally intriguing is Cotton's assertion that Matthias "ran off without any sufficient cause," a seemingly tacit admission that there might be legitimate reasons for apprenticed youths to flee their masters while rejecting that such was the case with Matthias.

Even settler Samuel Williams's bluntly named rebuttal to Nesbit, *Four Years in Liberia: A Sketch of the Life of the Rev. Samuel Williams; With Remarks on the Missions, Manners and Customs of the Natives of Western Africa; Together with an Answer to Nesbit's Book*, conceded just as Cotton's advertisement had that the Liberian system was fraught with opportunities for exploitation. "Wicked persons there [Liberia] do abuse the native youths. But why does Mr. Nesbit condemn the whole country and accuse all as slave holders, because a few abuse their power?" Intriguingly, Williams distinguished between the practice of binding African youths as wards of settler households, of which he approved, and the employment of cheap African labor at greatly reduced wages, which he denounced as an impediment to the advancement of Liberian settlers. Like Nesbit, Williams attributed this proclivity from "both gentlemen and ladies" for African servants as an inherited trait from the upbringing of the majority of the settlers in the American South. Williams, unsurprisingly, was a freeborn Pennsylvanian like Nesbit. In terms of hiring adult African laborers, Williams simply concluded, "This is wrong." But for Williams, the evangelizing benefits of taking African youths into Liberian households outweighed the abusive costs. Although "nearly all" of the Americo-Liberians had "natives as helps in their families," Williams concluded that "this is as it should be," dismissing those abusive relationships as simply indicative of the fact that "black people are no better than white people." Williams considered Liberia to be a "candle in a thick fog" and, like other settlers, pointed to the New Georgia settlement as indicative of their growing influence over Africans.[58]

Writing after Nesbit's scandalous account and after several exposés of

Liberia that did not paint the Americo-Liberians in a favorable light, Williams probably thought it ill-advised (or simply untruthful) to completely deny the abuse of laborers in Liberia. There were inklings of the problem, however, from earlier days of the colony. In 1835, two decades before Nesbit and Williams dueled in print, a series of newspapers printed a reported summary of an interview with Beverly Wilson, a freeman of color recently returned from Liberia. This published account found nothing but platitudes for the colony and reported as part of its assertions of American influence over the neighboring Africans: "A number of the natives, both men and boys (but no women) are employed by the colonists as servants or *helps*, in their families, work for wages by *the moon*, or month, which they are always careful to demand at the day, and are very sure to get."[59] While the belated assurance that the servants received their wages certainly raises eyebrows for modern readers, the authors of the piece seemingly blindly accepted this bit of good news without question. Just the year before, however, James Birney in his grand renunciation of his colonizationist roots, his *Letter on Colonization*, pointed to the indiscriminate abuses of African laborers as part of his reasoning for rejecting colonization. Quoting Samuel Jones, an African American dispatched by an Ohio colonization society to observe Liberia, Birney reiterated, "The relation between the colonist and native is very similar to that between master and slave." While Birney likewise noted the constitutional impediments to chattel slavery, "Yet," he wondered, "what kind of barrier does a paper prohibition oppose to a vitiated public sentiment?" The system was primed for exploitation, and Birney understood that the civilizing rhetoric surrounding Liberian labor provided a slippery slope that allowed culprits to further abuse the system. Based upon an argument that bringing African laborers into the settlement served missionary purposes, then, Birney pondered "how many plausible pretexts might be found" to bring in as many laborers as possible?[60]

Most settlers supported this argument that work in the colony brought "civilization" to the laborer and continued to employ Africans on the farms and in their homes in varying degrees of unfreedom. The arrangement of youthful labor—both African and American—within settler households proved susceptible not only to physical abuse but also to sexual indiscretions. Given Birney's fears that the missionary zeal surrounding the Liberian regime was instrumental to the expansion of exploitative practices, it is appropriate to note that one of the great scandals that rocked Maryland in Liberia not only centered on the activists of a missionary outpost but also was intimately tied to its workers.

* * *

The allegations surrounding the Mount Vaughan mission station, an outpost of the Episcopal Church, that shook the colony in 1837 centered on the actions of settler James Thomson, a British subject originally from British Guiana who, after a residence in England and New York, had set out for Liberia in 1832 aboard the *Jupiter* as a schoolteacher. Thomson had been picked up by James Hall when the governor touched at Monrovia before proceeding to Cape Palmas to establish the Maryland colony. Hall considered Thomson one of the "few . . . sterling good men" in his expedition and named him as a salaried employee of the colonization society, receiving $300 per annum for his services as colonial secretary, storekeeper, bookkeeper, and surveyor. His access to a regular salary and post as gatekeeper to the company's stores, and thus also keeper of the settlers' debts to the agency, did not endear Thomson to his fellow colonists, but Hall considered him an essential member of the colonial administration as a man possessing "more intelligence than any citizen of Liberia (Russwurm excepted)." Being a product of the British Empire, Thomson was a lay reader for the few Episcopalians in Monrovia, and Hall described him as a man possessing great "purity of heart." Thus, the Episcopal Board for Foreign Missions thought they had the perfect candidate for establishing a school for African children when they appointed Thomson a missionary in January 1836. By December the following year, Thomson was writing to his friend Oliver Holmes, the interim agent between Hall and Russwurm, seeking an advocate in Maryland with the board of the MSCS, as, Thomson wrote, "a rumor spread throughout the colony, that I had indulged myself in carnal intercourse with females, natives and colonists, and even with the girls of the mission school."[61]

In the spring of 1837, the head of the Episcopal mission, Thomas S. Savage, heard growing rumors surrounding his capable assistant. Things came to a boil when an Americo-Liberian teenager, Henry Harmon, was brought before Savage for attempting to seduce an unnamed girl living with Thomson's family.[62] Whether the "girl" was a bound African servant or orphaned American the written accounts did not record, but most bound girls in the colony were from settler families. Harmon, whom Thomson described as that "mischief-making, lying fellow," apparently attempted to ameliorate the charges laid against him by claiming that Thomson provided a poor role model and that a girl attached to the mission station had informed Harmon of illicit behavior by Thomson. Thomson traced down Harmon's source to a young orphan named Martha, "that girl who together with her grandmother, imposed themselves on my hospitality," reported the accused.[63] By the time Thomson found himself before the colony's Court of Quarter Sessions later that year, the accusations had expanded to illicit intercourse between himself and a "mulatto" girl, Sally, placed under his care; attempts at similar relations with two other children, Martha and Frances, placed with his family; sexual intercourse during a mission trip with an African woman of Robookah, located on the eastern edge of Maryland in Liberia's territory; and finally with a wife of "Jack," the headman of the African laborers attached to the Episcopal mission.

Despite the degraded position Africans held in the minds of most of the settlers, the charges involving African women were actually more legally threatening for Thomson than those involving American girls. As a married man, Thomson faced criminal charges for the crime of adultery under colonial jurisprudence, but under the ordinances for the newly established colony, "carnal illicit intercourse with native women shall be punished, on conviction, by fine and imprisonment"; if the convicted offender continued with sexual relations with African women, then the sentences would concomitantly increase in severity. This was an odd, paradoxical quirk of the colony's legal code. Aside from its gendered logic, which spent no time pondering the implications of settler relations with African men, it also placed an acknowledged barrier between Africans and African Americans. It is even more perplexing as the law code originated with the white colonizationist leadership in Baltimore, the very men arguing for a natural and inherent affinity between the inhabitants of Africa and the returning "children" of that continent.[64]

More than the alleged affair with "Jack's" wife, however, the community's uproar and court case centered on the incident at Robookah. This largely hinged on a confession wrangled out of Thomson by Savage. Thomson, claiming a heavily burdened soul, wrote, "[I am] conscious that I was guilty of one charge that was preferred against me. . . . I was powerfully impressed by conscience to make a candid acknowledgment of what, was really a fact—connection with that mulatto girl who lived with me . . . the one I had a law-suit about." Any particular details of that lawsuit, when it occurred and under what circumstances, Thomson omitted from his letter to Holmes. Thomson feared that the details of the Robookah incident circulating among the settlers were misleading and whipping the crowd into a mob calling for his blood. Of course, there was the problem that the charges had some veracity, although Thomson asserted, "They were erroneously impressed with the idea that, what had happened to me when I went to Robookah, which I thought they might have heard of, was an act so criminal as to deserve hanging." According to Thomson, he had traveled to Robookah to acquire "native scholars" for the mission school, but there had been confusion between him and the town's leaders. Thomson had been on the hunt for both African boys and girls, and the village headmen seemingly could not understand why Thomson would desire girls for his school. While Liberia's indigenous peoples were willing to let their sons adopt "white man's fash," the gendered moniker underscores how unwilling they were to do the same for their daughters. The "king" followed this logic and supposedly presumed that Thomson was there either for a wife or for a servant. Thomson claimed that he had grown frustrated with the African's intransigence or unwillingness to understand his mission and had retired to bed for the night. While Thomson dozed, an undisclosed African "female came & prostrated herself" by him. Such were the admitted crimes of Thomson.[65]

Savage decided that he could no longer employ the man in a missionary station, but he took a further step by requesting that Thomson remove himself from the colony entirely. Savage suggested a sort of self-imposed exile elsewhere in the British Empire, perhaps in Thomson's native Demerara, and then he could send for his wife after he had established himself. For all of the hardships of Africa, Thomson was remarkably uninterested in returning to South America, and he refused to abandon home or wife. Feeling scorned, Savage apparently began a smear campaign against Thomson and found fertile ground among those settlers with grudges against the old keeper of the company store and its accounts. Equally unfortunate for Thomson was the fact that the charges associated with him were of a criminal nature, and thus he found himself before the Court of Quarter Sessions, a three-judge panel presided over by Russwurm along with two other associate judges, Thomas Jackson and Joshua Stewart. This time Thomson pleaded not guilty to the charges, which focused on his relations with the orphan children placed at the mission station and the woman at Robookah.

As these were the two self-admitted incidents in Thomson's private confession and the fuel driving the gossip spread by Savage, the court case centered around them and ignored the other rumors circling around Thomson. Savage testified under oath but could not produce the original written confession, having dispatched it to the Episcopal missionary society headquarters in the United States; Thomson unsurprisingly disputed the veracity of Savage's court testimony. More significantly, the documents produced by Thomson reflected that in the correspondence between Thomson and Savage, Savage had requested the written confession, stating, "I must have your confession in your handwriting written in ink and signed by yourself. The world will not know it. The Board must—God already knows it." Savage supposedly concluded his request with the promise that the confession would be "sacred." Thomson's case was further buttressed by the testimony of one of the mission's girls—probably Martha—with whom he supposedly had had inappropriate relations. Under oath, she testified that Thomson had removed her blanket while she slept and hushed her when she made a noise, as his wife actually slept in the same room, but she stated before the judges that they had not engaged in sexual relations. The young woman's credibility was destroyed in the eyes of the judges, however, by testimony from others who claimed that Martha had told them different accounts of Thomson's behavior. Rather than viewing her testimony through the lens of a poor girl attached to the household of her attacker, the judges sternly dismissed the girl as unreliable and concluded the day's session.

That night, Russwurm and his fellow judges, assistant agent McGill, and colonial secretary Revey met at the Agency House to consult William Blackstone's *Commentaries on the Laws of England* and Edward Livingston's penal code originally prepared for the State of Louisiana, the sum total of the colony's law library. Martha's testimony was considered suspect, and little but hearsay could be gleaned from other witnesses. More significantly, the judges decided that confessions wrought by promises of secrecy could not be given juridical credence. Privately, Russwurm informed the managers of the MSCS that he believed Thomson to be guilty of the charges, but publicly he believed the judges were beholden to following the legal code, to prove that theirs was a society of law. The court found Thomson not guilty of the charges, the broader community was set alight by the verdict, and Russwurm sighed in a letter to his superiors, "There are peculiar difficulties surrounding an Agent here, he has to contend against the ignorance of the people at all times."[66]

Those people, it turned out, were not particularly impressed with the verdict of the court. Although both Thomson and Russwurm stated that certain individuals supported executing Thomson—and according to Russwurm, "the most lenient were for banishment and confiscation, while the law only required fine and imprisonment"—the male settlers of the colony actually adopted a more peaceful and legal approach: they petitioned a higher authority, the Managers of the MSCS.[67] On August 9, 1837, a gathering of settlers at the colonial schoolhouse produced a committee of five leading citizens to conduct their own plebian court of inquiry into Thomson's guilt and the behavior of the Court of Quarter Session. Reconvening in December, fifty-three male heads of families signed the resolutions written by a committee of five, a *"solemn protest"* against the proceedings of Thomson, which they "humbly hail to you [the Managers of the MSCS] across the Atlantic." As compared to the judges, the citizens did not believe the confessions were wrung out by promises of secrecy, and they were far more sympathetic to the testimony of the mission's children. As male heads of households, they adopted a paternal tone in addressing the managers and requested that the board think in the same terms. In addition to asking the board to "think of our poor children," the petitioners also deemed Frances and Martha, aged seven and fourteen, as trustworthy witnesses intimidated before the court "without friend or attorney." In short, they concluded that "James M. Thomson had confessed that he had cohabitated with a native woman and that he was tried for that offence but he got clear." For their part, the board sympathized with and applauded the settlers for their moral stance, but they upheld the legal decision of the judges as the proper course for a nation based upon law.[68]

The Thomson affair really shows the intimate connections of a tiny society in which few things could long remain private and the great inequalities in power that shaped day-to-day relations. The orphan girls were placed at the mission per the policies of the colony, which provided a limited, though very necessary, social security net for the inhabitants of that unhealthy settlement. Unfortunately, the legal status of the girls was never fully documented in the trial. While the missionaries were trying to bring African girls into their school, the language of their attachment both to the mission and to Thomson suggests they were apprenticed orphans. Harmon was "employed" by the mission, suggesting he received a wage. And finally, although glossed over by the court case, as Thomson seems to have omitted any mention of her from his confession, there was "Jack's" unnamed wife and the other African laborers attached to the mission station. For those who could seize it, there were advantages to be had in such a mishmash of social relations, an arrangement directly at odds with the efforts to geographically separate settlers from Africans, and Americo-Liberians like Thomson and McGill capitalized on their advantages to attain very different ends.

Yet, for all of the various indentured servants, orphans, and wage labor to be found in western Africa, it is important to remember that African laborers were conceived of differently than their American or culturally assimilated counterparts. For all of the debate surrounding an unknown woman at Robookah, very little ink was spilled in anger over "Jack's" wife. As laborers attached to the settlement, "Jack" and his wife would have been recognizable figures to the Americans. The silence in relation to a possible affair within the settlement, compared to the outrage of an admitted liaison, albeit with contested details, on the far reaches of the colony's territory with an unknown woman, is telling. For all of the labor options before them, Americo-Liberians reserved the drudgery for their African workers. Africans pulled the carts through Monrovia's streets and lived in the "negro quarters" behind the homes of the Americans.

* * *

It is equally important to remember that the cheapness of African labor was originally conceived as a selling point of the colony by those colonizationists who envisioned an idyllic agricultural settlement. African laborers were critical for the masculine agricultural mission of Liberia; little wonder then that many settlers saw the Liberian labor market as a rich exploitive field. In a widely published and reprinted letter from Eli Ayres, the colony's first governor, to Robert Stockton, the naval officer whose "encouragement" was so critical in securing the initial land cessation, Ayres laid out the advantages of Liberia for settlers. Ayres reiterated the old fantasy of the need for "legitimate commerce," an anti-Atlantic slave trade mainstay that held that the only thing standing between western nations freeing themselves from the productions of New World slavery and African involvement in the slave trade was the establishment of a "legitimate" commodity trade with Africa. In so doing, the Atlantic economy would not be deprived of the produce of the plantation economy even as the flow of enslaved Africans across the Atlantic would be extinguished by the bustling new economic opportunities in Africa.[69] Ayres painted a picture of Africans literally begging for employment opportunities ("waiting and longing for employment," in his words). He cataloged the exchange rates in Africa. Four pounds of tobacco or eight yards of the "cheapest calico" or two pairs of shoes or two pints of gunpowder or forty-eight gun flints would purchase "*a month*" (emphasis his) of work. A hat would secure two months. As Ayres transformed tobacco, hats, and flints into months of work, he calculated that an African could be kept working for less than one dollar a year.[70]

Yet before this testament of purely economic qualities, Ayres was extolling the civilizing virtues of this trade. In Sierra Leone, Africans had been trained as carpenters, blacksmiths, and ship builders, and they were in the process of constructing a stone church "that would be gazed at with astonishment in the city of New York." These skilled craftsmen were included in the same paragraph with other "young men" making progress in the attainment of Greek and Latin languages; the linkage between the laborers and the classics students was left for the reader to guess. Liberian labor was both commodity and civilizing mission, intriguing indices of the uneven market revolution and commodification of labor. Jehudi Ashmun followed in his predecessor's footsteps. In his final report of 1825, Ashmun noted that every colonist could "obtain the comforts of life" because "every family, and nearly every single adult person in the Colony, has the means of employing from one to four native labourers." The widespread availability of cheap and unfree labor provided a societal floor that elevated all settlers. Perversely, this was exactly the same theory of social bliss through inequality that undergirded George Fitzhugh's proslavery arguments before the American Civil War. Slavery was an unmitigated good for Fitzhugh because it removed economic competition among society's necessary lowest strata and, contrary to free market capitalism, enveloped these laborers within the protective embrace of paternalism while simultaneously elevating the entirety of white society above them. For Fitzhugh, slavery "is a form, and the very best form, of socialism." Paternal masters saw to the needs of the enslaved, thus sparing the lowest orders of society from cruel competition with their social peers. Much as slavery provided contentment to the enslaved according to Fitzhugh, African labor would find "civilization" through working for the colonists.[71]

Little wonder that Birney saw colonizationist rhetoric as a mere echo of the justifications for American slavery. Through this command of "negro" labor, the Americo-Liberians distinguished themselves from and elevated themselves above their African "servants" and the degraded labor they performed, much as degraded and enslaved black labor within the United States provided a unifying and elevating whiteness to those free from the taint of slavery. Or as Moses Sheppard informed Russwurm of his two sons, they "will be white men, that is they will have no tincture of the slave."[72]

This celebration of the civilizing mission of labor could produce strange bedfellows. Josiah Conder, the British editor, author, and abolitionist, displayed a nuanced understanding of colonizationist rhetoric and actually quoted supporters of colonization in his own approbation of free labor,

Wages or the Whip. Specifically, Conder was most fascinated with the praise for the New Georgians and used this example to extol the humanitarian effects of free labor elsewhere. He also understood that the heart of colonizationist thinking was a spatial understanding whereby occupancy in particular environments altered the inhabitants. Conder, however, turned the evidence of colonization's beneficence to Africans into an argument for abolition: "If, then, such be the actual transformation which the liberated slave exhibits on touching the shores of Africa . . . what is to prevent the slave from throwing off his very nature with his chains, on the western shores of the Atlantic or in the islands of the Caribbean Sea?"[73] Conder hoped that the superior "free labor" of New Georgia would prove the ability of former slaves to adapt. Conversely, while Conder demonstrated adept understanding of the changes wrought by "touching the shores" of Liberia, he failed to grasp the complexity of working in Liberia. Rather than the binary established in his title, colonial Liberia is better conceived as a place that employed both wages *and* the whip.

On the other end of the ideological spectrum, William Sleigh's unambiguously titled *Abolitionism Exposed!* employed the same colonizationist rhetoric to argue against abolitionism. Quoting from the *African Repository*, Sleigh celebrated Liberia's supposed stifling influence on the African slave trade within its territorial confines. Even more beneficial, several thousand Africans, "mostly youth," had "come into the colonies"—there seems to be no suggestion that any of these Africans may actually have been the original occupants of Liberia's territory—"to learn 'Merica fash,' and make themselves 'white men,' by conforming to the habits of civilization, and becoming subject to our laws."[74] In focusing specifically on the African youths in the colony, Sleigh was focusing on children like "Chancellor Walworth," who worked in Americo-Liberian households. Instead of the beneficence of free labor, Sleigh found a celebration of bound labor in his Liberian example. "Civilization" could be found through work in a "civilized" environment and at a "civilized" trade.

While Conder and Sleigh used Liberia as evidence for radically different conclusions, they share a rather generalized understanding of Liberian labor; there are no individuals in their works actually performing all this work. This absence of detail is in keeping with other Americo-Liberian writings. Simply, there is very little detailed mention of African wards or African laborers within the settlers' correspondence. On the other hand, generalized remarks on the use of such labor within the colony and early republic are common. Whether in scandalous vilifications of the colony, as in the case of Nesbit, or *apologias* in her defense, as in the example of Williams, all accounts provide broad generalizations with few explicit details. Detailed descriptions of the acquisition and naming of "Chancellor Walworth" are rare and exist only thanks to the prickly personality of a scorned McGill. What we are usually left with are in the model of David Bacon's remembrances of his years as a colonial physician in Monrovia, in which he described the cluster of buildings surrounding the government house as "a storehouse, on the street—behind that a small building, for the servants, and, a little further back the kitchen, then nearly rebuilt,—the whole being arranged on the Southern plan—of a dwelling-house distinct, with the domestic arrangements under separate roofs." This was the sole mention of the "negro quarters" behind the main house that so enraged Nesbit. Conversely, the various settler youths who were placed in his household serving as attendants and apothecary assistants were biographically described; Peter, for example, was originally from New Orleans and had been a "pet slave" of his enslaver, whose will dictated the teenager's passage to Liberia upon death.[75]

Such broad formulations served a purpose for the Americo-Liberians. By generalizing all Africans, aside from those most prominently attached to the Americans, into such nondescript blanket categories as "natives," "laborers," or "negroes," while likewise ensuring to consistently identify American settlers by name, the Americo-Liberians distinguished themselves from their African neighbors. Here, the rhetoric of African youths "coming" to the colonies is significant because it allowed settlers to argue that the Africans were seeking "civilization" by going to the Liberian settlements; that is, they were acquiescing control willingly to the Americo-Liberians. Regardless of the reality on the ground, and it was assuredly more complex than that simple construction, such fabrications provided the ideological underpinning for arguments supporting the labor system of Liberia as a "civilizing" influence. Focusing on African children within the settler households, which were largely under the domestic influence of settler women, further propelled this narrative. Obviously, those accounts that sought to disrupt and challenge this Liberian propaganda almost universally eschewed focusing on African children and instead directed attention to the lived experience of adult African laborers within the colony or the peculiar reinterpretation of the American South with its "negro quarters" behind the master's house.

There is also the question of elite Liberian women traveling abroad with their servants. If he or she was African, what did Russwurm's servant think of the United States? If this servant did travel with the family northward, did she perceive the same differences in the political and social contexts between Baltimore and Maine that so caught the attention of Sheppard and McGill? Or were her duties so regimented that it made little difference where on the globe she stood? It would be unwise to completely dismiss African Liberians as simply filled with wonderment at such American delights.

When one of these African visitors to the United States, Simleh Ballah, traveled to Baltimore, albeit under much better circumstances as the emissary of a needed ally, he had lived in Latrobe's household and climbed to the top of Baltimore's Washington Monument to observe the busy harbor below. He was obviously impressed, but he was also an apparently astute observer who either engaged thoroughly with his Baltimore hosts in questions about the city or understood English far better than he let on. After his return to Africa, while defending the Greboes in one of the numerous incidents of provocation between settler and African at Cape Palmas, Ballah claimed that the Board of Managers held their colony to too strict a standard. While there were certainly scrapes and confrontations in Liberia, such was the natural order of things: "Those occasional revolutions are inseparable from any state of society & [he] asks if the people in Baltimore did not pull down each others houses just before he went to America."[76] Clearly, the commercial might of the Chesapeake did not stupefy Ballah into believing that the United States was only a land of milk and honey, and he also conceived that there were parallels between the two societies no matter the distance. It seems likely that Russwurm's servant could easily have developed his or her own understanding of the Atlantic world after such a long residence in the United States. Indeed, if she ascribed to the practices of other West Africans like Ballah, then she would have already conceived of herself as having lived in a "little" United States and was simply visiting the larger version.

Another traveler in this Atlantic world sailing at roughly the same historical moment as Russwurm's servant was Horatio Bridge, the American naval officer who published his *Journal of an African Cruiser* under Nathaniel Hawthorne's guiding hand. Bridge predicted that "large plantations" in Africa could never compete "with those of Brazil and the West Indies" in the production of staple commodities. According to Bridge, "free labor in Africa will not soon be so cheap as that of slaves."[77] Bridge may have been right in asserting that Liberian plantations could never compete with their New World cousins, but he was duped by a false binary if he believed the farms he observed while on shore leave were maintained solely by "free labor." Perhaps the workers were not legally chattel, but they were also most certainly not entirely free either. And regardless of their respective abilities to compete with the sugar production of Barbados or coffee plantations in Brazil, Americo-Liberian settlers considered the acquisition of unfree laborers a stepping stone to acquiring their own economic freedom. Before he "returned to my labor among the heathen," missionary and Americo-Liberian Washington McDonogh spent several months assisting his brother in clearing and planting his farm. Of course, it was probably helpful that his brother possessed "about 24 or 25 bound boys; some of them were taken from on board of a slaver by an American man-of-war." This was undoubtedly the *Pons*, but it is important to note that only "some" of the "bound boys" originated from the slave ship.[78] That this windfall of labor could be justified as an exercise in "civilizing" the heathen provided an added bonus. Tellingly, despite apparently having a flock of sorts conveniently attached to his brother's farm, missionary McDonogh sought to go out beyond the American settlements to "labor among the heathen"; the presumption being that once the children found themselves bound to a Liberian household, conversion to Christianity was imminent. Space and labor worked hand in hand to transform the Americo-Liberians into the vanguards of civilized Christianity. That economic and social gain in Liberia came on the backs of degraded labor only disturbed those who dismissed the "civilizing" possibilities of that labor, the "legitimate commerce" argument writ small. But for the day-to-day lives of Liberia's inhabitants, the labor options were simply that: economic opportunities. It is perhaps best to conclude with a quote from settler Peyton Skipwith, who directly attributed his rising fortunes to the windfall of the overloaded *Pons*. He wrote his former enslaver, a well-suited correspondent for understanding the economic possibilities of unfree labor:

> I am very sorry that I did not turn my attention to farming when I first arrived to this Country, but It was Entirely out of my power as I was alone in a Manner & had no male kind to render me assistance. Now I Am very well Situated and has several apprentices with me Exclusive of some of the Barque Pons cargo of Congoes.[79]

For Skipwith, there was nothing civilizing or elevating about laboring on his farm. He simply needed male field hands to make his farm thrive. That he had the capacity and luck to acquire a multitude of laborers in various forms and stages of unfreedom to fulfill his agrarian demands and that his use of these laborers would be sanctioned by many individuals otherwise opposed to slavery was the benefit of being an Americo-Liberian, the great "civilizer" of a "heathen" continent.

4

"They Would Dearly Learn What It Was to Fight White Men"

Whitening through Violence in Liberia

For all of the assurances on the part of the white leadership of the ACS that colonization was practical, it easily devolved into a muddled affair. Such was the case when Virginia enslaver Aylett Hawes liberated more than one hundred people via his will upon condition of resettlement to Liberia. These formerly enslaved people found themselves auspiciously sailing from Norfolk on October 24, 1834; the day was propitious because it fell on the anniversary of William Penn's arrival in his New World colony in 1682. While the date probably bore little significance to the Virginians, it resonated with their patrons, the Young Men's Colonization Society of Pennsylvania (YMCSP), who relished the symbolism of establishing a new colony in West Africa on the same day that Penn had come ashore in North America. A "Mrs. Sigourney" composed a two-stanza hymn for the occasion; the first stanza celebrated the arrival of Penn, and the second echoed this motif by announcing, "A ship its sail is spreading, For that far tropic clime."

Partnering with the New York City Colonization Society, the YMCSP hoped to establish an independent colony just south of the mouth of the St. John River at a small inlet called Bassa Cove, or "Yorksylvania" as one apparently amused New York colonizationist named the effort. The partner institutions were anxious to demonstrate their antislavery agenda by sending out expeditions consisting entirely of manumitted persons and had received word of another band of potential emigrants in Savannah, Georgia. Following in the wake of the Marylanders' separation from the parent society, these northern societies were members of a broader separatist movement of state auxiliaries who were frustrated by the ACS's financial woes, mismanagement, and reluctance to take a firm stance in opposition to slavery. Although they retained their status as ACS auxiliaries, these societies increasingly retained control over their own funds and established their own independent colonies. The Bassa Cove settlement, named for the Liberian ethnic group who inhabited the area, was a short distance south of the ACS outpost of Edina, itself named in honor of the citizens of Edinburgh, Scotland, who had donated £100 to the ACS in 1833. And so it was that black Virginians set out to establish a new settlement under the governance of Pennsylvanians and New Yorkers who soon hoped to fill it with Georgians across the cove from an ACS settlement named in honor of a Scottish city.[1]

If any of the new settlers had possessed or examined the convenient 1830 map of the Liberian coast, based upon Jehudi Ashmun's observations, they would have discovered that their new neighbors, the Bassas, "are generally domestic, industrious and averse to war." The settlers probably would have found that description comforting as, per the large Quaker presence among the Pennsylvania colonization ranks, the new colony at Bassa Cove was to be founded on a principle of "total abstinence from trade in ardent spirits and arts of war." If any Northern benefactors had pushed into the hands of the literate settlers a curious book titled *Claims of the Africans: or History of the American Colonization Society*, published two years earlier by the Massachusetts Sabbath Union, they would have been reassured that their soon-to-be closest neighbor, "King Joe Harris," was "a good natured old man" who urged the settlement of missionaries among his people and begged "like a child" for the erection of schools. The early days of the Bassa Cove settlement seemed to justify the tactics of the auxiliary societies in establishing the separate colony. "Joe Harris" dispatched his son to be educated for three years in the United States. Over the course of three days in May, the Pennsylvanians and New Yorkers met in New York City to discuss the bright prospects of their settlement. "Joe Harris's" son was patronizingly introduced as "Master Harris," a budding scholar who had come to the United States in search of whiteness. The audience was informed, "He had come here to 'learn book,' and go back a white man—not in colour, but he trusted, in what surpassed all outward change, in having his sins washed away. (The lad smiled, as if he comprehended this accoun of him)."[2]

Less than one month later, "King Joe Harris" wiped Bassa Cove from the map, attacking the settlement on the night of June 10, 1835, killing eighteen settlers, and forcing a hellish flight on the part of the survivors into the surrounding woods. During the morning following the attack, Richard Davis, a fifty-five-year-old settler recently manumitted by Hawes—his former coach driver, in fact—scoured the woods in search of Lucretia Brant, his thirty-six-year-old unmarried daughter who was listed on the emigrant roll as a "spinster." Davis "found her out in the woods sitting on the ground looking as pal as death from great loss of blood from the many dangerous wounds she had recd. that night." Davis tried to move the woman by himself, but she suffered too greatly from his solitary efforts. He left her and sought additional aid in carrying his daughter away from harm. Somehow finding Edward Hankinson, a Quaker and the agent for Bassa Cove, Davis begged for assistance in securing the aid of the ever-present Kru to carry his daughter to safety. Hankinson himself had apparently escaped the devastation with the aid of one of the Kru. Davis "went immediately to Mr. Hankinson as ask him for something to pay the Kroomen to bring my child out of the woods. He very inhumanely sent me off without any thing say he had nothing for me notwithstanding my great distress his heart was iron-cased against my small request." Lucy Brant died in the forest.[3]

Most of the survivors fled to neighboring Edina. That small isolated outpost soon found itself engulfed in the conflict with "Harris." Unprepared to engage in a prolonged war and isolated from Monrovia, over fifty miles distant to the north, the citizens of Edina begged for aid from the colony and the ACS leaders in the States. In July, one correspondent inquired of "the board of managers whither they intend to forsake us all together Located in Edina." Despite the precarious situation, there were advantages to warfare. The superintendent in charge of Edina, W. L. Weaver, reported, "We stand at present in battle array wishing to obtain our ground the land which have been assigned to us we find is of no use on the east of this River purchased by Governor Mechlin. We have at all times been refused authority by the natives ... from whom the land was bought." The war provided the perfect opportunity to forcibly occupy the territory south of the St. John River to which the citizens of Edina clearly believed they were entitled. Of course, such a conflict would require some serious firepower, and the citizens formally petitioned the ACS for a dozen pieces of artillery and one hundred muskets.[4]

Even as they called for help, however, the Edina settlers were not content to remain holed up in their isolated village but rather moved up the river and attacked "Joe Harris's" forces near his town, losing one man as they inflicted an estimated twenty casualties on the enemy. Weaver informed the Board of Managers how a settlement in such desperate need of artillery and provisions was able to successfully go on the attack: "Bob Gray and King Yellow Will have proved themselves our devout friends in the War, they have taken almost the whole of it on themselves had several Battles with King Joe Harris and succeeded in repulsing him each time." "Bob Gray," whom one settler described in 1834 "as almost one of our citizens," and "Yellow Will," not to be confused with the Cape Palmas translator, were supporters of the American settlements who probably saw the war as an opportunity to curry favor with the Americans and simultaneously remove a rival—"Joe Harris"—from the south side of the river. While "Bob Gray" actively intervened in the war on the Americans' behalf, "Yellow Will" simply refused to aid "Harris," an act of defiance for which "Harris" burned his village. Although Bassa Cove was under the leadership of the Pennsylvania and New York societies, once Edina became engaged in the war, the authorities at Monrovia brought the entire colonial apparatus onto a war footing. Settler Nathaniel Brander served as vice agent, and following the resignation of John Pinney as governor in May, it was left to him to organize the ACS colonies' response to the attack on Bassa Cove before the board named Ezekiel Skinner to the post a few months later.[5]

Americo-Liberian volunteers along with their receptive African allies from New Georgia marshaled in Monrovia. On July 14, the colonial council declared war against "Harris" even as it held out the olive branch in the form of peace commissioners charged with the task of interviewing "Harris" in order to "demand . . . an explanation of his late conduct . . . demand reparation for his aggressions on the persons and property of Americans . . . demand security . . . for the future peace and safety of the Colony generally, and its citizens individually." The commissioners would be carrying a sizable stick with them in the form of more than one hundred volunteer soldiers who would immediately go to war with "Harris" if the commissioners did not feel their demands were adequately met. It was this colonial army that a young Samuel McGill joined before his medical career. The newly appointed colonial agent, Ezekiel Skinner, was not to be outdone by the citizens of Edina in asking for military supplies from his superiors; in addition to requesting field artillery pieces in case the settlers needed to "penetrate King Joes territories," quite the affirmation of this masculine mission, Skinner also asked the ACS for fifty rifles to form an elite rifle company. Ever the propagandists, the ACS officials in the States spun the war as evidence of the beneficial effects of colonization, as this simultaneous preparation for both war and peace "indicate a state of political advancement among" the settlers that was made possible only by their transformation into the civilizers of Africa.[6]

The peace commissioners had little time to ply their trade, as soon after arriving in the territory, a general engagement between "Harris" and the colonists led to the defeat of the Bassa leader and the burning of his town. Facing such odds, "Harris" made peace with the settlers and "Bob Gray," whom he considered only an auxiliary to the Americans, and promised not to interfere with Americo-Liberian efforts to resettle Bassa Cove or trade along the St. John River and to return the goods pillaged from the destroyed settlement. The ACS agent "dashed" "Bob Gray," "Young Bob"—presumably "Bob Gray's" son—and "Yellow Will" a smattering of trade goods, muskets, gunpowder, umbrellas, cloth, and snuff boxes to reinforce their connection to the American settlers, and by October 31 Skinner was walking among the unburied bodies of the Bassa Cove settlers with plans to reestablish the settlement.[7]

There was significant confusion regarding the cause of the assault, especially in light of the colonizationists' previous convictions that "Joe Harris" had embraced his American neighbors. In their July petition, the citizens of Edina ascribed "Harris's" motives to land disputes; by October, colonizationists in the United States were convinced that "Harris" was only a cog in the machinations of slave traders who had been forced to abandon their factory near Bassa Cove upon the arrival of the Americans. But most Americo-Liberians were positive that they understood the root cause of the betrayal: the principles of the settlement, namely, pacifism. On July 1, Hilary Teague informed his correspondent that the "unfortunate circumstances" of the destruction of the settlement and loss of lives was due "entirely to the principles on which the settlement was founded. I anticipated it and ventured to remark the same to Mr. Hankinson. He . . . imputed them to a want of faith." The cause was the inherent savagery of the surrounding Africans, who were kept in check only by force and the military strength of the colony. The June *Liberia Herald,* reporting immediately after receiving word of the attack, spoke for many of the settlers in explaining the problem with pacifist policies. Of neighboring Africans, the *Herald* proclaimed, "Such is the dastardly, unprincipled disposition of these half cannibals, that nothing but a knowledge of superiority, in point of physical force, on the part of foreigners, will keep them to the terms of any compact made with them."[8]

If properly managed with requisite shows of military might, the Africans would become pliable subservient neighbors, as their "dastardly souls like a humble spaniel will succumb into most willing obedience." According to the *Herald,* the Americo-Liberians were far more qualified to evaluate African character than distant colonizationists in the United States owing to their residence near and familiarity with Africans. In a letter labeled "private," settler Jacob W. Prout—soon to be secretary of the convention that declared Liberia's independence in 1847—affirmed the *Herald*'s perspective to the ACS: "I do not hesitate to say that the means of defence of the Settlement of Port Cresson will hereafter keep them in (the natives) in [*sic*] fear, as I well know that in order to keep them under subjection they must allways see some thing like a prepared state." There are echoes here of white Southerners' arguments that they were most qualified to "handle" the South's African American population because of similar claims to familiarity with savage blackness. Undoubtedly, arch-racist Samuel Cartwright did not know he echoed the *Liberia Herald* when he wrote nearly a decade later on enslaved African Americans that "no spaniel is more attached to his master or is truer to him, than is Canaan when properly managed."[9] Control could not only just be wrought from the map and bound labor, it also had to be created from cannon and sword, elegantly normalizing violence that ensured the smooth order of the society.

As variegated, shifting, and contested whiteness on the American mainland developed in opposition to black degradation and indigenous backwardness, elevated settler blackness—or African whiteness—emerged in opposition to black African savagery. And much as whiteness papered over many cultural, ethnic, economic, and social rifts within the elbowing ranks of European immigrants in nineteenth-century America, so too did "civilization" congeal fissures within settler society. Fractures developed among settlers as free-state and slave-state emigrants eyed one another suspiciously; freeborn settlers, who often emigrated with greater capital in terms of both money and educational resources that they could transform into government positions with regular salaries, often found themselves at odds with formerly enslaved colonists. Even racial differences among the supposedly homogenous "black" settlers, especially among the multitudinous mixed-race categorizations, cleaved society. And, of course, such identifying factors did not operate in a vacuum but rather built upon one another in dizzying constellations of power within the colonial setting. Controlling "half cannibals," as the *Liberia Herald* described Africans, usually took the form of the musket and provided the glue to cement these disparate elements of society together. With such an emphasis on violence, the colony enveloped itself in a masculine mission to tame savagery.

The control of black labor was foundational to the idea of Liberia. Such a large class of laborers, occupying the lowest strata of society because of their supposed lack of "civilization," obviously echoed the mixed free and enslaved organization of labor in the United States. And just as whites in the United States grumbled about the supposed attributes of enslaved and free African American workers, utilized violence to maintain their system of privilege, and legally constrained the mobility of African Americans, so too did the Americo-Liberians strictly enclose citizenship within the normalcy of American culture, engage in armed struggles against neighboring Africans, and denigrate the laborers who provided the economic backbone of the colony.

While the Africans were willing to see whiteness as an advantageous cultural identity, they were not supportive of this imported American construction of its concomitant relations of power. In some ways, the Americo-Liberians and Africans were not wholly dissimilar in their interpretations of whiteness. Clearly, whiteness was a privileged and highly prized commodity for the Africans that could strengthen their economic position. But they were unwilling to concede to the American style of whiteness conceived by the Americo-Liberian settlers in which they were degraded cheap labor cast out beyond the pale of citizenship or authority in Liberia.

The efforts on the part of the Americo-Liberians to enforce this relation of power led to conflicts with the Africans. These conflicts were often violent, and the wars and struggles between the settlers and neighboring African groups are a near constant in Liberian history. Even if the settlers and Africans avoided wars like the one that engulfed Bassa Cove, violence—or the threat of violence—was a ubiquitous presence in the colonies. The violence of Liberia was not limited to grand conflicts but shaped the day-to-day interactions of Americo-Liberian and African Liberian. This "landscape of violence" ranged from large-scale wars of conquest to intimate episodes among individuals. Both settlers and Africans, elbowing for space and power in western Africa, navigated a complex and evolving landscape.

Of course, there were peaceful alternatives to the sword, and one of the striking and understudied responses to this encroaching colonial power is how these Liberian Africans negotiated the laws of Liberian society to gain advantage. The ongoing negotiations between Maryland in Liberia and "Freeman" over thefts were prime examples of this exchange. As noted in chapter 1, before Governor Hall stepped down in favor of Russwurm, he had attempted to prevent thefts he attributed to Africans by threatening the indiscriminate confiscation of African goods of equal value to any good claimed by a colonist to have been stolen. The Greboes successfully parried that discriminatory system of justice by mobilizing their transatlantic experiences and arguing that Liberia was an extension of a "white man's country" and should replicate its legal codes. This legal defense led to the establishment of the Grebo constabulary.[10]

While the settlers desired to create a society in which they held such dominance, the reality on the ground often required negotiation. As in the case of the Bassa Cove expedition, Americo-Liberian military operations were often heavily reliant upon African auxiliaries, both Congoes and natives. The Grebo revolt in Maryland was initiated when an American Justice of the Peace summarily sentenced a Grebo to corporal and fiscal punishment without a means to challenge the ruling. The Greboes were able to negotiate a place in the colonial hierarchy owing to the Marylanders' relative lack of dominant force and need to hold on to Grebo allies for their excursions into the interior. Still, the desire for such power was a driving force among the colonists. In fact, such desires led Samuel McGill to advocate that the independent Maryland settlement request its own annexation by the larger Republic of Liberia. Maryland in Liberia declared its independence from the MSCS in a ceremony held in Baltimore on February 22, 1854. Like its other Liberian counterpart, the secession of Maryland in Liberia from the MSCS met with the full support of the parent society. Yet, as early as 1851, then-governor McGill was advocating merging with the government at Monrovia. His reasoning was straightforward: "The Colonists here should not be encouraged in their rejection of the idea of annexation to the Republic as a County for the following reasons. We require strength and numbers to control, and if necessary subdue our Native population."[11]

The projection of power and consolidating the force of all Americo-Liberians against native Africans was foremost in McGill's mind. Indeed, McGill suggested that "subduing" Africans was a particular specialty of Americo-Liberians. The letter would prove prophetic. In December 1856, Maryland in Liberia became embroiled in a war with its Grebo neighbors. After initially destroying Gbenelu at last and securing the aid of Rocktown Africans in their struggle, the settlers became bogged down in the military conflict, suffered setbacks, and eventually had to send for aid from Monrovia, whose military expedition resulted in the annexation of Maryland in Liberia in 1857, much as McGill predicted. Although the Americo-Liberians proved triumphant in the end, the seesawing conflict underscores the inability of the Liberian settlers to unilaterally project power at all times, everywhere. Instead, punch and counterpunch punctuate Liberian history. Africans burn Bassa Cove and have their town destroyed in turn;

Americo-Liberians order an African flogged, and his kinfolk break him out of jail.

* * *

This Liberian violence was all the more complicated by the multifaceted groups involved: European and American traders, Americo-Liberian settlers, rival colonizers, and numerous African nations and ethnicities, each with their own agenda. In 1831 Americo-Liberians at Grand Cape Mount, a one-thousand-foot-high promontory jutting into the Atlantic, hoped to capitalize on localized warfare to acquire the strategic point that lay beyond their legal claims, if not their ambitions. Just over thirty miles north of Monrovia, the towering peninsula and its environs were the homelands of the Vai people, a Manden ethnic group, who lived under Gola authority when the American settlers first arrived. By 1831, however, there were new rivals seeking control of the territory in the form of Charles Gomez and his allies, slave traders operating from the nearby Mano River, which today marks part of the border between Sierra Leone and Liberia. Elijah Johnson reported to Governor Mechlin, "Several of the parties are in favor of us having an establishment at this place particularly the Young men, and argue strongly in the palavers to support our *Mission*."[12] Johnson believed that Gomez was responsible for the opposition of "Fah Torah," a powerful warrior based at Cape Mount, to the Americans.[13] The complex war was further complicated by "Prince Peter," the heir of the Gola rulers, who hoped to retain authority over the Vai. "Peter's" father had secured his own position of power by amassing great wealth through the slave trade. Johnson inaccurately framed the conflict as a simplistic binary between supporters of slavery, namely, Torah and Gomez, and those who supported Peter and freedom.[14]

What Johnson described as a war between slaves and freemen was really a multifaceted conflict among the Vai, Gola, and Gomez for control of the lucrative slave-trading region. Johnson noted the possibility of another player in the region, a "Mr. Hornell," who Gomez claimed had gone to Sierra Leone to secure arms and munitions for Gomez to continue his war. But Johnson thought Hornell, presumably Robert Hornell, a prominent Freetown merchant, was trying to take possession of the territory for himself. Augustus Curtis, also at Cape Mount, likewise warned that "Gomez is about to sell the country to English men." Presumably, those young Vai leaders who Johnson believed were willing to deal with the Americans were probably hoping to locate strong enough allies to restore peace to a region ravaged by its location between two colonial powers, the presence of powerful slave traders, and competing indigenous and migratory peoples.[15]

While Cape Mount marked the northern terminus of Liberian land ambitions, similar problems plagued the southernmost colony. After their very rocky start, "Freeman" and Russwurm had eventually built a working relationship before being brought back into conflict in 1838. The immediate source of the problem was a prolonged drought combined with the arrival of two large expeditions of emigrants—one in January and another in July—that greatly taxed the food reserves of the colony; one of these expeditions owed its size to the rhetoric of Alexander Hance on his tour through Maryland discussed in chapter 1. In late February, after the arrival of the first expedition, Russwurm decided to make direct contact with the interior African town of Denah, several miles up the nearby Cavalla River, in hopes of opening a direct land route to the town to allow for the importation of foodstuffs. "Freeman" accompanied Russwurm on this expedition. While Russwurm thought that "Freeman's" presence would increase the prestige of the mission, the motives of "Freeman" are less well documented. Perhaps he desired to further cement the American settlement to his cause or he wanted to be present as the Americans interjected themselves into the coastal-interior trade that had traditionally been dominated by African go-betweens like himself. Or, perhaps more simplistically, he was also interested in opening up direct trade with the interior because his people were as hungry as the Americans. Regardless of "Freeman's" motives, the Africans living along the river were not receptive to this intrusion in their riparian trade. Before their arrival in Denah, the Maryland expedition was fired upon from the shore, dumped from their canoes, and ignominiously sent back down the river to nurse their pride. Despite their respective outrages, both African and American leaders knew they were in no shape to launch a war.[16]

In April, colonial secretary John Revey dutifully transcribed a message from "Freeman" dispatched through his interpreter Ballah. Despite the intervening month to cool his temper, "Freeman" clearly still seethed and informed the MSCS, "I want you please for send two schooners for fight them people & make them people no doo bad fash agin." As late as July, Russwurm still operated under the nominal assumption that "Freeman" was an ally of the colony, and he requested that the MSCS "send out a new suit of blue for King Freeman. His size is one of the largest." Russwurm did not record the results of this gift, but it seems likely that "Freeman" found a suit of the appropriate color a poor substitute for actually becoming a Grebo admiral.[17]

But even as the two leaders seemed to have developed some form of rapport, tensions worsened among the colony's inhabitants. J. Leighton Wilson, the missionary go-between for "Freeman" when he first met Russwurm, reported in July in revealing language that the "natives are becoming exceedingly uneasy as [to] the amount of lands appropriated by the colonists & they are apprehensive that they will be crowded out of their reservations." Once again, control of the territory and assumptions that the entire colonial territory was designated for the settlers aside from the "reservations" of the Africans resided at the forefront of the colony's conflicts. Letters dated from the lean summer of 1838 increasingly complained of thefts. For his part, Russwurm echoed the *Liberia Herald*'s summation of the Africans' assault on Bassa Cove and placed much of the blame for the thefts on the settlers. "Our people," he wrote that summer, "are also much to blame, as many houses have not proper fastenings, though they know the natives will steal." Just as pacifism failed to address African malevolence at Bassa Cove, so too did lackadaisical security invite African larceny.[18]

Unsurprisingly, the reports of the growing tensions in the colony were accompanied by increasing detail to the colonial militia. In April, an officer of the Latrobe Artillery—the company of men responsible for the cannon pointed at "King Freeman's" town—requested that the MSCS order uniforms more suitable to the climate, along with cartridge boxes and other military necessities. In July: "The muhtary [military] is moving. We have too uniform company and one mulitia, we can call one hundred men to arms. Lard is wanted and powder for the run of their quarterly parads as you know that we have men under arms some time that they never handled a musket and the drill officers find it very necessary that such thing are much wanted." Six months after arriving, schoolmaster Benjamin Alleyne reported in July 1838 a litany of problems with the colony: its stockpile of provisions, its governor, the supplies provided to settlers, and the lack of a prepared schoolhouse. About the only organization functioning well in the colony seemed to be its military structure, which Alleyne admitted had "quite a military appearance" and was "improving in discipline." At the same time, Russwurm was requesting one hundred cartridge boxes for the militia; the settler who carried his official correspondence to the United States was also entrusted to present to the Board of Governors a curiosity in the form of an African cartridge box. The underlying message seemed to be that despite the widespread availability of this African variant, the settlers would withdraw ammunition only from an American-style box.[19] The colony may starve, but the military would look good doing it, and they would do it dressed as Americans.

* * *

Despite the fact that their definition of the power within whiteness was contested, the Americo-Liberians found such broadly conceived identities as "white," "American," and "civilized"—contested claims when they were in the United States—to be useful tools for enveloping a disparate settler society. The survival of Liberia necessitated presenting a united front against divided African nations, and unfortunately Liberians had multiple fissures that produced deep divides into their society. There is no better example of these fissures than Russwurm himself. Although in charge of the Maryland colony, Russwurm was Jamaica-born and raised in New England. Freeborn Northerners who emigrated often attributed the colony's labor relations, poor educational opportunities, and lack of entrepreneurism to the majoritarian Southern settlers. Indeed, the problematic "Southern-ness" of Liberia was one of the few points that both William Nesbit and Samuel Williams, coincidentally both Pennsylvanians, agreed upon. In his scathing critique of Liberia, Nesbit scoffed at the condition of the "*Slave's Slave*" and highlighted how Liberians replicated the living arrangements of Southern slaveholders by housing natives in huts behind their main residences.

In his response to Nesbit, Williams essentially agreed that an abundance of Southerners was a problem: "The next objection that I find to Liberia, is the indolence or seeming indolence of many of the colonists. . . . This is to be attributed more to the kind of people who have settled them than to any other cause. They are principally emancipated slaves, who do not appreciate freedom in its proper light, but think that when once free they are at liberty to be industrious or otherwise, and many choose to be lazy. Now, if, in my opinion, the Northerners could be induced to go to Liberia, we would soon find quite a different state of things." The New Englander Russwurm was more cautious in his regional praises, if only because of his association with the colonization society from Maryland. Even before his appointment as governor, Russwurm rejoiced the arrival of an MSCS ship, noting, "The arrival of the Ann with emigrants for the settlement of Cape Palmas was with emigrants north of the District of Columbia; (for it cannot and ought not to be concealed that sectional feelings do prevail in our community) a subject of much rejoicing." Nesbit and Williams wanted settlers of more northerly stock, while Russwurm was contented if the colonists were simply from any area north of the capital or freeborn, but all three Northerners agreed that the colony was filled with far too many Southerners.[20]

Overlapping this regional divide among settlers was the question of whether individuals were freeborn or formerly enslaved. And this complicated web of division was further subdivided by the diversity of racial ancestry represented among the Americo-Liberians. These questions of race and condition related to practical matters. Freeborn settlers—or at least those who had been free for several years before their emigration—could accrue greater resources for life in Africa than many of their newly emancipated comrades, who were forced to rely on the colonization societies or their former enslavers.

The white-run colonization societies in the United States favored racially ambiguous settlers, who, in the words of Robert J. Breckinridge, as a "whole class of mulattoes is to be considered and treated as distinct from the blacks. They consider themselves so; the blacks consider them so, and all who have opportunity of comparing the two cannot doubt that the former are the more active, intelligent, and enterprising of the two."[21] For certain individuals of mixed ancestry, Liberia offered a perfect environment to obtain the power and influence denied them in the United States.

These relations of power meant that Liberia did not offer an escape from racialized tensions, even within settler society. Writing decades after his Liberian experiences, James Hall, who served as the ACS's doctor in Monrovia before becoming Maryland in Liberia's governor, explained how he came to learn of this fissure within Liberian society almost immediately. Shortly after arriving in the colony, the new colonial doctor was invited to a dinner hosted by the governor and attended by roughly twenty colonial officials and the colony's most prominent citizens. After more than two hours of wining and dining, the banquet concluded in good American fashion with a number of toasts to "The Governor," "The American Colonization Society," "Liberia," and so on deep into the night. All was well until one guest hoisted his glass and proclaimed, "'The *Fair* of Liberia'; which last created significant and not pleasant looks on the part of some very dark gentlemen present." Luckily, the governor stepped in and quickly suggested that surely the toaster had meant "The *Fair Sex* of Liberia," and the volatile situation defused. Hall added for any confused readers that "*Fair* is a specific term with Liberians, signifying the shade of color; as 'a little fair; *quite* fair; *very* fair; almost white, and so on.'" Related to these issues surrounding the "shade of color" was the former legal status of the immigrants.

Many freeborn Liberians believed the formerly enslaved to be unprepared for life on the frontier. One can hear the disappointment dripping from mixed-race governor Joseph J. Roberts, who would go on to be the first president of the Republic of Liberia, when he commented to a companion after observing a vessel of Kentucky émigrés disembarking, "Do not think much of the Kentucky delegates. . . . They appear to be rather self-consequential, blustering and ignorant—perhaps 'field hands.'"[22] To complicate this already messy society further, this emphasis on the supposed unpreparedness of the recently manumitted for life in Liberia was not only confined to those born free. Some pro-colonization slaveholders decided to educate or train enslaved settlers prior to their departure for Liberia, thus providing some newly freed settlers with the same literary and educational skills as their freeborn compatriots. Samson Caesar, who arrived in Liberia in 1834, was one. Although previously enslaved and a Virginian, Caesar thought the formerly enslaved Virginians of Liberia to be "the most Stupid Set of people in the place." He concluded that Liberia would never prosper so long as American enslavers kept the enslaved "as dum as horses" and sent them directly to Liberia without any additional training. Clearly, Caesar found no fault with the indictments of Nesbit, Williams, and Roberts regarding the quality of the emigrants.[23]

* * *

As governor, Russwurm joined this chorus of grumbles regarding the recently manumitted. After the arrival of the *Columbia* in July 1838, one of the vessels expediting the colony's food crisis, Russwurm complained to his superiors that the demographics of the ship were disappointing due to the high number of newly manumitted colonists onboard. "An acquaintance with people just emancipated," he reported, "knows that it is with the utmost difficulty, that males even can be driven to make the requisite exertions to maintain themselves." Russwurm's framing leads one to question the Liberian liberty that accompanied the act of manumission. The real problem with the *Columbia*, however, was the number of women. Unmarried women constituted too large of a percentage of the expedition, Russwurm fumed, voicing a complaint repeated by nearly every governor and agent of the colony. While the presence of unmarried women failed to match the masculine agriculture vision of a colony of farming families, the violence of the colony also factored into the gendered thinking of the governors. After noting that formerly enslaved men had to be "driven" to work, Russwurm added in a nod to the *Columbia*'s women, "how much greater then the difficulty where you have to deal with females without protectors."[24]

Surrounded by "savages," female settlers necessitated "protectors" in this line of thinking. Clearly, much of this rhetoric centered on fears that women could not provide for themselves economically or protect themselves from barbaric violence like that which befell Lucy Brant in this dangerous colonial environment. The high mortality rate of the colony exacerbated this masculine nightmare by producing large numbers of widows and fatherless families, male-led households being the society's assumed foundational unit. Formerly enslaved widows often found themselves in difficult situations. Such was the result for Rebecca Gibson, who wrote to the board of the MSCS on August 31, 1836, one year after her arrival in Maryland in Liberia, "I am a lone widow in a strange land" and whose pressing needs to feed and clothe her children had led her to confess, "Many a time I wished I had never left America." Gibson's husband had died four months after arriving in the colony, and his widow, burdened with six children all under the age of twelve, could simply no longer survive. She requested "a little aid any thing will be gratefully accepted old clothes for my children or any thing which the charitable feeling may compel them to do." Perhaps most tragically, Gibson had apparently left older children in bondage in Maryland. If the Maryland colonizationists could get one of her older sons to her in Africa, then she was certain that her lot would improve. It is a soul-crushing letter, all the more so for its concluding note seemingly underlining the reason for the Gibson family's relocation: "Joseph goes to school (my eldest boy) he is fond of his book and will make a good scholar."

In 1837, one year after writing for assistance from America, Gibson married William Dulany. In a testament to the microbial realities of Liberia, Dulany was dead one year later. Thus, the newly minted Rebecca Dulany once again directed a letter across the Atlantic in July 1838 to inform her correspondents that another husband had predeceased her. This time she dispatched a boxful of shells in hopes that the MSCS leadership would send her money and goods in advance and repay themselves through the sale of exotic African conchs.[25]

The widows usually framed their requests in relation to the poverty of the colony and their inability to harness enough labor to their farmsteads to make them self-sufficient. An impoverished economy and poor soils were the principal enemies. For all of their supposed weakness in this colonial society, Liberia's widows often exhibit remarkable grit in their letters. Even as Sally Ann Gibson, whose relationship to Rebecca is unknown,[26] asked for help in 1844 upon the death of her husband, she affirmed, "I have no desire to com back to America."[27]

While their respective economic contributions flustered colonizationists, women's presence in colonial Liberia added sexual politics to colonial dynamics. As governor, Russwurm could disparage the arrival of single women, but the sickly colony needed women for their reproductive capabilities. Simply, the high death rate of the colony placed a greater emphasis on births within the colony. The racialized regime of colonial Liberia altered American racial structures and subsequently fostered discourse among Euro-Americans in the United States that the colonial space encouraged an untoward familiarity between whites and blacks; sexual relations were of special concern. When the American Anti-Slavery Society publicly interviewed Thomas C. Brown, a disgruntled South Carolinian who found the colony wanting and returned to the United States after fourteen months in Liberia, some members of the audience coyly inquired about the number of white men present in the colony. Brown counted six white men connected with the colonial administration or missionary societies. The subsequent question—"Have there been any *mulatto children* born there?"—and Brown's unequivocal response—"There have certainly been mulatto children born there"—led to an immediate disruption as audience members howled "Shame! Shame!" from the balcony. The disruptive audience members, described in the published transcript as white men supportive of colonization, found the entire topic unseemly. Eventually quieted, the committee continued with the line of questioning, but Brown, obviously aware that at least a portion of the audience was hostile to even suggesting white officials engaged in sexual relations with female colonists, immediately backed away from his earlier claims. When further pressed, Brown's "mulatto children" became "one mulatto child," and Brown refused to reveal or speculate on the identity of the father. At no point did anyone inquire whether the children were the result of shared love or forced will, but the great disparities in power between a colonial official who controlled purse strings and a Liberian widow render such questioning practically meaningless.[28]

Clearly, the male-dominated audience—the published transcript does not mention whether it was a mixed-race audience—was divided over the propriety of airing the colony's dirty laundry in terms of sex. Equally clear, given the leading questions regarding the number of white men in the colony, the assumption by the interrogators and the implication put forward by Brown was that these mixed-race offspring were the result of white colonial officials' sexual liaisons with African American or African women. It is not difficult to imagine the desperation that could drive settler widows to seek relief through sexual relations with colonial administrators. Of course, married men and women were also susceptible. It is possible that the child Brown referred to belonged to Joseph Blake. In 1835, Blake wrote to colonization officials in the States that his wife had been seduced by the white ACS agent, Joseph Mechlin. Blake balked at the results of this affair; not only had Mechlin "left here for me to maintain a mulatto child," but the "criminal intercourse" between the governor and married woman included monetary gifts, which "made her haughty, insolent and disobedient to me [and] careless about my affairs." Blake sought compensation through the colonial officials by finding the father in the United States and securing restitution for the expenses involved in raising his child. Barring that, he requested a grant of land in order to build a shipyard, reestablishing his pecuniary resources as the family patriarch. Most intriguingly, Blake, in his listing the possibilities for his response as a wronged male head of household, explained to the board, "Had I killed the man in the night or day it would have been a stigma casted upon the colony." Clearly, Blake wanted to assert a claim to rightful violence on the white agent for disrupting and challenging his patriarchal place—indeed, one of the points of Liberia was to create black manhood through the colonizing mission—but his concerns for the colony's credibility prevented his actions. Violence against the white agent would hurt the image of the colony even as violence against black "savages" constituted a celebrated civilizing element.[29]

While the audience's assumptions that mixed-race children resulted from white officials' liaisons with black settlers reflected white masculine beliefs regarding the virtue of white womanhood and the licentiousness of black women, they also represented the reality of Liberian society in which white women were extremely uncommon and almost always the wives of missionaries. But a tantalizingly vague and undisclosed episode in Harper suggests the extent to which white and black could mingle in Liberia. Margaret McAllister was a single white woman about whom we know painfully little. She was apparently caught up in religious zeal and sought a missionary's life in Africa. The Baltimore Ladies' Society for Education in Africa subsequently hired her in 1835 to teach at their planned school in Maryland in Liberia, and she was in Africa before the close of the year. Although not officially attached to the MSCS, the society's agent, Hall, felt obliged to assist her in establishing her school. He initially attempted to have her board with the white missionary from South Carolina, J. Leighton Wilson, but

Wilson did not believe that he could accommodate another mouth at his mission station.

Thus, Hall wrote to the Board of the MSCS that he had procured a room and a nurse for her but made no mention of the specifics. McAllister was briefly mentioned in the Fourth Annual Report of the MSCS, penned January 15, 1836, roughly four months after her arrival in Harper. For the MSCS, McAllister, "a pious and benevolent lady of the M. E. [Methodist Episcopal] Church," was indicative of the progress that education and Christianity were enjoying in their little settlement. Right before publication of their report, the MSCS had received reports that McAllister was satisfied with the state of the colony, enjoyed good health, and was "comfortably accommodated in the house of one of the settlers." McAllister did not reside with Hall, Wilson, or any of the few white missionaries but rather with a "settler," a term reserved for the African American immigrants to Liberia, and one whose sex remained unidentified. Perhaps this was simply the room that Hall had arranged for her. Regardless of her dwelling, like so many other settlers, she would be dead in less than a year.[30]

And it was because of her early death that there is any record that something may have been amiss with the young woman. There should have been two colonial officials in Harper with medical training in 1836: the outgoing agent, Hall, and his replacement, Oliver Holmes, who had a dental practice in the United States. Unfortunately for McAllister, she took ill at the exact moment that Holmes was incapacitated with the African fever and Hall was away making his plans to return to the States. Additionally, a vessel filled with new emigrants arrived at the exact moment that McAllister took ill. Thus, McAllister's medical treatment fell into the hands of an overworked colonist, Joshua Stewart, who was William Polk's neighbor on Duncan Road. In Baltimore, Stewart had been a barber, tailor, and cooper, but he unfortunately possessed no medical training and had only the guidance of a feverish Holmes to assist him. Stewart misjudged the dosage and McAllister received a fatal quantity of mercury chloride. Her death at the hands of an unprepared colonist in a settlement greatly upset the missionary Wilson, a former slaveholder who was ill-disposed to see many settlers in a positive light.[31] While Wilson dispatched one letter outlining the tragic death of McAllister to a society official, he wrote a private letter to John H. B. Latrobe, the MSCS president. In a paragraph set aside as "inter nos" ("Between Ourselves"), Wilson strongly suggested that something was scandalous about McAllister.

And let me say (inter nos) do not consent again for a white woman in similar circumstances ever to come out in one of your vessels. The influence of enlightened xtian [Christian] females is much needed here, but when they come out unprotected they must encounter difficulties & have their influence contravened in ways & by means which neither they nor their friends can anticipate.[32]

This is the extent of Wilson's report about McAllister's actions in Liberia. Although the language is veiled, it does offer some suggestions about the nature of the scandal. In particular, the word "unprotected" has strong undertones of sexual predation. Whatever the relationship she held with the African American colonists, it was shockingly unanticipated and violated her "influence." This, combined with her peculiarly unspecified living arrangement with an undisclosed "settler," raises the possibility that McAllister did more than just reside with an African American. Obviously, Wilson found something about McAllister's presence in Liberia disconcerting enough to render a discreetly and vaguely worded letter as a "sacred" confidential report. Whatever the root of the scandal, the MSCS no longer accepted single white women as inhabitants in the colony, and the brief flash of the McAllister scandal faded from the record.

These disputes between newly freed and freeborn, Northerners and Southerners, light-skinned and dark-skinned, female and male not only reflected fractures within American society but also had practical real-world ramifications in Liberia as certain individuals arrived in the colony with greater economic support, a better network of acquaintances in the United States, and the literacy and racially ambiguous heritage to ensure promotion within the government. Given the advantages bestowed on individuals of mixed ancestry in Africa, it is little wonder that Harriet Beecher Stowe had her "mulatto" character George Harris immigrate to Liberia at the conclusion of *Uncle Tom's Cabin*. Such preferential treatment apparently led a few colonizationists to simply use the racial shorthand "are they black or mulatto?" when asking about the social status of certain individuals in Liberia.[33] Colonial Liberia, as the outpost of a semi-private society and thus lacking a national identity within itself, required a different identity to maintain societal cohesion in the face of so many disparate African nations surrounding its coastal settlements. Within European white settler societies, whiteness provided an adaptable identity with broad encompassing appeal, thus making it useful for colonial societies in which not every

European may have been an "Anglo-Saxon or "British." Whiteness was useful here at the boundaries of colonial society precisely because it was fluid, adaptable, and mobile.[34] Similarly, the whiteness, Americanness, and "civilization" of the Americo-Liberians provided a unifying identity around which to rally that at least offered some means to level this highly stratified society. Despite the relative advantages of certain settlers, they could all march forward against nonwhite, non-American, and "uncivilized" Africans while enjoying the fruits of those identities that were largely denied to them by the advantaged whites in the United States.

* * *

Russwurm encountered all of these fissures within his colonial outpost during the hungry and dry summer of 1838. Two sparks, one metaphorical and the other literal, set his settlement alight in late July. As he and "King Freeman" attempted to maintain peaceful relations amid the acrimonious thefts that month, a man from an interior town, Barrakah, walked along Maryland Avenue on the morning of July 24 accompanied by a sheep. Intending to trade the animal along with other goods at Harper, the Barrawe tragically encountered Eben Parker in his yard along the road. In his forties, the formerly enslaved Parker was the head of a farming household consisting of six other mouths in addition to his own and was in the position to know the quality of the animal and have many uses for it. He quickly purchased the sheep and the African continued on to Harper to conduct his trade. At some point later in the day, the Barrawe determined that Parker had cheated him and returned to the farm to demand the return of the sheep. Parker refused. The African walked into the yard to reclaim the animal; Parker walked into his house to grab his musket. Exiting his front door, Parker sighted the African as he left the farm and fired a round into the Barrawe's shoulder, wounding though not killing him. The gun's report sent Africans and Americans alike running, as everyone was especially tense during that long summer. The Africans joined in the Barrawe's outrage at being shot; the settlers commiserated with an angry Parker.

At that moment, Russwurm, "Freeman," and the Grebo leadership were engaged in negotiations at the Agency House, the seat of the colonial government, regarding the plague of burglaries. They were apparently unprepared for the arrival of a wounded man and his entourage. Russwurm dismissed the man after a brief interview, requesting that he return in the morning and "the palaver would be talked." With nightfall rapidly approaching, Russwurm ordered a colonial magistrate to arrest Parker and bring him before the colonial judiciary to explain his actions. This order was not completed, probably because, as Russwurm theorized, "Parker had threatened to shoot down any officer who should come on his premises for the purpose of arresting him." Relatives carried the Barrawe man to his home that night, and Russwurm was surprised to find both Parker free and the victim gone without justice. He reissued his arrest decree for Parker, this time with the new purpose of taking away his gun out of fear that he would shoot a civil officer of the colony.[35]

The second spark struck that night before Parker could be arrested. A cooking fire in Gbenelu set a thatch roof ablaze, and the conflagration spread and devoured most of the buildings. Such episodes usually sparked looting, and both African and American leaders were uninterested in providing additional opportunities to thieve. The colonial militia was once again called out to prevent lawlessness. Thus, when the pickets on the eastern edge of the settlement were approached by fifty Barrawe men, it should have aroused suspicion during those anxious hours. But when the officer in charge of the guard questioned the Africans' presence, they responded that they had simply come to see the destruction of Gbenelu. This apparently appeased the officer and he allowed the men to pass. Evidently, the wounded Barrawe had eschewed colonial justice to seek vengeance with disastrous results for the Parker family. The Barrawes repeated the journey of their kinsman and approached the Parker farm from Maryland Avenue. Parker, evidently in the yard, managed a rushed cry of warning to his wife in the house before he was cut down. His wife was able to escape out of the cabin's back window; two daughters were slain with their father in the yard. The Barrawes robbed the house before setting it on fire and fleeing into the countryside surrounding the small agricultural village.[36]

Charles Snetter, a freeborn man originally from Charleston, South Carolina, responded to the commotion with a group of militiamen under his command. Snetter had immigrated to Monrovia in 1832 and moved down the coast to Maryland in Liberia in 1836. He possessed a forceful character and had been commissioned an assistant agent by outgoing governor James Hall, before quarreling with Hall's briefly tenured replacement, Oliver Holmes, and then outright refusing to accept his demotion to storekeeper by incoming-governor Russwurm. He found employment with missionary Wilson while nursing his grudges against the colonial administration even as he retained his officer position within the colony's military structure; he was regarded, in fact, as one of the leading military minds among the settler ranks. The divide between Snetter and the administration deepened when the brig *Baltimore* arrived on July 4, 1837. A fourteen-year-old boy had stowed away and was not discovered until the vessel was out to sea. Evidently, there was confusion over whether the young man of color was free or enslaved, but the fearful captain was determined to return the youth to America lest he be charged in the loss of property. The boy, however, stole a boat and slipped ashore. American slavery splashed ashore in Liberia in a very real sense when the captain and crew went looking to reclaim the runaway.[37]

The sailors found the lad, bound him, and returned him to the vessel; many settlers were understandably perturbed and frustrated at the unwillingness of their assistant agent, George McGill (Russwurm being absent in Monrovia), to stop the manhunt. Magistrate and former vice-agent Thomas Jackson joined with the colonial administration in finding the results an unfortunate legal necessity: "The said boy has been delivered to the captain as we have no claim to him as greveous as it is we can but act in according with natural laws we trust in so doing we shall do justice to our selves and to our friends." Snetter, and many other settlers, arrived at a different conclusion. Writing to the MSCS Board of Managers, Snetter argued that as the laws of the colony forbade slavery, the boy was free after he "landed safe on this sand, which you have proclaimed to be of liberty." If fugitives could be chained and brought back to the States with a complicit administration, then the current situation made Liberia no better than the northern United States. Despite Snetter's angst and tearful tirades on the shore, to which he claimed the acting agent responded by "laughing at my weakness," the stowaway was returned to the ship. Snetter concluded the account with the promise, "I will remain untill no longer then freedom is maintained." Snetter was a lightning rod of a colonist, emotional and rash with a martial talent and equally gifted at inciting other settlers and angering administration officials. And he and his soldiers were the earliest responders to the Parker farm.[38]

Arriving at the scene of devastation, Snetter and his men spied a group of Grebo men and boys, at least one of whom carried a musket. Although they were Greboes returning from their outlying farms to see the destruction of their homes and not Barrawes, they were seized upon by the settlers, who were in no mood to differentiate between Africans. In a complete mirror image of white responses to supposed slave rebellions in the United States, a mob formed denouncing the innocent Greboes as the murderers; at that moment, any African would do to serve as the culprit. Snetter ordered the Greboes to march in front of his men. Apparently, the arrival of another band of militiamen proved too much for the fractured nerves of the Greboes; they made a run for the thicket along the settlement's edge. A hail of bullets followed in their wake, killing one and mortally wounding two. Initially, Russwurm was disposed to attribute the affair as an accident spurred by the anxiety-inducing setting. In the coming days, however, he sensed something far more sinister in Snetter's actions.[39]

In the weeks following the shooting of the Cape Palmas Africans, the militia continued to maintain its nightly vigilance. Curiously, on those nights in which Snetter commanded the watch at Mount Tubman, the easternmost colonial stronghold, Greboes reported multiple thefts of their cattle. Rumors spread of the Tubman family and guests at Mount Tubman dining on steak in the midst of famine; more intriguingly, Snetter, who dined with them, supposedly ate only rice and eschewed the beef. There seems to have been some suggestion that Snetter's culinary decisions stemmed from his desire to distance himself from the incriminating meal. Russwurm questioned Snetter, who denied the accusations. In the wake of the interrogations, Snetter supposedly gathered a group of settlers sympathetic to his vision of the colony and read the eighth chapter of the book of Joshua, which describes the Israelites' capture of the Canaanite city of Ai and begins with God's promise: "See, I have given into thy hand the king of Ai, and his people, and his city, and his land." "Freeman" was irate at the loss of cattle his people were suffering, as bullocks functioned as currency and trade goods for the Grebo economy and society.[40]

By August, Russwurm had had enough of both Snetter and "Freeman." He became increasingly suspicious that the "accidental" shooting of the Cape Palmas Africans actually reflected a long-standing and very intentional campaign of violence. He called together the colony's administration into a court of inquiry to investigate Snetter's behavior, a nebulous body not entirely established within the legal framework of the colony. Maryland in Liberia could ill afford a war with the Africans living literally in the middle of its settlement, and Russwurm was more interested in projecting power into the interior, an expedition that would require aid from "Freeman." Hence, the ten-man board of inquiry included both himself and those settlers either most loyal to Russwurm or most protective of Africans' rights. They concluded that Snetter had ordered the execution of the fleeing Greboes, although the confusion of the moment ameliorated his guilt. They turned the matter over to Russwurm for adjudication. To maintain order, Russwurm needed Snetter gone, but the colonist remained popular with many of the settlers. Rather than punish the quarrelsome officer,

Russwurm decided that removing him from the colony was the safest avenue. Despite this verdict, rampant rumors ran the length of Maryland Avenue that Russwurm planned to turn Snetter over to the Africans for execution, fueled, according to Russwurm, by Snetter and vice agent Anthony Wood. Provoked colonists flocked to Snetter's cause and set their grievances in writing. The governor was also under fire from his African neighbors, "Freeman" in particular, who likewise provoked Russwurm by challenging the governor's racial categorization. Writing on August 31, 1838, Russwurm fumed to the Board of Managers, "King Freeman having received his lesson from some quarter, has thrown it in my teeth that I am not a proper man for Governor—meaning that I am not a proper white man." In light of this loss of whiteness and beset by settler and African alike, Russwurm tendered his resignation.[41]

There are fascinating racial politics in this simple sentence attributed to "Freeman." For starters, Russwurm suspects that "Freeman" "received his lesson from some other quarter," but he suggests no culprits. Through Russwurm's eyes, "Freeman" equated whiteness with the ability to control the state. When he first arrived as colonial governor, Russwurm had originally suspected that Freeman did not register Russwurm as equivalent to a Euro-American, but in the intervening years the two had established a working relationship without cause to question Russwurm's race. Only at the moment in which his colony was on the verge of war with its neighbors and of his personal failure to protect Grebo property did "Freeman" challenge Russwurm's fitness to govern. What is really intriguing about Russwurm's wording is that he inserted the racialized language on behalf of "Freeman." Freeman supposedly only claimed Russwurm was not a "proper" man; it was Russwurm who extrapolated that that meant he was not a "proper white man." That definition, however, did not resonate with Liberian understandings of whiteness based upon western culture. This, then, may reflect the significance of "Freeman" receiving a "lesson from some quarter." Perhaps that "lesson" was in alternative definitions of whiteness from an American context. Or, more likely, Russwurm, so used to assuming that the whiteness granted to the African American settlers reflected the deference of Africans, simply also assumed that a loss of propriety would likewise lead to a loss of whiteness.

The board refused Russwurm's proffered resignation, affirmed their trust in the man, and denied any interest in turning over the colony to a Euro-American officer. The board presented an understanding of whiteness rooted in the American context even as they grappled with and pondered the African definitions of whiteness in the Liberian colonies. They assumed that "Freeman" and others were calling for a "white" governor as Americans understood the term, ignoring the complexity of the situation rendered by African definitions of the word.

This is especially odd given that the board was intimately aware of those African definitions. For example, one year before the Snetter incident, Moses Sheppard's letter to settler William Polk apparently so resonated with the white MSCS leadership that it was inscribed in the official MSCS letter book. In the far-ranging epistle, Sheppard confessed, "I am pleased with the meaning the native Africans give to the term 'white man' they make these words refer to intelligence rather than colour, the construction is a good one for knowledge is the same in all. minds [sic] as far as we know do not differ in complexion." The colonizationists clearly understood racial constructions in their West African colony, but they answered Russwurm's query in the form of American notions of whiteness. Convinced that they need only address their disgruntled agent in the form of American whiteness, they then reinforced the Atlantic nature of their project by reassuring him that "on this side of the atlantic you are acquiring a reputation which grows with the character of the colony." There is an implicit duality to Russwurm, and all Liberian settlers vicariously, here: with the expansion of power and prestige in the colonies came concomitant metaphorical power and prestige in the United States. The pathways to Liberia were not one-way streets, and the colonial space resided in the minds of Americans as much as it existed on a map or on the ground through force of arms. And to secure that power within the Atlantic world, all parties—African, settler, American—were willing to use force.[42]

Russwurm's efforts to appease the Africans within his colony did not go unappreciated by the majority of the rank and file settlers, who almost immediately after the announcement of Snetter's banishment banded together to protest the governor's actions. In many regards, the freeborn Snetter, a Charlestonian from the Deep South privileged with government patronage before Russwurm's arrival, was unrepresentative of Maryland in Liberia's settlers. But Russwurm's verdict struck a nerve with many outside his administration, and they nominated a committee of five men to voice their grievances. Betraying their enslaved pasts, several members could not sign their own names to the resulting document. But they found common cause with the elite Snetter in their opposition to Russwurm's pacific ways (at least pacific toward "Freeman," if not necessarily toward all Africans universally) and a shared commitment to masculine violence. They considered

Russwurm's move against Snetter "the first move to give the lives of our wives and Children into the hands of the Savages around us who thirsts for our Blood." To sacrifice the man whom they considered the best military mind in the colony would be "to oblige this savage ["Freeman" and the Greboes] who sirround us [and] . . . to be deprived of our Right Eye and then to lay down and die."[43] Surrounded and isolated among those whom they considered heathen, the fifty-six male signatories located manhood in their ability to protect their families against African violence. Clearly, the Parker family murder weighed heavily on their minds, and signatories like the formerly enslaved Maryland carpenter Ambrose Simpson and the freeborn North Carolinian Anthony Howard could join together in their violent efforts to tame and check the savagery that they believed threatened to swallow them whole.

Of course, the whole Atlantic world was in motion. As Russwurm tackled African whiteness and his settlers asserted their right to march against savagery, the colonization officials based in the United States likewise contemplated the recent violence within its settlement. The MSCS's response to the Snetter affair highlights the Afrocentric variations within colonizationist thought. While many white colonizationists conflated African with African American, the MSCS recognized differences in the "civilization" of the two groups but stubbornly refused to believe that race would divide the groups despite their awareness of African whiteness. In a response to a missionary desiring to know the official stance of the MSCS in regard to the Africans living within its colony, the MSCS reported, "Our wish is to raise them [the Africans] to the standard of civilization and to amalgamate them with the colonists." They took comfort from the "conviction on the part of king freeman, that the laws of the Americans, as the natives call the colonists, were better than the native laws."[44] The choice of "amalgamation" is intriguing; that was also the word Horatio Bridge used to describe settler/African relations. The reference to the African use of "American" to denote the settlers likewise highlights colonizationists' difficulty in establishing African American origins. To concede that the settlers were inherently American rather than to quantify the term as an African lexicon would jeopardize a foundational argument for colonization, and yet they also separated African from African American by highlighting the need for the two bodies to "amalgamate." The Liberian settlers somehow simultaneously straddle both Africa and America without ever touching either fully, encapsulated in a watery Atlantic.

Needless to say, the Snetter affair and the response of the settlers to

Russwurm's actions jarred MSCS leaders, who were somehow surprised at "the disposition of the colonists to ill treat the natives," despite the fact that colonial Liberia from its earliest days had been the site of consistent and constant violence between settler and African. The MSCS discussed solutions to this problem, and, ironically, for a body of men surprised to find such brutality in their planned Arcadia, arrived at the conclusion "that our *Executive* must have power; and 'power' is here used to mean *the power of armed men.*" To force peace upon the warring factions, the Marylanders proposed the creation of a "police guard," a military force answerable only to the governor as a counterbalance to the colonial militia. If the settlers and Africans would not "amalgamate" properly, then "armed men" would force them to. Much as free people of color were singled out as "negative influences" upon the enslaved by many white people within the United States, so too did the MSCS leadership seem to suspect that freeborn elites like Snetter were leading their formerly enslaved comrades astray. The "police guard" was designed to put "*it out of the power of evil designed men to create disturbances by imposing upon the ignorant.*" They attributed the settlers' petition regarding Snetter's sentence as a result of these designs rather than a competing affirmation of settlers' power and elevated place in the Atlantic world through their masculine colonizing spirit and willingness to protect women from savages. Knowing that the new executive's military might would be unpopular with the settlers, the MSCS recommended installing the police guard gradually, first by detailing a "night watchman" along Maryland Avenue to prevent African thefts, a move that would be popular with the settlers, and then by gradually growing the force into the guard. Further reinforcing that they understood the temperament of their settlers, the MSCS also ordered Russwurm to keep the matter private. Needless to say, Russwurm was pleased with the idea and noted that the other diasporic colonies along the coast—Monrovia and Sierra Leone—had employed similar institutions.[45]

* * *

Russwurm never received his police guard, as the funding could never be sufficiently secured to operate two military apparatuses in the colony (the guard and the militia) and the settlers did not receive the affirmation of their masculine right to violently oppose savagery or keep Snetter in their military apparatus. In January 1839, Snetter sailed for Monrovia and ACS governance. The ACS was far more comfortable in using every means available to tame the surrounding "savages" and promptly placed Snetter in command of the rifle company formed in the wake of the Bassa Cove massacre.

The newly appointed governor in Monrovia, Thomas Buchanan, a cousin of future American president James Buchanan, was forged in the same mold as Snetter and proved immediately willing to use force to bring the coast under Liberian control. While the territory around Little Bassa, a region lying between Monrovia and the site of the failed Pennsylvania–New York joint venture at Grand Bassa, had a complicated legal history and the ACS was unsure whether they held legitimate claim to the land, they *did* claim "jurisdiction over the territory along the seaboard, *as to foreigners especially.*" Before Buchanan's arrival in 1839, acting governor and settler Anthony Williams had already ordered away a slave trader operating in the area who refused to go; the trader was soon joined by an Englishman engaged in "regular trade." Buchanan determined to uphold the "rights of the Colony at all hazards." On July 18, less than five months after his arrival, the governor ordered a military parade and asked for forty volunteers to proceed immediately to Little Bassa to assert Liberian control. With his number of Americo-Liberian volunteers "more than complete," the governor asked for twenty-five Congo volunteers from New Georgia. Thirty-five recaptured Africans answered the call. The expeditionary force of roughly one hundred men was placed under the command of Elijah Johnson, a veteran from the first defense of Monrovia nearly two decades before, while a "fleet" of three schooners sailed with ammunition to resupply the land force if necessary. In the meantime, Buchanan ordered the colony's marshal, William N. Lewis, to proceed immediately to the slave trader's outpost, place him and his family under guard, seize all moveable property and place it aboard the schooners to relocate, liberate all enslaved persons held there, and then repeat for the English trading post so that "all the white men may be either driven *down* or *up* the coast, so that they are got rid of." Essentially, Buchanan hoped that Lewis would peacefully evict the traders from Little Bassa by giving him the negotiating tool of Johnson's slowly approaching force. This tactic of sending peaceful commissioners ahead of a lumbering violent menace had a history in Liberia and would become Buchanan's favored approach.[46]

It seems that while Lewis and Johnson were able to apprehend three Europeans at the slave barracoon without violence, the neighboring African villages under "Prince" and "Bah Gray" were not anxious to see the departure of their trading partners. Their combined assault led to the odd sight of the Americo-Liberian and recaptive Africans defending the slave barracoon—which they quickly renamed "Fort Victory"—while Bassas fired at them from neighboring forests. Buchanan and his fleet arrived from Monrovia and ordered the accompanying Kru to begin loading the property from the factories aboard the vessels while the battle raged around them. Buchanan's report possesses that curious distinction of command in which all activity is singularly ascribed to the governor's martial command—"I ordered the Kroomen . . ."; "I now ordered the houses without the palisade to be destroyed"; "I then directed . . . to . . . make a sally"—while all of the work is conducted by others; the Kru moved the goods, and the ubiquitous Elijah Johnson led the repeated assaults to clear the woods surrounding "Fort Victory" and was wounded twice in the effort. The end result of the battle was a treaty signed by "Bah Gray" in which he promised peace and conceded "supreme jurisdiction" of his territory to the Commonwealth of Liberia, as well as promised to stop participating in the slave trade and to pay for damages from the battle.[47]

The decision to sign a treaty with the Americo-Liberians put "Bah Gray" at odds with neighboring Africans. By January 1845, he was forced to write to Monrovia for assistance. The colonial council recorded that "the chiefs of the country had done and is now doing all in their power [to] destroy him and his people" and requested that the governor appoint two commissioners to proceed to Little Bassa. The commissioners were to meet with the enemies of their own enemy-turned-ally and "in as peaceable manner as circumstances will admit of" project colonial authority by asserting that the Liberian settlers would interpret any aggression against "Bah Gray" as aggression against the colony itself. Using their single treaty with "Gray" to establish broader jurisdictional claims, the colonial council also advised the Africans of Little Bassa that disputes with any Africans allied with the colony would require judgment from "proper authorities," namely, the colonial government. The Americo-Liberians were squeezing as much leverage out of the treaty with "Gray" as they could, and they clearly hoped to capitalize on it, as their final instruction to the governor was to purchase the territory around Little Bassa. This is a perfect example of how the decentralized and stateless nature of the indigenous African societies along the Liberian coast helped the weak colonies gain ever growing footholds along the coast.[48]

In his orders to Johnson during the first expedition to Little Bassa, Governor Buchanan had dictated that any disobedience from the soldiery should be swiftly punished. "But I am not willing to anticipate the smallest difficulty from such a base spirit," the governor noted, as assuredly "those who have so generously volunteered in the service of their country will do their duty like men, and do honor by their acts ... to the name they bear as citizens—soldiers of Liberia." It was not recorded whether Charles Snetter was among the volunteers for the Little Bassa expedition, but certainly those words would have been sweet music to his ears.[49]

Also in the same year that Snetter and Buchanan arrived in Monrovia, missionary George Brown established the Heddington mission station in the African interior northeast of the colonial capital. This eastward expansion from the coast brought the colony into conflict with an African leader, Getumbe, often spelled "Gay Toombay" by the settlers, who gathered a multiethnic coalition of natives to assault the isolated mission post in 1840. This assault pitted hundreds of natives against an American mission defended by Brown and two Americo-Liberian craftsmen, Sion Harris and Bennet Demery, employed in constructing the mission, Harris's wife, Martha, who was employed as a teacher, and two African students of the mission school. Additionally, the neighboring village upon which the Methodist station grafted itself likewise opposed "Gay Toombay's" martial airs. At daybreak on March 7, this small band found themselves surrounded by several hundred Africans led by a fierce Loma warrior named "Gotorah" or "Goterah." Fortunately, what the Americo-Liberians and their allies lacked in numbers, they more than made up for in available weaponry, as the defenders possessed between twenty to thirty muskets, which were constantly reloaded by Martha Harris. In the ensuing melee, "Zoda" and "Nicky," the two African schoolboys, were wounded, but Harris succeeded in killing "Gotorah," an act that threw the attackers into confusion and retreat.[50]

The subtle differences between Harris's account of the defense of Heddington, the official report of the governor published in the *African Repository*, and the edited version of Harris's letter also published in the *Repository* highlight the differing views of the colonial space and the violence it held.[51] In Harris's original account, the survival of the mission hinged upon the early warning of the assault from the neighboring African village: "I had hardly got down before I heard a gun fire at a half town[52] a mile off. I arose quickly & got to the window.... At that moment I head [heard] a voic crying war! war! is come, which appeared proved to be a woman and man from the half town." Governor Thomas Buchanan likewise considered the mission's survival to be the result of "the most signal interposition of Providence" but located that divine signal less in African warnings and more in his own good sense to supply the mission with muskets. Harris's account is, in fact, riddled with references to African allies engaged in the fighting beyond the mission's gate. Having sent two mission students into the village to ascertain the state of affairs, Harris reported that "by the time the boys got back crying war several picked up muskets and ran, the Headman with them at this I cried, if they did [not] bring back the guns, I wold shoot them, at this 4 only returned." What the four returnees did during this time went unrecorded, but "one of the four natives that stoped in town came in shot, by name Baker, and said Dady look, his bowels was out—and he left his gun by me." Clearly, "Baker" was engaged in the fighting elsewhere and it was with his loaded weapon, fortuitously dropped by Harris's side at the exact moment that "Gotorah" personally charged him, that killed the Loma chief. "Zoda" and "Nicky," presumably the two boys dispatched to the villages, fired from the upstairs window until both were shot. The two children were more engaged in the defense of the mission house than Brown was, according to Harris. Additionally, at the close of the battle "one of the two remaining country men" fired at a charging African in the mission yard.

In contrast to Harris's account, the governor's report largely removes these African allies in favor of an entirely American defense force: Brown, the Harrises, and Demery. The only point at which it was necessary to concede an African presence, the apparently disemboweled "Baker" who had somehow arrived at the mission with a loaded musket for Harris, was minimized in favor of making Harris larger than life. "GOTORAH made a desperate rush upon them, at the head of his best warriors. . . . HARRIS stood alone." His weapon discharged without time to reload as "Gotorah" rushed toward, the desperate Harris reached behind him to seize an axe and, instead, "struck a gun, which the moment before had been placed there by a wounded native of the town." The defense of the mission devolved into single combat between two warriors, akin to David and Goliath, accentuated by the printer's font choices and capitalization of the principal actors.[53]

Buchanan summed up the African allies of the Liberians in two sentences: "A few of BLACK TOM'S people behaved well in the battle, but they contributed very little to the result. Two of them were wounded, one of whom died the same day." In this war against "savages," Buchanan was uninterested in African heroes. Conversely, the ACS was also uninterested in turning their settlers into savages. Like many letters received by the ACS and subsequently published by them, Harris's printed account received a heavy dose of editing. While these white editors only occasionally altered wording (usually to fix grammatical errors), they were particularly adept at omitting damning information. Harris's original account details the shooting of Gotorah: "I took deliberate aim at him . . . and brought him to the ground cut off his knee shot him in the lungs, and cut off his privates." The line suggesting the mutilation of the African leader's genitalia is omitted from the *Repository*'s extracts and, indeed, can only be guessed at with modern eyes due to the editor's thick black line of ink striking through that final phrase.[54]

Conceiving of colonial Liberia as a civilizing space for both settler and African, the editors could rejoice in the murder of an unabashed "savage" described to readers as "the ferocious cannibal, GOTORAH, who had brought his pot for the purpose of cooking his breakfast of MR. BROWN," but the agents of this civilization, the settlers like Harris, could not be presented in the same uncivilized light by defacing the body of a fallen enemy. Equally intriguing, the body of "Gotorah" was removed some fifteen or twenty miles away from Heddington by the retreating army. Harris received this report from "fifteen of King Governor's men followed them ["Toombay's" retreating army] and found Goterah. . . . They returned about sundown, and wanted a head-man to go and cut of his head, they being common men would not." The arrival of fifteen "Americans" from Caldwell signaled the beginning of relief for Heddington, and luckily among the "Americans" was a Congo, "Zodaquee," who was perceived by his peers to be of high rank. It was actually this survivor of the Atlantic slave trade, relocated to Liberia, who collected the head of "Gotorah." The governor's report likewise did not expand upon these African contributions.[55]

"Gotorah's" skull seems to have had a strange journey after being separated from its body. After resting on a spike outside the mission as a warning against further attacks, the skull came into the possession of Dr. S.M.E. Goheen of the Methodist mission in Liberia. The preeminent collector of American skulls, Samuel George Morton, had written Ezekiel Skinner in 1835 that his collection lacked African subjects. Five years later, Goheen dispatched five skulls, including "Gotorah's," of warriors who fell attacking Heddington to find a place among Morton's growing cabinet of skulls in his Philadelphia study. Curiously, Morton cataloged the skull "1093, Golah Negro, warrior." Heddington mission lay outside Gola territory, and "Gotorah" is usually described as a Loma chief allied with the Condo confederacy, all interior peoples. Morton's expansive collection and his measurements of each skull for its respective cranial capacity launched the American obsession with craniometry and what has since been termed "scientific racism." Given the colonizing and "civilizing" rhetoric surrounding Liberia and its significance within American discourse, it is unsurprising that Morton sought assistance there in adding to his collection. It is perversely ironic, however, that Liberia, a space actively warping and shaping race and doing so in a blatantly observable manner, would play a not insubstantial role in the claims that racial difference was based upon biology and was scientifically observable. To further complicate matters, Morton also received the skull of a Bassa man executed for "committing some crime he was tried by the ordeal of drinking *red-wood water,* and found guilty, was cut in pieces, and thrown into the St. John's river, Grand Bassa."

The source of the Bassa skull was "Dr. Robert McDowell," who was almost certainly Dr. Robert McDowall, an Afro-Scottish physician in Liberia. McDowall found Liberia's racial ambiguity useful in his professional career and rarely identified himself in anything but professional terms in his writings (a practice that would result in a brief conflict with ACS officials, as detailed in chapter 5). It is likely that Morton received the gift of the Bassa skull without any idea that the sender was himself a racially ambiguous man. In many ways, the image of Dr. Morton carefully measuring the cranial capacity of the accused-witch to scientifically prove the intellectual inferiority of the "negro race" while remaining blissfully unaware that his work was being supported by a doctor of African descent who was intentionally manipulating the racial ambiguities of the mobile Atlantic was precisely what settlers like the McGills, Russwurms, and McDowalls envisioned for Liberia.[56]

Buchanan and the ACS also did not feel a need to establish a feminine hero, as the part taken by Martha Harris faded into the background of the raging battle between Harris and Demery, an "elegant marksman," and hundreds of oncoming savages. This was the ultimate example of masculine colonization, and the ACS celebrated the remarkable account of manly settlers defending both women and schoolchildren while downplaying the contributions of those women and children. Harris himself seemed to enjoy the results of his labors, reporting that after the battle "the natives came and licked my feet, said I had gree gree, and asked me for some. I told them I had none but what god gave me." This is a remarkable image of colonialism; the Christian settler, armed only with God's patronage, surrounded by groveling natives licking his feet in wonderment.[57]

The ACS lacked the Maryland society's ardent desires to maintain pacific settler-African relations. In light of the Heddington attack, Governor Buchanan reported on the relative confusion in determining the nature of the force opposed to the American settlements: "I found it quite impossible to gather any information of the enemy's movements or his forces." In this absence of information regarding the strength, size, and cohesion of "Toombay's" coalition, the ACS governor decided on a show of force and organized an expedition of three hundred men to attack "Toombay's" town and remove the irksome African from his seat of power. Of those three hundred men, sixty were the omnipresent Kru performing their usual task: carrying the army's baggage. Buchanan conceded that forty more soldiers were native allies, but he immediately belittled their contributions, noting that they "proved, instead of being useful, the greatest burden." At least one-third, then, of this "American" army proved to actually be African in origin.[58]

Marching toward "Toombay's" town, Buchanan associated the wild and savage forest—the antithesis of the mapped and orderly agricultural settlements of the Americans—with the uncivilized African. Clearly, the image of the uncultivated forest as the den of savagery was an old trope echoing the settlement of "wild" North America by the early colonists, and it had been employed from Liberia's earliest days. Given the rhetorical flourish in making Monrovia a parallel experience with Jamestown or Plymouth, it would seem easy to slot Africans into the roles of American Indians. And this was occasionally done, such as when the *African Repository* reprinted a British account of war in Sierra Leone that described Africans as moving through the woods in "Indian file" or in reports that the Berber language "bear[s] a strong analogy to those of our American Indians, particularly in the formation of compound verbs." Framing indigenous Africans as indigenous Americans was problematized, however, by the rhetoric that African American relocation to Africa would be a homecoming. As one colonizationist framed the advantages of Liberia over Jamestown, early English settlers were "almost entirely exterminated by their Indian enemies. But the African emigrant returns to the land of his fathers, and finds not only a climate congenial with his nature, but a people, with whom, in the process of time, he of necessity will become completely identified." While early American history provided colonizationists with an established language to justify and explain their colonial conflicts, they were largely unwilling to fully equate Bassa with Powhatan and weaken the claims that this colony, unlike Virginia or Massachusetts, would be a homecoming for the settlers.[59]

In his history of the first years of Monrovia, Jehudi Ashmun borrowed from this treasury of early American imagery and described an outpost surrounded by a dense forest chocked with undergrowth "so as to be nearly impracticable by any but the feet of savages." Ashmun described the

African tactic of disappearing into the forest to reload their weapons before reemerging to fire a single blast and then retiring into their sylvan refuge as a "mockery of ordinary warfare."[60] It was during this "mockery of ordinary warfare," namely, the hours of fighting in the jungle during the slow advance on "Toombay's" town, that Charles Snetter fell mortally wounded while leading the rifle company, "but his men rushed gallantly forward and dislodged the savages so quick that the march of the line was scarcely checked." Buchanan's report spotlights the various high-ranking colonial officials who were conspicuous in the destruction of "Toombay's" town.[61]

Always prefaced with their military rank: "General Roberts" (Joseph Jenkins Roberts) led the assault that captured the town; "Col. Wm. Lewis" served as the governor's aide and displayed conspicuous gallantry; "Captain Charles Johnson, of the artillery" and "Lieut. Richardson, of the Rifle Corps" were seriously wounded. All of the wounded, including the unnamed rank and file, "fell in the front rank, with theirs faces to the foe, fighting bravely!" The "savages" were defeated, although "the blood of the murdered WILSON and PEALE [two colonists who were executed by "Toombay"] still cries for justice," and the settlers had performed the deed with manly fortitude despite being burdened by what their governor would have his audience believe were the great weights of African allies. The report briefly deviated from martial affairs to discuss the economic exports of the colony before continuing on with a request for more weapons, blue cloth for officers' uniforms, another type of material to distinguish the rifle corps, and "additional articles for a *Liberia uniform* for our volunteer companies." The postscript of the report noted the need for a battle flag for the colonial military, preferably of silk, with the Liberian coat of arms, and perhaps also an eagle, near a palm tree and the sun rising over the whole scene. The governor seemed to have recognized that his flag design was a bit cluttered and addended, "or these objects arranged in some other way to accord with correct heraldic taste." Buchanan noted that the need for a military standard "may seem a trifle; but the lives of individuals and nations are made up of trifles, and we are all more influenced by small things than great ones."[62]

This may be an apt summation of colonial Liberia: a series of small things that added up to great ones. The military coat, a silk battle flag, the ability to write back to the United States about your manly stand against savagery: all of these elements were designed to elevate the settlers into the roles of masculine tamers of the African wilderness, much as the European descendants of white colonizationists believed their forefathers tamed the American wilderness. The possibilities for martial glory were one of the first lessons for male settlers. Such was the case for Joshua Stewart, the colonist who administered the lethal dose to Margaret McAllister; the first letter he wrote upon arriving in Africa's Maryland concluded with the signature "Joshua Stewart, First Sergeant of the Military[,] I have 45 men under my charge." The poignancy of that conclusion is all the more fortified by the fact that the letter was written to his mother's enslaver with the request that he pass on information of Stewart's respective health. There is obvious pride in Stewart's letter as he finalizes the text with his "respects to all the rest of your servants," before reaffirming his newly acquired rank and his own respective charges.63 Stewart understood the significance of his military rank and what claims it allowed him make on American audiences from his first moment in Liberia; he was not alone in drawing these conclusions after donning a Liberian uniform.

And for his own part, Buchanan was at least promised that flag he coveted. "I had the pleasure, on the last field day, of reading the complimentary resolution of the board to the assembled regiment," he reported in late 1840, "and also took occasion to inform them that, in consequence of their gallant and brave conduct, you had promised to present them with a standard." The assembled troops were apparently "highly satisfied." Buchanan trusted that along with the new battle flag, "rifles, brass cannon, and military equipments will be sent." Perhaps growing tired of waiting for heraldic experts to arrange all of the elements of the governor's banner, a "lady" of Monrovia produced a flag for Beverly Yates's company of volunteers with the simple motto "Forward" emblazoned on it. In a brief snippet titled "THE WAY THINGS ARE DONE IN LIBERIA," the *African Repository* quoted the *Liberia Herald*'s description of the ceremony surrounding the presentation of the flag. "The flag was made and presented in person, by a lady of this place. While mothers of such military spirit are found in Liberia, we cannot wonder at the prompt capture of Gay Toomba's town, nor need we fear in future, any Liberian will obey other than the watchword, 'forward,' to glory and victory."64

* * *

Buchanan's martial glory after Heddington reminded at least one colonist of the earliest days of the settlement when it first engaged in wars for its very existence. The clerk of the court, William W. Stewart (no apparent relation to Joshua), who arrived in Monrovia in February 1824 from his hometown of Petersburg, Virginia, aboard the *Cyrus*, praised Buchanan's efforts at reinvigorating the Liberian military to the martial glory it gained in the first defense of Monrovia. Even before the successful assault on "Toombay's" town, Stewart wrote, "Governor Buchanan a Gentlemen an lauded one, yes, for he puts me in mind of our General and Governor J. Ashmun that use to lead us to Battle and victory."[65]

Jehudi Ashmun had arrived in the infant colony of Liberia in 1822 at the head of an expedition of colonists and "recaptives." Ashmun nominally arrived in the colony as an agent for the U.S. government in charge of these recent victims of the illegal slave trade instead of as an agent of the ACS's operation. Soon after arriving in Monrovia, however, he was placed in charge of the government's recaptives and colony. The colonial beachhead had been established in December 1821 after ACS agent Eli Ayres and Navy Lieutenant Robert F. Stockton of the USS *Alligator* compelled local African leaders, "King Peter" being the most prominent, to cede Cape Mesurado. After establishing the foundations of the settlement at Cape Mesurado, Ayres departed for the United States to personally report on the colony's many wants, leaving Elijah Johnson in charge of the colonial outpost.[66]

At its sixth annual meeting held on February 20, 1823, in Washington, D.C., the ACS leadership held little fear of the disruption their infant colony might have had in African lives. They were pleased that a town had been initiated on "a regular plan" and "works thrown up for defence against the Barbarian powers." Despite the need for defenses against savages, the ACS remained unworried. "The natives are generally amicable," the Board of Managers informed their membership, "and were it otherwise, little apprehension would be felt, since a concerted attack is altogether improbable, and each King can command but a small force, destitute alike of conduct and courage."[67] Of course, little did the board know that four months previously their infant colony had suffered a concerted attack from the neighboring Vai, Dei, and Gola on November 11, 1822.

In his account of the earliest days of the colony, Ashmun claimed to present an accurate representation of the African war councils that preceded their attack on Monrovia. In one council of African "kings," "Peter" and "Bristol" opposed the assault because of the growing numbers of settlers—the colony at this moment numbered less than one hundred souls—and also because the colony was "not a settlement of foreigners and enemies, but of their countrymen and friends, as was proved by the identity of their colour." The supposedly authentic African voice in Ashmun's tale does not resonate with other Liberian African constructions of the settlers' identity. Perhaps the ACS agent suffered from wishful thinking, as such sentiments echoed the rhetoric of the colonizationists. Conversely, Ashmun frames these African voices as a minority opinion within the council of war. He explained, "Kings George, Governor, and all the other head-men of the tribe, contended that 'The Americans were strangers who had forgot their attachment to the land of their fathers; for if not, why had they not renounced their connexion with white men altogether, and placed themselves under the protection of the kings of the country?'" This contention perfectly reflected the opinions of most of the Liberians' African neighbors; an association with the cultural practices and maintaining their governance through the United States meant that these newly arrived settlers were neither countrymen nor necessarily "black" as they understood it. They were, in fact, "strangers." In his response to these African martial councils, Ashmun not only demonstrated a superb understanding of the racial structures in his new home but also reinforced them. Utilizing a neutral African as courier, Ashmun sent word to the African confederacy arrayed against the colony: "If they proceeded to bring war upon the Americans ... they would dearly learn what it was to fight white men."[68]

This fascinating message reveals how quickly Ashmun adapted to local customs. After but a month's residence in West Africa, he was describing the African American settlers in terms difficult to claim in the United States, "American" and "white." Surrounded by "savages," Ashmun—the only "white man" in the colony as he would have conceptualized it—evoked the identities, one racial and the other national, that could only be claimed outside the boundaries of the United States. For his assuredly confused readers, Ashmun provided an explanatory footnote to clarify that "white" denoted "a phrase by which civilized people of all colours and nations are distinguished in the dialect of the coast." Thus, with the wave of a seemingly magic wand, the newly arrived free people of color instantly became "civilized people," and white to boot.

Further complicating Ashmun's declaration that the Africans would soon fight white men was the enrollment of thirteen "African youths" of indeterminate young age from among Ashmun's expedition of recaptives into the "lieutenant's corps" for military drilling. Attacking Africans, then, faced not only "white" African Americans but also "white" African survivors of the illegal transatlantic slave trade. Did their relatively brief residence in the United States before arriving in Liberia place them on an accelerated trajectory akin to the African American settlers? Did mere loyalty to the colonial administration and residence in that space assure them a place among the ranks of "civilized peoples of all colours and nations" despite their African origins? Ashmun did not pause in his account of martial glory to ponder the implications of his own message.

Publishing his account in 1826, four years after the assault, Ashmun also ascribed a curiously nationalistic divine grace to the colony's survival: "As the cause was emphatically that of God and their country, they might confidently expect his blessing and success to attend the faithful discharge of their duty."[69] That the ordained Ashmun would see the workings of a Christian God supporting their efforts to tame and convert heathenism is unsurprising. But what country did Ashmun emphatically assert the settlers to be serving? Liberia was the colony of a private corporation (although certainly one heavily entwined with the U.S. government) that lacked a national identity within itself. In the correspondence of the African American settlers, very few adopt a Liberian identity during its colonial period, electing instead to lay claim to a national identity—American—that was only uncontested by their white audience because they had abandoned that nation. An independent Liberia was still more than twenty years away when Ashmun published his claim. Such construction suggests that Ashmun was a colonizationist in the expansionist mold of Henry Clay, who envisioned the tiny colony sprouting into a republican juggernaut in western Africa.

This was a manly endeavor for Ashmun and company, and the women kept getting in the way, of course. Although Ashmun repeatedly emphasized his prevailing illness that continually kept him bedridden during the colony's formative days, he always locates himself at the center of action during the attack. In his narrative, Ashmun singled out for praise particular settlers who exhibited courage in battle: Lott Cary, for rallying retreating settlers; Elijah Johnson, for leading a force of soldiers around the flank of the enemy.[70] Transgressions of military order, however, were left to anonymous settlers, such as the pickets charged with guarding the western approaches to the settlement who abandoned their post. Unfortunately, this retreat exposed several outlying dwellings to the African onslaught, and Ashmun chastised the settlers there, as he claimed to have given a command to vacate those premises, "The measures necessary to secure the proper observance of this order were unhappily omitted; and the rashness of the misguided individuals who disobeyed it, met with a signal punishment." The epicenter of the African attack fell upon several "helpless women and children" who had failed to heed the administrator's order, or maybe Ashmun had exaggerated the extent to which he had warned them to vacate the cabins.

Yet, while male failures were anonymous and collective, women were singled out individually for their faults and for placing their protective menfolk at risk of exposing their lives to protect the "helpless." Ann Hawkins, an "imprudent" woman who slept the night in her cabin, received thirteen wounds although she survived the ordeal. Minty Draper attempted to flee with her two small children in her arms but was wounded in the head from a cutlass and lost both of her children in the melee. Imprudently sleeping in their homes when such was forbidden, these women required heroic masculine protection in the forms of Cary and Johnson, even if their danger resulted from unnamed and generalized male negligence.

But even Ashmun's account contains hints that these women perhaps required less masculine protection than he suggested. Another named female transgressor, Mary Tines, boarded with another woman who was the mother of five children. When their cabin was surrounded by swarming Africans, they each seized an axe and prevented entry into the dwelling for several minutes. Tines died in this defense of the homestead, but the other woman escaped. Although Ashmun was forced to figuratively salute the actions of these "heroines," he clearly included the account to emphasize the character of the colony's foes, whom he described as "savage enemies" and "irresolute barbarians" in his retelling of the women's stand.[71] The death of Lucy Brant in the woods surrounding Bassa Cove, the escape of Eben Parker's wife from their cabin outside of Harper, the axe-wielding Mary Tines: all deeply underscore that the violence of colonial Liberia was deeply entwined with the home.

This violence, however, was gendered as masculine to provide uplift and "civilization" to the male settlers: the "black race" was interpreted through a gendered lens as the "black man." Even as women formed the critical reproductive backbone of the unhealthy colony and families served as the nucleus of the colonial project, African American men found elevation through their opposition and violent actions toward Africans. By violently taming African "savagery," the settlers distinguished themselves from natives. The automatic "civilization" bestowed upon African American settlers in this space stemmed from this binary; if male settlers protected women from black barbarians, then they themselves could not likewise be barbaric. They would have to be something else. Or to use Ashmun's phrase, the Africans would learn what it meant to fight white men.

Ignoring the Mary Tines of the colony, men usually framed their discussion of widows and single women in terms of the protection they required and exasperation at their continued presence aboard the colonization expeditions. Colonial Liberia, within this view, was no place for female heads of households. Hence, Russwurm's exasperation with the *Columbia*'s emigrants in 1838 stemmed not only from their enslaved past but also the ratio of the sexes. He also hoped that the Parker affair had taught the MSCS leadership a lesson in how they organized expeditions. With so much violence in the colony, Russwurm wrote to his supervisors, "I trust therefore that the fall expedition will be dispatched earlier than common; and that unusual care will be taken not to send out many women and children. We want able bodied men. We want two very light field pieces for immediate action—so light that 8 or 10 men may take them apart and carry them with ease."[72] For Russwurm, it was disastrous for the colony to be filled not only with ex-slaves but also with women without male guardians. Men in charge of households—preferably freeborn ones—were most likely to benefit from the uplift that relocation to Liberia provided.

* * *

Of course, this idea of violence as a whitening agent was contested and constantly in flux and deeply entwined in the impassioned debate over colonization. The attendees of the 1853 Colored National Convention believed they understood the meanings of violence in Liberia, at that point a six-year-old independent republic. The Colored Convention movement offered opportunities for African Americans to join together to strategize for racial justice. Nearly every convention since the movement's inception in the early 1830s passed a motion denouncing the ACS and colonization (see chapter 5). The 1853 "Report on Colonization," however, was a much longer document than those usually produced for these occasions that recorded the entire history of colonization in Africa beginning in the seventeenth century with the Dutch East India Company. When the report finally arrived at the nineteenth century and the creation of Liberia, it almost immediately turned to the issue of violence: "They tell of *reckless wars* upon the *natives* attended with both *rapine* and *bloodshed*, of legislation framed in a spirit of exclusiveness, not much less infamous than that of certain white slaveholding democracies." For any especially daft readers who failed to grasp the parallels that the Committee on Colonization, chaired by James W. C. Pennington,[73] was trying to draw, they further explained that the Liberians, "native whippers" and colonizers themselves, justified European encroachments in Africa.

The committee concluded that "the Liberians are in league with the worst enemies of Africa's dearest interest"; essentially, the Liberians and Europeans were cut from the same cloth and in league together to claim

Africa's riches from her native inhabitants. A laundry list of violence, wars, duplicitous dealings with Africans, and excessive punishments for African leaders committed by these Liberian "native whippers," another obvious allusion to white enslavers, provided the evidence to support their argument that the Liberians had gone over to the white side. To finally cement their claims, the committee quoted an 1827 address from the citizens of Monrovia to the free people of color in the United States: "'Tell us,' say the Liberians in their address to the free coloured people, 'which is the white man, who, with a prudent regard for his own character, CAN associate with one of you on terms of equality? Ask us which is the white man, who would decline such association with one of our number, whose intellectual and moral qualities are not an objection? We unhesitatingly answer both these questions by saying, the white man is not to be found.'" While the Liberians viewed this prospective equality as a virtue of their state, the 1853 convention discounted their independence from whites, believing instead that they remained marionettes with white hands pulling the strings, and denounced their aggression against Africans. Violence against African savagery, however, was one of the pillars by which the Liberians could claim equality with Anglo-Americans and Europeans, something they considered an unmitigated good.[74]

The 1853 report implicitly connected the violence waged in Liberia by the African American settlers to European colonial powers expanding into Africa and abusive slaveholders in the United States. Africa was an unappealing home for the committee who prophesized that the continent was "destined to be the theatre of bloody conflict, between her native sons, and intruding foreigners, black and white, for a century yet to come." Ironically, the Liberian settlers likewise conceived of their African home as a space for masculine violence and martial glory. It was a space in which James Hall, after picking up two settlers in Monrovia to aid in the establishment of Maryland in Liberia, blissfully wrote back to the board of managers that "two of Ashmun's veterans" had joined his expedition, assuring a contingent of seasoned colonizers accustomed to the violent episodes concomitant with the establishment of another Liberian settlement.[75] But whereas the delegates of 1853 saw the Liberians as simply the surrogates of expansionist white dreams in Africa, the Americo-Liberians conceived of violence as one of the great equalizing tools by which they could finally claim equality with America's whites on the other side of the ocean.

5

"Your Views Cross the Atlantic"

Black and White Responses to Settler Activism

The mobility of Liberian settlers, the ways in which they mapped their colony, how they put Africans to work there, and the violence that characterized it all profoundly shaped both supporters and opponents of colonization. Multiple schisms divided white colonizationists. Were free blacks inherently degraded or made so by American society? Was the ultimate goal of the movement abolition? And how should white Americans engage with a Liberian settler traveling through the United States? For their part, the settlers proved remarkably adept at holding colonizationist leaders accountable for their celebration of life in Africa. The Americo-Liberians identified those leaders most friendly to black uplift and used them as springboards, meaning most efforts by the colonization societies to support uplift were the direct result of settler agency.

That agency was a problem for colonization's opponents. While the overwhelming majority of black Americans rejected colonization, the Liberian settlers themselves presented a bit of an ideological problem. It was easy to denounce the ACS's white leadership, but what about the settlers themselves? The graduation of a man of color from Dartmouth's medical college was demonstrable evidence of black capacity, but that same doctor's disdain for free people of color who remained in the United States presented obvious obstacles to trumpeting his accomplishments.

Like all issues surrounding Liberia, these complex problems were further complicated by race and questions of "color." Of course, colonization was hardly the only nineteenth-century movement characterized by an obsession over racial ambiguities. Take, for example, the meeting of the American and Foreign Anti-Slavery Society in May 1854. On the first night of the convention, the delegates were regaled with speeches from America's leading lights of the abolitionist movement, including Frederick Douglass. One hundred people crowded into New York's Hope Chapel the following day to begin the proceedings, which began with William Lloyd Garrison gaveling the meeting to order at ten o'clock. Garrison stated that the purpose of the morning session revolved around two resolutions presented the day before: one proclaimed that "the grand vital issue to be made with the power is, the dissolution of the existing American Union," while the other was simply contented to call the South "in its pretended opposition to slavery, cowardly in its spirit, and spasmodic in its action." Robert Purvis signaled his desire to speak. The son of a free woman of color and a white English immigrant, Purvis was a member of Philadelphia's black elite. Educated at Amherst College and married to James Forten's daughter, Harriet, Purvis was a leading reformer who had joined with Garrison in establishing the American Anti-Slavery Society (AASS). He had served as president of the Pennsylvania branch of that society, and his household functioned as an epicenter for Philadelphia's Underground Railroad, moral reform, and black intellectualism. There were very few people in the nation, let alone in that room, more qualified to speak to the matter at hand. The floor was given to Purvis, and the wheels quickly fell off the convention.[1]

Instead of the resolutions before the convention, Purvis desired to mention an address given the night before by William Furness in which the speaker had evidently said that "Mr. Purvis was wealthy enough to purchase connection with a white skin, but with credit to himself he saw fit not to do so." While Furness correctly noted that economic conditions undergirded whiteness—that, in short, it could be purchased under certain conditions by certain racially ambiguous people—Purvis was not happy to be singled out in such a manner and wanted to know why such a claim had been presented in light of Purvis's pride "in his blood . . . of the fact that he had twenty-five per cent of negro blood in his veins." Instead of a particular color, Purvis claimed to desire to be known only as an "honest man." A white attendee attempted to defuse the situation by apologizing for Furness but concluded with a promise that Furness held "no color prejudice," missing Purvis's point that he wished to reject identities based solely on color. Speaking next, Samuel J. May seemed to grasp Purvis's point but twisted the knife instead. While he hoped to no longer discuss the issue of color, "Mr. Furness meant to say that Mr. Purvis was light enough to pass for a white man, but chose to pass as a colored man," an act for which Purvis should be commended. Thomas van Rensselaer, apparently in a desperate bid to right the convention's ship, said that these responses to Furness's address had soothed his uneasy conscience and hoped that the resolutions would now be taken up. Garrison rejected van Rensselaer's olive branch and contended that it was impossible *not* to discuss color. Purvis disagreed and found no compliment in acknowledging the fact of his "blood." Garrison thought "that was all very well; but still one could say—'Well done, good and faithful servant.'" That statement apparently did not have many admirers among the convention goers, leaving Wendell Phillips to opine that it *was* time to cease discussing color. "Who are the slaves? They are Americans of the second generation. The grandchildren of Thomas Jefferson are in slavery in Virginia. The *Tribune* talks about African slavery, when it should say American slavery." Van Rensselaer countered that it would be "difficult" for slavery's opponents to completely eschew color from their discussions, and, besides, he did not want to be "identified with the wicked white men of this society." Purvis bluntly replied, "I don't think there's much danger of that."[2]

And so the convention muddled forward in discord and disagreement regarding the propriety of addressing "color." After a mid-afternoon break, Frederick Douglass judged the crowd returning for the afternoon session "very small." The issue turned from color to religious institutions and then to the actual mechanics of the meeting, as members complained that sidebar issues had hijacked the convention and sent it down a myriad of paths unrelated to the issues at hand. The day lurched to an end amid confusion regarding whether one speaker could continue to respond to van Rensselaer's parting words that "the good of the slave was the only thing to be considered" and his hopes that future meetings adhered to that model. It was a lackluster display of organizational cohesion, although a typical one for the abolitionist movement, but it is telling that the issue of "color" sparked the initial derailment of the meeting. Could antislavery advocates discuss the issue without addressing color as Purvis, Phillips, and May desired? The response of van Rensselaer to this question suggests the widespread belief in normative whiteness in the mid-nineteenth-century United States. To no longer "have" a color was the same as to be "identified with" whites. Frederick Douglass's report of the meeting within his own paper underscores this conflation. Behind the name of every person of African descent speaking during the meeting, Douglass followed the conventions of the day and helpfully noted "(colored)" for his readership. Douglass did not offer the same annotation for Euro-American participants; the absence of color denoted a default to whiteness.

While the name of the American and Foreign Anti-Slavery Society clearly showed its focus on slavery and the American Colonization Society zeroed in on free people of color, neither organization could escape such racialized and colorized issues. Nearly twenty years before this question of color disrupted the annual meeting of the American and Foreign Anti-Slavery Society in New York, Robert McDowall wrote from Monrovia with many of the same complaints as Purvis. The recipient of McDowall's invective was Ralph R. Gurley, the colonization movement's jack-of-all-trades. At that moment in August 1835 when McDowall put ink to paper, he was most upset at Gurley in his capacity as the editor of the *African Repository*. An Afro-Scottish physician who had graduated from the University of Edinburgh, McDowall had left for Liberia in June 1834 in the employ of the ACS as a colonial physician. The immediate source of trouble for McDowall was the *African Repository*'s publication of the eighteenth annual report of the ACS in February 1835 and a letter from McDowall to Elliott Cresson in the following March issue. The problem lay less in the publication of these respective documents than in the biographical information they provided about young McDowall. Apparently writing to Gurley after perusing the latest issues of the *Repository* from his Liberian office, the doctor informed Gurley, "I have to request that in all official documents, wherein it may be necessary to mention my name that the epithet 'coloured gentleman' shall not be coupled with it." McDowall had apparently initially agreed that colonizationist propaganda could list his racial heritage, as "it was held out to me that my means of doing good and benefiting the cause would thereby be incalculably increased and much advantage to myself. . . . In this 'honour' I have been cruelly mistaken." McDowall believed that the inclusion of "coloured gentleman" set a "limit" on his abilities that greatly impeded both his current practice and his future prospects. "To be identified with the colonists here was never my intentions," he summed for Gurley, and then asked, "Should I . . . continue to place myself in a predicament, which I now see must forever prevent me from reaping any of its [his profession's] honors? and place me on a level with slaves?"[3]

For McDowall, to be labeled "colored" in the ACS publications placed him on the level of an enslaved person. Seemingly rejecting any possible coupling of "free" and "black," McDowall rejected the identity of "colored" as solely the possession of slaves. Once again, we see a Liberian seeking uplift through negation—simply not being racially marked—and seeking elevation through the normalizing tools of whiteness by which he apparently hoped, as was the case in Frederick Douglass's account of the antislavery convention, that the absence of "color" would lead the readers to default to normalizing whiteness or minimally assume elevation above a "colored" population. If "colored" could only equate to slavery, then McDowall wanted nothing to do with that particular moniker. McDowall had even contributed the skull of a Bassa man to Samuel Morton's collection without apparently any indication of his own identity. Given his response to the *African Repository*, it seems likely that McDowall presented himself in letters as a medical professional and left it up to his correspondent to ponder race. This was uplift through simply *not* being "colored."

Of course, the great irony was that McDowall was writing to the mouthpiece of the ACS. The colonizationists were the harbingers of unmitigated racial difference, to the point that they could not conceive of sharing a nation-state with free people of color. This was, after all, the very same organization that in its first annual report reprinted Robert G. Harper's description of free people of color as "for the most part idle and useless, and too often vicious and mischievous."[4] The coupling of "free" with "colored" could only create a vicious and idle class of people, as though the very words revolted from one another. How could McDowall ask the officers of an organization founded on unalterable racial divisions to acquiesce to his request for ambiguous racial identity when Purvis would fail to attain the same goal twenty years later within a multiracial abolitionist meeting?

He could expect this because Gurley was certainly no Harper, and the ACS was an evolving, multifaceted organization. One of the internal tensions tugging the colonization movement in various directions was the question of whether free people of color were degraded, vicious, and idle, and, assuming that they did possess these characteristics, whether these traits were inherent or the result of the undue strain placed on them by white-authored laws. This nagging question was visible even in the ACS's first report. Even as the report quoted Harper at length, it likewise republished the letter of an Indiana supporter who claimed to have a large group of black Indianans ready to go to Africa. The author reported them as being "in general industrious and moral. Some of them have landed property and are good farmers; and some can read and write. They are sensible of the existing degraded condition in which they are placed by our laws, respecting the right of suffrage, and other disabilities."[5] And so in 1836, the year following McDowall's original letter, the *African Repository* published a letter from "R. McDowall" regarding the attack on the settlement at Bassa Cove without any racial annotation. The pattern repeated in 1837, and by 1838, when the *Repository* published another McDowall letter, it described him as a colonial physician "with a candid and intelligent mind" and as one who has "recently returned to the United States," suggesting his "home" was the United States rather than Africa, the norm for colonizationist rhetoric.[6]

This is not to suggest a complete rehabilitation of the colonizationists.

This was an organization whose Board of Managers reported in their second annual meeting: "If, as is most confidently believed, the colonization of the free people of colour, will render the slave who remains in America more obedient, more faithful, more honest, and, consequently, more useful to his master, is it proper to regard this happy consequence to both, as the sole object which the Society hope to attain?"[7] Little wonder that most people of color would see the ACS as a pro-slavery organization, given this sort of rhetoric from the society's leadership.

The very few souls who embraced relocating to Liberia were usually people of color most able to take advantage of the ambiguity wrought by Atlantic mobility and Liberia's "in-between" racialized space. As such, it is unsurprising that so many of the greatest practitioners of this racial shape shifting—McGill, Russwurm, Roberts—were racially ambiguous individuals usually categorized as "mulattoes." With an existence already structured around racial liminality, these individuals were further buttressed by the racialized assumptions of Euro-Americans, who perceived them as elevated above the "purely black"; reflecting this thinking, the colonization societies tended to promote settlers of mixed ancestry into the upper ranks of colonial administration. The relationship between "mulatto" and "black" became a common query when discussing elite Americo-Liberians. When he visited the Republic of Liberia a few short years before the American Civil War, Alexander Cowan of Kentucky's colonization auxiliary sat down with the Roberts family to discuss the planned construction of the new Liberia College for which Joseph Roberts would serve as its first president. "I was much pleased with my social interview with the family. The husband and wife are bright mulattoes, especially the wife. I use the term with no disrespect. It is used to meet the often enquiry when speaking of persons in Liberia as to their standing, are they black or mulattoes?"[8] Although many settlers found their African whiteness useful in certain situations, regardless of their respective genealogies—Dempsey Fletcher, of "pure African" descent, being only the most obvious example—the mixed-ancestry elites of the colony were often the best poised and most able to cause that "colored" designation that so plagued Robert Purvis and Robert McDowall to evaporate.

Governor Roberts's 1844 tour of the United States underscores what Liberia could do with someone already identified as a "mulatto." He spoke at the annual conventions of two state colonization societies, Massachusetts and New York. In its annual report, the Massachusetts Society described Roberts: "This gentleman is a mulatto, with a highly intelligent countenance, and expressive eye, betokening him a man of talent. . . . He emigrated to Liberia from the vicinity of Petersburg, Va., when a boy, and received his education there, and may be considered of colony culture and growth." Relocation had transformed one of the numerous Petersburg "mulatto" youths into an exotic example of "colony culture:" foreign, "civilized," intelligent, and respectable. This performance was repeated in New York, whose colonizationists recorded, "Governor Roberts, a slightly colored gentleman of good appearance, being introduced, made some interesting statements, respecting an exploring tour he had recently made, in connexion with two or three white persons, and a number of colonists, into the interior." Here, Roberts related an account in which white individuals and black settlers jointly toured the African interior. Again, the effect was to distinguish settler culture in opposition to African savagery and to highlight the equal footing of "whites" and "blacks" in Liberia. Given this ideological framework, it is not surprising that the New York colonizationists determined that Roberts was only "slightly" colored. The descriptor perfectly encapsulates the result of these Liberian sojourns, whitening an individual into an indeterminate racial identity. If Roberts was not "white," then he was only "slightly" not so. And these identities were forged in the constant transatlantic exchange between the United States and Liberia, predicated upon Roberts's travels in the United States and his position of honor among the colonizationists, which served as a testament to their colony's capacity for improvement.[9]

The ACS was not a static, unified, or coherent organization in terms of race or slavery. In an effort to steer the society down an antislavery path with stronger support for black uplift, Ralph Gurley orchestrated a coup at the ACS's 1833 annual meeting. While reading the numerous bland reports of the national organization, which were routinely approved by the delegates without question, Gurley included, unnoticed, a reorganization of the managers. Unwittingly, the convention agreed to the removal of supporters of slavery from the Board of Managers and named them instead as vice presidents of the society, a more honorific position; they were replaced by a new antislavery slate of managers, including John H. B. Latrobe and Moses Sheppard.[10] Gurley also attempted to create a new directory body consisting of secretaries of auxiliary societies and individuals who donated $500 or more to the society. It was a system intentionally skewed to favor Northern colonizationists, who organized more auxiliaries and donated more money. Over the course of five separate meetings held between January 20 and February 8, the delegates contentiously debated these changes to the society. Even the published minutes of the society, intentionally scrubbed of the deep divisions within the organization, betray the confusion. Resolutions were submitted demanding a reconsideration of the Report of the Committee on the Election of Officers, the report by which Gurley had reorganized the Board of Managers; another proposal, subsequently voted down, authorized a committee to report on "whether there was any thing unfair, illegal, or dishonourable in the election of the officers of the Society." Finally, apparently deciding that under the Constitution nothing could be done that year to remove the newly appointed managers, the convention voted on a proposal to recommend that the new managers voluntarily resign their seats. The divisive resolution barely passed, sixty-three to fifty-seven. With the expected return of the status quo forthcoming, the delegates decided it was "inexpedient" to alter the constitution, and Gurley's 1833 antislavery revolt failed for the moment.[11] It was this failure that led the Maryland State Colonization Society to begin the antislavery auxiliary revolt from the parent organization the following year. Most abolitionists delighted in the schism of the society, noting that it undermined the oft-repeated refrain that colonization offered a path to emancipation. The front page of the *Liberator* crowed, "SIGNS OF THE TIMES!! *The great Babel tottering to its foundation!!!*"[12]

This schism is why McGill and so many Liberian settlers disdained abolitionists' focus on the ACS leadership. For them, it was more important to recognize that certain colonizationists would work toward African American uplift through their "once separate, equal" ideology and materially support *that* cause than to focus on the movement as a whole, which also included opponents of black equality. This was simply not possible for most free people of color in the United States, who saw themselves portrayed as degraded and unworthy of living in the land of their nativity.

For historians, the tale of free black rejection of colonization is standard fare: after initial dalliances with the schemes of Paul Cuffe on the part of a few black elites, such as James Forten, free people of color overwhelmingly rejected the white-led ACS. Instead of Cuffe's vehicle for black uplift, the ACS was perceived as propping up slavery while also denying black capacity for self-improvement in the States. Preferring to fight for liberty and equality in the land of their birth, free black people overwhelmingly rejected colonization during the 1820s and instead focused on the establishment of a national abolitionist community dedicated to immediate emancipation. As practically the only voices of opposition against colonization during that decade, African Americans were forced to create national networks to combat the national appeal of the ACS. Their efforts spawned the immediatist movement for white abolitionists during the 1830s—often former colonizationists shown the error of their ways, including James Birney, Gerrit Smith, Benjamin Lundy, and the Tappan Brothers—and fostered the creation of racially inclusive abolitionist societies.[13] This standard account is not inaccurate. Free African Americans *did* overwhelmingly reject colonization and organized nationally to combat the ACS.

* * *

The elite voices of the national convention movement ably support these scholarly conclusions. The national conventions, which began initially in 1830 with the sole purpose of debating the propriety of emigrating from the United States, evolved over the 1830s and 1840s to debate the best means to achieve racial equality. The published minutes of the twelve national conventions that met before the American Civil War provide ample material to explore elite black thinking in regard to colonization, as it proved a nearly ubiquitous topic of conversation. These national conventions were soon joined by many more state-level and local conventions addressing more regional issues. The question of Liberia, colonization, and emigration hung over these meetings as well.

Initially, the convention movement got off to a rocky start. The first gathering in 1830 proved to be a small affair numbering only a handful of delegates who were aware of its existence. Held in September, the idea for a national convention had been suggested only the April before; a formal announcement of the meeting went out in August. Hezekiah Grice, a Baltimore delegate who had published the original proposal for the meeting in April, arrived in Philadelphia to discover only five other men in attendance. It was not an auspicious beginning, and the small group was apparently interrupted periodically by visitors challenging the authority of the group to speak on behalf of America's people of color. Despite the missteps, the group recommended emigration to Canada in preference to Liberia and called for a future meeting in June 1831 to purchase land and create an organization to administer it. The next meeting was better attended and gradually evolved away from its emigrationist origins to include broader concerns for black uplift; soon the convention counted among its participants many of the nation's leading black intellectuals. In keeping with the tradition of the first meeting, however, a rejection of colonization became a staple of each annual convention regardless of its size or luminescence.[14]

In an early address produced by the 1831 convention, the delegates noted that "our forlorn and deplorable situation earnestly and loudly demand of us to devise and pursue all legal means for the speedy elevation of ourselves and brethren to the scale and standing of men." In its emphasis on the "deplorable situation" of African Americans within the United States and masculine conflation of uplift with the "scale and standing of men," the delegates' address echoed the rhetoric of many colonizationists. Yet, the delegates rejected African colonization despite the "great debt which these United States may owe to injured Africa" because the people of African descent were precisely that: people of African *descent*. The delegates contended that they were American by custom and birth and could not "consent to take [their] lives in [their] hands, and be the bearers of the redress offered by that Society to that much afflicted country." Further, a committee of inquiry established during the convention reported their belief that many of the "unconstitutional, unchristian, and unheard of sufferings" of African Americans stemmed from the rhetoric of the ACS. Finally, in a convention address, co-authors Belfast Burton, Junius C. Morel, and William Whipper suggested that the actions of the ACS inadvertently strengthened slavery rather than hindered the institution, argued that the delegates' forefathers had likewise fought for American liberty, and finally requested, "If we must be sacrificed to their philanthropy, we would rather die at home." The onus of their rejection of colonization lay in their cultural similarities with other Americans, the assumption that the ACS ran a deathtrap of a colony—a fair belief—and the debt of the United States to the people of color who had fought to secure its own liberty.[15]

Later conventions would build upon these themes with increasing vigor. By 1834, the convention's president declared that although colonizationists "put on the garb of angels of light," beneath that benevolent shell lay an inner darkness dedicated to "evil purposes." Ironically, the attempted 1833 coup by Gurley and other like-minded colonizationists who conceived of colonization as geared toward black uplift probably damaged the reputation of the ACS more than they encouraged African Americans to give the society a hearing. Instead of seeing the ACS as a divided organization with an internal power struggle, the convention goers saw only malevolence, believing that the ACS was "artful": "It suits itself to all places . . . it blows hot and cold." Given the disparate elements cobbled together under the broad "colonizationist" umbrella, there was a great deal of truth to these charges. The colonizationist hydra tended to undermine itself by swimming in multiple directions.[16]

By the 1840s, the convention had resolved that, theoretically, "it *may* be possible" that colonization had been founded by benevolent motives, but the actual accomplishments of the ACS had only "been fostered and sustained by the *murderous spirit of slavery* and prejudice." Regardless of its founders' motivations, the actions of colonization sustained the institution of slavery for the convention's participants and, returning to the theme of nativity established in the first convention, they were in favor of securing rights in the land of their birth. The 1853 convention summed this idea succinctly by declaring, "We are Americans, and as Americans, we would speak to Americans." Colonization had, in fact, played a significant role in the delegates' thinking in terms of their place in American society. Initially, the conventions had been established with the explicit purpose of securing territory outside the United States, preferably in Canada, to provide a haven for African American expatriates following the exodus of more than half the population of Cincinnati, Ohio's free people of color.

Following extensive mob violence in that city in 1829, between eleven hundred and two thousand of its free black residents established a colony in Canada they named Wilberforce in honor of the British abolitionist. After only two meetings, however, the convention delegates found their balancing act of encouraging relocation while simultaneously rejecting Liberia as a possible site for that relocation problematic. By 1832, a committee charged with examining resolutions supportive of relocation declared that, based upon their examination of the ACS, they had determined "that any express plan to colonize our people beyond the limits of these United States, tends to weaken the situation of those who are left behind, without any peculiar advantage to those who emigrate."[17] From that point forward, delegates would largely focus on black uplift within the United States, along with annual denunciations of the ACS program. Repeatedly, the conventions undermined the logic of colonization, decried the movement as a scheme that reinforced slavery, affirmed their American identity, and underlined their determination to secure their rights in the land of their birth; all of this scholars have accurately pinpointed as the basis of free black opposition to colonization.

Yet, there was initial hesitancy on the part of these elite African Americans to specifically pinpoint individuals. If the *movement* as a whole was soundly rejected along with its ideological underpinnings by these convention goers, then *individuals* within that movement were strangely absent from these denunciations. Given that colonization often functioned as a bridge to abolitionism for whites, these early formulaic denunciations are not surprising. The 1831 address, for example, qualified its rejection of colonization by noting that the convention did not doubt the "sincerity of many friends who are engaged in that cause." Much as they offered increasingly astringent denunciations of colonization with each passing year, the conventions likewise increasingly dropped any suggestion that certain individuals conceived of the project as one of uplift, especially in light of the desertion of white abolitionists from the ACS during the 1830s. The published accounts of the convention delighted in these defections, noting that these former colonizationists "are now busily engaged in tearing down the MONUMENT they assisted in erecting." Within just a few years, the convention's tone had changed from assuming that the society contained many friends to insisting that the constituent members had been duped by the insidious founders who kept their evil plans a closely guarded secret. Committees were formed to correspond with the figurehead vice-presidents of the ACS—positions created for men of national note without much regard for their actual opinions on colonization or dedication to the movement—to ascertain their opinion of the ACS and inform the officers of African Americans' estimation of the society.

In 1832, when Gurley spoke before the convention "with a view, as he said, of removing some erroneous impression in the minds of the people of color," he was challenged by several convention delegates and William Lloyd Garrison. Needless to say, the convention widely disagreed with Gurley's contention: "We have been told in this Convention, by the Secretary of the American Colonization Society, that there are causes which forbid our advancement in this country, which no humanity, no legislation and no religion can control. Believe it not."[18] But even as the ubiquitous denunciations of the ACS and colonization were written in increasingly acerbic tone, there remained a curious omission from the reports of these conventions: Liberia and Liberians. For all of the ink dedicated to decrying the white leadership of the ACS, the black convention leaders often found themselves tiptoeing around the actual colony and its settlers.

The 1833 report on colonization, for example, even as it crowed about former colonizationists turning on the society, briefly conceded one point before continuing its denunciation of the ACS. "The only exception to the rule is," the report noted, "those who are receiving an education, or preparing themselves for some profession, at the expense of the society." As an organization dedicated to black uplift, the convention could denounce colonization but had to make exceptions for those settlers who were acquiring educational uplift through the society. This was not an abstract problem. By the 1830s, the settlers had wrested concessions from the ACS and established a place for themselves in the governance of the colony, others were securing training on behalf of the society to administer the colonial bureaucracy, and still others were traveling the states stumping on behalf of the colonization societies and freeing family members from bondage. Indeed, the convention goers in 1832 who remained until the final session became intimately acquainted with the figure of the traveling Liberian settler, as "Mr. J. C. Morel introduced Major Barbour of Liberia to the Convention." What the delegates and Barbour discussed was not recorded in the minutes; this is especially unfortunate given that Barbour arrived at the same convention that so resoundingly rejected Gurley's arguments on behalf of the ACS.[19]

Barbour would have presented an intriguing contrast to the convention, simultaneously encapsulating the hope and tragedy of Liberian settlement. Originally from Petersburg, Virginia, James C. Barbour had emigrated to Liberia as a young man with his mother and nine siblings in 1824.[20] While the younger children enrolled in school in the colony, James and the older siblings found social, political, and economic success there. Eventually, James became a major of the colonial militia, was elected vice agent of the colony in 1835, and possessed a fine stone house on Broad Street in Monrovia. In the same year he was elected vice agent of the colony, the *African Repository* published Beverly R. Wilson's address to the free people of color in the United States. Wilson, visiting Norfolk, Virginia, before his return to Liberia, held up Barbour, along with Anthony Williams and Joseph J. Roberts, as an exemplar of the possibilities of Liberian relocation for creating paths parallel with those of elite whites in the United States. Liberia's "facilities held out for a comfortable living rarely equaled; industry and economy are sure to be rewarded and crowned with a generous competency, for proof of which I cite you to a Williams, to a Roberts, to a Barbour,—and to a number of others, who, a few years ago, possessed very limited means, but who now live all the affluence and style, which characterize the wealthy merchant and gentleman of Virginia."[21] In many regards, Barbour represented the potential of Liberia. Much of that lay in the future beyond his 1832 tour of the States, however, and even as James found his fortunes greatly elevated in the colony, the remainder of the large Barbour family struggled.

Agnes, James's mother and the matriarch of the clan, died of "decline" in 1828. William Barbour drowned in the same year; another sibling passed away two years later from a "deranged brain." During the same trip to the United States in which he visited the convention, Barbour also discussed the colony with a Virginia colonizationist who was dissatisfied with the results of the talk, unsurprising given the decimation of the Barbour family.[22] The high death rate would have reinforced most African Americans' beliefs that the colony was a deathtrap and would have found a receptive audience at the Philadelphia convention. Yet, Barbour himself was apparently not so disgruntled with his own opportunities in the colony, as he returned to Liberia and enjoyed a distinguished political and military career there. And the recorded introduction of "Major Barbour" to the convention is equally intriguing. As noted in chapter 4, Liberians embraced the martial airs that distinguished their civilized outpost from surrounding barbarian hordes. These positions of honor—officer ranks in the colonial militia along with their uniforms—were jealously guarded by Liberian settlers. Did Barbour introduce himself to the convention as an officer of the Liberian military establishment or demand that he be recorded as such? If so, it suggests the extent to which martial glory was a critical element for Liberians' self-defined "civilizing" mission. Of course, the use of military rank instead of proper name by the convention proceedings may reflect the delegates' desire to highlight black achievement. Not until Martin Delany also received a commission as major in 1865 would a man of African descent acquire a similar officer rank in the U.S. military. Conversely, it would have been remarkably hypocritical of the convention to capitalize on the elevating possibilities of Liberian emigration while simultaneously denouncing colonization as a secret proslavery plot and calling for African Americans to soundly reject the ACS. It is also intriguing that in the year after Gurley's defense of colonization and Barbour's last-minute introduction to the convention, the convention delegates approved a report on colonization that made an exception for those settlers reaping educational benefits from the colony.

Barbour embodied both the tragedy of Liberian emigration experienced by many settlers and also the possibilities that relocation provided. In that complexity lay problems for African American opponents of the ACS. Denouncing the colonization movement and its white supporters was a relatively straightforward affair, but what to do about the Barbours, the McGills, the Roberts, or the Fletchers who utilized Liberian emigration as a means to catapult themselves upward into society? Regardless of the desires of colonization leaders or their opinions of people of African descent, the agency of this assuredly elite settler class could not be dismissed—and should not be discounted by historians. Focusing too heavily upon the Euro-American leadership of the ACS ignores the contributions of individuals who forced the hand of the ACS to create a settler colonial bureaucracy and demanded access to educational and economic opportunities within the United States.

Colonization's opponents understood how central the promise of travel on equal footing with whites was for Liberia's supporters. The August 3, 1833, edition of the *Liberator*, under the heading "DISGRACEFUL," recounted the problems A. D. Williams, then vice agent of the colony, and Joseph J. Roberts, then High Sheriff, encountered in Boston. Williams and Roberts, the latter on his first return visit to the United States, had arrived in New York in April to engage in a northern speaking tour about Liberia. The two encountered difficulty in Boston when the stagecoach driver "would not carry *Niggers!* unless they would take an outside seat!" (meaning sitting on top of the coach with the luggage rather than in the cab with other passengers). The Liberians refused such an arrangement—"to their credit" as reported by the *Liberator*—and waited one day in Boston for a different coach to carry them to Providence. In summing the episode, Garrison displayed a remarkably deft understanding of colonization and attacked a central promise of the movement by concluding that "although Messrs. Williams and Roberts had been to Liberia, they met with the same treatment which is received by those of their color who remain in this country."

Even after Liberian independence, opponents still challenged the idea that Liberians' African status could return intact to the United States. When a convention of "colored citizens" of Ohio took up the question of emigrating from the United States in 1849, delegate J. L. Watson was adamantly opposed to Liberia. "Go to Liberia," he proclaimed to the convention, "become President, Senator, Judge or what not. Come to this country and see how the founders of this scheme will treat you." Watson and Garrison explicitly denied that relocation to Liberia would lead to a different relationship with the United States. Unsurprising, given how much colonizationists wished to distinguish settlers from African Americans, the 1833 episode involving Williams and Roberts was not reported in the ACS's *African Repository*. The following year's annual report simply stated that the two settlers' "visit to various places in this country during the last summer, rendered special service to the cause."[23]

The figure of a successful Liberian settler was a significant threat for those determined to battle for rights within the United States. Not only did settler success undermine the narrative of the duped and impoverished settler, but the possibility that the colony could attract the brightest minds and create a "brain drain" from among the African American population worried advocates of black uplift. Frederick Douglass made this point in a letter to Harriet Beecher Stowe, written in 1853 during a period of expanded emigrationist plans, that was also presented to the national convention that year. Douglass was especially concerned that the most educated of America's free black population would increasingly look overseas for intellectual opportunities. "It would see that education and emigration go together with us; for as soon as a man rises amongst us, capable, by his genius and learning, to do us great service, just so soon finds that he can serve himself better by going elsewhere. In proof of this, I might instance the Russwurms—the Garnetts—the Wards—the Crummells and others." Seeking better personal opportunities abroad, in Liberia for Russwurm, Alexander Crummell, and (in the last weeks of his life) Henry Highland Garnet, and in Great Britain, Canada, and Jamaica for Samuel Ward, these educated free men of color did a disservice to the broader African American community by robbing it of its best and brightest. Even heroes of the anti-colonization cause were not immune.[24]

When Thomas C. Brown, a former Liberian settler who disappointedly returned to the United States, gave a public interview regarding the pitfalls of Liberian emigration, he became an instant celebrity among abolitionists. It was his answer to the question of "mulatto" children born in the colony that had drawn jeers from the pro-colonization audience members. Brown, however, remained discontented with the United States and next tried relocating to Jamaica. *The Colored American*, edited by Samuel Cornish, Russwurm's former editorial partner, published a letter of Brown's extolling Jamaica's virtues. While editor Cornish reaffirmed his belief in Brown's "noble" spirit, he continued, "We contend that we have among us those who are MORE NOBLE STILL. One thing Brother Brown lackest; he should not count his life dear unto himself, but *stay in our midst*... Here is the spot. On this rock should we build, and if needs be, die martyrs to principle. No colored man, possessing the talent and soul of Thomas C. Brown, should leave the country." Cornish followed this up six months later with a denunciation of what he called the philosophy of "taking care of no. 1." This "unholy principle" led free blacks in the South to become slaveholders, retarded the social and political advances of African Americans broadly, and deterred black monetary contributions to philanthropic societies. Russwurm, of course, was Cornish's first example of this principle, a veritable traitor to people of color. "It is this Rock upon which we have always split. 'Take care of No. ONE' carried Mr. Russwurm to Liberia: it made Arnold sell his country, and it has plunged the South into all the guilt and shame of a cruel system of slavery."[25]

These accusations against individual settlers emerged mostly in the 1840s and 1850s, with Russwurm being an especially favorite target. In the earlier decades, elite African American opponents of colonization largely ignored the colony of Liberia in favor of denouncing the society's white leadership. Indeed, the only other notation regarding Liberians in minutes from the conventions before the 1840s, aside from the 1832 arrival of Barbour and the 1833 exemption made for settlers receiving educational training from the colonization societies, was in 1834, in which a committee was formed to correspond with settlers "to use every means for ascertaining the true situation of our brethren there colonized, how many are desirous to return to this country, but are prevented for want of means." Apparently, the duties of this committee were underperformed, as the following year it was reestablished with the new addendum to also locate settlers "who may have considered themselves deluded by the American Colonization Society." The adjustment in language—transitioning from an inspection of colonial society and settlers desirous of returning home to an inquisition of settlers believing themselves deceived by the Society—reflects the conventions' desires to keep the onus of their anti-colonization rhetoric centered on the white ACS leadership instead of the settlers themselves.[26]

This intellectual separation of the colony from the society that spawned it is a common motif in the writings of black elites. William Whipper, a driving force in the early convention movement, eulogized William Wilberforce in 1833 by praising the British abolitionist's opposition to colonization as the "*arch enemy* of liberty" and "Protean disciple of his Satanic majesty." Yet, Wilberforce battled the colonization *movement* "notwithstanding he loved the colony of Liberia, and the civilization of Africa."[27] Robert Purvis's tongue was far sharper than Whipper's when he included a denunciation of colonization in his own eulogy of a Philadelphia reformer. Noting the "farcical" idea of removing to their "native country" those "who were born in America," Purvis underscored how colonizationists sold relocation through promises of elevation: "You were ready to dub us Governors, Majors, Colonels, Sherriffs, & c. & c." He then moved on to address the broad reformist roof under which colonization could operate in creating "missionary Liberia, Temperance Palmas, Spiritualizing Bassa Cove, Quaker

Edina, and a host of Pennsylvanias, New Yorks, Marshalls, Marylands, and last though not least, Port or Fort Cresson." Finally, turning to the colonizationists themselves, Purvis concluded,

> Oh! When I think of these men, and their Liberia, forgive me, when I say, if I hate not them, I do hate their diabolical schemes, with a refined, a perfect hatred. . . . I would not wish to be understood, as having the most remote desire to denounce any part of God's created world, yet Liberia, (if you please, in the abstract,) as she is held out as the only appropriate home for the colored people of this country.[28]

Purvis's summation of colonization contains many of the elements of free black opposition and suggests, along with Whipper's eulogy of Wilberforce, the main thrusts of African American anti-colonization propaganda during the 1830s. Purvis mocks the spatial logic of colonization, denounces the appeal of high-ranking societal positions unavailable to African Americans within the United States, ridicules the reformist traditions that undergirded several of the Liberian settlements, underlines the violence, oppression, and warfare of the colony ("Port or Fort Cresson"), and concludes with broader denunciation of the entire enterprise. Yet, although seemingly said with a smirk, Purvis hates Liberia "in the abstract" instead of the material space. Once again, the brunt of the harangue is placed on the Euro-American colonizationists who "deceive and cheat" to bring settlers to their colony. Purvis makes this point clear by using the phrase, "Oh! When I think of these men, and *their* [emphasis mine] Liberia." Liberia could only be denounced as an abstract surrogate for the colonization movement; what existed of it on terra firma must be portrayed as filled with the formerly enslaved relocated without choice and unfortunate free people of color tricked into going there who lacked the necessary resources to return to the United States.

Of course, exceptions existed. One of the most scornful diatribes against the Americo-Liberian settlers graced the pages of *Freedom's Journal* in 1828. Senior editor Cornish would remain firm in his opposition to colonization throughout his life despite his son's emigration to Liberia;[29] junior editor Russwurm was still a year away from his public endorsement of colonization. Thus, the pages of the first African American newspaper were still fertile grounds in which to oppose the colonization movement. An unsigned editorial appeared on the third page of the January 25 edition responding to the publication of a "Liberian Circular" printed in the pages of the *African Repository* the December before. That circular, penned by a community-appointed committee of settlers that included George McGill and Barbour, was an address to the people of color of the United States that attempted to dispel the "many misrepresentations ... of a nature slanderous to *us*, and in their effects injurious to *them*."

Regardless of the lack of *direct* opposition against the settlers, the Liberians desired to contradict the overarching African American narrative. This is clear once they begin to list their corrections: "The first consideration which caused our voluntary removal to this country . . . is liberty." After affirming that their residence in Liberia was their choice, the settlers continued on to declare the West African coast healthy for those who survived the initial bout of fever, agriculturally fruitful, and economically viable. The response from *Freedom's Journal* was swift and pointed. To their "friends of Liberia," the editors again affirmed their determination to remain in the United States and continue the fight against slavery. Liberty, they thought, was a great thing, "but we were not aware that its value was superior in Liberia." From there, in a rare diversion from other elite critiques of colonization of the period, the editorial turned on both the ideology undergirding colonization and the colonists themselves, ridiculing their small numbers and the evidence presented in the circular regarding their perception of their African liberty: "Having laws of their own, and judges chosen from among their learned and enlightened *hundreds* are subjects of the greatest self-gratification to our Liberian friends." The colony must be a fairyland, they mused, for its seemingly magical abilities to transform America's degraded into such learned and respected civil officers. Finally, the editorial provided a theory as to why Liberian settlers believed they had escaped the "debasing inferiority" of American racial castes. "Half civilized themselves, with learning enough to render them conceited; in the midst of beings still more uncivilized; can we wonder that they meet with nothing to make them sensible of the least inferiority?"[30]

Such direct assaults on the settlers themselves were relatively uncommon. It is suggestive that it was a communication from a committee of settlers directly aimed at disputing the broad anti-colonization narrative regarding Liberia that sparked such a direct and pointed critique. So long as Liberian settlers were victims tricked into relocating to an unhealthy environment, they could be disregarded as critical agents in the movement while the Euro-American colonizationists received the brunt of the fervor. But once the settlers challenged this narrative and asserted their own actions in propagating colonization, African American opponents leveled their assaults against the literal colonial space, not just the abstract one.

Ironically, this became a necessity at the exact moment at which Liberia could most easily support arguments regarding African American intellectual capacity: when it became an independent republic.

* * *

Although several colonial governors had originated from the settler ranks, it was the Liberian Declaration of Independence, signed July 26, 1847, that delivered a critical blow to the argument that the settlers were deceived by the ACS. Without the direct control of the ACS managers in the States, it became difficult although not impossible to maintain the narrative of an abstract colonial space subservient to white demands. It is incredibly suggestive that of the twelve national conventions that met before the Civil War, the only one that did not include a single mention of Liberia or a denunciation of colonization in the published minutes was the 1847 meeting. Liberia was likewise omitted from the reports of William Cooper Nell regarding the convention that graced the pages of Frederick Douglass's the *North Star*. Nell concluded his account with the declaration, "We shall not be transported," but the statement seems to arise from his own editorial voice rather than from an official rendering of the meeting.[31] Certainly, colonization and Liberia had to be topics of conversation among the delegates, but such references are absent from all official reports. Implicitly, the delegates needed to reevaluate this new development and plot a new course of attack, especially as the legal landscape of the United States shifted dramatically.

Within only a few years of Liberian independence, the turbulent 1850s marked by the draconian Fugitive Slave Act of 1850, and the *Dred Scott* decision reinvigorated free black interest in emigration. Now heading for an independent republic, with Roberts installed as president, Liberia saw a growing number of passengers arriving on colonization ships. Still, Liberia bore the baggage of its past. The 1854 National Emigration Convention was not alone in calling for removal from the United States to anywhere on the globe except Liberia as convention goers pondered how to challenge the newly minted Republic of Liberia.[32]

* * *

One approach was simply to deny that the African republic was truly independent. The 1851 New York state convention, for example, seized upon Ralph Gurley's report of his 1849 visit to Liberia. Gurley reported that the Liberians were desirous of formal recognition by the United States and cognizant of the fact that recognition would be unpopular with proslavery Americans. Gurley reported, "The peculiarities of the condition of the free people of color, and others of the African race, in this country [meaning enslaved persons], they well know, and have no wish, by any relations which may be established between their government and ours, to cause inconvenience or embarrassment." To "accommodate" the American government, "as far as may be without exposure to dishonor or self-reproach," Gurley reported in vague passive voice that "it has been suggested" that the Liberians would be willing to designate an American citizen as their representative in the United States if the United States was willing to designate a Liberian citizen as their representative in Africa. Gurley was opaque in detailing the scheme—there was no indication of precisely who suggested it—but there is logic to it from an Americo-Liberian perspective.[33] Those same elite settlers who formed Liberia's government had been the privileged ones to travel in the United States. They intimately understood the ruckus their presence could cause in the States. A tit for tat exchange in which informal recognition could be secured through a willingness to designate citizens as pseudo-ambassadors certainly corresponds with the tactics of these individuals who excelled in ambiguous exchanges. Of course, the black New Yorkers were not buying it, and in denouncing the Liberian government's obsequiousness to the United States, they targeted one of the pillars of Americo-Liberian claims on the United States: mobility.

While besmirching Liberians' willingness "in substance, to bow slavishly to the worst sense, feelings, and views of the American government," what really irked the New Yorkers were the promises of international travel. Noting that the United States had refused to recognize Haiti, they (correctly) predicted that Liberian independence would likewise not be recognized. And lacking both colonial status and recognition of nationhood, Liberia could not guarantee its citizens "the power of locomotion; the protection of citizens of each country, at home or abroad; the mutual interchange of ministers, counsellors; security to commerce, &c., &c." Again, free people of color clearly understood that one of the more compelling reasons for free blacks to emigrate was not a renewed life in Africa but a renewed relationship with the United States.[34]

In painting an image of the Liberian republic as bowing to American slavery, the New Yorkers were following established tropes. One year after the Liberian Declaration of Independence, the pages of the *North Star* informed its readers that the new Liberian government could not be regarded by people of African descent as "making much progress onward—not even a respectable semblance of progress, while its heads and chief men, continue to beg the notice of American Colonizationists and slaveholders." Also noting the independence of Liberia, that "creature of Colonization," in the pages of the *North Star*, Martin Delany applauded the political move of the infantile republic "provided she is determined to exist without a *master* and *overseer*." Delany soon became disenchanted with the Liberian leadership's continued close relations with colonizationists in the United States, and the republic's politicians bore the brunt of Delany's disdain. After an official state visit to Europe by President Roberts to wrestle official recognition of Liberian independence, secure pecuniary aid, and receive military assistance to drive out slave traders in the newly acquired territory of New Cesters, Roberts sat down to write Anson G. Phelps, a prominent New England colonizationist, regarding the fruits of his labors. The letter was published in the thirty-second annual report of the ACS as evidence of the respect and courtesy Roberts had received from European heads of state. Delany seems to have taken offense to Roberts's tone, as he closed the letter, "I have not time, dear sir, to write another letter; I beg, therefore, that you will inform the Rec. Messrs. McLain, Pinney and Tracy and Mr. Cresson of my doings in Europe.... When I reach home, the Lord willing, I will send you and them a full account of my proceedings." Instead of a private letter from a head of state to a friend, Delany interpreted the account as the official report of an underling. "Like the slave; 'cap in hand, obedient to the commands of the dons who employ them,' bidden on an errand of his master, President Roberts no sooner concludes the business of his mission ... but he writes to A. G. Phelps ... giving him an official report of his proceedings as the Minister of Liberia, an independent nation! If ever the curse of slavery were manifest in the character of man, it has fully exhibited itself in this man Roberts." Delany expanded his metaphorical use of unfree labor systems by concluding that Roberts was simultaneously an American slave serving white masters and also a serf.[35]

In light of the racialized society evolving in Liberia, another intriguing response to Liberian independence was to argue that the Liberians had actually become the surrogates of whites themselves. As noted in chapter 4, the 1853 National Negro Convention adopted both strategies in a long report from its committee on colonization, which outlined the convention's opposition to colonization through a history of the settling of Africa by European and American powers. Not only was the committee horrified at the violent expansion of Liberia into the African hinterland, but it also demurred at the idea that Liberia was an independent nation freed from the reins of ACS leaders in the States. The Liberians had joined with the Europeans in colonizing Africa for their own profits: "The truth is, the Liberians are in league with the worst enemies of Africa's dearest interest."[36] It is especially intriguing that in their long denunciation of colonization, the 1853 convention committee referenced the nearly two-decades-old 1827 Liberian Circular, specifically the section trumpeting the ability of Americo-Liberians to "associate" with American whites "on terms of equality" established by their Liberian residence.[37]

The committee cast doubt on the African origins of this address due to its dismissal of those people of color who preferred American subjugation to Liberian liberty, believing instead that the circular's wording originated with white editors in the United States. The Liberian Circular presented a remarkably strong declaration.

> We solicit none of you to emigrate to this country; for we know not who among you prefers rational independence, and the honest respect of his fellow-men, to that mental sloth and careless poverty, which you already possess, and your children will inherit after you in America. But if your views and aspirations rise a degree higher—if your minds are not as servile as your present condition—we can decide the question at once; and with confidence say, that you will bless the day, and your children after you, when you determined to become citizens of Liberia.[38]

The phrasing could certainly have been altered through the editorializing of the *African Repository*. Conversely, statements by Liberian settlers washing their hands of intransigent African Americans who would not support the colony were not uncommon. Such ideas can even be found in the letters of initially critical settlers like Joshua Stewart, who writing nearly twenty years after his arrival in Liberia in 1834, admitted that he was initially daunted by problems with the colony. "But I have Braved thous dificulty &... now Sir, I am Ready to stand forth like a champion & defend the cause of my oppressed Brethren in Africa & etc. Where could the collard man in America feal what I injoy in Africa he would not stay their one day, but they have the Shadow, but not the substance."[39]

And therein lies the rub. For the vast majority of African Americans, the socio-spatial argument of the colonizationists, the idea that the degraded of the States could be the awe of Africa, was ludicrous and laughable. More so, the colonial *space* of Liberia seemed only to offer death and continuation of the relations of power within the United States. Residence in Liberia could not equate to genuine liberty if the young republic's officials still served at the beck and call of white colonizationists across the Atlantic. Even those who supported emigration usually preferred a nation in the western hemisphere over Liberia. Those who willingly chose emigration to Liberia saw potential in this geographic argument not for making claims for black "civilization" but for actually *performing* those actions: to chart their own maps, to receive liberal educations, to wear the uniform of a high rank. Russwurm explicitly underscored the importance of performance when he publicly announced his change of heart regarding colonization to the readers of *Freedom's Journal* in February 1829. "We ask every man of colour can any thing be more simple; here, is a land in which we cannot enjoy the privileges of citizen, for certain reasons known and felt daily; but there, is one where we may enjoy all the rights of freemen . . . in a word, where we may not only feel as men, but where we may also act as such." This performance of "Americanness" shaped the racial hierarchy of Liberia.[40]

* * *

The historical development of race in Liberia suggests the necessity of addressing whiteness as a "transnational force." What does it mean that the performative actions that denoted citizenship within the United States denoted whiteness in West Africa? And that, regardless of their explanations, these nineteenth-century observers were intimately aware of this transformative whiteness? Even if few embraced this definition of whiteness based upon performance and action to the same degree as Moses Sheppard, those who read the incalculable number of reports regarding life in Liberia were aware that race as understood by most Americans was altered there.

The settlers were certainly aware of the divisions within the colonization ranks and directed their requests and correspondence accordingly. It was not just simply their positions within the Societies that led to a preponderance of correspondence from Liberians to be directed to Sheppard, Gurley, Elliott Cresson, and Benjamin Coates; these were the colonizationists most committed to fulfilling the message of elevation after emigration, and they conducted far more correspondence with Liberian settlers than, say, Henry Clay, the long-serving president of the society. Such targeted correspondence reminds us to recognize the role that African American settlers had in shaping the colonization movement. We need to remember that it was McGill who first initiated contact to secure a medical degree, Hance who initially asked for assistance in freeing his family from bondage in Maryland, and Harris who first inquired about the state of affairs regarding

African American travel in his native Tennessee. Repeatedly, Liberians called colonizationists in the United States to task to actually support their own spatially based ideology, and they were savvy correspondents who knew where to direct their letters.

Of course, they favored those colonizationists who were committed to uplift and were critical of the continued presence of other members less enamored with black social mobility, and they notified their friends in the States that these members hurt Liberia. In 1840, Russwurm informed ACS agent Samuel Wilkeson, "Were all who call themselves Colonizationists, actuated by a right spirit, how different would now be the face of things in Africa.—their earnest desire would have not only to transport the people of color across the Atlantic, but to have made their home, in their fatherland, an inviting asylum." Samuel McGill made a similar distinction between colonizationists of "a right spirit" and the remainder of the movement in regard to Gurley, whom he met in 1849 when Gurley toured the newly independent nation. Gurley, McGill thought, was "not only a friend to colonization, but a friend to my race." Even more intriguing than McGill's summation of Gurley's commitment to the cause was his description of a "Mr. Webb," an African American from New York, who had come out to examine the infant republic. "He is one of those who has to abide the abuse of the both abolitionist and colonizationist. He desires the emancipation of his race in the states as much as any one can, and yet has no disposition to remain there to engage in the war of words by which it is to be effected. He is composed of the right material for our colonies at present."[41] It is fascinating that McGill transitions from Webb's liminal position between the abolitionist and colonizationist camps to a declaration that Webb is the sort of material needed in Liberia. McGill's sentence structure suggests that while Webb's unwillingness to fight within the States leads to his denunciation from abolitionists, his dedication to ending slavery leads colonizationists to dismiss him. Again, there is a clear recognition that not all colonizationists were cut from the same cloth as Gurley, but their presence in the organization and the ability of the Liberian settlers to hold all colonizationists accountable for their ideological elevation of the relocated African American were the critical lynchpins that fostered the support of men like Russwurm and McGill.

These Liberians, then, reveled in the gray world of indeterminate foreignness that provided them with access to previously unimagined opportunities. For colonizationists of "a right spirit," only through separation could uplift or equality be achieved. The colonizationists of New York City argued that Liberian emigration offered the *only* pathway to equality in a series of declarations in 1835: "That the Colonization in Africa of our free people of colour, tends to the immediate and essential improvement of their condition; that is in fact the only method by which they can be raised to political and social equality with the whites." The *African Repository* likewise gleefully reprinted a letter from Henry Duncan, the Scottish minister and founder of the first commercial savings bank, to the *Dumfires and Galloway Courier* defending the colonization movement in the wake of the 1833 anti-colonization rally in London. For Duncan, rather than deepening the chasm between whites and blacks in the States, colonization, in fact, actually ameliorated racial tensions. Referring to the role of Liberia in providing opportunities for uplift, Duncan concluded, "Let but a small portion of them [people of African descent] become civilized, intelligent, and influential, and from that small portion of respectability will be diffused over the whole mass—increase that portion and you will increase the respectability, till it become a matter not of doubtful theory, but of strong demonstration, that the black man stands naturally on an equality with his white brother in mental powers as well as in moral feeling, and has therefore a right to demand an equality of privileges and of station."[42] Having followed the prescription of colonizationists and removed themselves as threats to a purely Euro-American body politic in the United States, Liberian settlers demanded recognition from those colonizationists. Delany did not pay any attention to the conclusion of Roberts's letter to Phelps that so outraged him, but it suggests what Liberians found attractive about this Atlantic exchange. Roberts signed his letter:

> I beg that you will remember me kindly to all your family. Say to Messrs. Dodge, Stokes, Altenburg, and your son Anson, that I can never forget their kindness to me during my stay in New York. I shall entertain a grateful remembrance of them as long as I live. I am also under lasting obligations to your dear daughters.[43]

This simple ending of a letter to a colleague strikes at the heart of this Liberian narrative and the need to frame colonization within an Atlantic world of mobility (at least in potentiality if not actuality). Too often, colonization and Liberian emigration has been interpreted as a one-directional terminus. As noted in the national conventions and accounts of Liberia published by opponents of colonization, a recurring fear among free people of color regarding colonization was the belief that once they arrived in Africa, colonial authorities would endeavor to prevent their return to the United

States.⁴⁴ Colonizationists were certainly aware of these commonly held beliefs. For this reason, the managers of the MSCS were most distraught to observe a permit granted to Alexander Hance upon his return to the States to secure his family's freedom. As the Liberian colonies were especially cash-strapped, those few moneyed settlers in a position to serve as creditors were fearful of their debtors leaving the country without settling their accounts. The government of Maryland in Liberia seems to have rectified this dilemma by having the assistant agent issue permits certifying those who wished to leave the colony as being free from debt, much to the chagrin of the managers. Recognizing that the "dread among many colored persons in Maryland is, that if they go to Africa they will not be permitted to return," the board ordered the practice stopped. They informed Russwurm, "Emigration from Africa to Am:[erica] should be on the same footing as emigration *from* America."⁴⁵ These colonizationists certainly understood the significance of this transatlantic exchange between colony and the United States. While the colony was certainly sickly and impoverished and, thus, presented obstacles to uninhibited Atlantic mobility, it also opened opportunities for previously unattainable relationships within the United States for those settlers best poised to demand and secure them.

In writing to an ACS official in Washington, D.C., in 1840, Russwurm warned the man that "your views cross the Atlantic," underscoring the symbiotic relationship between Liberia and the United States. The building blocks of a western colony and young republic—the command of space, the control of black bodies, the claims to possessing a besieged "civilization" surrounded by "barbarity," the violence employed to uphold that "civilized" spot on the map, the neat renderings of the colonies on that map, the civil and military offices claimed by the settlers—all were ingredients in the African whiteness of the settlers, and parties on both sides of the Atlantic understood that racial alchemy occurred with each new expedition dispatched to Liberia. The question, then, hinged on how that African whiteness could cross the ocean and in what forms it could "return" to the United States. If the settlers understood the spatial confines of their whiteness in Africa, they also worked to secure the relationships necessary to occupy a liminal exotic and civilized blackness, not white but also not the blackness conceived in most whites' minds in the antebellum United States. This identity was often framed by establishing what they were *not*. By laying claim to an exotic, but civilized, blackness ironically attained through African whiteness, they secured previously unattainable educations, freed family members from bondage, and traveled with fewer hindrances and more options than other free people of color. A show of military might, an image of a tidy settlement surrounded by "savage" black bodies, the possession of a "plantation" complete with its "negro quarters," an American colleague who notifies friends to treat a visitor "as a white man": these were the little things of Liberia that combined to make great changes.

Afterword

At the beginning of the twenty-first century, Ghana's tourism ministry found itself in the midst of a cultural predicament. Although many of the country's citizens remained poor, with sparse or unreliable access to electricity or safe water, the West African nation 300 miles east of Liberia did enjoy a stable democratic government, economic growth, and broad international support. Taking Israel as its model, the Ghanaian government hoped to instantiate itself as the African "homeland" for the global African diaspora, encouraging people of African descent to vacation, retire, and invest in Ghana. The country laid the groundwork to begin offering special visas to the African diaspora and to relax citizenship requirements so that diasporans could secure Ghanaian passports. Surviving sites of the Atlantic slave trade, Cape Coast Castle in particular, were placed at the forefront of these efforts to foster pan-African identity as spaces for healing, reconciliation, and memory. Unfortunately for the ministry's efforts, those diasporans seeking a "return" to Ghana and Africa were often lumped together with visiting Europeans and white Americans and collectively called *oburoni* by Ghanaians. *Oburoni* may be translated as "someone born overseas," but it is most often translated as "white foreigner." Obviously, many diasporans have been put off by this appellation, as it emphasizes their foreignness from Africa at the same moment they are trying to establish an African identity; for diasporans, it diminishes their claims to this African "home," a critical point made by the Ghanaian government to encourage their "return."[1]

Similarly to the Africans who encountered nineteenth-century African American settlers to Liberia, the Ghanaians do not necessarily use *oburoni* in a derogatory manner but rather as a means of cultural differentiation. Much as nineteenth-century Liberian Africans used "white" and "countryman" to distinguish their cultural practices from those of the newcomers, so too do most Ghanaians assert the primacy of these practices over ancestry. Recognizing that race is a product of societies, these appellations are tools used by these West Africans to identify the cultural practices of the new arrivals from the Atlantic world and distinguish them from their own construction and self-identity of blackness. Hoping to increase the number of diasporans "returning" to their Ghanaian "home," the tourism ministry introduced to Ghanaians a new word for these diasporans, *akwaaba anyemi*, in hopes of changing the locals' tongues. A neologism created from an amalgamation of the Twi and Ga languages, *akwaaba anyemi* awkwardly translates as "welcome, sibling"; few Ghanaians used the new word to reference the visiting constituents of the black diaspora.[2]

It is not surprising that Ghana would lead the way in attempting to bring the African diaspora "home." Kwame Nkrumah, its first president after independence from Great Britain, had been a leading advocate of pan-Africanism. Nkrumah's pan-Africanism was fueled by his American education at Lincoln University in Pennsylvania, one of the United States' first historically black universities. Although the college adopted its name in 1866 following the presidency and assassination of Abraham Lincoln, it was actually established in 1853 as the Ashmun Institute, named in honor of Liberian governor Jehudi Ashmun. Founded by Presbyterians with an eye to producing African American missionaries, the Ashmun Institute was specifically organized to address "the wants of Liberia and the importance to its present and future welfare, of having suitably qualified men to fill its offices and posts of authority." The three students who constituted the academy's first class—two brothers, James and Thomas Amos, and one Liberian who had returned to the States for his education, Armistead Miller—were ordained as Presbyterian ministers in April 1859 and left for Liberia as missionaries one month later.[3]

The continued use of *oburoni* in the twenty-first century despite the government's best efforts to reduce use of the term and the nineteenth-century origins of America's black university system in a college dedicated to sending educated officials to the Republic of Liberia remind us to embrace the complexity of these mobile Atlantic societies. Settlers forced colonizationists to uphold bargains and make good on their rhetoric of black opportunity in Africa, and for certain colonizationists the fulfillment of those promises would have to begin and be continuously upheld in America. Liberia was not an end for many but only a way station. The actions on one side of the ocean resonated on the other, often with unintended consequences. The Jeremiahs of unending racial conflict helped blaze a trail for previously unattainable African American educational advancements.

John Brown Russwurm could write to his half-brother in 1834 that "color is nothing in Africa" and then fume in 1838 that the neighboring African leader did not conceive of him as a "proper man . . . meaning that I am not a proper white man." Black became white and then something else entirely. John H. B. Latrobe had an African houseguest with whom he toured Baltimore's Washington Monument. "Yellow Will" became William Hall. In the mind of a city planner, Emancipation Street could terminate in a well-designed fortification to protect civilization from the encircling barbarity that it was supposed to convert.[4]

When the founders of Ashmun Institute announced their plans for an institution of higher learning reserved solely for African American students, they explained the necessity of such a school in the United States. The arduous task of serving as missionaries and high officials in Africa necessitated advanced scholarly training for their African American pupils, and as far as the trustees were concerned, that could come from only one source. "But they must be prepared for the work, they must be prepared in this country, they must be prepared by white men, and they must be prepared mainly at the expense of white men. These points we need not argue. If white men are to be their teachers, they must live here, and here are the means of support and proper oversight while they are engaged in this preparation."[5] Perhaps they did not grasp the irony that the same words could be said of Africans by the Liberian settlers in their African home.

Notes

Introduction

1. Horatio Bridge, *Journal of an African Cruiser*, ed. Nathaniel Hawthorne (New York: Wiley and Putnam, 1845), 36–38.

2. Although the United States had been nominally engaged in suppressing the Atlantic slave trade for decades, the launching of Perry's squadron reflected the political realities of the Webster-Ashburton Treaty ratified the year before. The eighth article of the treaty between Great Britain and the United States reaffirmed their mutual commitment to suppressing the slave trade and ordered each nation to dispatch a naval force to Africa's western coast to intercept slavers. See Webster-Ashburton Treaty, The Avalon Project: Documents in Law, History and Diplomacy, www.avalon.yale.edu. For the vessels and duties of the Africa Squadron, see Donald L. Canney, *Africa Squadron: The U.S. Navy and the Slave Trade, 1842–1861* (Washington, D.C.: Potomac, 2006). Eugene S. Van Sickle has detailed the complicated relationship between Liberia and the U.S. Navy. See Eugene S. Van Sickle, "Reluctant Imperialists: The U.S. Navy and Liberia, 1819–1845," *Journal of the Early Republic* 31, no. 1 (2011): 107–34.

3. Bridge, *Journal of an African Cruiser*, v–vi; Patrick Brancaccio, "'The Black Man's Paradise: Hawthorne's Editing of the *Journal of an African Cruiser*," *New England Quarterly* 53, no. 1 (March 1980): 23–41.

4. Cuffe did not attend the first meeting of the ACS but did send a letter of support. Following his death, Cuffe's legacy, along with those of other early black supporters of colonization, became contested. See Matthew J. Hetrick, "Rewriting Their Own History; Or, the Many Paul Cuffes," in *New Directions in the Study of African American Recolonization*, ed. Beverly C. Tomek and Matthew J. Hetrick (Gainesville: University Press of Florida, 2017), 288–302.

5. Winston James, *The Struggles of John Brown Russwurm: The Life and Writings of a Pan-Africanist Pioneer, 1799–1851* (New York: New York University Press, 2010), 17–18.

6. Bridge, *Journal of an African Cruiser*, 37; Diana Skipwith James to Sally Cocke, March 6, 1843, in *Slaves No More: Letters from Liberia, 1833–1869*, ed. Bell I. Wiley (Lexington: University Press of Kentucky, 1980), 57.

7. David Kazanjian's *The Colonizing Trick: National Culture and Imperial Citizenship in Early America* ably highlights the significance of colonizationist rhetoric for the conflation of U.S. citizenship with whiteness. By assuming that black skin signified that

Africa was the true "home" of African Americans, colonizationists not only equated race with a specific nation but removed blacks from the possibility of American citizenship in favor of their "natural" African citizenship. Thus, antebellum "transatlanticism" refers to modes not only of exchange but also of white colonial dominance over nonwhites. See David Kazanjian, *The Colonizing Trick: National Culture and Imperial Citizenship in Early America* (Minneapolis: University of Minnesota Press, 2003).

8. Bridge, *Journal of an African Cruiser*, 156, 164.

9. Bridge, *Journal of an African Cruiser*, 107.

10. Tom W. Shick's *Behold the Promised Land: A History of Afro-American Settler Society in Nineteenth-Century Liberia* (1980) was a significant scholarly turning point, as it maintained such a tight focus on African Americans that even the white ACS authorities fade to the background. While indigenous peoples suffered due to Shick's tunnel vision and blanket acceptance of settler viewpoints, later scholars have built upon this foundation to better explain life in the colony for settlers and indigenous peoples. See Tom W. Shick, *Behold the Promised Land: A History of Afro-American Settler Society in Nineteenth-Century Liberia* (Baltimore, Md.: Johns Hopkins University Press, 1980), 99, 142–43; Claude A. Clegg III, *The Price of Liberty: African Americans and the Making of Liberia* (Chapel Hill: University of North Carolina Press, 2004); Marie Tyler-McGraw, *An African Republic: Black and White Virginians in the Making of Liberia* (Chapel Hill: University of North Carolina Press, 2007); James Campbell, *Middle Passages: African American Journeys to Africa, 1787–2005* (New York: Penguin, 2006); Bronwen Everill, *Abolition and Empire in Sierra Leone and Liberia* (New York: Palgrave Macmillan, 2013).

11. Winston James is one of the few scholars to examine a Liberian settler traveling in the United States as part of his biography of John Brown Russwurm and his edited collection of Russwurm's writings. James, *The Struggles of John Brown Russwurm*.

12. For Lamin O. Sanneh, Liberia "had America in its eyes while it turned its back on Africa"; see Lamin O. Sanneh, *Abolitionists Abroad: American Blacks and the Making of Modern West Africa* (Cambridge, Mass.: Harvard University Press, 1999), 215; James Campbell, *Middle Passages*, xxiv; James Sidbury, *Becoming African in America: Race and Nation in the Early Black Atlantic* (Oxford: Oxford University Press, 2007), 200–201; Bronwen Everill, "'Destiny Seems to Point Me to That Country': Early Nineteenth-Century African American Migration, Emigration, and Expansion," *Journal of Global History* 7 (2012): 60; Everill, *Abolition and Empire in Sierra Leone and Liberia*, 9–11, 55.

13. Beverly Tomek's history of colonization in Pennsylvania offers several useful case studies that illuminate the multitudinous personalities who were drawn at various points in their lives to the colonization schemes. Looking at New England reformers, Gale Kenny has argued that Christians supporting missionary efforts in Africa latched onto colonization as a means to ascribe to a rhetorical interracial equality while also allowing them to create actual physical separation between themselves and people of color. This was the appeal of colonization for one New England's leading colonizationists, Leonard Bacon. See Beverly Tomek, *Colonization and Its Discontents: Emancipation, Emigration, and Antislavery in Antebellum Pennsylvania* (New York: New York University Press, 2010); Gale Kenny, "Race, Sympathy, and Missionary Sensibility in the New England Colonization Movement," in *New Directions in the Study of African American Recolo-*

nization, ed. Beverly C. Tomek and Matthew Hetrick (Gainesville: University Press of Florida, 2017), 33–49; Hugh Davis, *Leonard Bacon: New England Reformer and Antislavery Moderate* (Baton Rouge: Louisiana State University Press, 1998).

14. Here, I join with Ben Wright, who also turns away from the question of slavery. Ben Wright, "'The Heathen Are Demanding the Gospel': Conversion, Redemption, and African Colonization," in *New Directions in the Study of African American Recolonization*, ed. Beverly C. Tomek and Matthew Hetrick (Gainesville: University Press of Florida, 2017), 50–69.

15. Quote is from Leslie M. Alexander, *African or American?: Black Identity and Political Activism in New York City, 1784–1861* (Urbana: University of Illinois Press, 2008), xix, 68–69. Alexander cites Floyd J. Miller's seminal *The Search for a Black Nationality* as the foundation for her distinction, but Miller never makes such a deterministic boundary between "colonization" and "emigration." Rather, he wrote, "'Colonization' and 'emigration' are used interchangeably throughout this work, in conformity with common practices in black history. However, most students of eighteenth- and nineteenth-century black migratory activities use 'colonization' to refer to those movements which are *largely* [emphasis mine] white-inspired—such as the American Colonization Society's efforts to found and maintain an African colony. There is a tendency to use 'emigration' to describe black-initiated movements, although 'colonization' has also been applied in these cases. While this usage has influenced me, I make no brief for any conceptual significance inherent in my terminology." Rather than arguing that all colonization activities must be the work of racist whites, Miller actually paid serious attention to the minority of African Americans who were attracted to colonization rather than dismissing them. See Floyd J. Miller, *The Search for a Black Nationality: Black Emigration and Colonization, 1787–1863* (Urbana: University of Illinois Press, 1975), vii, 54. Still, the white-led colonization/black-led emigration binary is commonly used by scholars. See, for example, Richard S. Newman, *The Transformation of American Abolitionism: Fighting Slavery in the Early Republic* (Chapel Hill: University of North Carolina Press, 2002), 96–104; John Stauffer, *The Black Hearts of Men: Radical Abolitionism and the Transformation of Race* (Cambridge, Mass.: Harvard University Press, 2002), 97–102; Ousmane K. Power-Greene, *Against Wind and Tide: The African American Struggle against the Colonization Movement* (New York: New York University Press, 2014), 4, 17–45.

16. Within the antislavery camp, Eric Burin and Beverly Tomek have led the charge. For Burin, not only was the ACS an inherently antislavery organization, but it also led a prolonged and direct assault on the institution. Tomek at least quantifies her study with an all-important "at least in Pennsylvania" when she makes her case for the antislavery credentials of colonizationists. See Eric Burin, *Slavery and the Peculiar Solution: A History of the American Colonization Society* (Gainesville: University Press of Florida, 2005), 5; Tomek, *Colonization and Its Discontents*, 1.

17. Clegg gets to the heart of the ACS agenda when he argues that colonization transcended slavery "since blackness itself, burdened with all of the degrading, brutalized, guilt-ridden meanings that bondage and history had encumbered it with, was the problem." See Clegg, *The Price of Liberty*, 33.

18. Nicholas Guyatt notes that both Indian Removal and colonization emerged at the

same historical moment, and both were supported by many Americans who conceived of themselves as "liberals" aiding nonwhites by ensuring their respective uplift via separation from whites. See Nicholas Guyatt, *Bind Us Apart: How Enlightened Americans Invented Racial Segregation* (New York: Basic, 2016); Brandon Mills, "'The United States of Africa': Liberian Independence and the Contested Meaning of a Black Republic," *Journal of the Early Republic* 34, no. 1 (2014): 83–84.

19. *The First Annual Report of the American Society for Colonizing the Free People of Color, of the United States*, 40; Marie Tyler-McGraw, *An African Republic: Black and White Virginians in the Making of Liberia* (Chapel Hill: University of North Carolina Press, 2007), 24; Clegg, *The Price of Liberty*, 30.

20. Joanne Pope Melish has observed that this train of colonizationist thinking bears a superficial resemblance to earlier arguments for environmental racism, the belief in the environment's capacity to mutate racial distinctions. Colonizationist arguments, however, focused on Africa as the "natural" place for African Americans; the environment does not reshape their race but rather provides the "natural" setting to nurture the essence of the African American settlers. Joanne Pope Melish, *Disowning Slavery: Gradual Emancipation and "Race" in New England, 1780–1860* (Ithaca: Cornell University Press, 1998), 195–97.

21. The study of whiteness flourished in the mid-1990s and early 2000s. At the height of this scholarly wave, whiteness studies were most useful in delineating the means by which "race" is and has been constructed throughout history and in reminding scholars to include "white" in their discussions of "race." The power of the argument lay in the contention that whiteness placed a dominant claim over class, gender, or political affiliation, such that being white provided a unifying bond over all other divergent identities. Yet, even in its early years, Peter Kolchin noted the tendency of whiteness scholarship to operate in dualities in which whiteness was both a contextual product of time and place and yet somehow pervasive, real, and unchanging after its formation. If initially determined to extricate studies of race from binaries, its users rapidly fell into "white/nonwhite" binaries themselves. Recently, scholars have sought to relocate whiteness studies beyond the confines of the United States and reestablish it as a global product of European colonialism. Such an approach also reminds us that the contours, definitions, performances, and behaviors associated with "whiteness" are not universal but rather products of certain places and times. The example of colonial Liberia suggests that it is possible to examine "whiteness" without necessarily focusing on "whites." See Alexander Saxton, *The Rise and Fall of the White Republic: Class Politics and Mass Culture in Nineteenth-Century America* (New York: Verso, 1990); David Roediger, *The Wages of Whiteness: Race and the Making of the American Working Class* (New York: Verso, 1991); Peter Kolchin, "Whiteness Studies: The New History of Race in America," *Journal of American History* 89, no. 1 (2002): 159; Leigh Boucher, Jane Carey, and Katherine Ellinghaus, eds., *Re-Orienting Whiteness* (New York: Palgrave Macmillan, 2009); Noel Ignatiev, *How the Irish Became White* (New York: Routledge, 1995); Ariela J. Gross, *What Blood Won't Tell: A History of Race on Trial in America* (Cambridge, Mass.: Harvard University Press, 2008).

22. Ariela J. Gross discusses this "twoness" of race in *What Blood Won't Tell*. She is

particularly struck by how the paradoxical components of race—the idea that race is an easily definable "clear-cut identity" and also an "ever-shifting category"—combine to form the "common sense of race." See Gross, *What Blood Won't Tell*, 16–72.

23. Samuel Wilkeson, *A Concise History of the Commencement, Progress and Present Condition of the American Colonies in Liberia* (Washington, D.C.: Madisonian, 1839), 45.

24. Whyte points to the Liberian term "Kwi," originally applied to whites and then to the settlers, which evolved in Liberian English to denote Westernization. In the colonial period, none of the correspondence coming from Liberia uses "Kwi," favoring instead the racialized term "white," and while this African whiteness was pliable, it was not necessarily easy to break into. Tunde Adeleke, *Unafrican Americans: Nineteenth-Century Black Nationalists and the Civilizing Mission* (Lexington: University Press of Kentucky, 1998); Christine Whyte, "Between Empire and Colony: American Imperialism and Pan-African Colonialism in Liberia, 1810–2003," *National Identities* 18, no. 1 (2016): 79–80.

25. Another name for the pepper, the "grains of paradise," yielded the alternative name of the region, the "Grain Coast."

26. See Elizabeth Stordeur Pryor, *Colored Travelers: Mobility and the Fight for Citizenship before the Civil War* (Chapel Hill: University of North Carolina Press, 2016).

27. Paul Gilroy, *The Black Atlantic: Modernity and Double Consciousness* (Cambridge, Mass.: Harvard University Press, 1993), 15.

28. For a strong overview of the criticisms of Gilroy's black Atlantic model, see Paul Tiyambe Zeleza, "Beyond the African Diaspora: Beyond the Black Atlantic," *African Affairs* 104, no. 414 (2005): 35–68. See also Paul Tiyambe Zeleza, "African Diasporas: Toward a Global History," *African Studies Review* 53, no. 1 (2010): 1–19.

29. Utilizing letters from settlers manumitted by John Hartwell Cocke, Ben Schiller has argued that ex-slaves' identities were intimately connected to their American homelands rather than as constituent members of a black or African diaspora. David Kazanjian makes a similar case, likewise utilizing letters from Liberia, but focusing on the former slaves of John McDonogh, to argue that "references to Africa as a homeland by emancipated black settlers in colonial and early national Liberia are exceedingly rare." These are not as rare as Kazanjian argues. Even in the article in which Kazanjian makes this claim, he also quotes the formerly enslaved Henrietta Fuller: "Liberia is the home for our race & as good a country as they can find, Industry & perseverance is only required to make a man happy & wealthy in this our Adopted country." There was great diversity of opinion among settlers regarding the identity of their "home." In his biography of John Brown Russwurm, Winston James was particularly struck by the "extent to which Russwurm had become attached to his new African home, his corresponding bemused detachment from the United States, and his eagerness to return [to] his 'free home' in Liberia." See Ben Schiller, "US Slavery's Diaspora: Black Atlantic History at the Crossroads of 'Race,' Enslavement, and Colonisation," *Slavery & Abolition* 32, no. 2 (June 2011): 208–9; David Kazanjian, "The Speculative Freedom of Colonial Liberia," *American Quarterly* 63, no. 4 (2011): 882; James, *The Struggles of John Brown Russwurm*, 238–42.

30. On the federal government's involvement with Liberia, see David F. Ericson, "The American Colonization Society's Not-So-Private Colonization Project," in *New Directions in the Study of African American Recolonization*, 111–28; Padraic X. Scanlan, *Free-*

dom's Debtors: British Antislavery in Sierra Leone in the Age of Revolution (New Haven: Yale University Press, 2017), 14–25.

31. Lisa A. Lindsay's study of James Churchill Vaughan is illustrative of the possibilities. A freeman of color originally from South Carolina, Vaughan emigrated to the Republic of Liberia in 1853. He did not like life in Liberia and secured passage to Yorubaland—modern-day Nigeria—with a group of missionaries. He found success there and subsequent generations of Vaughans became Nigerian elites. The Vaughans integrated so well into Nigerian society that a family story emerged that "Church," Vaughan's father, had actually been Yoruba and, thus, this constituted the sort of "homecoming" favored by colonizationists. The story, in fact, was not true, but it is suggestive of the alchemic possibilities of transatlantic travel. See Lisa A. Lindsay, *Atlantic Bonds: A Nineteenth-Century Odyssey from America to Africa* (Chapel Hill: University of North Carolina Press, 2017).

32. In his discussion of the colonization movement's gendered rhetoric, Bruce Dorsey has argued that colonizationists, both white and black, presented a masculine framework that emphasized politics and open forums and thus limited the roles available to women when compared to abolitionist groups. See Bruce Dorsey, *Reforming Men and Women: Gender in the Antebellum City* (Ithaca, N.Y.: Cornell University Press, 2002), 136–64.

33. This is especially underscored by Bronwen Everill building upon the work of Burin and Clegg. See Everill, "'Destiny Seems to Point Me to That Country,'" 55–57.

34. See Diane Frost, "Ethnic Identity, Transience and Settlement: The Kru in Liverpool since the Late Nineteenth Century," *Immigrants & Minorities* 12, no. 3 (1993); Frederick D. McEvoy, "Understanding Ethnic Realities among the Grebo and Kru Peoples of West Africa," *Africa: Journal of the international African Institute* 47, no. 1 (1977): 62–80; Jane Martin, "Krumen 'Down the Coast': Liberian Migrants on the West African Coast in the 19th and 20th Centuries," *International Journal of African Historical Studies* 18, no. 3 (1985): 401–23. For a broader history of the Kru during the period of Liberian settlement, see George E. Brooks, Jr., *The Kru Mariner in the Nineteenth Century: An Historical Compendium* (Newark, Del.: Liberian Studies Association, 1972).

35. This work owes a debt to V. Y. Mudimbe, who suggested that colonialism be understood through three "main keys": "the procedures of acquiring, distributing, and exploiting lands in colonies; the policies of domesticating natives; and the manner of managing ancient organizations and implementing new modes of production." Mudimbe recognized the problematic colonial space presented by Liberia, founded by settlers who were both products of and rejected by white Westerners, but he attempted to address it through an examination of the writings of Edward Wilmot Blyden. The West Indies–born Blyden was a brilliant thinker and writer who served at various points in both Liberia and Sierra Leone as a newspaper editor, college professor, missionary, and government official. Curiously, Mudimbe attempted to separate this "strange and exceptional man" from his own "historical or sociological climate" in order to mine Blyden's works as an "archeological viewpoint" in order to better understand the "nineteenth-century atmosphere." Mudimbe found Blyden's emphasis on "civilizing" Africa through black colonization as simply opposing one racist view by presenting an alternative racist view. While Blyden was exceptional, within the context of Liberia's colonial history he

was certainly not "strange." V. Y. Mudimbe, *The Invention of Africa: Gnosis, Philosophy, and the Order of Knowledge* (Bloomington: Indiana University Press, 1988), 2, 111–47.

36. Nicholas Guyatt, *Bind Us Apart*, 11–12.

37. Bronwen Everill and William E. Allen are the scholars who have most closely examined Liberia's agriculture. See Bronwen Everill, "'The Colony Has Made No Progress in Agriculture': Contested perceptions of Agriculture in the Colonies of Sierra Leone & Liberia," in *Commercial Agriculture, The Slave Trade & Slavery in Atlantic Africa*, ed. Robin Law, Suzanne Schwartz, and Silke Strickrodt (Woodbridge, U.K.: James Currey, 2013), 192–202; William E. Allen, "Rethinking the History of Settler Agriculture in Nineteenth-Century Liberia," *International Journal of African Historical Studies* 37, no. 3 (2004): 435–62.

38. In modern Liberia, "Congo" is used to denote the descendants of both Americo-Liberians and recaptured Africans. This reflects their status as nineteenth- and twentieth-century migrants to the Liberian coast as well as the historical trajectory in which Congo communities increasingly became allied with the Americo-Liberians. See Ayodeji Olukoju, *Culture and Customs of Liberia* (Westport, Conn.: Greenwood, 2006), 3.

39. In his survey of Liberian agriculture, William E. Allen calls for greater investigation of Liberia's labor shortages as the probable cause of the colony and republic's poor agricultural output. See Allen, "Rethinking the History of Settler Agriculture in Nineteenth-Century Liberia," 453–58.

40. On the use of "colored" rather than "African," see Patrick Rael, *Black Identity and Black Protest in the Antebellum North* (Chapel Hill: University of North Carolina Press, 2002), 82–117. Baltimore has had a particularly prominent place in the discussion on black citizenship, given what Martha S. Jones has termed a "radical strain of colonization" in Maryland. See, for example, Martha S. Jones, *Birthright Citizens: A History of Race and Rights in Antebellum America* (Cambridge, Mass.: Cambridge University Press, 2018); and Andrew K. Diemer, *The Politics of Black Citizenship: Free African Americans in the Mid-Atlantic Borderland, 1817–1863* (Athens: University of Georgia Press, 2016), 11–46.

41. I concur with Ariela J. Gross's argument that "mixed race," although possessing historical precedent, suggests an inherent reality to race that I do not support. I have followed her suggestion and utilize "racially ambiguous" or "mixed ancestry" whenever appropriate to convey the sentiments of the individuals of this study without inadvertently ascribing to their theories of inherent racial identity and "blood." I use "mixed race" in the text only when it is necessary to reinforce the viewpoints of historical figures. See Gross, *What Blood Won't Tell*, ix–x.

42. Eric Burin, for example, utilized the attempted coup of the antislavery faction in 1833 to support his broader argument that the ACS was an antislavery organization. See Burin, *Slavery and the Peculiar Solution*, 23–24.

43. Today, the former Maryland in Liberia is Maryland County, the southeasternmost county of Liberia neighboring Côte d'Ivoire.

44. Scholars examining the colonization movement have always faced the problem of the sheer enormity of the scale of operations upon which the colonization societies operated. The records of the ACS housed in the Library of Congress contain 190,000

items, to say nothing of the hundreds of other caches of documents deposited across the country. Adding additional problems to archival research, a series of civil wars in Liberia raging between 1989 and 2003 dramatically damaged the infrastructure of the country and makes conducting research in Liberia difficult. In 2009, the staff of the National Archives estimated that 60 to 75 percent of their collection was lost to looting or destroyed during the war. Those documents that were saved by relocating them to the J. J. Roberts house do constitute more than one thousand boxes of materials, but there is no catalog or system of organization. See Myles Osborne, "A Note on the Liberian Archives," *History in Africa* 36 (2009): 461–63.

45. Beverly C. Tomek has joined with Eric Burin in studying colonization in Pennsylvania. Richard L. Hall and Penelope Campbell have examined Maryland. Clegg's work focuses on North Carolina; Alan Huffman has published a history of Mississippi in Africa; Tyler-McGraw focuses on Virginia. In addition to the previously cited works by these scholars, see Richard L. Hall, *On Afric's Shore: A History of Maryland in Liberia, 1834–1857* (Baltimore: Maryland Historical Society, 2003); Penelope Campbell, *Maryland in Africa: The Maryland State Colonization Society, 1831–1857* (Urbana: University of Illinois Press, 1971); Alan Huffman, *Mississippi in Africa: The Saga of the Slaves of Prospect Hill Plantation and Their Legacy in Liberia Today* (New York: Gotham, 2004). There is an unpublished dissertation on the colonization movement in Kentucky; see Charles Raymond Bennett, "All Things to All People: The American Colonization Society in Kentucky, 1829–1860" (Ph.D. diss., University of Kentucky, 1980).

46. Michael Gomez and James Sidbury have argued that the concept of a unified African identity was a product of forced relocation and slavery rather than of the continent itself, where individuals would have retained their ethnic identities. Leslie M. Alexander has written on the political and social discourse within the United States among African Americans about whether to emphasize their "African" or "American" identity in the early nineteenth century. The transition away from the once-popular "African" is largely attributed to the colonization movement. See Sidbury, *Becoming African in America*; Michael A. Gomez, *Exchanging Our Country Marks: The Transformation of African Identities in the Colonial and Antebellum South* (Chapel Hill: University of North Carolina Press, 1998); Alexander, *African or American?*

47. Olukoju, *Culture and Customs of Liberia*, 3–5.

48. Delany had provided the introduction to William Nesbit's scathing 1855 critique of Liberia, *Four Months in Liberia or, African Colonization Exposed*. In his introduction, Delany thanked Nesbit for exposing "the true state of things in that miserable hovel of emancipated and superannuated slaves, and deceived colored freemen, controlled by the intrigues of a conclave of upstart colored hirelings of the slave power in the United States." See William Nesbit, *Four Months in Liberia, or African Colonization Exposed* (Pittsburgh: J. T. Shryock, 1855), 5.

49. For Delany's thinking on emigration, see "Call for a National Emigration Convention of Colored Men to Be Held in Cleveland, Ohio, on the 24th, 25th and 26th of August, 1854," in *Martin R. Delany: A Documentary Reader*, ed. Robert S. Levine (Chapel Hill: University of North Carolina Press, 2003), 240; James Campbell, *Middle Passages*, 57–98.

50. Martin R. Delany, *Official Report of the Niger Valley Exploring Party* (New York: Thomas Hamilton, 1861), 12.

51. Ifeoma Kiddoe Nwankwo, *Black Cosmopolitanism: Racial Consciousness and Transnational Identity in the Nineteenth-Century Americas* (Philadelphia: University of Pennsylvania Press, 2005), 9–15, 56–74; Martin Delany, *Blake: Or, the Huts of America* (Boston: Beacon, 1970), 110–17, 237–38, 245–48.

52. Martin Delany, "Political Destiny of the Colored Race on the American Continent," in *Proceedings of the National Emigration Convention of Colored People* (Pittsburgh: A. A. Anderson, 1854), 39–41.

Chapter 1. "To Be Called a Free Colored Man in the States Is Synonymous with What We Here Term Slavery": Transformative Mobility and Liberian Travels through the United States

1. The confusion engendered by this awkward arrangement of government and society agents would be rectified in the future by naming the governor of the colony as agent both of the ACS and of the United States government.

2. An Act in Addition to the Acts Prohibiting the Slave Trade, chap. 101, 3 *Stat.* 532–34; Floyd J. Miller, *The Search for a Black Nationality: Black Colonization and Emigration, 1787–1863* (Urbana: University of Illinois Press, 1975), 59–61.

3. Floyd J. Miller described Coker as a man who had lived much of his life in a netherworld between white and black. Floyd J. Miller, *The Search for a Black Nationality: Black Emigration and Colonization, 1787–1863* (Urbana: University of Illinois Press, 1975), 55–65.

4. Miller, *The Search for a Black Nationality*, 31–55. For a history of the American traders along the Rio Pongo, see Bruce L. Mouser, *American Colony on the Rio Pongo: The War of 1812, the Slave Trade, and the Proposed Settlement of African Americans, 1810–1830* (Trenton, N.J.: Africa World Press, 2013).

5. African Institution, *Barrow's Voyage to Cochinchina* (London: Ellerton and Henderson), 71–77; Samuel Mills, "Abstract of a Journal of the Late Rev. Samuel John Mills, Written While in Africa," in *The Second Annual Report of the American Society for Colonizing the Free People of Color in the United States* (Washington, D.C.: Davis and Force, 1819), 24–31.

6. Elijah Johnson, "Extracts from Elijah Johnson Esq's Journal," trans. Christian Wiltberger, Manuscript Division, Library of Congress, Washington, D.C.

7. Miller, *The Search for a Black Nationality*, 62–63; Johnson, "Extracts from Elijah Johnson Esq's Journal."

8. Miller, *The Search for a Black Nationality*, 54–63; Christian Wiltberger Diary, Manuscript Division, Library of Congress, Washington, D.C.

9. Ephraim Bacon, *Abstract of a Journal Kept by E. Bacon*, 4th ed. (Philadelphia: Clark & Raser, 1824), 18–22, 42–43.

10. Ralph R. Gurley, *Life of Jehudi Ashmun, Late Colonial Agent in Liberia: With an Appendix, Containing Extracts from his Journal and Other Writings; With a Brief Sketch of the Life of the Rev. Lott Cary* (Washington, D.C.: James C. Dunn, 1835), 114–15; December 10–December 15, 1821, Wiltberger Diary.

11. Wiltberger Diary; Miller, *The Search for a Black Nationality*, 69–72; Ashmun, *History of the American Colony in Liberia*, 5–9.

12. Following repeated settler protests, this provision would eventually be altered to a policy where settlers received rations and supplies by agreeing to cultivate and improve their respective allotments.

13. On the Constitution of 1820 and laws of Liberia before the 1824 reorganization, see Charles Henry Huberich, *The Political and Legislative History of Liberia* (New York: Central Book Co., 1947), 1:145–55.

14. See the Constitution of 1820 and Ashmun's response in Huberich, *The Political and Legislative History of Liberia*, 1:147, 319.

15. Huberich, *The Political and Legislative History of Liberia*, 1:145–55; *The Seventh Annual Report of the American Society for Colonizing the Free People of Color of the United States* (Washington, D.C.: Davis and Force, 1824), 13–24; Gurley, *Life of Jehudi Ashmun, Late Colonial Agent in Liberia*, 180–215; Miller, *The Search for a Black Nationality*, 72–74; P. J. Staudenraus, *The Colonization Movement, 1816–1865* (New York: Columbia University Press, 1961), 88–97.

16. Nathaniel Brander to Ralph R. Gurley, May 21, 1839, ACS.

17. *Liberia Herald*, September 21, 1842, 3; George McGill to Maryland State Colonization Society, March 8, 1834, MSCS.

18. Martin R. Delany, *Official Report of the Niger Valley Exploring Party* (New York: Thomas Hamilton, 1861), 27, 71.

19. Diana Skipwith to Sally Cocke, November 7, 1839, in Wiley, ed., *Slaves No More*, 49; Robert Leander Sterdivant to John H. Cocke, August 13, 1857, in Wiley, ed., *Slaves No More*, 83; Nancy Smith McDonogh to John McDonogh, July 3, 1848, in Wiley, ed., *Slaves No More*, 150.

20. Edlie L. Wong, *Neither Fugitive nor Free: Atlantic Slavery, Freedom Suits, and the Legal Culture of Travel* (New York: New York University Press, 2009), 183–262; Ifeoma Kiddoe Nwankwo, *Black Cosmopolitanism: Racial Consciousness and Transnational Identity in the Nineteenth-Century Americas* (Philadelphia: University of Pennsylvania Press, 2005), 9–15, 56–74; *An Act for the Better Regulation and Government of Free Negroes and Persons of Color; And for Other Purposes, South Caroline Statute No. 2277, in The Statutes At Large of South Carolina*, ed. J. McCord (Columbia, S.C.: A. S. Johnston, printer, 1840), 7:461–62.

21. Nwankwo, *Black Cosmopolitanism*, 57–60; Martin Delany, *Blake: Or, the Huts of America* (Boston: Beacon, 1970), 247–48.

22. *An Act for the Better Regulation and Government of Free Negroes and Persons of Color; And for Other Purposes, South Caroline Statute No. 2277, in The Statutes at Large of South Carolina*, ed. J. McCord (Columbia, S.C.: A. S. Johnston, printer, 1840), 7:461–62; *An Act the More Effectually to Prohibit Free Negroes and Persons of Colour from Entering this State; And for Other Purposes, South Carolina Statute 2319 in The Statutes At Large of South Carolina*, ed. J. McCord (Columbia, S.C.: A. S. Johnston, printer, 1840), 7:463–66; *An Act to Amend "An Act the More Effectually to Prohibit Free Negroes and Persons of Color from Entering into This State"; and for Other Purposes, South Carolina Statute 2361*

in the Statutes At Large of South Carolina, ed. J. McCord (Columbia, S.C.: A. S. Johnston, printer, 1840), 7:466–67.

23. On passports and African American travels, see Elizabeth Stordeur Pryor, *Colored Travelers: Mobility and the Fight for Citizenship before the Civil War* (Chapel Hill: University of North Carolina Press, 2016), 104–25.

24. Geographer Tim Cresswell highlights the constraints of mobility for most subjects by emphasizing an examination of what he terms the "prosthetic subject." These are individuals incapable of initiating and controlling their own movements. For Cresswell, the prosthetic subject is constrained by the availability of modes of transportation; see Tim Cresswell, *On the Move: Mobility in the Modern Western World* (New York: Routledge, 2006), 198–99; "Inhumanity," *Freedom's Journal*, March 23, 1827, 3.

25. Moses Sheppard to William Polk, May 10, 1837, Moses Sheppard Papers, Friends Historical Library, Swarthmore College, Swarthmore, Penn.

26. Sion Harris to Samuel Wilkeson, April 16, 1840, in Bell I. Wiley, ed., *Slaves No More: Letters from Liberia, 1833–1869* (Lexington: University Press of Kentucky, 1980), 220–23; Ezekiel Birdseye to Gerrit Smith, October 11, 1841, in *An Abolitionist in the Appalachian South: Ezekiel Birdseye on Slavery, Capitalism, and Separate Statehood in East Tennessee, 1841–1846*, ed. Durwood Dunn (Knoxville: University of Tennessee Press, 1997), 185–87.

27. At least, Harris claimed in his letter that he left no immediate family in the United States. In his letter to Gerrit Smith, Ezekiel Birdseye claimed that Harris was visiting a brother in eastern Tennessee. This may reflect subterfuge on the part of Harris to emphasize his lack of connections to the United States and thus reaffirm his commitment to returning to Liberia. More likely, Birdseye was unaware that Harris was visiting his wife's relatives.

28. "Agents," *African Repository and Colonial Journal* 18, no. 16 (August 15, 1841): 250.

29. Sion Harris to Samuel Wilkeson, April 16, 1840, in Wiley, ed., *Slaves No More*, 220–23; "Departure of the Mariposa," *African Repository and Colonial Journal* 18, no. 10 (August 1842): 262; "Massachusetts Colonization Society," *African Repository and Colonial Journal* 18, no. 11 (September 1842): 298; Ezekiel Birdseye to Gerrit Smith, October 11, 1841, in *An Abolitionist in the Appalachian South*, 187–88.

30. "Information Wanted," *Maryland Colonization Journal* 1, no. 7 (December 1841): 102.

31. The records of the MSCS list the Hances as freeborn residents of Calvert County, Maryland, at the time of their departure. The subsequent dealings between Hance and the owner of his daughters suggest that this was unlikely. Their classification as "freeborn" in the settler records probably reflected an error on the part of the scribe, who either mistook a currently free person of color for someone born free, assumed that the legal status of the patriarch applied to the entire family, or was tricked by the Hances in an intentional effort on the part of the Hance family to obscure their enslaved past. Alexander Hance to the Maryland State Colonization Society, September 11, 1837, MSCS.

32. Alexander Hance to William McKenney, March 14, 1835, MSCS; Alexander Hance to William McKenney, August 30, 1835, MSCS.

33. Richard L. Hall, *On Afric's Shore: A History of Maryland in Liberia, 1834–1857* (Baltimore: Maryland Historical Society, 2003), 446–47; Alexander Hance to the Maryland State Colonization Society, September 11, 1837, MSCS; Minutes of the Meeting of the Board of Managers of the Maryland State Colonization Society, September 29, 1837, MSCS.

34. Hall, *On Afric's Shore*, 53–55, 169–71; Alexander Hance to John H. B. Latrobe, April 7, 1838, MSCS.

35. Samuel F. McGill to Moses Sheppard, January 20, 1846, Moses Sheppard Papers; John B. Russwurm to John H. B. Latrobe, January 24, 1846, MSCS; David Hughes to James Hall, May 30, 1846, MSCS; Moses Sheppard to James Hall, July 13, 1846, MSP; James Higgins to James Hall, August 25, 1846, MSCS.

36. Charles Scotland to James Hall, September 21, 1846, MSCS; Charles Scotland to James Hall, October 1, 1846, MSCS; Charles Scotland to James Hall, October 15, 1846, MSCS; J. W. Reynolds to James Hall, November 17, 1846, MSCS.

37. Penelope Campbell, *Maryland in Africa: The Maryland State Colonization Society, 1831–1857* (Urbana: University of Illinois Press, 1971), 64–74, 119; Hall, *On Afric's Shore*, 117–18, 130–33.

38. "The Colony and Colonization," *African Repository and Colonial Journal* 11, no. 11 (November 1835): 321–24; Samuel F. McGill to Moses Sheppard, October 9, 1835, MSP.

39. In requesting a medical education, McGill joined with other Liberian settlers who recognized the great want of medical professionals in the sickly colony. See Joshua Chase to Board of Managers of the ACS, [unknown month] 26, 1836, Records of the American Colonization Society, Manuscript Division, Library of Congress, Washington, D.C.; Jacob W. Prout to Ralph Gurley, March 12, 1835, ACS.

40. Moses Sheppard to Samuel F. McGill, January 12, 1836, MSCS.

41. Moses Sheppard to Samuel F. McGill, January 12, 1836, MSCS.

42. Students to the Faculty of the Washington Medical College, December 12, 1836, MSCS.

43. H. McCulloch et al. to the Faculty of the Washington Medical College, undated, MSCS.

44. Committee of the Maryland State Colonization Society to R. E. Harrison, December 17, 1836, MSCS; H. McCulloch et al. to the Faculty of the Washington Medical College, undated, MSCS; Edward E. Phelps to Ira A. Easter, January 9, 1837, MSCS.

45. Ira A. Easter to Samuel F. McGill, January 11, 1837, MSCS; Moses Sheppard to Thomas Edmonds, January 31, 1837, Moses Sheppard Papers; Moses Sheppard to Samuel F. McGill, May 29, 1837, Moses Sheppard Papers.

46. Samuel F. McGill to Ira A. Easter, August 11, 1837, MSCS; Samuel F. McGill to Moses Sheppard, August 18, 1837, Moses Sheppard Papers; Samuel F. McGill to Moses Sheppard, August 29, 1837, Moses Sheppard Papers.

47. Samuel F. McGill to Moses Sheppard, June 15, 1837, Moses Sheppard Papers; Samuel F. McGill to Ira Easter, April 16, 1839, MSCS.

48. While David Jones Peck is usually credited as being the first African American to receive his degree from an American institution, he did not graduate from Chicago's Rush Medical College until 1847.

49. The colonization societies usually hoped to send out two expeditions in a year, one in the spring and one in the fall. Chronically short of funds, however, the societies could rarely maintain this quixotic scheduling, and by 1838 there was discussion among the MSCS leadership of only sending out a solitary expedition each year. Indeed, there would be no spring 1839 expedition from Baltimore. McGill left for Liberia aboard the *Oberon* on November 22, 1838. The next expedition for Harper left Baltimore aboard the *Boxer* on December 12, 1839. See Hall, *On Afric's Shore*, 433–516.

50. John Stauffer, ed., *The Works of James McCune Smith* (New York: Oxford University Press, 2006), x–xi; Records of the Faculty of Medicine in Dartmouth College, 1819–1838, Dartmouth College Archives, Rauner Special Collections Library, Dartmouth College, Hanover, New Hampshire; Moses Sheppard to Samuel F. McGill, November 30, 1838, MSP.

51. Samuel F. McGill to H. B. Goodwin, March 15, 1845, MSCS.

52. Samuel F. McGill to Moses Sheppard, July 10, 1842, MSP.

53. Moses Sheppard to George R. McGill, January 12, 1836, MSCS; Moses Sheppard to Samuel F. McGill, January 12, 1836, MSCS; Campbell, *Maryland in Africa*, 119–21; Samuel F. McGill to Ira A. Easter, October 16, 1838, MSCS.

54. Michael Sappol, *A Traffic of Dead Bodies: Anatomy and Embodied Social Identity in Nineteenth-Century America* (Princeton, N.J.: Princeton University Press, 2002), 2–12, 122–30.

55. The illicit cadaver trade that McGill tapped into is detailed more completely in Robert Murray, "Bodies in Motion: Liberian Settlers, Medicine, and Mobility in the Atlantic World," *Journal of the Early Republic* 39, no. 4 (2019): 615–46.

56. The MSCS leadership was particularly worried in light of Lewis Wells, a black doctor in Baltimore, who had secured training by promising to emigrate before electing to remain in the United States. Moses Sheppard to Samuel F. McGill, January 12, 1836, MSCS.

57. Samuel F. McGill to Ira A. Easter, October 16, 1838, MSCS.

58. Samuel F. McGill to Ira A. Easter, January 29, 1838, MSCS.

59. For George Thompson's opposition to colonization, see *Speeches Delivered at the Anti-Colonization Meeting in Exeter Hall, London, July 13, 1833* (Boston: Garrison and Knapp, 1833); *Discussion on American Slavery, Between George Thompson, Esq. . . . and Rev. Robert J. Breckinridge . . . Holden in Rev. Dr. Wardlaw's Chapel, Glasgow, Scotland* (Boston: Isaac Knapp, 1836). For another man of mixed ancestry's perception of Thompson and abolitionists' opinions on mixed-race unions, see William G. Allen, *The American Prejudice Against Color* (London: W. and F. G. Cash, 1853).

60. Samuel F. McGill to Henry Goodwin [Goodwyn], March 15, 1845, MSCS; Samuel F. McGill to Ira A. Easter, January 29, 1838, MSCS.

61. In a letter to a Quaker friend and correspondent, Moses Sheppard confided that Nickolson broke off the engagement twice before agreeing to marry McGill. While Sheppard was happy for McGill, he seemed rather unimpressed with the new bride, writing, "There is nothing in her appearance or manner more than common, I have seen hundred of yellow girls quite as fascinating, but suppose love laughs at reason as well as at locksmiths." Moses Sheppard to Benjamin F. Taylor, December 14 and 15, 1842, MSP.

62. Two years after Lydia's death, McGill married again. His second wife, the seventeen-year-old orphan of early settler Francis Devany, was an Africa-born Liberian. After her death, McGill married a freeborn Virginian who had removed to Liberia as a missionary. In each marriage partner, McGill sought freeborn women who had attained some level of education. See Samuel F. McGill to Moses Sheppard, January 14, 1845, MSP; Samuel F. McGill to Moses Sheppard, June 15, 1848, MSP.

63. Samuel F. McGill to John H. B. Latrobe, January 13, 1844, MSCS; Hall, *On Afric's Shore*, 223.

64. Samuel F. McGill to Sheppard, June 15, 1837, MSP; Moses Sheppard to Samuel F. McGill, May 29, 1837, MSP.

65. Hall, *On Afric's Shore*, 218–20.

66. Samuel F. McGill to Moses Sheppard, May 18, 1839, MSP; Hall, *On Afric's Shore*, 324–25.

67. Even Richard Hall, who makes the argument that McGill is a pan-African forefather, admits that although he found portraying one useful in the United States, McGill did not like Africans. See Hall, *On Afric's Shore*, 197.

68. Samuel F. McGill to John H. B. Latrobe, June 8, 1840, MSCS.

69. Samuel F. McGill to Henry Goodwin [Goodwyn], March 15, 1845, MSCS; William Polk to Capt. Hooper, November 29, 1835, MSCS.

70. William Polk to Captain Hooper, November 29, 1835, MSCS; Moses Sheppard to William Polk, March 14, 1836, MSP.

71. William Polk to William McKenney, August 30, 1836, MSCS.

72. George R. McGill to Board of Managers of the Maryland State Colonization Society, May 13, 1837. MSCS; Horatio Bridge, *Journal of an African Cruiser*, ed. Nathaniel Hawthorne (New York: Wiley and Putnam, 1845), 163–64.

73. Moses Sheppard to George R. McGill, January 12, 1836, MSCS; Moses Sheppard to Matthews & Hopkins, January 18, 1837, MSP; Edward E. Phelps to James Hall, October 5, 1836, MSP; Moses Sheppard to George W. Light, January 28, 1837, MSP; Moses Sheppard to Thomas Edmonds, January 31, 1837, MSP; Unknown [probably Moses Sheppard] to Samuel F. McGill, June 29, 1841, MSP.

74. Claude A. Clegg III, *The Price of Liberty: African Americans and the Making of Liberia* (Chapel Hill: University of North Carolina Press, 2004), 67–68, 213.

75. Hall, *On Afric's Shore*, 257–58.

76. Richard L. Hall argues that Fletcher and McGill's personalities clashed and this partly led to Fletcher's threats that he would quit his position unless he received a formal medical education in the United States. Although McGill would later write disparagingly of Fletcher, these characterizations do not appear in McGill's correspondence when Fletcher was a student of his. Although not flushed with praise, McGill did request that Sheppard aid Fletcher in his American travels. While it is certainly conceivable that McGill was condescending toward Fletcher as reflective of his general *joie de vivre*, in this instance it seems that Hall is reading McGill's later thoughts backward in time to the earliest days of their partnership. See Hall, *On Afric's Shore*, 257–58, 280–81, 582–83; Samuel F. McGill to Moses Sheppard, November 12, 1844, MSP.

77. Samuel F. McGill to Moses Sheppard, October 27, 1839, MSP; Dempsey Fletcher to John H. B. Latrobe, September 1, 1844, MSCS; Moses Sheppard to B. F. Taylor, website, March–September 1850; Minutes of the Board of Managers of the MSCS, March 20, 1845, MSCS; Dempsey Fletcher to James Hall, January 14, 1844, MSCS.

78. See Records of the Faculty of Medicine in Dartmouth College, 1845–1862, August 4, 1846, Faculty meeting minutes.

79. Edward E. Phelps to James Hall, January 28, 1846, MSCS.

80. Moses Sheppard to B. F. Taylor, March 23, 1850, http://triptych.brynmawr.edu/cdm/compoundobject/collection/HC_QuakSlav/id/11002/rec/1; Dempsey R. Fletcher to Moses Sheppard, November 11, 1845, MSP; Moses Sheppard to Dempsey R. Fletcher, January 10, 1846, MSP.

81. Dempsey R. Fletcher to Moses Sheppard, September 16, 1850, MSP.

82. Dempsey R. Fletcher to Moses Sheppard, February 24, 1846, MSP; Dempsey R. Fletcher to Unknown [Probably James Hall], September 25, 1845, MSCS.

83. Edward E. Phelps to James Hall, October 21, 1846, MSCS.

84. The MSCS expeditions were sporadic after 1838 until the start of the annual trips of the *Liberia Packet* in 1846. See Hall, *On Afric's Shore*, 433–516.

85. See Records of the Faculty of Medicine in Dartmouth College, 1845–1862, October 29, 1846, Faculty meeting minutes. Also November 17–18, 1846, Faculty Minutes; Hall, *On Afric's Shore*, 280–81; Samuel F. McGill to Ira Easter, May 6, 1837, MSCS; Hall, *On Afric's Shore*, 489.

86. See Records of the Faculty of Medicine in Dartmouth College, 1845–1862, October 29, 1846, Faculty meeting minutes. Also November 17–18, 1846, Faculty Minutes; Hall, *On Afric's Shore*, 280–81; Samuel F. McGill to Ira Easter, May 6, 1837, MSCS.

87. Robert Breckinridge, "Hints on Colonization and Abolition; with reference to the black race," *Biblical Repertory and Theological Review* 5, no. 3 (July 1833): 282–83.

88. Elizabeth Pryor's etymology of "nigger" is particularly enlightening here, as she notes the word's use by whites to contain and control black mobility by making public spaces uncomfortable for black travelers. Given the experiences of Liberian travelers, Sheppard's closing remark is all the more poignant. Moses Sheppard to Benjamin Franklin Taylor, March–September 1850, MSP; Moses Sheppard to W. W. Handy, November 16, 1846, MSP; Moses Sheppard to Dempsey R. Fletcher, June 20, 1850, MSP; Elizabeth Stordeur Pryor, *Colored Travelers: Mobility and the Fight for Citizenship before the Civil War* (Chapel Hill: University of North Carolina Press, 2016), 10–43.

89. Dempsey R. Fletcher to John H. B. Latrobe, January 27, 1846, MSCS.

90. Robert J. Breckinridge, *The Black Race: Some Reflections on Its Position and Destiny, as Connected with Our American Disposition; A Discourse Delivered Before the Kentucky Colonization Society, at Frankfort, on the 6th Day of February, 1851* (Frankfort: A. G. Hodges, 1851), 17.

91. The reasons for training settlers as colonial physicians, according to the ACS's official organ, was "that it will ultimately diminish the expenses of the Board; that it will impress the free people of color with the truth, that they are to be encouraged in Liberia in the liberal professions; and that it is the wish of the Board, that they should share *there*

[emphasis mine], in all honourable pursuits, and rise to the highest distinction." See "Medical Education of Young Men of Color for Liberia," *African Repository and Colonial Journal* 8, no. 9 (November 1832): 285–86.

92. "Major Anthony Wood," *Maryland Colonization Journal* New Series 2, no. 11 (May 1844), 162–63; Samuel F. McGill to Moses Sheppard, February 13, 1844, MSP; Moses Sheppard to Samuel F. McGill, November 12, 1844, MSP; Gurley, *Life of Jehudi Ashmun, Late Colonial Agent in Liberia*, 153; Untitled article, *Connecticut Mirror*, January 24, 1829, 3; Major Bolin [Bolon] to James Hall, January 21, 1846, MSCS.

93. Moses Sheppard to Samuel F. McGill, November 17, 1845, MSP.

94. Andrew Hall to Unknown, January 24, 1847, MSCS.

95. These last names stem from the principal towns of which their respective fathers were headmen. They were also known, respectively, as "John Baphro" (son of Baphro or "King Joe Holland") and "Charles Bolio" (son of Weah Bolio or "King Will").

96. James Hall to John H. B. Latrobe, February 23, 1834, MSCS; Hall, *On Afric's Shore*, 42–46; Minutes of the Board of Manager of the Maryland State Colonization Society, April 26, 1834, MSCS.

97. Garrison referred to the Africans as "humbugs" in a private letter detailing his altercations with the colonizationist delegation. He does not explicitly state whether he thought the Africans were frauds or whether their manipulation by the MSCS was the fraud, but his word choice has confused at least one editor, Walter M. Merrill. See Walter M. Merrill, *The Letters of William Lloyd Garrison: I Will Be Heard!* (Cambridge, Mass.: Belknap, 1971), 1:384–87, 396–98.

98. Robert Breckinridge to Moses Sheppard, August 7, 1834, MSP.

99. "Memorandums"; journal, 58, Moses Sheppard Papers; "Died," *Baltimore Patriot & Mercantile Advertiser*, November 19, 1834, 2.

100. Nathan Lee to John H. B. Latrobe, July 5, 1838, MSCS; Samuel F. McGill to John H. B. Latrobe, June 8, 1840, MSCS.

101. Ballah is an intriguing character. Although occasionally called "Bill Williams" in correspondence, Ballah is one of the rare African figures who was largely called by his name. Since he was often referenced by name, I have elected to follow suit, although he is certainly more of an exception than a rule.

102. "Selim Ballah," *African Repository and Colonial Journal* 13, no. 3 (March 1837): 101–3.

103. The missionary J. Leighton Wilson, who transcribed the letter for "Freeman," explained to the board that the Greboes referred to the United States as "big Merica." The unspoken corollary to this formula would be that the colony clinging to the shores of Africa must be some sort of small America. J. Leighton Wilson and "King Freeman" [Pah Nemah] to the Board of Managers of the MSCS, September 5, 1836, MSCS.

104. J. Leighton Wilson to John H. B. Latrobe, June 25, 1836, MSCS; Minutes of the Board of Managers of the MSCS, June 23, 1836, and July 8, 1836, MSCS; Pah Newmah [King Freeman] to the Board of Managers of the MSCS, September 5, 1836, MSCS; Hall, *On Afric's Shore*, 52–53.

105. James Hall to John H. B. Latrobe, May 1, 1836, MSCS. Also printed in Hall, *On Afric's Shore*, 107–8.

106. Winston James, *The Struggles of John Brown Russwurm: The Life and Writings of a Pan-Africanist Pioneer, 1799–1851* (New York: New York University Press, 2010), 5–25; Hall, *On Afric's Shore*, 136–50.

107. John B. Russwurm to John H. B. Latrobe, February 12, 1837, MSCS.

108. Hall, *On Afric's Shore*, 149.

109. In his history of Liberia, Clegg notes that because of their long association with European and American merchants, their close proximity to the American colonies in Liberia, and the fact that the entire colonial population and its wares passed through their hands, the Kru functioned as both literal and cultural "middlemen" for the colony. Clegg, *The Price of Liberty*, 77.

110. "Kroomen," *African Repository and Colonial Journal* 5 (July 1829): 156–57.

111. John B. Russwurm to Samuel Wilkeson, January 4, 1840, ACS; Sion [Zion] Harris to William McLain, January 5, 1848, ACS.

Chapter 2. "All Those Things Desirable for a Map to Show": Space, Cartography, and Control in Colonial Liberia

1. Henry Clay, "Speech of the Hon. Henry Clay, before the American colonization society, in the Hall of the House of Representatives, January 20, 1827" (Washington, D.C.: Columbian, 1827).

2. Robert J. Breckinridge, *The Black Race: Some Reflections on Its Position and Destiny, as Connected with Our American Disposition; A Discourse Delivered Before the Kentucky Colonization Society, at Frankfort, on the 6th Day of February, 1851* (Frankfort: A. G. Hodges, 1851), 17; Peachy Grattan, "The Rev. Leonard Bacon's Plea for Africa, and an Address in Behalf of the Colonization Society, by Peachy Grattan, Esq," *African Repository and Colonial Journal* 1, no. 6 (August 1825): 174.

3. Bruce Dain and Nicholas Guyatt have both noted this antebellum focus on space. Dain focused more on the lingering environmentalist assumptions of nineteenth-century racism, while Guyatt focused on the parallels between Indian Removal and Colonization. Bruce Dain, *A Hideous Monster of the Mind: American Race Theory in the Early Republic* (Cambridge: Harvard University Press, 2002), 81–83, 104–5; Nicholas Guyatt, "'The Outskirts of Our Happiness': Race and the Lure of Colonization in the Early Republic," *Journal of American History* 95, no. 4 (2009): 986–88, 998–1000; Nicholas Guyatt, *Bind Us Apart: How Enlightened Americans Invented Racial Segregation* (New York: Basic, 2016).

4. David Kazanjian, "The Speculative Freedom of Colonial Liberia," *American Quarterly* 63, no. 4 (2011): 875.

5. Kazanjian, "The Speculative Freedom of Colonial Liberia," 882; Abraham Blackford to Mary C. Blackford, February 14. 1846, in Bell I. Wiley, ed., *Slaves No More: Letters from Liberia, 1833–1869* (Lexington: University Press of Kentucky, 1980), 24–25; Sezer Chue [Caesar Chew] to Unknown, September 2, 1835, MSCS; Paul Sansay to Unknown, January 16, 1839, MSCS; The book of Micah 4:1–13, New International version.

6. "An Address to the Public, By the Managers of the Colonization Society of Connecticut," *African Repository and Colonial Journal* 4, no. 4 (June 1828): 121.

7. See, for example, Hayden White, "The Forms of Wildness: Archaeology of an Idea,"

in *Tropics of Discourse: Essays in Cultural Criticism* (Baltimore, Md.: Johns Hopkins University Press, 1978), 150–82; T. Carlos Jacques, "From Savages and Barbarians to Primitives: Africa, Social Typologies, and History in Eighteenth-Century French Philosophy," *History and Theory* 36, no. 2 (May 1997): 190–215. My thinking here is heavily indebted to Karen Piper, *Cartographic Fictions: Maps, Race, and Identity* (New Brunswick, N.J.: Rutgers University Press, 2002).

8. Jacques, "From Savages and Barbarians to Primitives," 204–14.

9. "Report to the Pennsylvania Legislature," *African Repository and Colonial Journal* 16, no. 9 (May 1840): 137; "Colonization Society," *African Repository and Colonial Journal* 1, no. 10 (December 1825): 302.

10. Washington McDonogh to John McDonogh, December 28, 1845, in Wiley, ed., *Slaves No More*, 138; George R. McGill to Maryland State Colonization Society, July 12, 1832, MSCS; Matilda Lomax to Sally Cocke, July 4, 1848, in Wiley, ed., *Slaves No More*, 67; John B. Russwurm to John H. B. Latrobe, June 26, 1843, MSCS. Lomax's disparaging remarks were not directed toward the natives of Liberia but rather toward a group of recently arrived "Congoes."

11. Samuel F. McGill to John H. B. Latrobe, August 11, 1837, MSCS; Samuel F. McGill to John H. B. Latrobe, April 28, 1838, MSCS.

12. William Polk to William McKenney, February 5, 1836, MSCS; Edward Pembleton, James Rice, Isiah Shockley, et al., February 3, 1833, MSCS; Richard L. Hall, *On Afric's Shore: A History of Maryland in Liberia, 1834–1857* (Baltimore: Maryland Historical Society, 2003), 16–27.

13. William Thornton, "Town plan for Mesurado, Liberia," Library of Congress, www.loc.gov; Sidbury, 200–201.

14. While Nicholas Guyatt has noted the allure of this vision of colonial Liberia as an African United States, Brandon Mills has focused on the "contested meanings" of this "mirror" republic with the creation of an independent Republic of Liberia. See Guyatt, "'The Outskirts of Our Happiness,'" 986–1011; Brandon Mills, "'The United States of Africa': Liberian Independence and the Contested Meaning of a Black Republic," *Journal of the Early Republic* 34, no. 1 (2014): 79–107.

15. Franco Farinelli makes a similar argument for Amerigo Vespucci's maps of the Americas. Franco Farinelli, "Why America is Called America," in *Envisioning Landscapes, Making Worlds: Geography and the Humanities*, edited by Stephen Daniels et al. (New York: Routledge, 2011), 3–10.

16. Jehudi Ashmun, "Map of the West Coast of Africa from Sierra Leone to Cape Palmas, including the Colony of Liberia" (Philadelphia: A. Finley, 1830); James C. Minor to John Minor, February 11, 1833, in Wiley, ed., *Slaves No More*, 17.

17. This relationship between territorial sovereignty of the state and personal possession by an individual is highlighted in Piper, *Cartographic Fictions*, 6–14.

18. Moses Sheppard to Samuel F. McGill, May 18, 1843, MSP.

19. The settlers were correct. West African soils are susceptible to leaching, a process that greatly reduces the nutrients in the soil. See William E. Allen, "Rethinking the History of Settler Agriculture in Nineteenth-Century Liberia," *International Journal of African Historical Studies* 37, no. 3 (2004): 458–59.

20. "From Liberia," *African Repository and Colonial Journal* 14, no. 9 (September 1838): 271; Ralph R. Gurley, *Life of Jehudi Ashmun, Late Colonial Agent in Liberia: With an Appendix, Containing Extracts from his Journal and Other Writings; With a Brief Sketch of the Life of the Rev. Lott Cary* (Washington, D.C.: James C. Dunn, 1835), appendix 132.

21. "Latest from Liberia," *African Repository and Colonial Journal* 2, no. 3 (May 1826): 76–77; Report of the Citizens of Maryland in Liberia, October 24, 1844, MSCS; Moses Jackson to Eliott West, March 22, 1846, Shelby Family Papers, University of Kentucky, Lexington.

22. In the defense of the ACS, they were quoting from the internal propaganda machine of the colony, the *Liberia Herald*, published in Monrovia.

23. "Mississippi Colonization Society," *African Repository and Colonial Journal* 15, no. 5 (March 1839): 88; "Annual Report of the American Colonization Society," *African Repository and Colonial Journal* 16, no. 4 (February 1840): 66.

24. Thomas Winterbottom, "Agriculture of Africa," *African Repository and Colonial Journal* 1, no. 4 (June 1825): 101; "Description of Bornou from Clapperton's Narrative," *African Repository and Colonial Journal* 2, no. 8 (October 1826): 259.

25. Samuel Bacon, "Extracts from the Journal of the Reverend Samuel Bacon, Agent to the Colonization Society," ACS.

26. For the 1824 law code, see "Digest of the Laws Now in Force in the Colony of Liberia, August 9th 1824," in *Constitution, Government and Digest of the Laws of Liberia, as Confirmed and Established by the Board of Managers of the American Colonization Society, May 23, 1825* (Washington, D.C.: Way & Gideon, 1825), 11.

27. Anthony D. Williams, "Intelligence from Liberia: From the Lieutenant Governor, Anthony D. Williams," *African Repository and Colonial Journal* 14, no. 3 (March 1838): 67.

28. "Digest of the Laws Now in Force in the Colony of Liberia, August 19, 1824," in *Constitution and Digest of the Laws of Liberia, as Confirmed and Established by the Board of Managers of the American Colonization Society, May 23, 1825* (Washington, D.C.: Way & Gideon, 1825), 10–11.

29. Tolbert Major to Joseph Major, September 1836, and Tolbert and Austin Major to Benjamin Major, August 7, 1843, both letters can be found in Major Collection, McLean County Museum of History, Bloomington, Illinois, www.mchistory.org; Jehudi Ashmun to R. R. Gurley, June 21, 1826, in *African Repository and Colonial Journal* 2, no. 9 (November 1826): 263–64; Gurley, *Life of Jehudi Ashmun, Late Colonial Agent in Liberia*, 130–46, appendix 131–32; Lewis Crook to Ralph R. Gurley, March 3, 1835, ACS.

30. By 1826, Jehudi Ashmun was desperately asking the ACS to send out forms to record all these complicated dealings as he could only purchase forms from a Sierra Leone press as at "immoderate price." Jehudi Ashmun to R. R. Gurley, June 21, 1826, in *African Repository and Colonial Journal* 2, no. 9 (November 1826): 263–64.

31. John Revey's maps are located in the archives of the Maryland Historical Society. Unfortunately, their size, orientation, and deterioration, which make their digitized versions readable only through zooming and manipulation, make them impossible to reproduce in this work. Hall, *On Afric's Shore*, 327–30.

32. The settlers renamed Auburn Island in honor of Russwurm. After war with the Greboes in 1857 led to the annexation of the colony into the larger Republic of Liberia,

the cessation of Grebo burials on Russwurm Island was the final constituent element of the peace treaty signed between the Greboes and Americo-Liberians. See "Treaty of Peace between the Government of Maryland in Liberia and the Grebo People," *Maryland Colonization Journal* New Series 8, no. 24 (May 1857): 374–75.

33. John B. Russwurm to John H. B. Latrobe, December 8, 1839, MSCS; John Revey to John H. B. Latrobe, January 20, 1840, MSCS.

34. Hall, *On Afric's Shore*, 539–40.

35. Samuel F. McGill to Moses Sheppard, April 25, 1849, MSP. Sierra Leone and Liberia were both products of vast transatlantic networks of exchange, and McGill was not alone in comparing and contrasting the two colonial bodies. Bronwen Everill's *Abolition and Empire in Sierra Leone and Liberia* critically examines these two spaces together, both in terms of transatlantic antislavery networks and in terms of the interactions of their respective inhabitants. See Bronwen Everill, *Abolition and Empire in Sierra Leone and Liberia* (New York: Palgrave Macmillan, 2013).

36. Map of the West Coast of Africa from Sierra Leone to Cape Palmas, including the Colony of Liberia (Philadelphia: A. Finley, 1830). Library of Congress, www.loc.gov.

37. Map of Liberia (Baltimore, Md.: E. Weber & Co., 1845). Library of Congress, www.loc.gov.

38. Hall, *On Afric's Shore*, 82–84.

39. Guyatt, "'The Outskirts of Our Happiness,'" 986–88; Guyatt, *Bind Us Apart*.

40. Hilary Teague's proposal perfectly reinforces Nicholas Guyatt's argument that colonization and Indian Removal were symbiotic movements. Minutes, Legislature, 1845–1847, January 10, 1846, Liberian Government Archives. Indiana University; Andrew Jackson, "First Annual Message to Congress, December 8, 1829."

41. John Peacock, "Principles and Effects of Puritan Appropriation of Indian Land and Labor," *Ethnohistory* 31, no. 1 (Winter 1984): 39–44. The eighth annual report of the ACS, for example, claimed that colony was "already to the African tribes, like 'a city set upon a hill which cannot be hid.'" The tenth report made the connection between Jamestown, New England, and Liberia even more explicitly: "How was it with the two great Colonies of this country? Did they support themselves? Did Jamestown go on in its early period, without assistance? No, sir . . . I will now come nearer home, and consider the condition of the fathers of New England. The feeble Colonists of Plymouth could never have sustained themselves without other aid than their own." See *The Eighth Annual Report of the American Society for Colonizing the Free People of Color of the United States* (Washington, D.C.: J. C. Dunn, 1825), 14; *The Tenth Annual Report of the American Society for Colonizing the Free People of Color of the United States*, 8. This conflation of Monrovia with Jamestown or Plymouth Rock has also been noted by Nicholas Guyatt; see Guyatt, "'The Outskirts of Our Happiness,'" 986–87, 991, 999.

42. Jehudi Ashmun, "A Journal during the Negotiations for the St. Pauls Land, May 1825," ACS.

43. Marie Tyler-McGraw, *An African Republic: Black and White Virginians in the Making of Liberia* (Chapel Hill: University of North Carolina Press, 2007), 72–73.

44. William McLain to James Hall, July 14, 1845, MSCS.

45. "View of Colonial Settlement at Cape Montserado," *African Repository and Colonial Journal*, volume 3.

46. ACS images of colonial Liberia were often framed from the perspective of the Atlantic Ocean and usually incorporated a ship, visually reinforcing both the connection of the colony to Atlantic commerce and also the origins of Liberia as an American product, that is, it is seen from the American side across the water. The Republic of Liberia replicated this ocean and ship motif but reversed the perspective and presented the ship as seen from the African shore.

47. "A View of Bassa Cove," Library of Congress, www.loc.gov.

48. Images of Cape Mesurado and Bassa in University of Virginia Special Collections.

49. Stephen Smith to Zachariah Tippett, July 5, 1838, MSCS. "Cooney" seems to be a slip of Smith's pen, as elsewhere in the letter he spells the word "coloney."

50. Sampson Caesar to David Haselden, February 7, 1834, UVA website.

51. February 1840 and February 1841 Sessions for Court of Montserrado County, Monthly Court Records, Liberian Government Archives, Indiana University.

52. Revey Map.

53. Tolbert Major to Benjamin Major, October 17, 1840, Major Collection of Letters from Liberia, McLean County Museum of History, Bloomington, Illinois, in www.mchistory.org/ (accessed October 25, 2012)

54. Moses Jackson to Eliott West, March 22, 1846, Shelby Family Papers, University of Kentucky, Lexington, Kentucky; George Crawford to John M. McCalla, September 25, 1836, in Wiley, 252.

55. John B. Russwurm to John H. B. Latrobe, December 8, 1839, MSCS. William E. Allen has dispelled the dual myths that Liberian settlers were uninterested in African agricultural productions specifically and agriculture broadly. See Allen, "Rethinking the History of Settler Agriculture in Nineteenth-Century Liberia," 435–62.

56. Tolbert Major to Benjamin Major, October 17, 1840, Major Collection of Letters from Liberia, McLean County Museum of History, Bloomington, Illinois, in www.mchistory.org/ (accessed October 25, 2012); James Hall to John H. B. Latrobe, February 23, 1834, MSCS; William E. Allen, "Liberia and the Atlantic World in the Nineteenth Century: Convergence and Effects," *History in Africa* 37 (2010): 7–11, 24–40.

57. "Yellow Will" of Cape Palmas can easily be confused with "Yellow Will," the Bassa leader who resided near Edina. Not only do they share the same sobriquet suggesting racial ambiguity, but they were also staunch supporters of the American occupation.

58. James Hall provided a brief biography of "Yellow Will" in his May 1, 1836, report to the MSCS. In it, he noted that "Yellow Will" "had formerly been a head-workman, among the natives employed by the English at Fernad[o] Po." This information, coupled with the timing of events and the behavior of Fernando Po's "Yellow Will," suggests that he and the Cape Palmas "Yellow Will" were one and the same. See James Hall to MSCS, May 1, 1836, MSCS. Also printed in Winston James, *The Struggles of John Brown Russwurm: The Life and Writings of a Pan-Africanist Pioneer, 1799–1851* (New York: New York University Press, 2010), 119–20, 287.

59. Once working aboard an English vessel, "Yellow Will" would have been defined as a "Krumen." Levi Scott, "Remarks of Bishop Scott, at the Anniversary of the Missionary

Society of the M.E. Church, at Cincinnati," *African Repository and Colonial Journal* 30, no. 6 (June 1854): 181–82; James Holman, *Travels in Madeira, Sierra Leone, Teneriffe, St. Jago, Cape Coast, Fernando Po, Princes Island, etc. etc.*, 2nd ed. (London: George Routledge, 1840), 68.

60. *State Papers, Relating to Slaves in the Colonies; Slave Trade. Session: 5 February–23 July 1830*, vol. 33 (Oxford: Bodleian Library, 1830), 117–39.

61. A native African of Sierra Leone, "James Paterson" had apparently received a thorough colonial education, probably in a missionary school. He not only claimed to be a Christian but also could read and write in English fluently. Robert Jameson, the colonial judge of Dominica, who recorded the depositions of the Africans regarding the *Neirseé* affair, singled out "Paterson" as possessing a remarkable command of English. In the official state papers, the signatures of the other Africans include the ubiquitous "the mark of" to denote that they could not sign their English names. "James Paterson" was apparently the only one who could write his own signature. See Robert Jameson, "Deposition of Negroes, in Case of the 'Neirseé' or 'Estafette,'" *State Papers, Relating to Slaves in the Colonies*, 123–25.

62. Jameson, "Deposition of Negroes, in Case of the 'Neirseé' or 'Estafette,'" 117–39.

63. Jameson, "Deposition of Negroes, in Case of the 'Neirseé' or 'Estafette,'" 117–39.

64. Hall, *On Afric's Shore*, 42–46.

65. Horatio Bridge, *Journal of an African Cruiser*, ed. Nathaniel Hawthorne (New York: Wiley and Putnam, 1845), 63.

66. James Hall to John H. B. Latrobe, May 1, 1836, MSCS.

67. Levi Scott, "Remarks of Bishop Scott, at the Anniversary of the Missionary Society of the M.E. Church, at Cincinnati," 181–82; Jane Jackson Martin, "The Dual Legacy: Government Authority and Mission Influence among the Glebo of Eastern Liberia, 1834–1910" (Ph.D. diss., Boston University, 1968), 98–100.

68. Revey Map; Yellow Will to John H. B. Latrobe, June 8, 1837, MSCS; Yellow Will to John H. B. Latrobe, January 21, 1840, MSCS; Yellow Will to Oliver Holmes, Jr., May 22, 1839, MSCS; Moses Sheppard to Yellow Will, December 13, 1842, MSP.

69. *First Annual Report of the American Society for Colonizing the Free People of Color, of the United States*, 37, 40.

70. Some colonizationists said free people of color were seen as inherently degraded, while others presumed their degradation was a result of the society. Others invoked the language of disease to sow fear that "degradation" could spread. For a sample of the range of colonizationist theories of "degradation," see *The Fourth Annual Report of the Kentucky Colonization Society, with an Address, by Rev. John C. Young* (Frankfort, Ky.: Albert G. Hodges, 1833), 19; Nathaniel Bouton, *Christian Patriotism: An Address Delivered at Concord, July the Fourth, 1825* (Concord, N.H.: Shepard & Bannister, 1825), 14–17; *Proceedings of the Convention of the Friends of African Colonization, Held in the Capital at Washington, May 4, 1842* (Washington, D.C. [?]: 1842 [?]), 58; *First Report of the New-York Colonization Society* (New York: J. Seymour, 1823), 19; Cassius M. Clay, "What Is to Become of the Slaves in the United States?" *Lexington True American*, August 12, 1845.

71. Wilson Moses argues that Afrocentrism—the argument that Africa is central to the identity of African Americans and all members of the black diaspora—was not an

inherently black phenomenon and points to the arguments of white colonizationists who utilized these Afrocentric arguments to justify their plans to remove African Americans to their "natural" environment. See Wilson Moses, *Afrotopia: The Roots of African American Popular History* (New York: Cambridge University Press, 1998).

72. *First Annual Report of the American Society for Colonizing the Free People of Color of the United States*, 33, 37.

73. *The Fourteenth Annual Report of the American Society for Colonizing the Free People of Color of the United States* (Washington, D.C.: James C. Dunn, 1831), 6.

74. "Influence" was the word of choice for white and black colonizationists, whether it was a string of reports from the colonial governors—white and black—or colonization boosterism at home. For examples see *The Fifteenth Annual Report of the American Society for Colonizing the Free People of Color of the United States* (Washington, D.C.: J. C. Dunn, 1832), 4; Joseph J. Roberts, "Governor Roberts' Message," *African Repository and Colonial Journal* 19, no. 6 (June 1843): 176; *Tenth Annual Report of the American Society for Colonizing the Free People of Color of the United States* (Washington, D.C.: Way & Gideon, 1827), 46.

75. The colonization movement was filled with evangelical Christians who conceived of the colonial endeavor as one great missionary outpost. The northern societies in particular were driven by religious fervor, and one of the principal fundraising drives of the ACS was the annual Fourth of July collection taken up by sympathetic ministers. See Daniel Mayes, "Address," in *The Proceedings of the Colonization Society of Kentucky with the Address of the Hon. Daniel Mayes, at the Annual Meeting, at Frankfort, December 1st, 1831* (Frankfort: Commentator, n.d.), 23.

76. *The Twelfth Annual Report of the American Society for Colonizing the Free People of Color of the United States* (Washington, D.C.: James C. Dunn, 1829), 8.

77. John B. Russwurm to John H. B. Latrobe, December 8, 1839, MSCS; This letter is also reproduced by Winston James, but James unfortunately relies solely on transcriptions from the *African Repository and Colonial Journal* (in this case, the June 1840 issue). The reliance on printed sources leads James to overemphasize Russwurm's pan-Africanism. To their credit, the colonizationists were skillful and usually honest transcriptionists when publishing accounts from Liberia. But as producers of a work of propaganda, they were equally talented editors who chose to omit anything that challenged their narrative of pan-African unity within the colony. It is easy to see the editorial hand of the colonizationists at work; there are copyediting marks on the report in the MSCS collection to denote which sections to excise. In this instance, the editors removed the section where Russwurm dismissed the Greboes as liars and thieves. This is not to suggest that Russwurm lacked for early pan-Africanist thoughts or consistently dismissed Africans, but he was not so consistent and singular in his praise for the continent as James or the colonizationist editors portrayed. See John B. Russwurm to James Hall, September 26, 1842, MSCS. See also James, *The Struggles of John Brown Russwurm*, 246–49.

78. The "*Vandalia* Affair" is further detailed by Eugene S. Van Sickle. It unsurprisingly was the result of reported African thefts. The missionaries and naval officers attempted to bypass the colonial authorities by making demands for restitution directly to "Freeman."

See Eugene S. Van Sickle, "Reluctant Imperialists: The U.S. Navy and Liberia, 1819–1845," *Journal of the Early Republic* 31, no. 1 (2011): 119–20.

79. John B. Russwurm to James Hall, September 26, 1842, MSCS; Samon Caesar to Henry F. Westfall, August 3, 1835, *Liberian Letters*, Electronic Text Center, University of Virginia Library, www.etext.lib.virginia.edu/subjects/liberia/index.html; Jehudi Ashmun, *The Liberia Farmer*, in Gurley, *Life of Jehudi Ashmun, Late Colonial Agent in Liberia*, 64–79; Peyton Skipwith to John H. Cocke, February 10, 1834, in Wiley, 36–37.

Chapter 3. "Nearly All Have Natives as Helps in Their Families, and This Is as It Should Be": The "Civilizing" Mission of Unfree Labor

1. Toyin Falola and Paul E. Lovejoy, "Pawnship in Historical Perspective," in *Pawnship, Slavery, and Colonialism in Africa*, ed. Paul E. Lovejoy and Toyin Falola (Trenton, N.J.: Africa World, 2003), 1–26. For a discussion of the evolution of pawnship practices in the twentieth century, see Martin Ford, "Indirect Rule and the Brief Apogee of Pawnship in Nimba, Liberia, 1918–30," in *Pawnship, Slavery, and Colonialism in Africa*, ed. Paul E. Lovejoy and Toyin Falola (Trenton, N.J.: Africa World, 2003), 283–98.

2. McGill's Maryland in Liberia, for example, explicitly included the relationship between "master and servant" under its legal definition of "Domestic Relations." See *Constitution and Laws of Maryland in Liberia; with an Appendix of Precedents*, 2nd ed. (Baltimore: John D. Toy, 1847), 9, 32, 37, 188, 204, 211.

3. "To the Editors of the N. E. Puritan," *New England Puritan*, October 1, 1842, reprinted in "Report of Chancellor Wolworth, Chairman of a Committee of the American Board of Commissioners for Foreign Missions, to Whom was Referred the Community of the Secretary Relative to the Cape Palmas Mission," *Maryland Colonization Journal*, 260–63.

4. The "general militia" was made distinct from the "volunteer militia," which was to consist of distinct uniformed companies reflective of American militia companies. Also, although the ordinance named all males of the appropriate age group living within the colony to serve in the general militia, the settlers did not consider the colony's African residents as suitable for service except for the handful of "civilized" Africans, such as "Yellow Will," who fully embraced American cultural practices. See *Constitution and Laws of Maryland in Liberia*, 21.

5. "Report of Chancellor Wolworth, Chairman of a Committee of the American Board of Commissioners for Foreign Missions, to Whom Was Referred the Community of the Secretary Relative to the Cape Palmas Mission," *Maryland Colonization Journal* 1, no. 17 (October 15, 1842): 257–59.

6. Episcopal Church, Foreign Committee, *An Historical Sketch of the African Mission of the Protestant Episcopal Church in the U.S.A.* (New York: Foreign Committee, 1884), 9, 13, 61.

7. "Chancellor Walworth," *Maryland Colonization Journal* 2, no. 3 (September 1843): 33–35.

8. "Chancellor Walworth," 33–35.

9. Scholars have debated the extent to which Africans and African Americans controlled their own naming practices, retained their own names in addition to new ones

projected onto them by slavery, and emulated the Euro-American naming system of their enslavers. See John Thornton, "Central African Names and African-American Naming Patterns," *William and Mary Quarterly* 50, no. 4 (October 1993): 727–42; Jerome S. Handler and JoAnn Jacoby, "Slave Names and Naming in Barbados, 1650–1830," *William and Mary Quarterly* 53, no. 4 (October 1996): 685–728; John Inscoe, "Carolina Slave Names: An Index to Acculturation," *Journal of Southern History* 49, no. 4 (November 1983): 527–54.

10. Campbell, *Middle Passages*, 71.

11. "Our Autumnal Expedition," *Maryland Colonization Journal* 4, no. 3 (September 1847): 33; "Sailing of the Packet, Emigrants, & c.," *Maryland Colonization Journal* 5, no. 2 (August 1849): 17.

12. Andrew N. Wegman, "'He Be God Who Made Dis Man': Christianity and Conversion in Nineteenth-century Liberia," in *New Directions in the Study of African American Recolonization*, ed. Beverly C. Tomek and Matthew J. Hetrick (Gainesville: University Press of Florida, 2017), 70–89.

13. Psalm 68:31 (King James Version).

14. See Wilson Moses, *The Golden Age of Black Nationalism, 1820–1925* (1978; repr., New York: Oxford University Press, 1988); Wilson Moses, ed., *Classical Black Nationalism: From the American Revolution to Marcus Garvey* (New York: New York University Press, 1996); Moses, *Afrotopia: The Roots of African American Popular History* (New York: Cambridge University Press, 1998).

15. John Revey to John H. B. Latrobe, January 20, 1840, MSCS.

16. In her study of settler women, Debra Newman Ham focuses on institutions—schools, benevolent societies, churches—to examine the role women played in African education. She does not dedicate space to households, unsurprising given the dearth of sources that speak directly to how settler women oversaw African children. See Debra Newman Ham, "'Teaching Them to Observe All Things': African American Women, the Great Commission, and Liberia in the Nineteenth Century," in *New Directions in the Study of African American Recolonization*, ed. Beverly C. Tomek and Matthew J. Hetrick, 90–105 (Gainesville: University Press of Florida, 2017).

17. Diana Skipwith James to Sally Cocke, March 6, 1843, in Bell I. Wiley, ed., *Slaves No More: Letters from Liberia, 1833–1869* (Lexington: University Press of Kentucky, 1980), 57; Diana Skipwith to Louisa Cocke, May 20, 1839, in Wiley, ed., *Slaves No More*, 46; Diana Skipwith James to John H. Cocke, March 7, 1843, in Wiley, ed., *Slaves No More*, 58; Bruce Dorsey, *Reforming Men and Women: Gender in the Antebellum City* (Ithaca, N.Y.: Cornell University Press, 2002), 136–64.

18. The Russwurms had one daughter, Angelina, and four sons, George Stockbridge, Francis Edward, Samuel Ford, and James Hall Russwurm. In his biography of Russwurm, Winston James builds upon the work of Mary Sagarin to conclude that James Russwurm probably died in infancy soon after his birth in 1836. In his June 15, 1848, letter, however, McGill requests assistance from Moses Sheppard in paving the path for his sister's residence in the northern states. As an aside, he notes, "James knows but little of the U. States." Given the familial context and the fact that James Russwurm was born in Liberia and would not have visited the United States, it seems likely that James Russwurm

did not die in infancy but rather lived to at least 1848. Angelina had accompanied her mother to the United States in 1847, but there is no record of her presence in the 1848 journey. For whatever reason, it seems that only Samuel Ford accompanied his parents to the United States in 1848. The *Maryland Colonization Journal* announced the arrival of the *Liberia Packet* on the front page of its August issue, noting the ship carried "Gov. Russwurm and lady, child and servant." Russwurm noted that Samuel Ford was with him in North Yarmouth, Maine, as they unpleasantly shared a similar bout of diarrhea. When father and son returned to Africa that year, the servant remained with Sarah Russwurm. For James Hall Russwurm, see Samuel F. McGill to Moses Sheppard, June 15, 1848, MSP; Winston James, *The Struggles of John Brown Russwurm: The Life and Writings of a Pan-Africanist Pioneer, 1799–1851* (New York: New York University Press, 2010), 80–83, 292; Samuel F. McGill to Moses Sheppard, June 15, 1848, MSP. For Angelina Russwurm's 1847 accompaniment of her mother, see John B. Russwurm to James Hall, October 1, 1847, MSCS; "Fifteenth Annual Report of the Board of Managers of the Maryland State Colonization Society," *Maryland Colonization Journal* 3, no. 24 (June 1847): 371. For Samuel Ford Russwurm's presence and medical ailments in Maine, see "Arrival of the Liberia Packet," *Maryland Colonization Journal* 4, no. 14 (August 1848): 217; John B. Russwurm to James Hall, August 21, 1848, MSCS, this letter also reprinted in James, *The Struggles of John Brown Russwurm*, 238–39.

19. Samuel F. McGill to Moses Sheppard, March 31, 1848, MSP.

20. Moses Sheppard to George R. McGill, January 12, 1836, MSCS. Sheppard's half of this transatlantic correspondence has been saved, and fortuitously the curmudgeonly merchant made sure to acknowledge the receipt of Russwurm's packages and their contents when dispatching his own to Liberia. Moses Sheppard's letter book records several letters and packages, along with their contents, dispatched to Sarah Russwurm before her prolonged stay in Baltimore on May 30, 1823; November 25, 1837; April 6, 1838; November 20, 1838; November 10, 1841; December 12, 1842; and April 6, 1848, all in MSP.

21. Moses Sheppard to Samuel F. McGill, August 25, 1848, MSP.

22. John B. Russwurm to James Hall, August 21, 1848, MSCS, this letter also reprinted in James, *The Struggles of John Brown Russwurm*, 238–39.

23. John B. Russwurm to John H. B. Latrobe, November 22, 1848, MSCS; this letter also reprinted in James, *The Struggles of John Brown Russwurm*, 239–40.

24. Moses Sheppard to Samuel F. McGill, February 16, 1849, MSP.

25. John B. Russwurm to James Hall, October 18, 1849, MSCS.

26. "Our Autumnal Expedition," 33; John H. B. Latrobe, *Maryland in Africa: A History of the Colony Planted by the Maryland State Colonization Society under the Auspices of the State of Maryland, U.S. at Cape Palmas on the South-West Coast of Africa, 1833–1853* (Baltimore: John Murphy & Co., 1885), 72. Latrobe's extract regarding Russwurm's banquet is also reprinted in James, *The Struggles of John Brown Russwurm*, 242.

27. For a discussion of the significance of interpreters or "talk men" for coastal trading in West Africa, see George E. Brooks, Jr., *The Kru Mariner in the Nineteenth Century: An Historical Compendium* (Newark, Del.: Liberian Studies Association, 1972), 18–25.

28. "Deed No. 1 from King Freeman and King Will, of Cape Palmas," MSCS; Hilary Teague, "Native Children," *Liberia Herald* 24 (January 1844).

29. March 1838 Court Session; November 1839 session of the court of Montserrado County, Monthly Court Records, Liberian Government Archives, Indiana University.

30. Fett, *Recaptured Africans*, 175.

31. "Natives Apprenticed to Colonists," Cabinet Minutes, January–April 1838, Liberian Government Archives, Indiana University.

32. For a history of these recaptured Africans before their arrival in Liberia, see John T. Noonan, Jr., *The Antelope: The Ordeal of the Recaptured Africans in the Administrations of James Monroe and John Quincy Adams* (Berkeley: University of California Press, 1977); Sharla Fett's *Recaptured Africans* is the most systematic examination of recaptured Africans seized in the years immediately preceding the Civil War. See Sharla M. Fett, *Recaptured Africans: Surviving Slave Ships, Detention, and Dislocation in the Final Years of the Slave Trade* (Chapel Hill: University of North Carolina Press, 2017).

33. "Died," *Liberia Herald*, September 30, 1843. It should be noted that the high standing of the New Georgians was not limited to the settlers but was likewise embraced by colonizationists in the United States as examples of the colony's civilizing influence. See *Third Annual Report of the Managers of the Colonization Society of the State of Connecticut* (New Haven: Baldwin and Treadway, 1830), 17–18; "Report," *The Fourteenth Annual Report of the American Society for Colonizing the Free People of Color of the United States*, 4–5.

34. "From Capt. Bell to the Secretary of the Navy," *Extracts from Letters Respecting the Capture of the Slave Ship "Pons," on the Coast of Africa, and the Landing of the Captured Slaves in Liberia on the 16th of the Twelfth Month, 1845* (1845?), Triptych, Tri-College Digital Library, http://triptych.brynmawr.edu/cdm/compoundobject/collection/SC_Broad/id/2124/rec/6; Matilda Skipwith Lomax to Sally Cocke, July 4, 1848, in Wiley, ed., *Slaves No More*, 67; "A Feat," *Liberia Herald*, July 3, 1846; "The Africans by the Pons," *Liberia Herald*, July 17, 1846; "The Africans by the 'Pons,'" *Liberia Herald*, December 4, 1846. For an examination of the *Pons* shipmates in relation to other recaptured Africans, see Fett, *Recaptured Africans*, 161–64.

35. *The First Annual Report of the American Society for Colonizing the Free People of Color, of the United States*, 15.

36. As the agent of the U.S. government, James Lugenbeel was assigned to oversee the "return" of recaptives to Liberia. Joseph Roberts, who served as the governor of the colony, was the agent of the ACS. See "From the *Monrovia Herald* of 'December 28th, 1845,'" *Extracts from Letters Respecting the Capture of the Slave Ship "Pons."*

37. "The Africans by the 'Pons,'" *Liberia Herald*, December 4, 1846.

38. *Examination of Mr. Thomas C. Brown, A Free Colored Citizen of S. Carolina as to the Actual State of Things in Liberia in the Years 1833 and 1834* (New York: S. W. Benedict and Co., 1834), 12.

39. The term "negro" has an evolving and contested history. For Americo-Liberians, it seems that "negro" was attached to accompanying associations of debased labor, and they rarely used the word. See Anita Henderson, "What's in a Slur?" *American Speech* 78, no. 1 (2003): 55–56; Joanne Pope Melish, "The Racial Vernacular: Contesting the Black/White Binary in Nineteenth-Century Rhode Island," in *Race, Nation, and Empire*

in American History, edited by James T. Campbell, Matthew Pratt Guterl, and Robert G. Lee (Chapel Hill: University of North Carolina Press, 2007), 17–39.

40. Samuel Williams, *Four Years in Liberia: A Sketch of the Life of the Rev. Samuel Williams; With Remarks on the Missions, Manners and Customs of the Natives of Western Africa; Together with an Answer to Nesbit's Book* (Philadelphia: King and Baird, 1857), 16–17; Alexander M. Cowan, *Liberia as I Found It, in 1858* (Frankfort, Ky.: A. G. Hodges, 1858), 40.

41. Cowan, *Liberia as I Found It, in 1858*, 43–44.

42. "Cabinet Minutes," November 29, 1838, Liberian Government Archives, Indiana University; February 1841 session of the Court of Montserrado County, Monthly Court Records, Liberian Government Archives.

43. November 1838 Session, Monthly Court Records, 1838–1842, Liberian Government Archives, Indiana University. During the August 1840 session, the court did try John Clark for "improper correction" of one of his servants, but the court simply returned the servant to Clark with a reprimand that "he should not so abuse the said apprentice in like manner again."

44. "Manual Labor School," *African Repository and Colonial Journal* 13, no. 9 (September 1837): 282–83. The court bound several children to the White Plains Manual Labor School. Owen Outland, aged sixteen years and four months, Burgess Washington, age thirteen, Zachariah Outland, fourteen, and [illegible] White, age fourteen, were all apprenticed to Beverly Wilson, the school's superintendent, during the July 1839 session. July 1839 Session, Monthly Court Records, 1838–1842, Liberian Government Archives, Indiana University.

45. February [or March] 1840 Session, County Court of Montserrado, Monthly Court Records, 1838–1842, Liberian Government Archives, Indiana University. Sabry Trueblood had indentured her seven-year-old son to Seys for identical terms in March 1840. Joseph Craig, a sixteen-year-old without a guardian, signed his own indenture on April 27, 1841. Presumably, he was an orphan. While Craig's requirements remained identical to the Trueblood, Seys promised to give Craig only what the law required once he had served his term.

46. Seth Rockman, for example, examines the many different types of labor to be found in the port city of Baltimore. See Seth Rockman, *Scraping By: Wage Labor, Slavery, and Survival in Early Baltimore* (Baltimore: Johns Hopkins University Press, 2008).

47. January–June 1838 Colonial Account Books, MSCS; Ladies School House Acct., July–December 1839 Colonial Account Books, MSCS; John B. Russwurm to John H. B. Latrobe, 1 November 1838, MSCS; Fortification Account, July–December 1838, Colonial Account Books, MSCS.

48. For information on the Davenports, see William McKenney to Managers of the Colonization Fund, July 9, 1836, MSCS; see also Richard L. Hall, *On Afric's Shore: A History of Maryland in Liberia, 1834–1857* (Baltimore: Maryland Historical Society, 2003), 454–55. "Farm Account, January–July 1838, Colonial Account Books, MSCS; Contingent Expenses, January–July 1838, Colonial Account Books, MSCS.

49. James Lugenbeel to James Hall, May 26, 1846, MSCS; John B. Russwurm to John H. B. Latrobe, December 30, 1845, MSCS.

50. William Nesbit, *Four Months in Liberia, or African Colonization Exposed* (Pittsburgh: J. T. Shryock, 1855), 15, 32. Both pauper and child apprenticeship had long histories in the American colonies and the United States before the settlers arrived in Liberia. The system was expansive and certainly would not have been foreign to nineteenth-century Americans even as they adapted it to their African context. See Ruth Wallis Herndon and John E. Murray, ed., *Children Bound to Labor: The Pauper Apprentice System in Early America* (Ithaca, N.Y.: Cornell University Press, 2009).

51. Nesbit, *Four Months in Liberia, or African Colonization Exposed*, 15, 39–40.

52. Nesbit, *Four Months in Liberia, or African Colonization Exposed*, 39–41.

53. "Two Cents Reward!" *Liberia Herald*, February 24, 1842.

54. "Six Cents Reward," *Liberia Herald*, September 21, 1842, 3.

55. June 1838 Records, "Monthly Court Records, 1838–1842," Liberian Government Archives, Indiana University.

56. March 1839 Records, "Monthly Court Records, 1838–1842," Liberian Government Archives, Indiana University.

57. Like many emigrant rolls, there is some confusion with the names. There are two Isaiah Holisters listed in the 1843 census, one eighteen and the other twenty years of age, and both are listed as "apprentices." Although the emigrant role for the *Roanoke* does not list Isaiah, it does include his surviving sister, Loretta, and Sally Ogon. While the ship's list includes an age-appropriate "Josiah Hollister," he does not appear elsewhere in the archives, suggesting the possibility of a mistaken identity. See U.S. Government, *Tables Showing the Number of Emigrants and Recaptured Africans Sent to the Colony of Liberia by the Government of the United States* (Washington, D.C.: N.p., 1845), 333, 357, 368; "Information Relative to the Operations of the United States Squadron on the West Coast of Africa, the Condition of the American Colonies there, and the Commerce of the United States Therewith," *Public Documents Printed by Order of the Senate of the United States, Second Session of the Twenty-Eighth Congress* (Washington, D.C.: Gales and Seaton, 1845), 9: 152–393; Claude A. Clegg III, *The Price of Liberty: African Americans and the Making of Liberia* (Chapel Hill: University of North Carolina Press, 2004), 99.

58. Williams, *Four Years in Liberia*, 16–17, 59.

59. "Liberia," *Richmond Enquirer*, June 12, 1835. The article, originally published in the *Norfolk* (VA) *Herald*, was also republished in the *Pittsfield Sun* on June 18, 1835, and the *New Bedford* (MA) *Mercury* on June 19, 1835. It was likewise published in the August 1835 edition of the *African Repository*.

60. James G. Birney, *Letter on Colonization: Addressed to the Rev. Thornton J. Mills, Corresponding Secretary of the Kentucky Colonization Society* (New York: American Anti-Slavery Society, 1838), 37–39.

61. Hall, *On Afric's Shore*, 112–14, 157–68, 512; James Hall to John H. B. Latrobe, February 9, 1834, MSCS; James Hall to John H. B. Latrobe, February 23, 1834, MSCS; James Hall to John H. B. Latrobe, April 24, 1834, MSCS; James Thomson to Oliver Holmes, December 28, 1837, MSCS.

62. Harmon was a son of the Nathan Harmon who received the wages of certain "boys'" labor on the public farm.

63. James Thomson to Oliver Holmes, December 28, 1837, MSCS.

64. *Constitution and Laws of Maryland in Liberia*, 23.

65. James Thomson to Oliver Holmes, December 28, 1837, MSCS. On the lack of indigenous women trained in English, see Ham, "'Teaching Them to Observe All Things,'" 93–95.

66. John B. Russwurm to John H. B. Latrobe, December 27, 1837, MSCS; "Extract of Letter from George R. McGill," MSCS. The letter in full is George R. McGill to John H. B. Latrobe, December 25, 1837, MSCS.

67. George McGill claimed the petition to be of Savage's rendering and even Russwurm described the committee of citizens as meeting with Savage to receive his advice on how they should proceed, but the actual petition outlines a settler-initiated project.

68. Petition of Citizens of Maryland in Liberia, August 9, 1837, MSCS; Thomas Savage to Charles Snetter, September 15, 1837, MSCS; Petition of Citizens of Maryland in Liberia, December 21, 1837, MSCS; Board of Managers of the MSCS to Petitioners of Maryland in Liberia, March 26, 1838, MSCS.

69. James T. Campbell has a useful discussion of the significance of the "legitimate commerce" argument in undergirding the establishment of Sierra Leone and Paul Cuffe's own efforts at emigration. See James T. Campbell, *Middle Passages: African American Journeys to Africa, 1787–2005* (New York: Penguin, 2006), 15–56.

70. "American Colony in Africa," *Trenton Federalist*, September 6, 1824.

71. Fitzhugh actually did address colonization and Liberia in a few of his published works. Although he found Liberia to be a better run society than Haiti, he did not see colonization as a viable alternative to the benefits of slavery. Ironically, he based this criticism on the fact that Liberia was a colonizing space that would need to conquer its neighbors to make room for African Americans. See George Fitzhugh, *Sociology for the South, or, The Failure of Free Society* (Richmond, Va.: A. Morris, 1854), 277.

72. Moses Sheppard to John B. Russwurm, August 7, 1837, MSP.

73. Josiah Conder, *Wages or the Whip: An Essay on the Comparative Cost and Productiveness of Free and Slave Labour* (London: George Woodfall, 1833), 14–16.

74. William Sleigh, *Abolitionism Exposed!: Proving the Principles of Abolitionism Are Injurious to the Slaves Themselves, Destructive to This Nation, and Contrary to the Express Commands of God* (Philadelphia: D. Schneck, 1838), 83.

75. David Francis Bacon, *Wanderings on the Seas and Shores of Africa* (New York: Joseph H. Harrison, 1843), 1:104–6.

76. J. Leighton Wilson to John H. B. Latrobe, June 6, 1837, MSCS; John H. B. Latrobe to King Freeman, May 1837, MSCS; "Selim Ballah," *African Repository and Colonial Journal* 13, no. 3 (March 1837): 101–3.

77. Horatio Bridge, *Journal of an African Cruiser*. Edited by Nathaniel Hawthorne (New York: Wiley and Putnam, 1845), 45.

78. Washington W. McDonogh to John McDonogh, October 7, 1846, in Wiley, ed., *Slaves No More*, 141.

79. Peyton Skipwith to John H. Cocke, June 25, 1846, in Wiley, ed., *Slaves No More*, 63–64.

Chapter 4. "They Would Dearly Learn What It Was to Fight White Men": Whitening through Violence in Liberia

1. J. R. Tyson, *A Discourse before the Young Men's Colonization Society of Pennsylvania* (Philadelphia, 1834); "Colonization Meeting," *African Repository and Colonial Journal* 11, no. 1 (January 1835): 17; "Intelligence," *African Repository and Colonial Journal* 9, no. 2 (April 1833): 58; Colonization Society of the City of New York, *Proceedings of the Colonization Society of the City of New York, at Their Third Annual Meeting* (New York: William A. Mercein & Son, 1835), 4–10, 25.

2. "Colonization Meeting in New York," *African Repository and Colonial Journal* 11, no. 7 (July 1835): 206; Tyson, *A Discourse before the Young Men's Colonization Society of Pennsylvania*, 59; anonymous, *Claims of the African: Or the History of the American Colonization Society* (Boston: Massachusetts Sabbath School Union, 1832), 245; "Colonization Meeting in New York," 206.

3. Richard Davis to H. J. Woodbury, October 7, 1835, ACS.

4. Hanson Leiper to the Board of Managers of the ACS, July 10, 1835, ACS; W. L. Weaver et al. to Ralph R. Gurley, July 10, 1835, ACS.

5. Nathaniel Brander to Ralph R. Gurley, May 21, 1839, ACS.

6. W. L. Weaver to Ralph R. Gurley, July 12, 1836, ACS; "Letter from a Colonist," *African Repository and Colonial Journal* 10, no. 8 (October 1834): 244–45; Ezekiel Skinner to Elliott Cresson, October 31, 1835, ACS; "Latest from Liberia," *African Repository and Colonial Journal* 11, no. 11 (November 1835): 337–39; Ezekiel Skinner to Ralph R. Gurley, August 24, 1835, ACS; "Proceedings of the American Colonization Society, at the Nineteenth Meeting," *African Repository and Colonial Journal* 12, no. 1 (January 1836): 23–25.

7. Ezekiel Skinner to Elliott Cresson, October 31, 1835, ACS.

8. "Relief of the Sufferers at Bassa Cove," *African Repository and Colonial Journal* 11, no. 12 (December 1835): 371; Hilary Teague to Unknown [probably Ralph R. Gurley], July 1, 1835, ACS.

9. "Latest from Liberia," *African Repository and Colonial Journal* 11, no. 11 (November 1835): 338; Jacob W. Prout to Ralph R. Gurley, January 8, 1836, ACS; Samuel A. Cartwright, *Essays* (Vidalia, La.: N.p., 1843), 40.

10. James Hall to John H. B. Latrobe, May 1, 1836, MSCS. Richard Hall, 107–8, 136–50; Winston James, *The Struggles of John Brown Russwurm: The Life and Writings of a Pan-Africanist Pioneer, 1799–1851* (New York: New York University Press, 2010), 5–25.

11. For an overview of Maryland in Liberia's independence, time as a republic, and eventual annexation by Liberia, see Richard Hall, 370–431. Samuel F. McGill to John H. B. Latrobe, January 6, 1851, MSCS.

12. Elijah Johnson to J. Mechlin, December 6, 1831, Liberia Government Archives, http://webapp1.dlib.indiana.edu/findingaids/view?doc.view=entire_text&docId=VAB6927#;

13. Fah Torah was also called Fan Tolo, Fana Toro, and Gotolo, indicating again the complexities of determining African names through western sources. By the 1840s, Torah/Tolo would come to dominate the Vai at the cape.

14. Elijah Johnson to J. Mechlin, December 6, 1831, Liberia Government Archives, http://webapp1.dlib.indiana.edu/findingaids/view?doc.view=entire_text&docId=VAB6927#.

15. Augustus Curtis to Joseph Mechlin, December 14, 1831, Liberia Government Archives; Curtis agreed with Johnson and believed that the acquisition of territory could be completed in just a few days. See Augustus Curtis to J. Mechlin, November 15, 1831, Liberia Government Archives, http://webapp1.dlib.indiana.edu/findingaids/view?doc.view=entire_text&docId=VAB6927#. John Saillant has published a useful commentary and transcriptions of several documents within the Liberia Government Archives. These archival documents were first photocopied and transcribed by Svend Holsoe in Monrovia. Unfortunately, the damage to the National Archives during the civil wars means that often these transcriptions and copies are the sole surviving records. The haphazard nature of their preservation also presents issues. Beginning with the fourteenth document transcribed by Saillant, there are a series of unsigned drafts that Saillant guessed may have originated from Curtis, as they immediately followed his letters to the governor. These drafts, however, are from Governor Mechlin, and their finalized editions arrived in the States and were dutifully recorded into the correspondence records of the ACS. John Saillant, "Letters and Notes on Liberia, 1828–1834," *Vestiges: Traces of Record* 3, no. 1 (2017): 1–44.

16. Their subsequent inability to march an army upon the guilty party, the Barboes, led to the hiring of "Yellow Will" to kidnap a Barbo in order to bring them to the negotiating table to answer for their actions.

17. For a description of the Maryland expedition to Denah, see Richard Hall, 169–72; King Freeman to John H. B. Latrobe, April 27, 1838, MSCS; John B. Russwurm to John H. B. Latrobe, July 7, 1838, MSCS.

18. J. Leighton Wilson to Ira Easter, July 5, 1838, MSCS. In terms of thefts, newly returned settler Alexander Hance commented upon the growing problem: "The natives can get troublesome in stealing the poultry of the Colonist and the like, thou trying we must expect it from them who do not know that jesus Christ is truly the son of the living god." See Alexander Hance to Unknown, July 5, 1838, MSCS. John B. Russwurm to John H. B. Latrobe, July 7, 1838, MSCS.

19. Anthony Wood to John H. B. Latrobe, April 27, 1838, MSCS; Alexander Hance to Unknown, July 5, 1838, MSCS; Benjamin Alleyene to John H. B. Latrobe, July 10, 1838, MSCS; John B. Russwurm to John H. B. Latrobe, July 7, 1838, MSCS.

20. William Nesbit, *Four Months in Liberia, or African Colonization Exposed* (Pittsburgh: J. T. Shryock, 1855), 38–39; Samuel Williams, *Four Years in Liberia. A Sketch of the Life of the Rev. Samuel Williams: With Remarks on the Missions, Manners and Customs of the Natives of Western Africa; Together with an Answer to Nesbit's Book* (Philadelphia: King and Baird, 1857), 16–17; John B. Russwurm to John H. B. Latrobe, February 23, 1834, MSCS.

21. Robert Breckinridge, "Hints on Colonization and Abolition; with Reference to the Black Race," *Biblical Repertory and Theological Review* 5, no. 3 (July 1833): 282–83.

22. James Hall, "My First Visit to Liberia [Concluded]," *African Repository* 62, no. 1 (January 1886): 1–2. Also quoted in James, *The Struggles of John Brown Russwurm*, 69–71; John Lewis to ACS, June 19, 1848, ACS, quote also in Marie Tyler-McGraw, *An African Republic: Black and White Virginians in the Making of Liberia* (Chapel Hill: University of North Carolina Press, 2007), 152.

23. Samson Caesar to Henry F. Westfall, June 2, 1834, *The Liberian Letters*, http://etext.virginia.edu/subjects/liberia/samson.html.

24. John B. Russwurm to John H. B. Latrobe, July 7, 1838, MSCS. On colonial administrator's complaints regarding single women, see Debra Newman Ham, "'Teaching Them to Observe All Things': African American Women, the Great Commission, and Liberia in the Nineteenth Century," in *New Directions in the Study of African American Recolonization*, ed. Beverly C. Tomek and Matthew J. Hetrick, 90–105 (Gainesville: University Press of Florida, 2017), 90–93.

25. Sally An Gipson [Sally Ann Gibson] to James Hall, January 19, 1844, MSCS; Richard Hall, 450; Rebecca Gibson to William McKenny, August 31, 1838, MSCS; Rebecca Delanie [Dulany], July 9, 1838, MSCS.

26. The Gibson family, a large clan originally from Talbot County, Maryland, relocated to the colony in 1835. The colony's high death toll usually led to multiple marriages for individuals, which subsequently make genealogical connections difficult to make. The tragic account of Rebecca Gibson turned Rebecca Dulany is indicative of the problems facing researchers.

27. Rebecca Gibson to William McKenney, August 31, 1836, MSCS; Sally Ann Gipson to James Hall, January 19, 1844, MSCS.

28. *Examination of Mr. Thomas C. Brown*, 12.

29. Joseph Blake to Ralph Gurley, March 9, 1835, ACS; Joseph Blake to Ralph Gurley, May 13, 1835, ACS. Joseph Blake's account and the implications for African American masculinity is also examined by Bruce Dorsey. See Bruce Dorsey, *Reforming Men and Women: Gender in the Antebellum City* (Ithaca, N.Y.: Cornell University Press, 2002), 136–64.

30. James Hall to John H. B. Latrobe, August 25, 1835, MSCS; "Fourth Annual Report of the Maryland State Colonization Society," January 15, 1836, MSCS.

31. Richard Hall, 109, 127.

32. J. Leighton Wilson to John H. B. Latrobe, June 25, 1836, MSCS.

33. Harriet B. Stowe, *Uncle Tom's Cabin, or Life Among the Lowly* (New York: Penguin, 1981), 609–12; Alexander M. Cowan, *Liberia as I Found It, in 1858* (Frankfort, Ky.: A. G. Hodges, 1858), 159–60.

34. Such is the argument presented by Warwick Anderson in one of the scholarly works attempting to examine whiteness outside of the boundaries of the West. Warwick Anderson, "Traveling White," in *Re-Orienting Whiteness*, 65–70.

35. Richard Hall, 181–85; John B. Russwurm to John H. B. Latrobe, August 21, 1838, MSCS.

36. Richard Hall, 184–87.

37. Richard Hall, 101–4, 128, 144–46, 162–63; Charles Snetter to John H. B. Latrobe, July 9, 1837, MSCS. In examining Liberia, David Kazanjian, building on Saidya Hartman's ideas regarding the relationship between past, present, and future in which slavery and freedom are not antipodal constructions but rather simultaneous experiences, raises "the question of what kind of ongoing relationship with U.S. slavery Liberian freedom requires." See David Kazanjian, "The Speculative Freedom of Colonial Liberia," *American Quarterly* 63, no. 4 (2011): 869–75.

38. Thomas Jackson to Unknown, July 6, 1837, MSCS; Charles Snetter to John H. B. Latrobe, July 9, 1837, MSCS.

39. Richard Hall, 185–89; John B. Russwurm to John H. B. Latrobe, November 1, 1838, MSCS.

40. Richard Hall, 186–88; Joshua 8:1–2 (King James).

41. Richard Hall, 187–90; John B. Russwurm to John H. B. Latrobe, August 31, 1838, MSCS; John B. Russwurm to John H. B. Latrobe, November 1, 1838, MSCS.

42. John H. B. Latrobe to John B. Russwurm, July 17, 1839, MSCS; Moses Sheppard to William Polk, May 15, 1838, MSCS.

43. Richard Hall, 188–91; "Remonstrance of Citizens of Maryland in Liberia," September 12, 1838, MSCS.

44. John H. B. Latrobe to Launcelot Minor, November 14, 1839, MSCS.

45. John H. B. Latrobe to John B. Russwurm, November 21, 1839, MSCS; John B. Russwurm to John H. B. Latrobe, January 15, 1841, MSCS.

46. "Despatches from Liberia," *African Repository and Colonial Journal* 15, no. 17 (October 1839): 276–87.

47. "Despatches from Liberia," 276–87.

48. Legislature, Minutes, 1845–1847, "January 1845, the seventh session of the colonial council," Liberian Government Archives, Indiana University.

49. "Despatches from Liberia," *African Repository and Colonial Journal* 15, no. 17 (October 1839): 276–87.

50. Sion Harris to Samuel Wilkeson, April 16, 1840, ACS, also in Bell I. Wiley, ed. *Slaves No More: Letters from Liberia, 1833–1869* (Lexington: University Press of Kentucky, 1980), 220–23.

51. George Brown also published an account of the assault that portrayed himself as one of the heroic defenders, but Harris grumbled in a private letter that Brown had shut himself into his second-story bedroom and did not participate in the fight except to discharge four muskets on Harris's command. See Sion Harris to Samuel Wilkeson, April 16, 1840, ACS, also in Wiley, ed., *Slaves No More*, 223.

52. A "half town" refers to a settlement without an established headman or "king." These were satellite villages that owed their allegiance to another town.

53. Thomas Buchanan, "Latest from Liberia," *African Repository and Colonial Journal* 16, no. 12 (June 1840): 178.

54. Thomas Buchanan, "Latest from Liberia," *African Repository and Colonial Journal* 16, no. 12 (June 1840): 179; Sion Harris to Samuel Wilkeson, April 16, 1840, ACS.

55. Thomas Buchanan, "Latest from Liberia," *African Repository and Colonial Journal* 16, no. 12 (June 1840): 178; Sion Harris to Samuel Wilkeson, April 16, 1840, ACS.

56. Ann Fabian, *The Skull Collectors: Race, Science, and America's Unburied Dead* (Chicago: University of Chicago Press, 2010), 37, 229.

57. Sion Harris to Samuel Wilkeson, April 16, 1840, ACS.

58. Buchanan, "Latest from Liberia," 179–80.

59. Buchanan, "Latest from Liberia," 180–81; "Narrative of the Ashantee War," *African Repository and Colonial Journal* 9, no. 5 (July 1833): 134; "Communication: Letters of Wm. B. Hodgson, Esq. on the Berber Language," *African Repository and Colonial Journal* 7,

no. 4 (June 1831): 113; "Mr. Toler's Address," *African Repository and Colonial Journal* 9, no. 10 (December 1833): 300.

60. *First Annual Report of the American Society for Colonizing the Free People of Color of the United States*, 18; Jehudi Ashmun, *History of the American Colony in Liberia, from December 1821 to 1823* (Washington, D.C.: Way & Gideon, 1826), 6–10.

61. Buchanan, "Latest from Liberia," 180.

62. Buchanan, "Latest from Liberia," 179–88.

63. Joshua Stewart to Doctor Macaulay, [February?] 10, 1834, MSP.

64. "Despatches from Liberia," *African Repository and Colonial Journal* 17, no. 1 (January 1, 1841): 5–6; "THE WAY THINGS ARE DONE IN LIBERIA," *African Repository and Colonial Journal* 17, no. 20 (October 15, 1841): 312. A draft copy of Buchanan's September 30, 1840, report is in the Liberian Government Archives, General Correspondence, 1840–1841.

65. William W. Stewart to Ralph R. Gurley, January 28, 1840, ACS.

66. Ashmun, *History of the American Colony in Liberia, from December 1821 to 1823*, 6–16; "American Colonization Society," *African Repository and Colonial Journal* 1, no. 1 (March 1825): 3–5.

67. *The Sixth Annual Report of the Society for Colonizing the Free People of Color of the United States* (Washington, D.C.: Davis & Force, 1823), 13.

68. Ashmun, *History of the American Colony in Liberia, from December 1821 to 1823*, 23–25.

69. Ashmun, *History of the American Colony in Liberia, from December 1821 to 1823*, 26.

70. It should be noted that Ashmun's account of the battle in which he is front and center was contested by several colonists there. David Francis Bacon, a white doctor who served as colonial physician in Monrovia, recorded his surprise at the way in which certain settlers remembered Ashmun. See David Francis Bacon, *Wanderings on the Seas and Shores of Africa*, vol. 1 (New York: Joseph H. Harrison, 1843), 120–21.

71. Ashmun, *History of the American Colony in Liberia, from December 1821 to 1823*, 28–30.

72. John B. Russwurm to John H. B. Latrobe, July 7, 1838, MSCS; John B. Russwurm to John H. B. Latrobe, August 6, 1838, MSCS.

73. That Pennington served as chair of this committee is unsurprising. Sharla Fett has argued that the literature, imagery, and spectacle of the Atlantic slave trade and recaptured Africans inspired Pennington to develop an alternative theory of human rights that emphasized the unity of humanity. See Sharla Fett, *Recaptured Africans: Surviving Slave Ships, Detention, and Dislocation in the Final Years of the Slave Trade* (Chapel Hill: University of North Carolina Press, 2017), 101–25.

74. "Proceedings of the Colored National Convention, Held in Rochester, July 6th, 7th, and 8th, 1853," in *Minutes of the Proceedings of the National Negro Conventions*, Howard Bell, ed., 55–56. These assumptions that Liberia provided equal footing with whites worked themselves into the everyday thinking of many Liberian settlers. For example, settler Jacob W. Prout functioned as a medical officer in Monrovia, nursing newly arrived settlers through the acclimating fever. In addition to settlers, Prout reported in 1836 that

his ward contained a number of white European sailors, two of whom died after apparently refusing to follow Prout's prescribed treatment. Not only did Prout assume that white and black bodies were analogous by prescribing the same treatment for settlers and Europeans, but he also completely reversed the power structures of western medicine by conducting an autopsy of a European to prove his case. See Jacob W. Prout to Unknown, December 16, 1836, ACS.

75. "Proceedings of the Colored National Convention, Held in Rochester, July 6th, 7th, and 8th, 1853," in *Minutes of the Proceedings of the National Negro Conventions*, ed. Howard Bell, 55; James Hall to John H. B. Latrobe, February 9, 1834, MSCS.

Chapter 5. "Your Views Cross the Atlantic": Black and White Responses to Settler Activism

1. "American Anti-Slavery Society. Second Day—Morning Session. Spirited Debate on the Color and Infidelity Questions—Lucretia Mott Against the Abolitionists," *Frederick Douglass' Paper*, May 19, 1854; *The Letters of William Lloyd Garrison*, vol. 6, 59. Robert Purvis would split with Garrison and many other male abolitionists in 1868 over his opposition to the Fifteenth Amendment's gendered language, but that schism lay years in the future. See Margaret Hope Bacon, *But One Race: The Life of Robert Purvis* (Albany: State University of New York Press, 2007), 158–59; Margaret Hope Bacon, "'The Double Curse of Sex and Color': Robert Purvis and Human Rights," *Pennsylvania Magazine of History and Biography* 121, no. 1/2 (Jan.–Apr. 1997): 53–76.

2. "American Anti-Slavery Society. Second Day—Morning Session. Spirited Debate on the Color and Infidelity Questions—Lucretia Mott Against the Abolitionists," *Frederick Douglass' Paper*, May 19, 1854.

3. Robert McDowall to Ralph R. Gurley, August 4, 1835, ACS.

4. *The First Annual Report of the American Society for Colonizing the Free People of Color of the United States*, 14.

5. Even the racial warping of Liberia was contested among white colonizationists. In 1825, still early in the colony's history, Reverend Nathaniel Bouton described free people of color as "the most ignorant, degraded and vicious class in the community. . . . You may call them *free*; you may enact laws to make them free, but 'you cannot bleach them into the enjoyment of freedom.'" But, of course, Liberia *could* bleach its inhabitants. See Nathaniel Bouton, *Christian Patriotism: An Address Delivered at Concord, July the Fourth, 1825* (Concord, N.H.: Shepard & Bannister, 1825), 15–16; *The First Annual Report of the American Society for Colonizing the Free People of Color of the United States*, 26.

6. "Annual Report," *African Repository and Colonial Journal* 12, no. 1 (January 1836): 24; "Latest from Liberia," *African Repository and Colonial Journal* 12, no. 2 (February 1836): 44; "Testimony Concerning Liberia," *African Repository and Colonial Journal* 14, no. 7 (July 1838): 201–6.

7. *The Second Annual Report of the American Society for Colonizing the Free People of Color in the United States* (Washington, D.C.: Davis and Force, 1819), 9.

8. Alexander M. Cowan, *Liberia as I Found It, in 1858* (Frankfort, Ky.: A. G. Hodges, 1858), 160. Marie Tyler-McGraw likewise argues that "self-selected" mixed-race emigrants, usually freeborn, who chose to relocate to Liberia were motivated by different

factors than were other Liberian settlers. See Marie Tyler-McGraw, *An African Republic: Black and White Virginians in the Making of Liberia* (Chapel Hill: University of North Carolina Press, 2007), 66–68.

9. "Massachusetts Colonization Society," *African Repository and Colonial Journal* 20, no. 7 (July 1844): 213–14; "N.Y. State Colonization Society," *African Repository and Colonial Journal* 20, no. 7 (July 1844): 215–16.

10. In his brief notation of the 1833 annual meeting, Eric Burin claims that despite the objections of the deposed managers and their supporters, the decision stood and the proslavery faction was replaced with Northerners. Neither is entirely accurate. Francis Scott Key and Walter Jones, both slaveholders, were back on the board the following year, while Samuel H. Smith, another manager whom Gurley attempted to oust, remained as a vice president. While Latrobe and Sheppard's understanding of colonization more closely aligned with Northern colonizationists and both were born in Philadelphia, they were Baltimoreans by the time of their appointments. See Eric Burin, *Slavery and the Peculiar Solution: A History of the American Colonization Society* (Gainesville: University Press of Florida, 2005), 23–24.

11. *The Sixteenth Annual Report of the American Society for Colonizing the Free People of Color of the United States* (Georgetown, D.C.: James Dunn, 1833), iii–xxii; P. J. Staudenraus, *The Colonization Movement, 1816–1865* (New York: Columbia University Press, 1961), 78–79, 207–9. Moses Sheppard was unenthused about his predicament and disliked the idea of traveling from Baltimore to Washington for the meetings. Latrobe prevailed upon him to at least attend the meeting in late February, but Sheppard was already planning to submit his resignation by March. See Moses Sheppard to John H. B. Latrobe, February 20, 133, MSP; Moses Sheppard to Charles Howard and Robert G. Harper, February 24, 1833, MSP; Moses Sheppard to John H. B. Latrobe, March 22, 1833, MSP.

12. "Signs of the Times!!" *Liberator*, February 23, 1833, 1. Of course, colonizationists were equally aware of the divisions exposed by the 1833 meeting. See John H. B. Latrobe to Cortland Van Rensselaer, July 10, 1833, MSCS.

13. With only slight alterations, this has largely been the standard narrative since at least Floyd J. Miller's *The Search for a Black National Identity*. See Miller, 82–90.

14. "The First Colored Convention," *Anglo-African Magazine* 1, no. 10 (October 1859) in *Minutes of the Proceedings of the National Negro Conventions, 1830–1864*, ed. Howard Holman Bell (New York: Arno, 1969), i–vi. Ousmane K. Power-Greene likewise uses the Colored Conventions to gauge free black resistance to colonization. Although he does not note the problem that Liberian independence created in the resistance rhetoric, he does note concerns regarding the ACS's popularity when Liberian independence in 1847 combined with black frustrations of the 1850s. Ousmane K. Power-Greene, *Against Wind and Tide: The African American Struggle against the Colonization Movement* (New York: New York University Press, 2014), 95–128.

15. *Constitution of the American Society of Free Persons of Colour. . . . Also the Proceedings of the Convention, with their Address to the Free Persons of Colour in the United States* (Philadelphia: J. W. Allen, 1831), in *Minutes of the Proceedings of the National Negro Conventions, 1830–1864*, ed. Bell, 9–10, 5, 15.

16. *Minutes of the Fourth Annual Convention, for the Improvement of the Free People of Color, in the United States* (New York: 1834), in *Minutes of the Proceedings of the National Negro Conventions, 1830–1864*, ed. Bell, 4–5.

17. *Minutes of the National Convention of Colored Citizens* (New York: Piercy and Reed, 1843), in *Minutes of the Proceedings of the National Negro Conventions, 1830–1864*, ed. Bell, 19–20; *Proceedings of the Colored National Convention* (Rochester, N.Y.: Frederick Douglass, 1853), 8; *Minutes and Proceedings of the Second Annual Convention, for the Improvement of the Free People of Color of these United States* (Philadelphia: Martin and Boden, 1832), in *Minutes of the Proceedings of the National Negro Conventions, 1830–1864*, ed. Bell, 18. For the relocation of Cincinnati's free people of color to Canada, see Nikki Taylor, "Reconsidering the 'Forced' Exodus of 1829: Free Black Emigration from Cincinnati, Ohio to Wilberforce, Canada," *Journal of African American History* 87 (Summer 2002): 283–302.

18. *Constitution of the American Society of Free Persons of Colour*, 10; *Minutes and Proceedings of the Third Annual Convention, for the Improvement of the Free People of Color in these United States* (New York: 1833), 9, 27, 35; *Minutes and Proceedings of the Second Annual Convention*, in *Minutes of the Proceedings of the National Negro Conventions, 1830–1864*, ed. Bell, 9, 27, 35.

19. *Minutes and Proceedings of the Third Annual Convention*, in *Minutes of the Proceedings of the National Negro Conventions, 1830–1864*, ed. Bell, 26; *Minutes and Proceedings of the Second Annual Convention*, in *Minutes of the Proceedings of the National Negro Conventions, 1830–1864*, ed. Bell, 30.

20. Marie Tyler-McGraw identifies him as James B. Barbour. See Tyler-McGraw, *An African Republic*, 145.

21. "Latest from Liberia," *African Repository and Colonial Journal* 12, no. 1 (January 1836), 31; W. Hutton, "Mr. Hutton's Letter," *African Repository and Colonial Journal* 13, no. 5 (May 1837): 160–61; Beverly R. Wilson, "To the Free Coloured People of the United States," *African Repository and Colonial Journal* 11, no. 8 (August 1835): 245.

22. Tyler-McGraw, *An African Republic*, 145.

23. "DISGRACEFUL," *Liberator*, August 3, 1833; "Latest from Liberia," *African Repository and Colonial Journal* 9, no. 5 (July 1833): 158; "Report," *African Repository and Colonial Journal* 9, no. 12 (February 1834): 12. This episode is also noted in Elizabeth Stordeur Pryor, *Colored Travelers: Mobility and the Fight for Citizenship before the Civil War* (Chapel Hill: University of North Carolina Press, 2016), 67. *Minutes and Address of the State Convention of the Colored Citizens of Ohio, convened at Columbus, January 10th, 11th, 12th, & 13th, 1849*, 7–8. www.coloredconventions.org.

24. *Proceedings of the Colored National Convention held in Rochester, July 6th, 7th, and 8th, 1853*, in *Minutes of the Proceedings of the National Negro Conventions, 1830–1864*, ed. Bell, 35.

25. "Thomas C. Brown," *New York The Colored American*, July 15, 1837; "Take Care of Number One!" *New York The Colored American*, January 27, 1838.

26. *Minutes of the Fourth Annual Convention*, in *Minutes of the Proceedings of the National Negro Conventions, 1830–1864*, ed. Bell, 12–17; *Minutes of the Fifth Annual Convention for the Improvement of the Free People of Color in the United States*, in *Minutes of*

the *Proceedings of the National Negro Conventions, 1830–1864*, ed. Howard Holman Bell (New York: Arno, 1969), 6.

27. William Whipper, *Eulogy on William Wilberforce, Esq.: Delivered at the Request of the People of Colour of the City of Philadelphia in the Second African Presbyterian Church, on the Sixth Day of December, 1833* (Philadelphia: William P. Gibbons), 28.

28. Robert Purvis, *A Tribute to the Memory of Thomas Shipley, the Philanthropist* (Philadelphia: Matthew and Gunn, 1836), 14–15.

29. This relocation caused Cornish a bit of consternation in 1848, when his son took over as head teacher of a school sponsored by the Ladies Association of Baltimore at Cape Palmas under the supervision of Russwurm. Cornish received word from his son that his wages were meager, thus leading the protective father to write to the MSCS to request assistance in dispatching trunks of clothing and goods to the settlement and increasing his son's wages. As a result, Cornish found himself awkwardly requesting aid from the society against which he had railed for nearly three decades, and in his letter Russwurm changed from a Benedict Arnold looking out for "Number One" to "my old friend and brother." Cornish needed such assistance in dispatching goods to his son from Baltimore because he did not want to go to Baltimore personally, as he lacked freedom papers, was accustomed to traveling without them, and feared what might happen to him in Baltimore. Cornish conceded, inadvertently highlighting one of the reasons that Liberian emigration appealed to certain free people of color, that the idea of traveling with such restrictions was "a painful" idea. No doubt, the McGills of Baltimore would have agreed. See Samuel Cornish to James Hall, March 20, 1848, MSCS; Samuel Cornish to James Hall, March 27, 1848, MSCS; Samuel Cornish to James Hall, April 30, 1848, MSCS.

30. "Address of the Colonists to the Free People of Color in the U.S.," *African Repository and Colonial Journal* 3, no. 10 (December 1827): 300–307; "Liberian Circular," *New York Freedom's Journal*, January 25, 1828.

31. William C. Nell, "The Colored Convention," *Rochester (NY) The North Star*, December 3, 1847.

32. When Indiana's free black men met in convention in August 1851, they suggested to Indiana's free people of color that if the laws of that state should "become oppressive as to be intolerable," then "we recommend our people to emigrate to Canada or Jamaica, in preference to Liberia." The convention reiterated the decades-old arguments that relocation to Liberia would actually strengthen slavery, although some supporters of moving there surely possessed pure motivations, "though misguided by wrong impressions." *The Minutes of the State Convention of the People of Color of the State of Indiana* (Indianapolis, Ind., 1851), www.coloredconventions.org. Brandon Mills has also detailed black critics of Liberian independence who viewed it as "a manipulative exercise in political theater." See Brandon Mills, "'The United States of Africa': The Contested Meaning of a Black Republic," 100–107, quote on 101.

33. "Report of the Rev. R. R. Gurley," *African Repository* 28, no. 2 (February 1851): 36–37.

34. *Proceedings of the State Convention of Colored People: Held in Albany, New-York, on the 22d, 23d, and 24th of July, 1851*, 23–24. www.coloredconventions.org.

35. "Republic of Liberia," *Rochester (NY) The North Star*, August 21, 1848; Martin Delany, "Editorial Correspondence," *Rochester (NY) The North Star*, February 4, 1848; "Thirty-Second Annual Report of the American Colonization Society," *African Repository and Colonial Journal* 25, no. 2 (February 1849): 43–45; Martin Delany, "Liberia," *Rochester (NY) The North Star*, March 2, 1849.

36. *Proceedings of the Colored National Convention*, in *Minutes of the Proceedings of the National Negro Conventions, 1830–1864*, ed. Bell, 55–56.

37. *Proceedings of the Colored National Convention*, in *Minutes of the Proceedings of the National Negro Conventions, 1830–1864*, ed. Bell, 56–57; also in "Address of the Colonists to the Free People of Colour in the U.S.," 301–2.

38. "Address of the Colonists to the Free People of Colour in the U.S.," 301–2.

39. Joshua H. Stewart to Moses Sheppard, April 12, 1852, MSP.

40. John B. Russwurm, "Liberia," *New York Freedom's Journal*, February 21, 1829; James Sidbury, *Becoming African in America: Race and Nation in the Early Black Atlantic* (New York: Oxford University Press, 2007), 201.

41. John B. Russwurm to Samuel Wilkeson, January 4, 1840, ACS; Samuel F. McGill to Moses Sheppard, October 16, 1849, MSP.

42. "Report," *Proceedings of the Colonization Society of the City of New York, at Their Third Annual Meeting*, 14; "The Protest," *African Repository and Colonial Journal* 9, no. 10 (December 1833): 295.

43. "Thirty-Second Annual Report of the American Colonization Society," 45.

44. The published transcript of a public questioning of returned settler Thomas C. Brown organized by the American Anti-Slavery Society, for example, almost immediately turned to this line of questioning: "How much more did they charge to bring you back than to carry you out?"; "Was there any opposition made to your coming away?" See *Examination of Mr. Thomas C. Brown*, 8–10.

45. John H. B. Latrobe to John B. Russwurm, October 24, 1837, MSCS.

Afterword

1. Lydia Polgreen, "Ghana Wants Once-Enslaved Diaspora," *New York Times*, December 27, 2005; Katharina Schramm, *African Homecoming: Pan-African Ideology and Contested Heritage* (Walnut Creek, Calif.: Left Coast Press, 2010), 142.

2. Schramm, *African Homecoming*, 142.

3. "The Ashmun Institute" Broadside and "Ashmun Institute Trustee Record Book #1," both available via HBCU Library Alliance Digital Collection, http://www.hbcudigitallibrary.auctr.edu.

4. John B. Russwurm to Francis E. Russwurm, March 31, 1834, John Sumner Russwurm Papers, Tennessee State Library and Archives, Nashville, Reel 1.

5. "The Ashmun Institute" Broadside.

Bibliography

Manuscript Collections

American Colonization Society Records. Manuscript Division, Library of Congress, Washington, D.C.
John Sumner Russwurm Papers, 1786–1914. Tennessee State Library and Archives, Nashville, Tenn. Microfilm edition.
Liberian Government Archives, 1828–1911. Indiana University, Bloomington, Ind.
The Library Company, Philadelphia, Pa.
Major Collection, McLean County Museum of History, Bloomington, Ill.
Maryland State Colonization Society Papers, 1827–1871. Maryland Historical Society, Baltimore, Md.
Moses Sheppard Papers. Friends Historical Library, Swarthmore College, Swarthmore, Pa.
Records of the Dartmouth Medical School. Rauner Special Collections Library, Dartmouth College, Hanover, N.H.
Shelby Family Papers, University of Kentucky, Lexington, Ky.

Published Primary Sources

African Institution. *Barrow's Voyage to Cochinchina*. London: Ellerton and Henderson, c. 1807.
Allen, William G. *The American Prejudice Against Color*. London: W. and F. G. Cash, 1853.
Anonymous. *Claims of the African: Or the History of the American Colonization Society*. Boston: Massachusetts Sabbath School Union, 1832.
Anonymous. *The Trial of Reuben Crandall, M.D.* Washington, D.C., [1836].
Ashmun, Jehudi. *History of the American Colony in Liberia, from December 1821 to 1823*. Washington, D.C.: Way & Gideon, 1826.
Bacon, David Francis. *Wanderings on the Seas and Shores of Africa*. Volume 1. New York: Joseph H. Harrison, 1843.
Bacon, Ephraim. *Abstract of a Journal Kept by E. Bacon*. 4th ed. Philadelphia: Clark & Raser, 1824.
Bell, Howard Holman, ed. *Minutes of the Proceedings of the National Negro Conventions, 1830–1864*. New York: Arno and the New York Times, 1969.

Bennett, Charles Raymond. "All Things to All People: The American Colonization Society in Kentucky, 1829–1860." Ph.D. diss., University of Kentucky, 1980.

Birney, James G. *Letter on Colonization: Addressed to the Rev. Thornton J. Mills, Corresponding Secretary of the Kentucky Colonization Society.* New York: American Anti-Slavery Society, 1838.

Bouton, Nathaniel. *Christian Patriotism: An Address Delivered at Concord, July the Fourth, 1825.* Concord, N.H.: Shepard & Bannister, 1825.

Breckinridge, Robert J. *The Black Race: Some Reflections on Its Position and Destiny, as Connected with Our American Disposition; A Discourse Delivered Before the Kentucky Colonization Society, at Frankfort, on the 6th Day of February, 1851.* Frankfort: A. G. Hodges, 1851.

———. "Hints on Colonization and Abolition; with Reference to the Black Race." *Biblical Repertory and Theological Review* 5, no. 3 (July 1833): 281–305.

Bridge, Horatio. *Journal of an African Cruiser.* Edited by Nathaniel Hawthorne. New York: Wiley and Putnam, 1845.

Cartwright, Samuel A. *Essays.* Vidalia, La.: N.p., 1843.

Colonization Society of the City of New York. *Proceedings of the Colonization Society of the City of New York, at Their Third Annual Meeting.* New York: William A. Mercein & Son, 1835.

Conder, Josiah. *Wages or the Whip: An Essay on the Comparative Cost and Productiveness of Free and Slave Labour.* London: 1833.

Constitution and Laws of Maryland in Liberia; with an Appendix of Precedents. 2nd ed. Baltimore: John D. Toy, 1847.

Constitution, Government and Digest of the Laws of Liberia, as Confirmed and Established by the Board of Managers of the American Colonization Society, May 23, 1825. Washington, D.C.: Way & Gideon, 1825.

Cowan, Alexander M. *Liberia as I Found It, in 1858.* Frankfort, Ky.: A. G. Hodges, 1858.

Crandall, Reuben. *The Trial of Reuben Crandall, M.D.* New York: H. R. Pierce, 1836.

Delany, Martin R. *Blake: Or, the Huts of America.* Boston: Beacon, 1970.

———. *Official Report of the Niger Valley Exploring Party.* New York: Thomas Hamilton, 1861.

Discussion on American Slavery, Between George Thompson, Esq. . . . and Rev. Robert J. Breckinridge . . . Holden in Rev. Dr. Wardlaw's Chapel, Glasgow, Scotland. Boston: Isaac Knapp, 1836.

Dunn, Durwood, ed. *An Abolitionist in the Appalachian South: Ezekiel Birdseye on Slavery, Capitalism, and Separate Statehood in East Tennessee, 1841–1846.* Knoxville: University of Tennessee Press, 1997.

The Eighth Annual Report of the American Society for Colonizing the Free People of Color of the United States. Washington, D.C.: J. C. Dunn, 1825.

Episcopal Church, Foreign Committee. *An Historical Sketch of the African Mission of the Protestant Episcopal Church in the U.S.A.* New York: Foreign Committee, 1884.

Examination of Mr. Thomas C. Brown, A Free Colored Citizen of S. Carolina as to the Actual State of Things in Liberia in the Years 1833 and 1834. New York: S. W. Benedict and Co., 1834.

Extracts from Letters Respecting the Capture of the Slave Ship "Pons," on the Coast of Africa, and the Landing of the Captured Slaves in Liberia on the 16th of the Twelfth Month, 1845. 1845[?].

The Fifteenth Annual Report of the American Society for Colonizing the Free People of Color of the United States. Washington, D.C.: J. C. Dunn, 1832.

The First Annual Report of the American Society for Colonizing the Free People of Color, of the United States. Washington, D.C.: D. Rapine, 1818.

First Report of the New-York Colonization Society. New York: J. Seymour, 1823.

Fitzhugh, George. *Sociology for the South: Or, the Failure of Free Society.* Richmond, Va.: A. Morris, 1854.

The Fourteenth Annual Report of the American Society for Colonizing the Free People of Color of the United States. Washington, D.C.: James C. Dunn, 1831.

The Fourth Annual Report of the Kentucky Colonization Society, with an Address, by Rev. John C. Young. Frankfort, Ky.: Albert G. Hodges, 1833.

Fox, Early Lee. *The American Colonization Society, 1817–1840.* Baltimore: Johns Hopkins University Press, 1919.

Gurley, Ralph R. *Letter on the American Colonization Society.* [Washington?]: 1832.

———. *Life of Jehudi Ashmun, Late Colonial Agent in Liberia: With an Appendix, Containing Extracts from his Journal and Other Writings; With a Brief Sketch of the Life of the Rev. Lott Cary.* Washington, D.C.: James C. Dunn, 1835.

Holman, James. *Travels in Madeira, Sierra Leone, Teneriffe, St. Jago, Cape Coast, Fernando Po, Princes Island, etc. etc.* 2nd ed. London: George Routledge, 1840.

Key, Francis Scott. *A Part of a Speech Pronounced by Francis S. Key, Esq., on the Trial of Reuben Crandall, M.D.* Washington, D.C., 1836.

Latrobe, John H. B. *Maryland in Africa: A History of the Colony Planted by the Maryland State Colonization Society under the Auspices of the State of Maryland, U.S. at Cape Palmas on the South-West Coast of Africa, 1833–1853.* Baltimore: John Murphy, 1885.

Levine, Robert S., ed. *Martin R. Delany: A Documentary Reader.* Chapel Hill: University of North Carolina Press, 2003.

Liberian Letters. University of Virginia Electronic Text Center. https://search.lib.virginia.edu/catalog.

Martin, Jane Jackson. "The Dual Legacy: Government Authority and Mission Influence among the Glebo of Eastern Liberia, 1834–1910." Ph.D. diss., Boston University, 1968.

Merrill, Walter M., ed. *The Letters of William Lloyd Garrison: I Will Be Heard!.* Volume 6. Cambridge, Mass.: Belknap, 1971.

Nesbit, William. *Four Months in Liberia, or African Colonization Exposed.* Pittsburgh: J. T. Shryock, 1855.

Opimius [pseud.]. "Opimius, No. 3." *Controversey between Caius Gracchus and Opimius in Reference to the American Society for Colonizing the Free People of Color of the United States.* Georgetown, D.C.: James C. Dunn, 1827.

The Proceedings of the Colonization Society of Kentucky with the Address of the Hon. Daniel Mayes, at the Annual Meeting, at Frankfort, December 1st, 1831. Frankfort, Ky.: Commentator, n.d.

Proceedings of the Convention of the Friends of African Colonization, Held in the Capital at Washington, May 4, 1842. Washington, D.C. [?]: 1842 [?].

Proceedings of the National Emigration Convention of Colored People. Pittsburgh: A. A. Anderson, 1854.

Public Documents Printed by Order of the Senate of the United States, Second Session of the Twenty-Eighth Congress. Washington, D.C.: Gales and Seaton, 1845.

Purvis, Robert. "The American Government and the Negro." In *Lift Every Voice: African American Oratory, 1787–1900.* Edited by Philip S. Foner and Robert James Branham. Tuscaloosa: University of Alabama Press, 1998.

———. *A Tribute to the Memory of Thomas Shipley, the Philanthropist.* Philadelphia: Matthew and Gunn, 1836.

The Second Annual Report of the American Society for Colonizing the Free People of Color in the United States. Washington, D.C.: Davis and Force, 1819.

The Sixteenth Annual Report of the American Society for Colonizing the Free People of Color of the United States. Georgetown, D.C.: James Dunn, 1833.

The Sixth Annual Report of the Society for Colonizing the Free People of Color of the United States. Washington, D.C.: Davis & Force, 1823.

Sleigh, William. *Abolitionism Exposed!: Proving the Principles of Abolitionism are injurious to the Slaves Themselves, Destructive to this Nation, and Contrary to the Express Commands of God.* Philadelphia: D. Schneck, 1838.

Speeches Delivered at the Anti-Colonization Meeting in Exeter Hall, London, July 13, 1833. Boston: Garrison and Knapp, 1833.

State Papers, Relating to Slaves in the Colonies; Slave Trade. Session: 5 February–23 July 1830. Volume 33. Oxford: Bodleian Library, 1830.

Stowe, Harriet B. *Uncle Tom's Cabin, or Life Among the Lowly.* Reprint, New York: Penguin, 1981.

Tenth Annual Report of the American Society for Colonizing the Free People of Color of the United States. Washington, D.C.: Way & Gideon, 1827.

Third Annual Report of the Managers of the Colonization Society of the State of Connecticut. New Haven: Baldwin and Treadway, 1830.

The Twelfth Annual Report of the American Society for Colonizing the Free People of Color of the United States. Washington, D.C.: James C. Dunn, 1829.

Tyson, J. R. *A Discourse before the Young Men's Colonization Society of Pennsylvania.* Philadelphia, 1834.

Webster-Ashburton Treaty, The Avalon Project: Documents in Law, History and Diplomacy. www.avalon.yale.edu.

Whipper, William. *Eulogy on William Wilberforce, Esq.: Delivered at the Request of the People of Colour of the City of Philadelphia in the Second African Presbyterian Church, on the Sixth Day of December, 1833.* Philadelphia: William P. Gibbons, 1833 [?].

Wiley, Bell I., ed. *Slaves No More: Letters from Liberia, 1833–1869.* Lexington: University Press of Kentucky, 1980.

Wilkeson, Samuel. *A Concise History of the Commencement, Progress and Present Condition of the American Colonies in Liberia.* Washington, D.C.: Madisonian, 1839.

Williams, Samuel. *Four Years in Liberia. A Sketch of the Life of the Rev. Samuel Williams: With Remarks on the Missions, Manners and Customs of the Natives of Western Africa; Together with an Answer to Nesbit's Book.* Philadelphia: King and Baird, 1857.

Secondary Sources

Adeleke, Tunde. *Unafrican Americans: Nineteenth-Century Black Nationalists and the Civilizing Mission.* Lexington: University Press of Kentucky, 1998.
Alexander, Leslie M. *African or American?: Black Identity and Political Activism in New York City, 1784–1861.* Urbana: University of Illinois Press, 2008.
Allen, William E. "Liberia and the Atlantic World in the Nineteenth Century: Convergence and Effects." *History in Africa* 37 (2010): 7–49.
———. "Rethinking the History of Settler Agriculture in Nineteenth-Century Liberia." *International Journal of African Historical Studies* 37, no. 3 (2004): 435–62.
Bacon, Margaret Hope. *But One Race: The Life of Robert Purvis.* Albany: State University of New York Press, 2007.
Berlin, Ira. *Many Thousands Gone: The First Two Centuries of Slavery in North America.* Cambridge, Mass.: Belknap, 1998.
Boucher, Leigh, Jane Carey, and Katherine Ellinghaus, eds. *Re-Orienting Whiteness.* New York: Palgrave Macmillan, 2009.
Brancaccio, Peter. "'The Black Man's Paradise': Hawthorne's Editing of the *Journal of an African Cruiser.*" *New England Quarterly* 53, no. 1 (March 1980): 23–41.
Brooks, George E., Jr. *The Kru Mariner in the Nineteenth Century: An Historical Compendium.* Newark, Del.: Liberian Studies Association, 1972.
Buettner, Elizabeth "'We Don't Grow Coffee and Bananas in Clapham Junction You Know!': Imperial Britons Back Home." In *Settlers and Expatriates: Britons Over the Seas,* ed. Robert Bickers, 302–28. New York: Oxford University Press, 2010.
Burin, Eric. *Slavery and the Peculiar Solution: A History of the American Colonization Society.* Gainesville: University Press of Florida, 2005.
Campbell, James T. *Middle Passages: African American Journeys to Africa, 1787–2005.* New York: Penguin, 2006.
Campbell, Penelope. *Maryland in Africa: The Maryland State Colonization Society, 1831–1857.* Urbana: University of Illinois Press, 1971.
Canney, Donald L. *Africa Squadron: The U.S. Navy and the Slave Trade, 1842–1861.* Washington, D.C.: Potomac, 2006.
Clegg, Claude A., III. *The Price of Liberty: African Americans and the Making of Liberia.* Chapel Hill: University of North Carolina Press, 2004.
Cresswell, Tim. *On the Move: Mobility in the Modern Western World.* New York: Routledge, 2006.
Dain, Bruce. *A Hideous Monster of the Mind: American Race Theory in the Early Republic.* Cambridge, Mass.: Harvard University Press, 2002.
Davis, Hugh. *Leonard Bacon: New England Reformer and Antislavery Moderate.* Baton Rouge: Louisiana State University Press, 1998.
Diemer, Andrew K. *The Politics of Black Citizenship: Free African Americans in the Mid-Atlantic Borderland, 1817–1863.* Athens: University of Georgia Press, 2016.
Dorsey, Bruce. *Reforming Men and Women: Gender in the Antebellum City.* Ithaca, N.Y.: Cornell University Press, 2002.
DuBois, Laurent, and Julius S. Scott, eds. *Origins of the Black Atlantic.* New York: Routledge, 2010.

Everill, Bronwen. *Abolition and Empire in Sierra Leone and Liberia.* New York: Palgrave Macmillan, 2013.

———. "'The Colony Has Made No Progress in Agriculture': Contested Perceptions of Agriculture in the Colonies of Sierra Leone & Liberia." In *Commercial Agriculture, The Slave Trade & Slavery in Atlantic Africa.* Ed. Robin Law, Suzanne Schwartz, and Silke Strickrodt, 180–202. Woodbridge, U.K.: James Currey, 2013.

———. "'Destiny Seems to Point Me to That Country': Early Nineteenth-Century African American Migration, Emigration, and Expansion." *Journal of Global History* 7, no. 1 (2012): 53–77.

Fabian, Ann. *The Skull Collectors: Race, Science, and America's Unburied Dead.* Chicago: University of Chicago Press, 2010.

Falola, Toyin, and Paul E. Lovejoy. "Pawnship in Historical Perspective." In *Pawnship, Slavery, and Colonialism in Africa,* ed. Paul E. Lovejoy and Toyin Falola, 1–26. Trenton, N.J.: Africa World, 2003.

Farinelli, Franco. "Why America Is Called America." In *Envisioning Landscapes, Making Worlds: Geography and the Humanities,* ed. Stephen Daniels, et al. New York: Routledge, 2011.

Fett, Sharla. *Recaptured Africans: Surviving Slave Ships, Detention, and Dislocation in the Final Years of the Slave Trade.* Chapel Hill: University of North Carolina Press, 2017.

Ford, Martin. "Indirect Rule and the Brief Apogee of Pawnship in Nimba, Liberia, 1918–30." In *Pawnship, Slavery, and Colonialism in Africa,* edited by Paul E. Lovejoy and Toyin Falola, 283–98. Trenton, N.J.: Africa World, 2003.

Frost, Diane. "Ethnic Identity, Transience and Settlement: The Kru in Liverpool since the Late Nineteenth Century." *Immigrants & Minorities* 12, no. 3 (1993): 8–106.

Gilroy, Paul. *The Black Atlantic: Modernity and Double Consciousness.* Cambridge, Mass.: Harvard University Press, 1993.

Gomez, Michael A. *Exchanging Our Country Marks: The Transformation of African Identities in the Colonial and Antebellum South.* Chapel Hill: University of North Carolina Press, 1998.

Gross, Ariela J. *What Blood Won't Tell: A History of Race on Trial in America.* Cambridge, Mass.: Harvard University Press, 2008.

Guyatt, Nicholas. *Bind Us Apart: How Enlightened Americans Invented Racial Segregation.* New York: Basic, 2016.

———. "'The Outskirts of Our Happiness': Race and the Lure of Colonization in the Early Republic." *Journal of American History* 95, no. 4 (2009): 986–1011.

Hall, Richard L. *On Afric's Shore: A History of Maryland in Liberia, 1834–1857.* Baltimore: Maryland Historical Society, 2003.

Ham, Debra Newman. "'Teaching Them to Observe All Things': African American Women, the Great Commission, and Liberia in the Nineteenth Century." In *New Directions in the Study of African American Recolonization,* edited by Beverly C. Tomek and Matthew J. Hetrick, 90–105. Gainesville: University Press of Florida, 2017.

Handler, Jerome S., and JoAnn Jacoby. "Slave Names and Naming in Barbados, 1650–1830," *William and Mary Quarterly* 53, no. 4 (October 1996): 685–728.

Henderson, Anita. "What's in a Slur?" *American Speech* 78, no. 1 (2003): 52–74.

Herndon, Ruth Wallis, and John E. Murray, ed. *Children Bound to Labor: The Pauper Apprentice System in Early America*. Ithaca, N.Y.: Cornell University Press, 2009.

Huberich, Charles Henry. *The Political and Legislative History of Liberia*. New York: Central Book, 1947.

Huffman, Alan. *Mississippi in Africa: The Saga of the Slaves of Prospect Hill Plantation and Their Legacy in Liberia Today*. New York: Gotham, 2004.

Ignatiev, Noel. *How the Irish Became White*. New York: Routledge, 1995.

Inscoe, John. "Carolina Slave Names: An Index to Acculturation." *Journal of Southern History* 49, no. 4 (November 1983): 527–54.

Jacques, T. Carlos. "From Savages and Barbarians to Primitives: Africa, Social Typologies, and History in Eighteenth-Century French Philosophy." *History and Theory* 36, no. 2 (May 1997): 190–215.

James, Winston. *The Struggles of John Brown Russwurm: The Life and Writings of a Pan-Africanist Pioneer, 1799–1851*. New York: New York University Press, 2010.

Jones, Martha S. *Birthright Citizens: A History of Race and Rights in Antebellum America*. Cambridge: Cambridge University Press, 2018.

Kazanjian, David. *The Colonizing Trick: National Culture and Imperial Citizenship in Early America*. Minneapolis: University of Minnesota Press, 2003

———. "The Speculative Freedom of Colonial Liberia." *American Quarterly* 63, no. 4 (2011): 863–93.

Kolchin, Peter. "Whiteness Studies: The New History of Race in America." *Journal of American History* 89, no. 1 (2002): 154–73.

Kramer, Neil S. "The Trial of Reuben Crandall," *Records of the Columbia Historical Society, Washington, D.C.*, 50 (1980): 123–59.

Lindsay, Lisa A. *Atlantic Bonds: A Nineteenth-Century Odyssey from America to Africa*. Chapel Hill: University of North Carolina Press, 2017.

Martin, Jane. "Krumen 'Down the Coast': Liberian Migrants on the West African Coast in the 19th and 20th Centuries." *International Journal of African Historical Studies* 18, no. 3 (1985): 401–23.

McDaniel, Antonio. *Swing Low, Sweet Chariot: The Mortality Cost of Colonizing Liberia in the Nineteenth Century*. Chicago: University of Chicago Press, 1995.

McEvoy, Frederick D. "Understanding Ethnic Realities among the Grebo and Kru Peoples of West Africa." *Africa: Journal of the International African Institute* 47, no. 1 (1977): 62–80.

Melish, Joanne Pope. *Disowning Slavery: Gradual Emancipation and "Race" in New England, 1780–1860*. Ithaca, N.Y.: Cornell University Press, 1998.

———. "The Racial Vernacular: Contesting the Black/White Binary in Nineteenth-Century Rhode Island." In *Race, Nation, and Empire in American History*, edited by James T. Campbell, Matthew Pratt Guterl, and Robert G. Lee. Chapel Hill: University of North Carolina Press, 2007.

Miller, Floyd J. *The Search for a Black Nationality: Black Emigration and Colonization, 1787–1863*. Urbana: University of Illinois Press, 1975.

Mills, Brandon. "'The United States of Africa': Liberian Independence and the Contested Meaning of a Black Republic." *Journal of the Early Republic* 34, no. 1 (2014): 79–107.

Moses, Wilson. *Afrotopia: The Roots of African American Popular History.* New York: Cambridge University Press, 1998.

———, ed. *Classical Black Nationalism: From the American Revolution to Marcus Garvey.* New York: New York University Press, 1996.

———. *The Golden Age of Black Nationalism, 1820–1925.* 1978. Reprint, New York: Oxford University Press, 1988.

Mouser, Bruce L. *American Colony on the Rio Pongo: The War of 1812, The Slave Trade, and the Proposed Settlement of African Americans, 1810–1830.* Trenton, N.J.: Africa World, 2013.

Mudimbe, V. Y. *The Invention of Africa: Gnosis, Philosophy, and the Order of Knowledge.* Bloomington: Indiana University Press, 1988.

Newman, Richard S. *The Transformation of American Abolitionism: Fighting Slavery in the Early Republic.* Chapel Hill: University of North Carolina Press, 2002.

Noonan, John T., Jr. *The Antelope: The Ordeal of the Recaptured Africans in the Administrations of James Monroe and John Quincy Adams.* Berkeley: University of California Press, 1977.

Nwankwo, Ifeoma Kiddoe. *Black Cosmopolitanism: Racial Consciousness and Transnational Identity in the Nineteenth-Century Americas.* Philadelphia: University of Pennsylvania Press, 2005.

Olukoju, Ayodeji. *Culture and Customs of Liberia.* Westport, Conn.: Greenwood, 2006.

Osborne, Myles. "A Note on the Liberian Archives." *History in Africa* 36 (2009): 461–63.

Peacock, John. "Principles and Effects of Puritan Appropriation of Indian Land and Labor." *Ethnohistory* 31, no. 1 (Winter 1984): 39–44.

Piper, Karen. *Cartographic Fictions: Maps, Race, and Identity.* New Brunswick, N.J.: Rutgers University Press, 2002.

Power-Greene, Ousmane K. *Against Wind and Tide: The African American Struggle against the Colonization Movement.* New York: New York University Press, 2014.

Pryor, Elizabeth Stordeur. *Colored Travelers: Mobility and the Fight for Citizenship before the Civil War.* Chapel Hill: University of North Carolina Press, 2016.

Rael, Patrick. *Black Identity and Black Protest in the Antebellum North.* Chapel Hill: University of North Carolina Press, 2002.

Rockman, Seth. *Scraping By: Wage Labor, Slavery, and Survival in Early Baltimore.* Baltimore: Johns Hopkins University Press, 2008.

Roediger, David. *The Wages of Whiteness: Race and the Making of the American Working Class.* New York: Verso, 1991.

Sanneh, Lamin O. *Abolitionists Abroad: American Blacks and the Making of Modern West Africa.* Cambridge, Mass.: Harvard University Press, 1999.

Sappol, Michael. *A Traffic of Dead Bodies: Anatomy and Embodied Social Identity in Nineteenth-Century America.* Princeton, N.J.: Princeton University Press, 2002.

Saxton, Alexander. *The Rise and Fall of the White Republic: Class Politics and Mass Culture in Nineteenth Century America.* New York: Verso, 1990.

Scanlan, Padraic X. *Freedom's Debtors: British Antislavery in Sierra Leone in the Age of Revolution.* New Haven: Yale University Press, 2017.

Schiller, Ben. "US Slavery's Diaspora: Black Atlantic History at the Crossroads of 'Race,' Enslavement, and Colonisation." *Slavery & Abolition* 32, no. 2 (June 2011): 199–212.

Schramm, Katharina. *African Homecoming: Pan-African Ideology and Contested Heritage*. Walnut Creek, Calif.: Left Coast, 2010.
Shick, Tom W. *Behold the Promised Land: A History of Afro-American Settler Society in Nineteenth-Century Liberia*. Baltimore: Johns Hopkins University Press, 1980.
Sidbury, James. *Becoming African in America: Race and Nation in the Early Black Atlantic*. New York: Oxford University Press, 2007.
Staudenraus, P. J. *The Colonization Movement, 1816–1865*. New York: Columbia University Press, 1961.
Stauffer, John. *The Black Hearts of Men: Radical Abolitionism and the Transformation of Race*. Cambridge, Mass.: Harvard University Press, 2002.
———, ed. *The Works of James McCune Smith*. New York: Oxford University Press, 2006.
Taylor, Nikki. "Reconsidering the 'Forced' Exodus of 1829: Free Black Emigration from Cincinnati, Ohio to Wilberforce, Canada." *Journal of African American History* 87 (Summer 2002): 283–302.
Thornton, John. "Central African Names and African-American Naming Patterns." *William and Mary Quarterly* 50, no. 4 (October 1993): 727–42.
Tomek, Beverly C. *Colonization and Its Discontents: Emancipation, Emigration, and Antislavery in Antebellum Pennsylvania*. New York: New York University Press, 2010.
Tomek, Beverly C., and Matthew J. Hetrick, eds. *New Directions in the Study of African American Recolonization*. Gainesville: University Press of Florida, 2017.
Tyler-McGraw, Marie. *An African Republic: Black and White Virginians in the Making of Liberia*. Chapel Hill: University of North Carolina Press, 2007.
Van Sickle, Eugene S. "Reluctant Imperialists: The U.S. Navy and Liberia, 1819–1845." *Journal of the Early Republic* 31, no. 1 (2011): 107–34.
Wegman, Andrew N. "'He Be God Who Made Dis Man': Christianity and Conversion in Nineteenth-Century Liberia." In *New Directions in the Study of African American Recolonization*, edited by Beverly C. Tomek and Matthew J. Hetrick, 70–89. Gainesville: University Press of Florida, 2017.
White, Hayden. "The Forms of Wildness: Archaeology of an Idea." In *Tropics of Discourse: Essays in Cultural Criticism*. Baltimore, Md.: Johns Hopkins University Press, 1978.
Whyte, Christine. "Between Empire and Colony: American Imperialism and Pan-African Colonialism in Liberia, 1810–2003." *National Identities* 18, no. 1 (2016): 71–88.
Wong, Edlie L. *Neither Fugitive nor Free: Atlantic Slavery, Freedom Suits, and the Legal Culture of Travel*. New York: New York University Press, 2009.
Wright, Ben. "'The Heathen Are Demanding the Gospel': Conversion, Redemption, and African Colonization." In *New Directions in the Study of African American Recolonization*, edited by Beverly C. Tomek and Matthew Hetrick, 50–69. Gainesville: University Press of Florida, 2017.
Zeleza, Paul Tiyambe. "African Diasporas: Toward a Global History." *African Studies Review* 53, no. 1 (2010): 1–19.
———. "Rewriting the African Diaspora: Beyond the Black Atlantic." *African Affairs* 104, no. 414 (2005): 35–68.

Index

Page numbers in *italics* refer to illustrations.

Abolitionism, 50, 60–61, 148, 202, 205; and New Georgia, 148; relationship to colonization, 17, 59, 202, 219

Adams, Jonathan, 26–27

Advertisements, runaway servant, 137–38

Africa: as black "homeland," 3, 10–11, 41, 77–78, 178, 186, 199, 223, 227n7, 231n29, 232n31, 248n71; colonizationists views on, 7, 75–76, 80, 110, 156; and Ethiopianism, 11, 109, 117; and European and American Colonization, 16, 193–94, 216–17, 232; travel between United States, 4, 31–32, 34, 41–42, 63–64, 118, 120–21, 150, 220–21

Africans: bound children, 15, 113, 115–16, 118, 123–24, 134, 137, 139–40, 148–49; bound laborers, 124, 127, 129; children, 9, 15, 66–67, 113, 115–16, 118, 132, 134, 137, 139–41, 143, 145, 148–49; and "civilization," 14, 47, 62, 80, 117, 127, 157, 172, 250n4; compared to American Indians, 94, 186; identities, 18–20, 107, 149, 189–90, 223; in imagery, 98–99; as laborers, 13, 15, 102, 111–12, 117–18, 123–24, 127, 129–30, 132–33, 136–37, 139–42, 145–49, 151–52; Liberia as "America," 68–69, 160, 242n103; perceptions of western culture, 8–9, 66, 102, 107, 109, 113, 122–23, 159, 231n24; relations with settlers, 100–101, 125–26, 136, 142, 154, 157–59, 163, 178–79, 181, 186, 192; as "savages" or "heathens," 12, 19, 46–47, 52, 80, 84, 126, 128, 178, 183–84, 187, 189; as settler allies, 160, 182–83, 185; settler perceptions, 80, 100, 111, 126, 142, 160, 194, 201; sexual relations with settlers, 128, 142–46, 169; and thievery, 68–70, 100–101, 103, 111, 126–27, 130–31, 133, 159, 163, 249n78, 258n18; transatlantic travels, 64–66, 68, 71–72, 103–6, 150, 242n97,

248n61; as wage laborers, 129–33, 139–40, 146–47

Africa Squadron, 1, 111, 227n2

Agriculture: African, 86–87, 94, 96, 102; colonial, 14, 84, 86–89, 99, 102, 111–12, 130, 151–52; in imagery, 99

American African Union Society, 28

American and Foreign Anti-Slavery Society (AFASS), 195, 197–98

American Anti-Slavery Society (AASS), 168, 196, 266n44

American Board of Commissioners for Foreign Missions (ABCFM), 114

American Colonization Society (ACS), 1–2, 5, 18, 110, 180, 199–200, 221; and colonial violence, 179, 183, 185, 189; founding, 1, 227n4; on land, 87–89; maps, 93, 95, 97–98; relationship to federal government, 23, 235n1; relations with Africans, 72, 109; relations with settlers, 26, 29–30, 87, 216; and slavery, 6, 17, 75–76, 153, 200–202, 229n16, 229n17, 233n42

Americo-Liberians (settlers and descendants): and anti-colonization, 16–17, 20, 212; definition, 20, 233n38; divisions within society, 158, 179; identities, 12, 129, 159, 164–65, 172; and labor, 15, 129–32, 135–36, 138–40, 145–48, 158; and land, 24, 87–89, 94, 96, 110–11, 129, 163; military, 114, 157, 163–64, 175, 179, 187–88, 208, 250n4; as missionaries, 4, 92, 109, 113–17, 136, 151–52; and mobility, 5, 9, 32, 34–35, 42, 46, 54–55, 57, 61, 63–64, 72–73, 77, 209; perceptions of Africans, 3, 46–47, 70–71, 79–80, 84, 91, 93, 123, 125, 127–29, 149, 151, 157; racial ambiguity, 26, 51, 57, 158, 165, 171, 200–201; relationship to United States, 10, 31–32, 34, 36, 42, 56, 72, 174, 201, 215; relationship

Americo-Liberians—*continued*
  with African Americans, 51, 53, 55, 213, 217; rhetoric of controlling Africans, 14, 76, 110, 149, 158; role in colonization movement, 9–10, 17, 30, 40, 59, 73, 195, 202, 209, 213, 216–20; social divisions, 15, 72, 164–66, 171; use of "negro," 64, 72, 128–29, 136–37, 146, 149, 253n39; and violence, 15–16, 159–61, 182, 187, 192, 194; and whiteness, 4, 7–8, 10, 12–14, 66, 71, 121
Amos, James, 224
Andrus, Joseph, 27
Anti-colonization, 16, 20, 77, 193–95, 202–6, 208, 210–14, 216–17, 220, 265n32
Ashmun, Jehudi, 29, 86, 96, 111, 147, 186, 189–92, 261n70
Ashmun Institute, 224
Auburn Island, 92
Ayres, Eli, 27–29, 146–47, 189

Bacon, Ephraim, 27
Bacon, Leonard, 76
Bacon, Samuel, 23, 25–27
"Bah Gray," 180–81
Ballah, Simleh ("Bill Williams"), 67–70, 150, 242n101
Barbour, James, 207–8, 211, 213
Bassa (ethnic group), 185
Bassa Cove, 99, 99–101, 153–54; 1835 attack, 42, 111, 154–57, 159, 163, 199
Birdseye, Ezekiel, 36–38, 237n27
Birney, James G., 140
Black Atlantic, 4, 10, 12, 21, 32–33, 77, 102, 121, 231n29; scholarship, 10–11; and whiteness, 12
Blackford, Abraham, 78
Blake, Joseph, 169, 259
Blyden, Edward Wilmot, 232n35
Bolon, Major, 63
Brander, Nathaniel, 30, 156
Breckinridge, Robert, 61–62, 65, 76
Bridge, Horatio, 2–4, 55, 150–51
Brown, Dixon B., 131, 138
Brown, George S., 36, 38, 182–83, 260
Brown, Thomas C., 128, 168, 210, 266n44
Buchanan, Thomas, 180–83, 185–88
Bushrod Island, 126

Caesar, Samson, 111, 166
Caldwell, Liberia, 57
Cape Mount, Liberia, 161–62
Cary, Lott, 28–29, 192
Clay, Henry, 75–78, 109

Coker, Daniel, 24–26, 28, 235n3
Colonization: and agriculture, 86–88, 96, 102, 146; and Christianity, 38, 65, 78, 117, 191, 249; and "degraded," 7–8, 34, 62, 75–76, 78, 109, 127, 199, 248n70; and emigration, 2, 6, 203, 209, 218, 229n15; and gender, 12, 72–73, 78, 87–88, 93, 118, 169, 232n32; ideologies, 3, 6, 62–63, 76–77, 80, 109–10, 146, 148, 213, 217, 219–20, 228n13, 230n20; and Indian Removal, 94, 96, 163; "Maryland Plan," 18, 153; and race, 3–4, 7–8, 13, 58, 61, 64, 165, 171, 177–78, 195, 199, 201, 227n7; Relationship to Indian Removal, 77, 94, 96, 229n18, 243n3; and slavery, 6, 110, 117, 198, 200–202, 205, 229n16; views on "civilization," 7, 12, 14–15, 62, 76–77, 79–80, 109–10, 117, 127–28, 147, 149, 178, 192
Conder, Josiah, 147–48
Connecticut Colonization Society, 78
Cook, William, 100
Cornish, Samuel, 210, 265n29
Cotton, James, 138
Cowan, Alexander, 130, 136, 200
Cresson, Elliott, 198, 218
Crook, Lewis, 89
Crozer, Samuel, 23
Cuffe, Paul, 2, 16, 24, 202
Curtis, Augustus, 161

Davenport, Thomas, 134
Davis, Richard, 154–55
Delany, Martin R., 11, 20–22, 31, 33, 52, 208, 216, 220, 234n48
Dominica, 104–6
Douglass, Frederick, 11, 195, 197–98, 210, 214
Dulany, William, 167
Duncan, Henry, 220

Edina, Liberia, 154–57, 212
Elizabeth expedition, 23–27, 87, 91
Erskine, George, 36–37

Fitzhugh, George, 147, 256
Fletcher, Dempsey, 57–62, 200, 240n76
Freedom's Journal, 2, 34, 69, 212–13, 218
Friendly Society of Sierra Leone, 24–25
Furness, William, 196

Garnet, Henry Highland, 210
Garrison, William Lloyd, 65, 196–97, 206, 209, 242n97
Gbenelu ("King Freeman's Town"), 67, 69–70, 90–91, 93, 160, 173

Getumbe ("Gay Toombay"), 182, 184, 186–87, 189
Ghana, 223–24
Gibson, Rebecca, 167
Gilroy, Paul, 10–11
Goheen, S. M. E., 184
Gomez, Charles, 161
"Gotorah," 182–84
Grand Bassa, 27, 71, 127, 160, 180, 185
Grebo (ethnic group), 19, 31, 39, 64, 68, 107, 150; and colonial administration, 69, 111, 133, 159–60, 176; conflicts with settlers, 70, 160, 172, 174–75, 178; and maps, 90–91, 93–94, 103
Guadeloupe, 103–6
Gurley, Ralph R., 29–30, 36, 117, 198–99, 201–2, 204, 206, 208, 214–15, 219

Hall, Andrew, 64, 129
Hall, James, 42–43, 57–58, 64, 67–69, 120–21, 141, 165, 169–70, 194
Hance, Alexander, 38–40, 54, 73, 162, 218, 221, 237n31
Hankinson, Edward, 155, 157
Harper, Maryland in Liberia, 39, 67–68, 90–91, 107, 172
Harris, Martha, 36, 182, 185
Harris, Zion ("Sion"), 36–38, 73–74, 182–85, 237, 260n51
Hawthorne, Nathaniel, 1–2, 150
Heddington Mission Station, 36, 182–84
Hoffman River, 90, 92
Holmes, Oliver, 108, 141, 170, 173
Hornell, Robert, 161

Jackson, Moses, 86, 102
James, Diana Skipwith, 3, 118
Johnson, Elijah, 25, 28, 161, 180–81, 189, 191–92

Kentucky Colonization Society, 62, 200
"King Bob Gray," 155–57
"King Freeman," 20, 37, 64, 67–68, 70–71, 123, 133, 159, 162–63, 172, 175–78
"King Governor," 184
"King Joe Harris," 42, 154–57
"King Joe Holland," 64, 123, 242n95
"King Yellow Will" (Bassa Cove), 155
Kizell, John, 24–27
Krumen (Kru), 19, 71–72, 105–6, 155, 181

Labor: African practice of pawnship, 15, 113; and "civilization," 14–15, 117–18, 129, 140, 147, 149, 151–52, 159; comparisons to slavery in Liberia, 14, 116, 129, 136–37, 140, 147; in Liberia, 14, 113, 116–17, 127–29, 133–35, 147–48, 151, 158–59; as punishment, 130–31; and Recaptured Africans, 125, 127–28
Ladies' Society for Education in Africa, 90, 133, 169
Lafayette expedition, 81
Land: African spaces, 92, 94, 96, 163; distributed to settlers, 87–89, 169; negotiations with Africans, 24, 26–27, 96, 155; possession, 84, 86, 88, 94, 96, 98, 111, 180
Latrobe, John H. B., 47, 67, 114, 117, 121–22, 170, 201
Latrobe, Maryland in Liberia, 70, 90–91
Lee, Nathan, 66, 71, 132
"Legitimate commerce," 2, 146–47
Lewis, William N., 180, 187
Liberator, 65, 202, 209
Liberia, 18, 82, 84, 101, 116, 123, 130, 135–36, 139–40, 148, 159, 188, 218; and "American" identity, 5, 81, 102, 107–9, 112, 133, 164, 172, 178, 184, 190; and anti-colonization, 86, 205, 209–14, 216; and Black Atlantic, 10–11, 102; as "civilizing" space, 1, 7–8, 15, 31, 75, 77, 81, 109, 117, 149, 151; colonial administration, 26, 29, 63, 200; and colonialism, 9, 15, 19, 110, 159, 169, 180–81, 194, 216; commonwealth of, 18, 100, 181; constitutions, 18, 29, 113, 130; court cases, 100–101, 143–44; ethnic groups, 19; images of settlements, 98–100, 247n46; imagined geography, 79, 84, 91–92, 97–98, 163; independence of, 16, 20, 73, 81, 209, 214–16; and maps, 79, 82, 84, 95, 97–98; and masculinity, 78; mortality in, 51, 96, 167; as new United States, 5, 13, 75–76, 81–82, 94, 96, 112, 186, 246n41; orphans, 116, 131–32, 135, 139, 146; and race, 46, 55, 57, 70, 77, 159, 165, 169, 185, 200–201, 218; sexual relations, 141–42, 144, 168–71; and Sierra Leone, 11, 93; systems of labor, 113, 116, 123–25, 129, 131–32, 134–35, 140, 151; territorial expansion, 27, 155, 161, 180–81, 216; and women, 118, 135, 149, 166, 168, 192–93, 251n16
Little Bassa expedition, 180–81
Lugenbeel, James W., 134–35

Maps, 79, 82, 107, 112, 221; 1830 map of Liberia, 83, 83–84, 93, 97, 154; 1845 map of Liberia, 93–95, 95; and African spaces, 84, 92–94, 96–98, 100–101, 103, 109; and "civilization," 14, 84, 91–92; and colonial expansion, 92, 94, 97–98, 101, 107; Maryland in Liberia, 91–92, 97–98, 101, 108–9, 117

Maryland in Liberia, 2, 17–18, 91, 221; and agriculture, 39, 86; colonial accounts, 132–33; expedition to Denah, 162; founding, 64, 123, 164, 194; independence, 160; and missionaries, 113–15; Public Farm, 90–91, 102, 134–35; relations with Africans, 67–69, 100, 107, 111, 133–34, 150, 159, 175; war with Greboes, 160

Maryland State Colonization Society (MSCS), 2, 17, 60, 160; and Africans in colony, 178–79; and Africans in the United States, 64–67; communications with settlers, 92, 144–45, 167, 179, 221; employing settlers as spokesmen, 38–40; "Maryland Plan," 18, 153, 160, 202; and McAllister Affair, 170–71; relations with missionaries, 114; and Russwurm, 121, 179; supporting settler education, 43, 45–46, 48, 57–58, 62

Massachusetts Colonization Society, 200

McAllister, Margaret, 169–71, 188

McDonogh, Washington, 151

McDowall, Robert, 99, 185, 198–200

McGill, George R., 31, 42, 55–56, 144, 174, 213

McGill, James, and Africans, 137

McGill, Samuel F.: and abolitionism, 50, 53, 202, 219; and African Americans, 48–54; and Africans, 46–47, 52–53, 115–16, 118, 160, 240; and Bassa Cove Attack, 42; birth and emigration, 42; and bound African children, 113–16, 118, 149; at Dartmouth, 45–49, 56; and Dempsey Fletcher, 57–60, 240n76; as governor, 52, 160; marriages, 51, 239n61, 240n62; and Sarah Russwurm's American travels, 119–20, 150, 251n18; travels to the United States, 43–44, 48, 114; at Washington Medical College, 42–45; and whiteness, 51, 56–58, 60–61, 120, 200

Mechlin, Joseph, 155, 169

Missionaries, 30, 36, 67–68, 70, 86, 108, 115, 117, 123, 154; and maps, 92, 94; and Maryland in Liberia, 114–15, 163, 170, 249n78; Thomson Affair, 141–45; training, 224–25; women, 169–70, 240n62

Monrovia, Liberia, 2, 21, 80–81, 89, 156, 165, 186; 1822 attack, 189, 191–92; African inhabitants, 100–101, 130, 135, 149; compared to Jamestown or Plymouth, 5, 96, 186, 246n41; images, 98–100; and maps, 81–82, 85, 93–94

Morton, Samuel George, 184–85

Mount Tubman, 91–92, 175

National Emigration Convention, 21, 214

Nautilus expedition, 25–27

Negro Seamen Act, 33

Neirseé affair, 103–6, 248n61

Nesbit, William, 135–37, 139, 149, 164

New Georgia, 125–26, 128–29, 139, 148, 156, 180, 253n33

New York City Colonization Society, 153–54, 200–201, 219

Nickolson, Lydia, 50–51, 57, 239n61

Ohio Colonization Society, 140

Pan-Africanism, 53, 224

Parker, Eben, and incident with Barrawe, 172–74

Paterson, James, 104, 106, 248n61. *See also* *Neirseé* affair

Paul, Thomas, 49–50

Pennsylvania Colonization Society, 99

Perry, Matthew, 1

Perseverance Island, 28

Phelps, Anson G., 216, 220

Phelps, Edward E., 45, 56, 60

Pinney, John, 30, 156, 216

Polk, William, 35, 54–55, 80, 90–91, 170, 177

Pons, 126–29, 136, 151

Posey, Francis, 27–28

Posey, Lucy, 27–28

Prout, Jacob W., 158, 261–62

Purvis, Robert, 196–99, 211–12, 262n1

Recaptured Africans ("Congoes"), 15, 125–28, 151, 156, 160, 184, 189–90, 253n36, 261n73

Revey, John, 91–94, 97, 100–101, 103, 108, 117, 144

Rio Pongo, 24

Roberts, Joseph Jenkins, 30, 138, 166, 200–201, 207–9, 214, 216, 220

Robookah, 142–43, 146

Russwurm, Angelina, 251–52

Russwurm, James Hall, 251–52

Russwurm, John Brown, 1–2, 69–71, 111, 114–16, 119–22, 132–33, 135, 141, 143–44, 162–66, 172–79, 193, 210–12, 218–19, 23n291, 249n77, 251–52n18, 256n67; and anti-colonization, 210–11; background, 69; and bound children, 115–16; as co-editor of *Freedom's Journal*, 35, 212, 218; dinner with Bridge, 1–2; as governor, 69, 135, 143–44, 159, 163–64, 166, 172–73, 176, 179, 193; honored by MSCS, 121–22; and missionaries, 114; regarding Africans, 80, 111, 163, 177, 179; relations with "King Freeman," 69–71, 133, 162–63, 172, 175–77; and Snetter Affair, 175–78; travels to the United States, 119–20;

and whiteness, 71, 122, 147, 164, 176, 225; and "Yellow Will," 133
Russwurm, Samuel Ford, 251–52n18
Russwurm, Sarah, 119–20, 122, 252n20; travels to the United States, 116, 119–22

Sansay, Paul, 78
Savage, Thomas, 108, 141–44
Savagery: and gender, 88, 158, 167, 169, 178–79, 187, 192; and Liberian landscape, 126–27, 186–87; versus "primitive," 79–80
Schools: in Liberia, 52–53, 66–67, 90–92, 123, 132–33, 141, 143, 145, 154, 167, 169; White Plains Manual Labor School, 131–32
Scotland, Charles, 40–41, 54, 73
Seys, John, 132, 254
Sheppard, Moses, 8, 35, 63, 65, 201, 218; and Dempsey Fletcher, 58–59, 61–62; and Sarah Russwurm, 119–22, 150; sponsors McGill, 43–48, 51; and whiteness, 46, 54, 56, 108, 118, 147, 177, 218; and "Yellow Will," 108
Sherbro Island, 24–27, 87
Sierra Leone, 11, 13, 24, 83, 93, 103, 147, 161, 186; comparisons with Liberia, 93, 179; and *Elizabeth* expedition, 24–27
Sierra Leoneans and *Neirsee* affair, 103, 105–6
Skinner, Ezekiel, 30, 156–57
Skipwith, Peyton, 151
Slavery, 147, 174, 197; as "apprenticeship," 62; slave trade in Liberia, 2, 24, 28, 157, 161, 180–81, 216, 227n2
Slave Trade Act of 1819, 23
Sleigh, William, 148
Smith, Gerrit, 36, 203
Smith, James McCune, 47
Smith, Stephen, 100
Snetter, Charles, 173–76, 178–80, 187
Stewart, Joshua, 143, 170, 188, 217
Stewart, William W., 188–89
Stowe, Harriet Beecher, 171, 210

Thompson, George, 50
Thomson, James, 141–45
Thornton, William, 81–82, 85
Tines, Mary, 192
Titler, Ephraim, 35
Tolbert Major, 89, 101

U.S. government, and Liberia, 11, 23–24, 26–27, 189, 191
U.S. Navy, 1, 15, 125, 227n2

USS *Alligator*, 28
USS *Saratoga*, 1
USS *Vandalia*, 111

Van Rensselaer, Thomas, 196–97
Violence, 15–16, 159, 182, 194; and anti-colonization, 193–94, 212, 216; and gender, 166, 169, 177, 192–94; and MSCS, 114, 179; and Receptives, 128; and "savagery," 80, 128, 158, 187, 221; and Snetter Affair, 175, 178; and women, 167, 185, 191–93

Warner, D. B., 101
Washington Medical College in Baltimore, 43–45, 47, 51, 58
Weaver, W. L., 155
Webster-Ashburton Treaty, 227n2
Whipper, William, 204, 211
Whiteness, 5, 76, 97, 109, 121, 158, 171–72, 197–98, 218; African constructions, 2–5, 8–9, 12–14, 18, 27, 31, 56–57, 66–67, 71, 109, 118, 158–59, 176–78, 190, 200–201, 221; and Americo-Liberians, 72, 136; and anti-colonization, 16, 136–37, 194, 196–97, 216; and Black Atlantic, 10, 12, 121; and colonization, 8–10, 54, 154, 177, 262n5; definitions, 7–8, 13–14, 20, 67, 71, 176, 218; and gender, 12, 122, 143; and mobility, 42, 54, 56, 61, 72, 195; scholarship, 10–11, 230; and settlers, 81, 109–10, 112, 137, 147, 159, 164, 176–77, 221
Wilkeson, Samuel, 8
Williams, Anthony D., 88, 124, 180, 207, 209
Williams, Samuel, 129–30, 139–40, 149, 164, 166
Wilson, Beverly R., 207
Wilson, J. Leighton, 113–14, 163, 169–71, 242n103
Wiltberger, Christian, 25–29
Women, 12, 78, 87, 118–19, 166, 168; African, 15, 87, 128, 142; and colonization rhetoric, 78, 118, 166, 179, 185, 191–93, 232n32; and labor, 15, 87, 140; and travels to the United States, 12, 118–19, 122, 150; widows, 131, 167, 169, 192
Wood, Anthony, 63, 70, 91, 176

"Yellow Will" (Bassa Cove), 156–57, 247
"Yellow Will" ("William Hall"), 106–9, 112, 123, 133–34, 156; *Neirsee* affair, 103, 105–6
Young Men's Colonization Society of Pennsylvania (YMCSP), 99, 153–54

ROBERT MURRAY is associate professor of history at Mercy College in Dobbs Ferry, New York.

www.ingramcontent.com/pod-product-compliance
Lightning Source LLC
Chambersburg PA
CBHW052056230426
43662CB00037B/1906